Culloden

The History and Archaeology
of the
Last Clan Battle

Edited by Tony Pollard

Pen & Sword
MILITARY

Published in 2009 and reprinted
in this format in 2011 by
Pen & Sword Military
an imprint of
Pen & Sword Books Ltd
47 Church Street
Barnsley
South Yorkshire
S70 2AS

ISBN 978 1 84884 687 6

A CIP catalogue record for this book is available from the British Library

Typeset in Ehrhardt by Phoenix Typesetting, Auldgirth, Dumfriesshire

Printed and bound by CPI Group (UK) Ltd, Croydon, CR0 4YY

Pen & Sword Books Ltd incorporates the imprints of
Pen & Sword Aviation, Pen & Sword Maritime, Pen & Sword Military,
Wharncliffe Local History, Pen & Sword Select,
Pen & Sword Military Classics and Leo Cooper,
Remember When, Seaforth Publishing and Frontline Publishing

For a complete list of Pen & Sword titles please contact
PEN & SWORD BOOKS LIMITED
47 Church Street, Barnsley, South Yorkshire, S70 2AS, England
E-mail: enquiries@pen-and-sword.co.uk
Website: www.pen-and-sword.co.uk

Contents

List of Figures and Plates

Figures

Plates

About the Authors

David Blackmore was born in Crickhowell, south Wales, in 1955. Until recently he worked for the Royal Armouries, and he is now a museum consultant and writer and researcher concentrating on the period from the English Civil War to the mid-eighteenth century and cavalry in particular. A lifelong interest in military history and rugby led him into re-enactment. From 1989 to 1995 he was Lord General of the Roundhead Association, and he now rides with Cobham's Dragoons, c.1746. He is the author of *Arms and Armour of the English Civil Wars*, lives in Doncaster, South Yorkshire, and rides whenever he can.

Dr Christopher Duffy is a military historian and former lecturer at the Royal Military Academy Sandhurst and the Army Staff College. Between 1996 and 2001 he was Research Professor in the History of War at De Montfort University. He has published widely on many aspects of military history, of most relevance being *The '45: Bonnie Prince Charlie and the Untold Story of the Jacobite Rising*, published in 2003 by Cassell.

Jill Harden is employed by the National Trust for Scotland to provide archaeological advice and undertake archaeological work for properties across the Highlands and Islands. She has worked intensively on the Culloden Battlefield Memorial Project over the last five years, with the aim of ensuring challenging yet accurate information for visitors to the battlefield. Although most of her studies over the past twenty years have been associated with cultural heritage management, in landscapes and museums, she has also worked on the sites of conflict at Auldearn, Glencoe and Glenshiel.

Elspeth Masson was Principal Teacher of History and Modern Studies at Crieff High School in Perthshire, and developed a particular interest in the Forty-Five and its effect upon Highland life, producing much of the material which she used with second-year classes. After eight months in Ghana, where she had been given the responsibility of raising academic standards in a rural mission school, she – with her husband, David – returned to live in the Highlands. Having volunteered to produce educational material for use in the new Culloden Visitors' Centre, she was instead given the opportunity to research the battlefield memorials, a task which she found both challenging and rewarding.

Dr Tony Pollard studied archaeology at the University of Glasgow, at both undergraduate and postgraduate level (MA 1987, PhD 1995). He worked as a Senior Project Manager for both GUARD (Glasgow University Archaeological Research Division) and the Field Unit of University College London. Along with Neil Oliver he co-presented the BBC television series *Two Men in a Trench*, which between 2002 and 2004 introduced battlefield archaeology to an international audience. He was appointed Director of the Centre for Battlefield Archaeology at Glasgow University in early 2006. Over the last ten years he has carried out archaeological projects on battlefields in South and North Africa, South America, Europe and the UK, including several seasons of fieldwork at Culloden. He has written widely on archaeology and history and is co-editor of the *Journal of Conflict Archaeology*.

Stuart Reid was born in Aberdeen, Scotland, and educated at Aberdeen Grammar School and Robert Gordon University, Aberdeen (1974–7), where he studied librarianship, majoring in historical bibliography and local history. He worked as a librarian before going on to more exciting things as a boatman, diving support technician, soldier (Royal Regiment of Fusiliers, 1980–86), cartographer and surveyor. Has also cut down trees, built bridges, climbed mountains, jumped out of helicopters and worked in the movies, as well as doing various other jobs once considered essential prerequisites for writing books. His numerous works on military history include: *Like Hungry Wolves: Culloden Moor, 16 April 1746*.

Dr Jeffrey Stephen worked as a historical researcher on the Culloden redevelopment project and is currently employed as a Research Fellow in the Department of History at the University of Strathclyde. His research interests include Presbyterianism in Scotland from the Reformation to the Disruption, the post-revolution church, Anglo-Scottish union and Jacobitism/anti-Jacobitism. He is the author of

Scottish Presbyterians and the Act of Union, 1707 (Edinburgh University Press, 2007).

Dr Daniel Szechi is a graduate of the University of Sheffield and St Antony's College, Oxford. After eighteen years as a Professor at Auburn University in Alabama, he was appointed Professor of Early Modern History at the University of Manchester in 2006. He is a Fellow of the Royal Society of Edinburgh and the Royal Historical Society. His books include: *1715: The Great Jacobite Rebellion* (Yale University Press, 2006); *George Lockhart of Carnwath, 1689–1727: A Study in Jacobitism* (Tuckwell Press, East Lothian, 2002); *The Jacobites: Britain and Europe, 1688–1788* (Manchester University Press, Manchester, 1994); with Prof. G. Holmes, *The Age of Oligarchy: Pre-Industrial Britain, 1722–1783* (Longman, 1993); and *Jacobitism and Tory Politics, 1710–14* (John Donald Press, Edinburgh, 1984).

Robert C. Woosnam-Savage studied art history at the University of Manchester before becoming Curator of European Arms and Armour at Glasgow Museums (1983–97). There he curated the major UK exhibition of 1995–6 commemorating the 250th anniversary of the '45, *Bonnie Prince Charlie: Fact and Fiction* and was editor of the accompanying book, *1745: Charles Edward Stuart and the Jacobites*. He has been Curator of European Edged Weapons at the Royal Armouries since 2001 and has been heavily involved since 2004 with the Culloden Battlefield Memorial Project, which opened in 2008.

Introduction

The Battle of Culloden –
More than a Difference of Opinion

TONY POLLARD

Well over two and a half centuries after the event, the Battle of Culloden, fought on 16 April 1746, still means many things to many people. To Scottish expatriates, no matter how many times removed, it is an emotional touchstone to their Scottish identity and commonly regarded as the opening act of the epic tragedy of the Highland Clearances; to those with nationalist inclinations it is held up as an example of England's terrible maltreatment of its northern neighbour; to Unionists it is seen as the final gasp of a divisive movement hell-bent on returning Britain to monarchical despotism; to romantics it marks the end of one of those great lost causes, pitching the Highland underdog against the might of the Hanoverian war machine.

Discussions of Culloden can be passionate and heated, even among academics. This volume does not attempt to reconcile these various view-points, some of which obviously sit in direct opposition to one another, nor does it ignore them. Indeed, acknowledgement of these contrasting perceptions and preconceptions is vital in any attempt to provide a meaningful reassessment of a battle which has already spawned an extensive literature. And so it is that some of those writing here may appear to be partisan, their stance detectable perhaps through a turn of phrase or the choice of one term over another. Any attempt by me as editor to remove these idiosyncrasies would be sailing uncomfortably close to censorship.

Nevertheless, neutral terminology can be hard to find: do we refer to the '45 as an 'uprising' or a 'rebellion'? Was it the 'government army', 'Hanoverian army' or 'British army'? Was the son of the exiled James VII 'James VIII' or the 'Old Pretender'; was his son Charles Edward Stuart 'Bonnie Prince Charlie' or the 'Young Pretender'? As far as the army is concerned, in my own contribution I have adopted 'government' through nothing more than force of habit after working for so long with the National Trust for Scotland – that is the term it uses. However, as Stuart Reid points out, it was the British army which faced the Jacobites on Culloden Moor,[1] and not a Hanoverian army. George II may have been Hanoverian but his army was not; Germanic elements were present in the form of 6,000 Hessians on hire from Prince Friedrich of Hesse, but these troops were elsewhere when the battle was fought.[2] The issue of national identity with specific reference to the term 'British' is discussed more fully below.

Before proceeding, a little background to this volume would not go amiss. A vital impetus has been the archaeological investigation of the battlefield, which has been carried out on a sporadic basis since 2000. This is the first time that the results of this archaeological work have been published in any detail, and because of this no apologies are made for the archaeological chapter being slightly longer than the others. This is not to belittle the more historically based chapters, which in themselves make an important contribution to a fresh understanding of an event which has not wanted for scholarly attention. Most of the contributors served on one or more of the academic panels and discussion groups which accompanied the long process of bringing together the content for the new National Trust for Scotland visitor centre. Research into various aspects of the battle by these leading experts was carried out under the auspices of what became known as the Culloden Battlefield Memorial Project, but not all of this could be reflected in the on-site displays and exhibitions, and on this basis it seemed only right to give them an outlet in published form. The present volume is the end result; it may not be the last word on Culloden but it is certainly the latest.

Culloden was the first battlefield in Scotland to be subject to any form of archaeological investigation, and is still one of relatively few in Britain. The first project featured in the BBC television series *Two Men in a Trench*, co-presented by me, which for the first time brought battlefield archaeology to a wide audience.[3] The results of that preliminary work, which took place in 2000, and included topographic, geophysical and metal detector surveys as well as some excavation, established that archaeological techniques could be used to shed new light on the battle and its landscape context. This knowledge further encouraged an embryonic initiative by the National Trust for Scotland – which, as Masson and Harden's contribution will discuss, has for many years had in its care a significant portion of the site – to enhance the presentation and interpretation of the battlefield for the visiting public. The fruits of these labours were officially unveiled on 16 April 2008 when a new, state-of-the-art visitor centre was opened alongside the reinterpreted battlefield.

The results of several seasons of archaeological research have fed directly into the visitor centre, with the display of recovered artefacts providing a direct link to the fighting, killing and dying which created the hallowed ground outside the building. Perhaps more importantly, the surveys have provided a fuller understanding of the battlefield itself, and Culloden represents one of the first examples of the full integration of archaeological research with historic accounts in the presentation of a battle site to the public.

During the initial fieldwork it became obvious that there were some inaccuracies in the pre-2008 on-site interpretations, as reflected through display boards showing unit locations and flags marking the position of the Jacobite and government lines. Taking these findings into consideration, the National Trust for Scotland has provided revised on-site interpretation, making readjustments where required and providing footpaths more appropriate to a fuller understanding of the site as visitors walk around it. The simple act of removing field fences which isolated some parts of the site has done much to give a truer sense of scale and return the place to something more like the relatively open landscape of the mid-eighteenth century. Although it is impossible to recreate the battlefield entirely, an important contribution of the archaeological survey to this process was in identifying surviving elements of the 1746 landscape.

As reference to Woosnam-Savage's chapter on the contemporary maps will highlight, the battle was fought within a landscape occupied by a number of distinct features. Perhaps the most obvious of these are the high stone walls of the enclosures, the one to the north, known as Culloden Parks, and the one to the south, the Culwhiniac enclosures. These disappeared during the nineteenth century as agricultural improvements took place. Also present were a number of settlements, most of which have either disappeared or been subsumed within modern farms, such as Culchunaig to the west of the battlefield. A possible exception to this is the Leanach farmstead, which according to most of the maps consisted of three buildings and was located somewhere close to the left of the government line. Although two of the buildings no longer exist it has traditionally been thought that Leanach Cottage (often referred to as Old Leanach Cottage), which has for a long time been integrated within the NTS presentation of the battlefield, was one of these buildings (though see Chapter 6 for a fuller discussion).

Establishing where these enclosures and buildings stood was an important objective of the investigation as they provided important anchor points for the troops on both sides, with the Jacobite front line strung out between the enclosure walls and the government left standing close to the farmstead.

Other features also played a role in the battle, notably the road which is shown on several of the maps cutting across the battlefield between the two armies, passing beneath the Jacobite centre and running just to the north of the farmstead, close to the government left. This feature has been almost entirely overlooked by historians, but as the archaeological survey progressed, it became apparent that the road – which, though marked as the 'Muir road to Inverness' on Sandby's map, was unlikely to have been more than a dirt track – played a vital part in the battle. Given that the road travels along a spine of high ground which may have afforded Jacobite troops charging to the south of it some cover from government fire and roughly corresponds to the main thrust of the Jacobite charge from the centre and right, which converged on the government left, it seems reasonable to suggest that at least some Jacobites advanced along it.

Not least among the inaccuracies in the pre-2008 NTS presentation of the battlefield was the location of the opposing battle lines. The front line of the Jacobite army was marked by an alignment of red flags displaying the white cockade, and the government line with yellow flags adorned with the black cockade (although probably entirely coincidental the choice of yellow flags, with all that the colour signifies in relation to behaviour in battle was not lost on some visitors). The location of the government line was largely in accord with that depicted on contemporary battle maps, at least in the association of the left flank sitting forward of the Leanach farmstead. However, the Jacobite line, as marked by the flags and regimental markers, was located around 150m closer to the government line (to the east) than was the case on 16 April 1746. This error can be traced back to the attempt in the 1960s by the NTS to present the site to the public, a process begun in the early 1880s by Duncan Forbes of Culloden. Battle maps which appeared in several popular history books published in the early 1960s,[4] which themselves were based on nineteenth- and early twentieth-century maps, including that by Sir D.Y. Cameron (Figure 1), may be partly responsible for this misalignment, perhaps along with the temptation to place as much of the battlefield as possible within the NTS property holding. Whatever the case, the revised presentation of the battlefield has pushed the Jacobite line westward, and in doing so it makes even more apparent the great distance over which the Jacobites charged before coming to grips with the enemy on the government left, all the while under fire. At the southern ends of the lines (Jacobite right and government left) the distance has been increased from around 400m to near 550m; the distance is even greater at the northern end, as the lines did not sit quite parallel to one another.

This revised reading of the landscape gives us a better understanding of

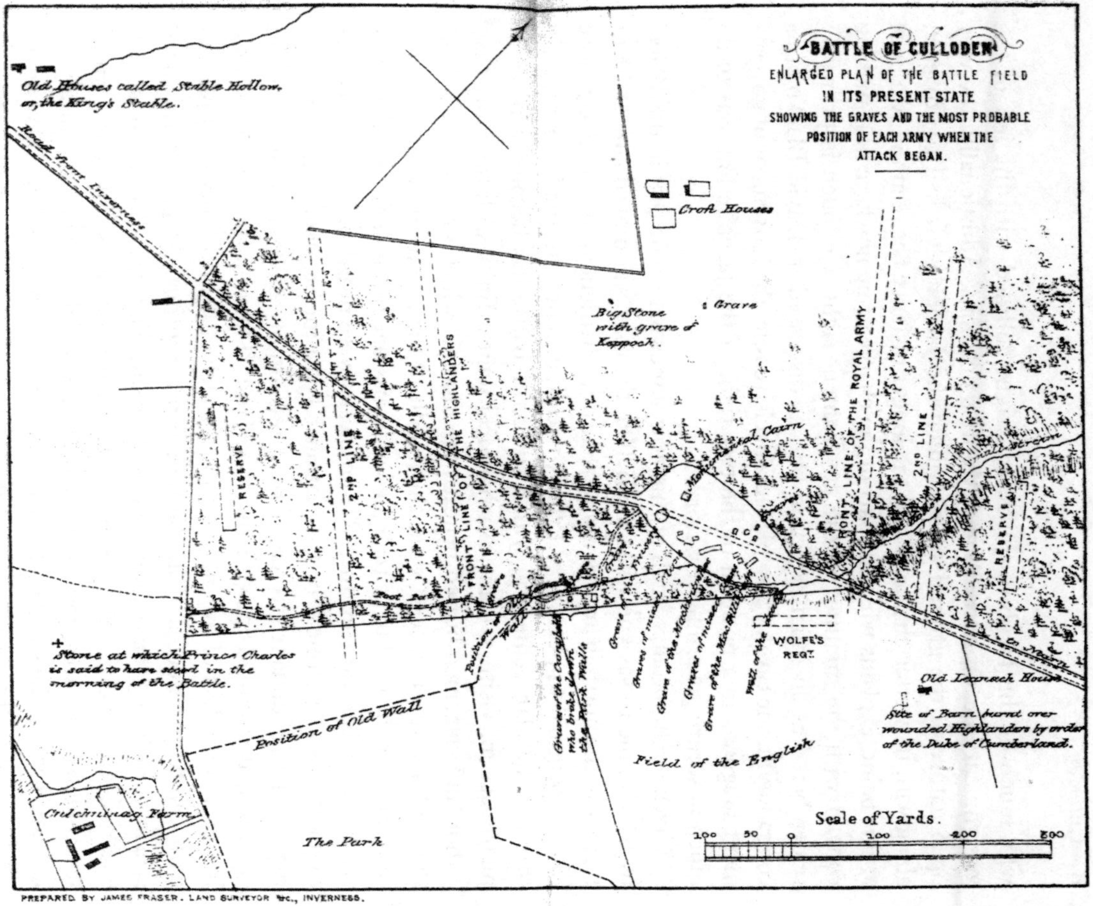

Figure 1. Map of the battlefield prepared by Sir D. Y. Cameron RA (1865–1945), showing the position of the battle lines which provided the basis for the site layout until 2008. Note the Jacobite right anchored on the junction of the Culwhiniac and Leanach enclosures. (© National Trust for Scotland)

why much of the Jacobite centre and right collided with the left of the government line, on Barrell's and Monro's positions. Additionally, the very open nature of the ground across which the Jacobite left had to advance, along with its wetter character and the longer distance between the two lines at this point, explains why this part of the charge came nowhere near making contact with the infantry on the government right. Culloden is primarily remembered as an infantry action but, as discussed in David Blackmore's contribution, the cavalry also played a decisive role: the movement of government dragoons to a position to the rear right of the Jacobite line was to do much to secure government victory.

Given its importance in all of this, it is somewhat ironic that in the 1980s, by which time it was known as the B9006, the road was moved almost 300m further to the north in an attempt to return the battlefield to something more like its original appearance. Prior to realignment, the road ran directly through the clan cemetery, which since the battle has become a place of pilgrimage for visitors, many of whom feel some affinity with the more than a thousand clansmen buried beneath the mounds which sat at either side of the road. However, at least since the middle of the nineteenth century, there were calls for the road to be realigned as its passage through the cemetery was regarded as disrespectful. In 1982 those calls were heard and, after a request to the Roads Department by the National Trust for Scotland, the move took place. The redundant stretch of road was simply covered with earth and encouraged to blend in with the moorland. The moorland itself is also, however, a product of the modern era, as much of the battlefield was planted with coniferous woodland in the nineteenth century. As part of the same scheme which saw the realignment of the road, the trees were also removed, and tree stumps can still be seen among the heather, gorse and birch which has colonized the area since deforestation (the aerial photograph reproduced in Plate 9 shows the site largely cleared of trees but the road still following its original course through the clan cemetery).

When studying a specific battle, especially through the medium of archaeology, there is always a danger of focusing on the microscopic and the particular to the cost of an understanding of the broader picture. Accordingly, an essay on the wider European background to the '45 has been provided here by Daniel Szechi, while the history of the campaign preceding the battle is covered by Christopher Duffy.

Looking back to the origins of the Jacobite movement, it could be argued that Culloden occurred in the first place only because almost sixty years earlier another, much bigger engagement did not. This great 'battle that never was' might have decided the future of the Stuart dynasty at a stroke, and one way or another staved off the uncertainty of an unsettled life in exile for its male members. In November 1688 some 20,000 troops under the Catholic James II advanced toward an invading army of 15,000 under William of Orange, somewhere near Salisbury Plain. Although popular history would have us believe that William stood at the head of a Dutch force flying Orange flags, it was in fact multinational and included large numbers of English and Scottish troops; indeed the leading division was commanded by Major General Hugh Mackay, a Highlander from Sutherland.[5]

Had it not been for defections among key elements of his army, including influential officers such as Marlborough, then James and his superior numbers might have been able to push the invaders back into the sea. But abandoned and then fleeing into exile,[6] James was reaping the whirlwind he had sown with his refusal to recognize that the world had changed with the beheading of his father, Charles I, in 1649. Of course, if James had acted in such a way as to inspire loyalty among his armed services then the invasion would never have taken place, at least not with the collusion of his subjects (his attempts to purge the army of Protestants certainly did not help). But history is full of 'what ifs' (the most popular in the case of the '45 undoubtedly being what if Charles and the Jacobites had not turned back at Derby?).

It was the partly pre-planned dissolution of the Royal army while in the field in November 1688 which prevented bloodshed and gave what was effectively a *coup d'état* the misnomer of the 'Glorious Revolution'. It was, however, only a temporary respite, and between 1689 and 1746 much blood was to be shed across Ireland, Scotland and England (the latter getting off lightly with only two small engagements, Preston in 1715 and Clifton Moor in 1745, and with minimal impact on the civilian population).

It has already been noted that Culloden is not a history readily consigned to books and the peaceful environment of the library. It is a live issue which has refused to be pacified over the passing years, as shown by listeners' complaints in response to my remarks on clan graves recently made on BBC radio. In the programme concerned I had proposed that the clan graves were not exclusively given over to particular clans, as suggested by the inscribed gravestones erected by Duncan Forbes of Culloden in 1881, but contained anonymous bodies of uncertain affiliation, as it would be impossible to distinguish, with perhaps a few exceptions, which dead Jacobite belonged to which clan. There are several reasons for believing this: the bodies were not buried until several days after the battle; for the most part they were not buried by people who knew them; there are accounts of bodies being stripped naked; even if clothing, in the form of tartan plaids and so on, did remain then it would provide little clue as to identity, as tartan designs particular to a specific clan did not come into being until the nineteenth century. It was this last statement which caused the greatest objection, from at least one listener, a tartan-wearing descendant of a MacDonald who fought on the day.

David Morier's famous painting *An Incident in the Rebellion of 1745*, showing the Jacobite attack on the left flank of the government line, on Barrell's position, has been used to demonstrate how tartans known today were present on the field in 1746 (Plate 1). However, the tartan pattern makers of the nineteenth century may simply have used the painting as a source of inspiration when it came to making up patterns, or setts as they are known. This fits well with the school of thought that tartans could be identified with localities in the early eighteenth century – owing to the appearance of local patterns and the availability of certain dyestuffs – but not with specific clans or families. This latter development, it is believed,[7] did not come until the nineteenth century when tartan and the kilt became fashionable again once the Jacobite threat was safely in the past.

This renaissance, of course, followed the ban on the wearing of tartan, introduced as a modification to the Disarming Act in 1747 and, with the exception of those patterns authorised for military use (British army), enforced until the 1780s. Is it the case, though, that we have the visit of George IV to Edinburgh in 1822, organized by Sir Walter Scott, to thank for the clan tartans we see today? Certainly at the time the great and the good were falling over themselves to be seen draped in the chequered fabric, and pattern books from the period show an increasing multitude of designs. Some original patterns do appear to have survived the enforced hiatus, and others were no doubt reconstructed from visual sources such as Morier's painting. Despite claims to the contrary, however, there does not seem to be a straightforward and reliable way of establishing whether or not these original forms represented familial clan tartans or regional forms which were later to provide inspiration for those identifying the wearer as the member of a specific clan.

I would not be the first to point out that Morier's painting and various others show individual Highlanders wearing several patterns of tartan as part of the same costume, with some of them differing from those current today. This mix-and-match approach would certainly not suggest adherence to recognized clan setts. Alternatively, it could be suggested that the painting post-dates the battle by several years and so the mix of tartans may represent not the authentic costume of the day but merely the miscellaneous collection of garments available to the artist and his models at that time.

With specific reference to clan affiliation, there is additionally an account from Culloden of tartan-clad soldiers from both sides being indistinguishable without the presence of the white or black cockade in the bonnet, but as this comes from James Ray,[8] an Englishman, we should perhaps consider him unable to 'read' tartan – to him one pattern would look pretty much like the next.

As a native of Skye, Martin Martin may be a more reliable source. In the late seventeenth century he wrote in his *Description of the Western Islands of Scotland*: 'Every Isle differs from each other in their fancy of making Plads as to the stripes in breadth and colours. The humour is as different thro the main-land of the Highlands, in so far that they who have seen those places are able at the first view of a man's Plad, to guess the place of his residence.'[9] This statement has been subject to differing interpretations. To those who do not believe that clan tartans existed prior to 1746 it provides evidence for patterns associated with region rather than clan. However, as Adam points out in his classic work *The Clans, Septs and Regiments of the Scottish Highlands*, familial and clan links were very much tied into land and territory: in short, clan and region are one and the same.[10] Adam's argument is compelling, and, though the case for clan tartans in the early eighteenth century may remain unproven, I am swayed enough to accept that at least some clan tartans did exist and were worn on the field at Culloden.

But if the dead of Culloden were stripped of their garb before burial then the issue of tartan and its role in associating the graves with specific clans becomes academic. In *The Lyon in Mourning* Robert Forbes recorded the testimony of Alexander MacIntosh of Essech, 'who received above twenty wounds on the field of Culloden, was stript naked as he was born, all to the short hose, and reckoned amongst the Dead. However, he came to himself again, and got off the field in the Dead of Night, as his limbs were sound and untouched.'[11] And further: 'He told me likewise, that, after stripping of the dead and Wounded, a party of Dragoons came riding over the Field, with their bayonets fixed.' The dragoons then proceeded to pierce one of MacIntosh's buttocks; he made no sound or movement and so was left for dead.

This account notwithstanding, there is at least one problem with the theory relating to the anonymous nature of the burials. The first edition Ordnance Survey map of the area, which was surveyed in 1868, shows all the grave mounds, and some of them are marked with clan names – MacGillivray, MacIntosh and Fraser (graves of the Campbells are also marked in the vicinity of the Leanach enclosure). The graves of the Stuarts and the Camerons, which appear on later editions of the map, are not, however, marked on this first edition. Despite the incomplete nature of the annotation, specific associations are clearly in place prior to Forbes of

Culloden's intervention in 1881. Whether the inscribed headstones were preceded by wooden markers is unknown: there is certainly no mention of such in early- to mid-nineteenth-century accounts of the site, including the Ordnance Survey Name Book. The associations may be based on local oral tradition, and we should not underestimate public interest in the battlefield prior to the late nineteenth century. In one tourist's account from 1836, which again makes no mention of graves associated with specific clans, a local guide digs a turf from one of the mounds in a quest for bones, and tells his clients that visitors often go away from the place with bones as souvenirs.[12]

The image of men of the same clan sharing a grave, brother lying along-side brother, father alongside son, appeals to the imagination; it gives a neat ending to an event which was anything but. Named graves give descendants, however distant, somewhere to lay their wreaths or sprigs of heather, or in some cases even a last resting places for their own scattered ashes.[13] But when the circumstances surrounding the burials are weighed together it seems likely that the reality is less palatable. Naked, decaying bodies were dragged from the wagons in which they had been collected and dumped into pits with the minimum of fuss, a task probably carried out by frightened locals under the uncaring eyes of victorious government troops. Only later, when calm returned and it was once again safe to walk the moor, did these grass-covered mounds become associated with particular clans and provide a physical and metaphorical platform for the telling of their brave deeds – associations to be set in stone by Forbes nearly a century and a half later. As the later discussion of the archaeology makes plain, no such immortality was to be accorded the graves of the fifty or so government soldiers who died on the field, which to this day lie unmarked and untended somewhere in the 'Field of the English'.

The expression of strong feelings is by no means limited to the passionate ancestor; Scottish academic Alan MacInnes has compared the aftermath of the battle, which saw a cruel repression extend across the Highlands, as 'ethnic cleansing'.[14] Brutal acts of violence were visited on wounded Jacobite soldiers on the field, on civilians caught up in the immediate aftermath, and then on the wider population of the Highlands in the months that followed. Closely identified with these acts is the Duke of Cumberland, otherwise known as 'the Butcher' because of his perceived role in them. His greatest crime was probably to engender in his men a real contempt and hatred for the Jacobite, and the Highlander in particular. This lack of humanity was perhaps a useful quality in those about to face a daunting enemy in battle, but when elements of that same army are let off the leash with less than specific orders once the fighting is over then the result is surely predictable. It was also Cumberland who recommended that troublesome clans be transported to the colonies (although the policy was first suggested by Duncan Forbes of Culloden, who at the time of the battle was Lord President of Scotland and, unlike his nineteenth-century descendant was a strident anti-Jacobite). James Wolfe, the later hero of Quebec and aide-de-camp to Hawley at Culloden, saw a more practical application for these belligerent people, and in reference to the benefits of the Highlander to the British army observed that they 'make little mischief when they fall'.

But cruel as these acts were, it has been suggested in some quarters that MacInnes's highly charged language, which has much in common with that used to describe acts of unequivocal genocide in more recent times, is out of place in the consideration of punitive actions carried out in the mid-eighteenth century. (Scottish academics are certainly not alone in passing Nuremberg-like judgements on historical events, the latest being a group of French historians who have accused the English army of Henry V of war crimes during the Agincourt campaign.)[15]

Certainly, as we consider Culloden and its aftermath from the comfort of a stable and relatively secure west in the early part of the twenty-first century, we would do well to remember that these events occurred in a very different time and place, where the barbarous ritual of hanging, drawing and quartering was reserved for crimes against the state (nine English Jacobites from Manchester suffered this fate in 1746). Warfare in the mid-eighteenth century was a brutal business and the Geneva Convention was still over a century away. The first convention of 1864 covered the treatment of wounded soldiers, while prisoners of war had to wait until the third convention of 1929; concern for civilians in time of war was not incorporated until the fourth convention of 1949. That said, though, rules of war did exist in 1746, and the Scottish and Irish soldiers in regular French service who surrendered after the battle were the only captives treated as *bona fide* prisoners of war, as Britain was at war with France at the time. The rest were regarded as rebels and treated as such, many of them dying in the horrendous conditions of their captivity.[16]

The Highland Clearances are another greatly emotive issue and have come to be regarded in the popular imagination as a continuation of the suppression which came in the wake of the '45. Under the guise of agricultural 'improvements' they took place over a century from the 1760s onwards, and undoubtedly included tragic incidents and acts of cruelty by landowners and their factors, but it is an oversimplification to regard them as a direct result of the '45 and Culloden. Despite this it seems highly unlikely that recent attempts to rehabilitate Cumberland's reputation[17] will cut much ice north of the Highland line, where memories are long, nor in many other parts of

Scotland where the image of 'the Butcher' sits comfortably within a popular perception of Scottish history.

What Jacobite defeat at Culloden did bring about was the emasculation of the clan system, an outcome which finds much common ground with the military objectives of British imperial campaigns, such as those in Sudan and Zululand in the later part of the nineteenth century. The greatest impacts were obviously felt in the Highlands, where the clan system, which operated through a complex network of feudal and familial allegiances and obligations, had long controlled the nature of social relations and economy in the region. We should, however, resist the temptation, fostered by the romantic image, to see life under the old clan system as an Arcadian idyll. There are, for instance, accounts of clan chiefs and tacksmen threatening eviction and violence against their tenants and dependants if they ignored the call to arms and 'come out' during the '45 and earlier risings (see Reid, Chapter 3, this volume).[18]

Movements of populations at the behest of powerful landowners wishing to maximize the income from their holdings were not confined to the Highlands, or indeed to Scotland, and economic migration in the face of increasing urbanization outweighed forced removal (Scottish cities saw dramatic growth and expansion during this period). But neither can they be uncoupled entirely; the battle and its aftermath helped to lay the ground-work, quite literally in some cases, by facilitating the confiscation of estates and creating a conflicted social milieu within which the introduction of agri-cultural improvements was to be a much more tumultuous process than elsewhere.[19]

We should not though ignore the reality behind such sanitised statements, especially as it impacted on the common people who suffered most during the depredations wrought on the Highlands during the search for the fugitive Charles and the suppression of areas still regarded as hotbeds of rebellion. In the immediate wake of the '45, and prior to what we today understand as 'the clearances', entire communities were made homeless and deprived of the means to feed themselves through the theft of cattle or destruction of crops. The notorious General 'Hangman' Hawley, who had suffered defeat at the hands of the Jacobites at Falkirk in January 1746, reckoned that by June 1746 upwards of 7,000 homes had been burned, before speculating gleefully that, 'There's still so many more houses to burn, and I hope still some to put to death.'[20] It seems hard to believe that, even with the likes of the infamous Captain Caroline Scott, Captain John Fergusson and Major Lockhart in command of punitive expeditions,[21] so many houses were destroyed, but when these statistics are penned by high-ranking officers, terms such as 'genocide' and 'ethnic cleansing' may not seem such an uncomfortable fit after all.

A relatively recent trend has been to frame the '45 within the wider context of the War of Austrian Succession, a pan-European conflict which at its core saw France pitched against Britain (see Szechi's chapter for a lucid overview). France saw an opportunity to destabilize the British mainland through the back door of Scotland, hence its support of the Jacobite cause during the conflict. Such a perspective is to be welcomed, and it is certainly one adopted by the new NTS visitor centre in its portrayal of events. Associated with this is what could be termed a revisionist view of the conflict as it played out in Scotland, with the focus being on a struggle between Scots, with Lowlander pitched against Highlander, Presbyterian against Catholic and Episcopalian.

The concept of the '45 as a Scottish civil war is as valid as it has been useful in countering the enduring misconception that Culloden was a straightforward England versus Scotland affair, in the same mould as battles such as Bannockburn and Flodden. Like Bannockburn, which plays host to an annual rally by the Scottish National Party, Culloden has become something of a focus for nationalist sentiment. An early suggestion of this goes back to the 1950s, when letters in the NTS archive refer to the daubing of nationalist graffiti on the stone traditionally associated with Cumberland's position during the battle. The new visitor centre at Culloden has rightly attempted to present a balanced and nuanced picture of a battle which has in certain quarters been falsely cast as a fight between Scotsmen in kilts and Englishmen in red coats. As Stuart Reid points out in Chapter 3, there were at least four Scottish regiments among the sixteen infantry battalions fielded by Cumberland, with many more Scots distributed among the 'English' regiments. There were also small numbers of English Jacobites on the field – there could have been more, but most of these had been left behind to defend Carlisle, and were to suffer badly for doing so.

But convenient archetypes die hard, and some might argue that this 'spreading of blame' is a result of political correctness or a result of Anglocentric bias. Whatever its root, the civil war model does effectively serve to diffuse those uncomfortable accusations of ethnic cleansing.[22] Difficult as it is for an English academic who regards himself as a naturalised Scot to admit, they do have a point. The '45 was in part a civil war and a theatre within a wider European war, but there can be no denying that it was perceived as something else by many of those caught up in it. Jacobite letters and journals often refer to the enemy as English (see quote regarding Falkirk in Blackmore, p.92, also Jeffrey Stephen's contribution, Chapter 8, for a revealing overview of other aspects of the contemporary accounts). And if there is any doubt that the view from England, where there was a misapprehension that the majority of Scots were for the Stuart cause, was any different, then one needs only to refer to the notorious verse from 'God save the King' which in late 1745 was being sung with gusto in the Drury Lane Theatre, London:

> Lord grant that Marshal Wade,
> May by thy mighty aid,
> Victory bring,
> May he sedition hush and like a torrent rush,
> Rebellious Scots to crush,
> God save the King.

The issue is also etched into the landscape at Culloden, where the place name 'Field of the English' is given to the area where the government dead were buried. The label is at least as old as the association of the clan graves with clan names, no matter that at least some of these fifty or more men were Scots.

Disquiet over the Union of 1707 was certainly a part motivator for the flurry of Jacobite activity which was to punctuate the first half of the eighteenth century. Deeply rooted ideas that Scottish independence so hard won in the wars of the early fourteenth century was 'bought and sold for English gold'[23] may have undergone some reconsideration of late, but the Union undoubtedly served as an effective recruiting sergeant for the Jacobite cause. Indeed, as Whatley has suggested, one of the defining motivations for the Union was the desire by Scottish Protestants to extinguish Catholic influence, and these two groups were clearly at odds during the '45.[24] It was not for nothing that many of the broadsword blades imported from the continent were inscribed with slogans such as 'Prosperity to Schotland and No union' (the spelling of course is indicative of the blades' Germanic origins).

Perhaps ironically, the Union came into being while a Stuart, James VII's daughter Queen Anne, was on the throne, and hopes that her reign would secure the return of the Stuart dynasty were misplaced. The Jacobite leader during the '15, John Erskine, the 22nd Earl of Mar, was a loyal servant of Anne, who appointed him Secretary of State for Scotland, but he was equally willing to serve George I when the Elector of Hanover came to the throne in 1714 – this willingness to switch allegiances earned him the less than flattering nickname of 'Bobbing John'. The Hanoverian George did not, however, trust a Tory who had previously served a Stuart, and so he was denied a position. Affronted by this rejection, Mar became a fervent Jacobite and led the rising in 1715, but in no small part because of his poor generalship it was a lost cause, which even the presence in Scotland of James, the Old Pretender, in the winter of 1715 could not revive. It goes almost without saying that personal opportunism and political pragmatism like that displayed by Mar, rather than blind loyalty or deeply held beliefs, were to be the prime motivators for many key players on both sides during the Jacobite conflicts.

The purpose of the foregoing has not been to unreservedly resuscitate the old 'Scotland versus England' paradigm, with all the accompanying nationalist baggage, nor even to downplay the importance of internecine conflict in driving the '45, but merely to demonstrate that the issue is more complex than any single model of interpretation would have us believe.[25] There are, as with every conflict, unpalatable truths here, and they need to be faced up to rather than brushed under the carpet.

Ethnic cleansing or no, the Union certainly brought with it an attempt to suppress any expression of Scottish national identity. This perhaps most obviously manifested itself through the renaming of the country as 'North Britain' on maps of the period.[26] Maps were also the business of the surveyor General Roy, who in the aftermath of the '45 was set the task of creating detailed maps of Scotland. Today, these are an extremely valuable resource to archaeologists and historians, as they show every farmstead, village, field and road, or at least set out to do so. They were not, however, created for the benefit of those wishing to travel or learn more about geography, but in order to provide information on where threats to the state were likely to originate and the routes likely to be taken by an enemy force, and even to provide an idea of how many troops any locality could support through its food resources (it wasn't just his fine eye for detail which prompted him to show ploughed fields). Roy's remarkable maps are a prime example of how cartography can be used as a tool of suppression and control, and to this day this military role is reflected in the term Ordnance Survey. In the same way, Field Marshal Wade had earlier been given the task of building roads throughout the Highlands, not for the benefit of the locals but to ensure that troops could be marched to any trouble spot with the maximum of haste (there is perhaps poetic justice in the fact that one of the first beneficiaries of these military roads were the Jacobites, who used them to great effect during their lightning campaign in the autumn of 1745).

All roads, it would seem, lead to Culloden, and any way you look at it the battle was a bloody mess, but as the above has demonstrated, our understanding of it today is none too tidy either. To assist readers in picking their way through this palimpsest of opinion and viewpoint and to draw their own conclusions, this volume has gathered together a series of studies which deal with both specific and general issues, with the main focus throughout being the last pitched battle fought on the British mainland.

NB: Dates are in 'old style' (Julian) rather than the 'new style' (Gregorian) fully adopted in Britain in 1752 but prior to 1745 in Europe – new-style dates were eleven calendar days in advance of the old style. While some archaic name spellings have been standarized (e.g. 'Monro' is sometimes today referred to as 'Munro' but the old form has been retained), some variation is present; e.g. both the 'Argyle' and 'Argyll' variants have been used by different authors.

Acknowledgements

Thanks are due to a large number of people, all of whom have had some influence on this book. Alexander Bennett managed the Culloden Battlefield Memorial Project on behalf of the National Trust for Scotland and was supportive throughout the archaeological work which accompanied the project, as was Jill Harden, NTS archaeologist and contributor to the present volume. Other participants in the Culloden project are noted in the acknowledgements which follow the archaeology chapter. Angus McClellan was a source of much stimulating conversation and plentiful food for thought. Rupert Harding at Pen and Sword saw the potential for this volume at an early stage and displayed much patience during its preparation. Jen Novotny provided a first copy-edit, followed by Merle Read for Pen and Sword. Special thanks go to Pamela Covey for her proofreading services. The two maps which accompany Christopher Duffy's chapter (Figures 2 and 3) were created by Ingrid Shearer. A number of individuals and institutions provided permissions for illustration reproduction. The various examples of the wonderful Penicuik drawings are provided with the kind permission of Sir Robert Clerk of Penicuik House. The sources of other illustrations are credited as they appear. Natasha Ferguson of the Centre for Battlefield Archaeology at the University of Glasgow did much to arrange reproduction permissions.

The photographs of the 'battle' which adorn the cover of this volume and appear as plates were taken by Danny Carr during the filming of the video display which can now be seen at the Culloden Visitor Centre. It was directed by Craig Collinson and produced by Nobles Gate, and was the first serious attempt to create a filmed reconstruction of the battle since Peter Watkins made his influential drama-documentary in the 1960s.

Chapter 1

The '45 Campaign

CHRISTOPHER DUFFY

The story of the Jacobite rising of 1745–6 will probably be familiar, at least in outline. Perhaps less well known will be the connections between the processes and key decisions that explain why the culminating battle at Culloden was fought when, where and how it was.

By 1745 Britain had lived through decades of political and religious upsets, beginning in 1688 when King James II (VII of Scotland), an ardent Catholic convert, was forced from his throne by the 'Glorious Revolution'. This usurpation existed in an international context, for the Dutch Prince William of Orange, now installed in London as King William III, was motivated primarily by a desire to gather Britain into a league against Louis XIV of France. Catholics were actually a minority among what became known as the 'Jacobites', who were the many men and women throughout the British Isles who concluded that the Revolution had been a 'fix', engineered by small groups of powerful interests, and that the laws of God and man had thereby been set aside.

William III had married James's daughter Mary, and a semblance of Stuart continuity was preserved when Mary's sister, Anne, succeeded as queen, reigning from 1702 to 1714. However, the biggest 'fix' of all had already been engineered by virtue of the Act of Settlement (1701), which determined that after the death of the childless Anne the crown must pass to the heirs of the Electress of Hanover, a granddaughter of James I of England (VI of Scotland), and so guarantee the succession of a Protestant line. Anne died in 1714, and the throne was duly inherited by Elector George of Hanover, who but for the Act of Settlement would have had only a remote claim to the succession. Continental priorities, in this case the security of the Electorate of Hanover, were the main concern of this first of the Georges, and of his son George II, who came to the throne in 1727.

Conversely, the unrest in Britain every now and then served the interests

17

of France and Spain. The French first intervened on behalf of the Jacobites in March 1689, when they deposited James II on the coast of Ireland with a body of 4,000 French troops. The subsequent fight of the Irish Jacobites outlasted the resistance in Scotland and the departure of King James, and came to an end only when the defenders of Limerick surrendered on favourable terms on 3 October 1691.

The celebrated Jacobite rising of 1715 was in measurable terms the largest of the four (1689, 1715, 1719, 1745), embracing much of northern England and Lowland Scotland, but it lacked cohesion and leadership, and was launched at a time of general European peace, when neither France nor Spain was inclined to intervene. In 1719 the Spanish did indeed put a small force ashore in the Western Highlands, but the troops and their Scottish supporters made scarcely any progress inland before they were defeated at Glenshiel on 10 June. The Scots dispersed, and the Spaniards were left to surrender.

In the longer term the Jacobite connections with Spain and more particularly with France proved to be a source of underlying strength, as was to be revealed in 1745. Exiled Irish Jacobite shipowners, rich from the profits of trade, slaving and privateering, proved willing to put their resources at the disposal of a new Stuart leader, Prince Charles Edward Stuart, who was more single-minded and energetic than anything that his house had produced in recent generations. Something of a Stuart army in exile had come into being in the French military service in the shape of the formidable Irish Brigade and the Regiment of Royal Ecossois, while clansmen and young Highland gentlemen circulated between Scotland and France and Spain, and so helped to build up the fund of military expertise available to the Scottish Jacobites in their homeland.

In 1743 a fresh war pitted France against Britain and its Austrian, Dutch and German allies, and at a time when the new generation was coming to the fore (for a more detailed account of the War of the Austrian Succession, see Szechi, this volume). In the theatre of war in the Austrian Netherlands (corresponding roughly to present-day Belgium), the command passed to King George's second son, William Augustus, Duke of Cumberland. He was brave and enthusiastic, but he was no match for the French under the Marshal de Saxe, and on 11 May 1745 he was defeated at Fontenoy, which inaugurated a run of reverses that opened the Channel coast as far as Ostend as a potential base for the invasion of Britain.

How well placed were the Jacobites to take advantage of their opportunities? Since 1701 their hopes had been invested in James II's son and heir, James Francis Edward, known as 'King James III' to his supporters but 'The

Old Pretender' to his enemies. Over the course of time James III lost the credibility, will and energy to lead an armed Jacobite restoration, and the lead in militant Jacobitism was taken by his son Prince Charles Edward Stuart, the Bonnie Prince Charlie of history and legend. The Prince Charles of 1745 was a world removed from the comatose Polish–Latin hermaphrodite as conveyed in caricatures like that in Peter Watkins's celebrated 1964 film, *Culloden*. On the contrary, the prince was clear-headed and determined, he was flexible enough to adapt himself to the most varied people and circumstances, and he had a rare gift for raising sunken spirits. Physically he had trained himself for his role by a taxing regime of hunting and exertion, showing a self-discipline that abandoned him entirely in later years.

Expecting a French invasion of Britain early in 1744, Prince Charles hastened from Rome to join the expedition. The project was cancelled at the last moment, which caused him to lose faith in official French help, and he invested his hopes instead in his contacts among the Irish traders. On 4 June 1745 his privately-financed expedition came together when the nimble privateer *Le du Teillay* met the ex-British battleship *Elizabeth* off the coast of Brittany, and the two sailed together for Scotland, bearing artillery, muskets, broadswords, cash and 700 troops of the Irish Brigade. This was well short of the invasion force of 6,000 that had been demanded by the prince's potential supporters in Scotland and England, and the expedition became even more of a gamble after it encountered the British warship HMS *Lyon* on 9 July. The *Elizabeth* took such a battering in the following action that she had to turn back to France with all the troops. *Le du Teillay* sailed on alone, landing Prince Charles first on the little isle of Eriskay in the Outer Hebrides on 23 July, and then in the afternoon of the 25th on Arisaig on one of the most secluded coasts of the western Scottish mainland.

The prince was putting his sympathizers to a very severe test when he came ashore with his tiny group of ill-assorted associates, the 'Seven Men of Moidart'.[1] Some of the clan chiefs were hostile, while the others were uneasy about the lack of French assistance, but the prince had working for him the ancient Scottish loyalties to the House of Stuart, and the resentment which many Scots felt against the political union with England in 1707. Deploying all his persuasive charm, Prince Charles made a valuable conquest in the form of Donald Cameron of Lochiel, who commanded much respect among the western clans; he also won over the old and bent John Gordon of Glenbucket, who was the first of the eastern lairds to declare himself. On 19 August the first sizeable force assembled at Glenfinnan at the head of Loch Shiel, and the Jacobites raised their standard of red and white.

On the next day the prince's men began their eastward march, while the government's commander in Scotland, Lieutenant General Sir John Cope, set out from Stirling for the Highlands with a scratch force of about 1,500 troops. A battle seemed to be in the making, for the rivals were converging from opposite sides on the great grey ridge of the Monadhliath Mountains, which separated the Great Glen from upper Strathspey. At this juncture Cope lost his nerve. On 27 August he abandoned his attempt to gain the high Corrieyairack Pass, and over the following days he fled north-east to Inverness, convinced that the Jacobites were at his heels.

On 28 August, a day of blazing heat, Prince Charles crossed the Corrieyairack unopposed and descended into Strathspey. He was playing for high stakes. He rightly rejected the opportunity to chase and beat Cope, for by removing himself from the scene that gentleman had left open the road to the Lowlands. On 29 August the Jacobites arrived at Dalwhinnie at the head of the new military road which led so conveniently to the south. They were at Blair Castle in Atholl on 1 September. Two days later they traversed the narrows of Killiecrankie, and on the 4th they reached Perth, where they rested and gathered strength until the 11th. They came to Dunblane on 12 September, and the next day they reached the Lowlands when they passed the upper Forth at the Fords of Frew, a step of great symbolic and practical importance.

The Jacobites were stepping out with some urgency, for they knew that Cope had come to his senses, had marched from Inverness to Aberdeen and was taking ship there in the hope of reaching Edinburgh before Prince Charles. He was now moving as fast as he could, but he was delayed by adverse winds and tides, and he did not arrive in the Firth of Forth until after dark on 16 September. By that time Prince Charles and his 1,800 or so men were already outside the city.

Edinburgh, unlike the solidly Whig Glasgow, was divided between partisans of the houses of Hanover and Stuart. The Whigs could put precious little trust in their primitive town walls, hardly any in the hastily assembled trained bands, town guards and volunteers, and none at all in the only available regular troops, namely two regiments of dragoons who now fled the neighbourhood in panic. Early on the 17th a party of Highlanders gained entry by way of the Netherbow Port, and the prince arrived to an ecstatic welcome later in the day.

On 20 September 1745 two armies were moving to contact in the country to the east of Edinburgh. They numbered about 2,400 men each. The one was under the command of Lieutenant General Sir John Cope. Having embarked at Aberdeen, he had landed his troops on the 17th and 18th at Dunbar, the nearest secure port to Edinburgh. On shore he met the two

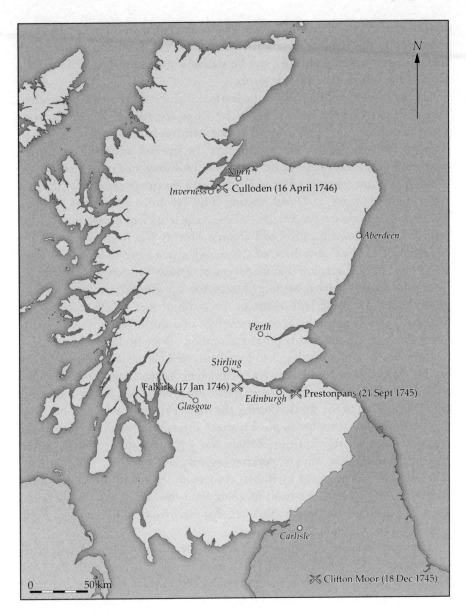

Figure 2. Location of the battles of the '45.

shaken regiments of dragoons that had so far failed to offer any show of resistance to the Jacobite advance. Cope had shrunk from doing battle with the Jacobites in the Highlands, but he was now determined to strike off the head of the rebellion at a single stroke.

On the morning of the 20th Cope learned that the other army in question, that of Prince Charles, was on the move. Cope accordingly halted his westward march on the open ground that extended from a morass north of Tranent towards the sea. He trusted that the flat and unobstructed terrain would act to the advantage of his troops, and his dragoons in particular.

Early the same morning Prince Charles and his troops set out for the east from their bivouacs at Duddingston. The Jacobites continued through Fisherrow and crossed the Esk by the spectacular ancient bridge that carried the road onto Musselburgh. Lord George Murray was in the lead with the regiment of Lochiel, and directed the march around the south of the town and Pinkie Park. Learning that Cope was at or near Prestonpans (Figure 2), he at once made for what he judged to be the key ground: the long, smooth grassy ridge of Falside Hill, rising to the south of that village. Early in the afternoon the Jacobites arrayed themselves in a north-facing line of battle along the high ground and as far as the mining village of Tranent.

Cope had his troops well in hand, and adjusted his positions repeatedly to accord with what he could discover of the enemy movements. The day ended with his original west-facing line of battle changed to one facing the marsh (the 'Meadows') to the south. During the night Prince Charles and his principal officers debated what to do. To attack directly across the stretch of the Meadows immediately in front of them was a physical impossibility, and so they began to think of ways of working around Cope's position from the east. The solution was provided by Robert Anderson, the son of the owner of the Meadows, who was in the habit of going wild-fowling in the marshes, and knew of a difficult but practicable track that ran by way of Riggonhead Farm and across the far end of the Meadows.

The long Jacobite column set off just before four in the morning of 21 September 1745. The Duke of Perth made good progress with the Clan Donald regiments, which according to ancient custom made up the right wing and on this occasion had the lead. Lord George commanded the left wing, which came up behind and was accompanied by Prince Charles. In leaping one of the ditches the prince fell to his knees, and had to be hauled to his feet. In spite of this bad omen, both wings of the main force were clear of the marsh at dawn, and formed in line of battle.

Towards five the redcoats saw indistinct forms on the near side of the swamp, and in the half-light the Highlanders in their dark plaids looked like nothing so much as a line of bushes. Once he had grasped what was afoot, Cope responded with some speed. He wheeled his main force of infantry to the left by platoons, and marched them to form a 670-pace line of battle parallel to the advancing Jacobites, with the two regiments of dragoons in support. His feeble artillery consisted of four light mortars and six little 'galloper' cannon, and was posted on the far right. There were just two officers to serve them, and the action opened when the pair ran along the line of pieces and touched them off one by one, like pyrotechnicians at an old-fashioned firework display. After that, the dragoons opened a fire by volleys with their carbines.

As commander of the Jacobite right wing, the Duke of Perth had been concerned to leave plenty of space to allow the left under Lord George to form up on the northern side of the marsh, with the result that the duke's wing outflanked the long line of redcoats by a useful 100 paces. This impetus gave added effect to the three regiments of Clan Donald as they advanced in good order and closed with the enemy. Men and horses began to fall among Hamilton's regiment of dragoons (the 14th), and the sight of Lieutenant Colonel Wright being pinned beneath his horse helped to provoke a general flight which carried the reserve squadron along with it.

Cope's centre and right were already staggering under Lord George's attack. Cope's artillery was overrun, and the three squadrons of supporting dragoons (Gardiner's 13th) fled one by one. The line of redcoat infantry was now exposed, and the platoons disintegrated in succession from their right flank.

The fleeing troops crowded towards the parks of Preston and Bankton, and their panic was heightened when they lapped around the tall enclosing walls of stone. Some of the dragoons made off west towards Edinburgh, 'with their horses all in fro' and foam', and a party actually galloped up the High Street and into the Castle.[2] The rest of the fugitives hurried south by way of 'Johnny Cope's Road' past Bankton House, and the flight continued almost without intermission all the way over the Lammermuir Hills and on to Berwick-upon-Tweed. Brigadier Thomas Fowke and Colonel Lascelles caused great scandal by arriving ahead of their men.

Between 150 and 300 of Cope's troops had been killed, most of them mutilated in the heat of action by broadswords and Lochaber axes, and the abandoned field looked as if a hurricane had spread the contents of a slaughterhouse over the ground. The number of the redcoat prisoners was disproportionately high, at probably more than 1,300, which indicates a collapse of morale. Prince Charles forbade any gloating at the defeat of his father's subjects, and ordered all possible care to be taken of the wounded, though nothing could be done for the gallant old Colonel Gardiner, a local man, who died of his wounds.

The appalled Whig clergyman Alexander Duncan lamented that 'since the days of the Reformation a more dismal day did not shine on the friends of liberty and the Protestant interest in North Britain, than on the 21st of September 1745, the day of the Battle of Preston'.[3] In the international context, the little battle at Prestonpans bears direct comparison with Washington's victories at Trenton and Saratoga in 1776 and 1777, which energized the anti-British party among the colonists, shook the British and persuaded potential allies that the Revolutionary Army was a force to be reckoned with. For the Jacobites in 1745, their victory at Prestonpans enabled them to argue their case with renewed conviction among the French, who so far had been content only to observe the progress of the Highland Army, and in the next month the French pledged their formal support in the Treaty of Fontainebleau.

The first news of Prestonpans had already prompted the French to renew their plans to invade England. However, the difficulties of bringing troops and shipping together on the Channel coast repeatedly postponed the attempt until, by 26 December, the Royal Navy had been given time to redeploy its forces in the narrows. The diversionary effect was nevertheless significant, and it might have been decisive if the French had been able to co-ordinate the threat with the Jacobite advance on London. More immediately, the French began to ship support direct to Scotland by instalments. The first four vessels reached the eastern coast between 9 and 19 October, bearing small arms, artillery, ammunition and specialist military personnel.

Meanwhile the beaten redcoat army fell prey to recriminations, of officers against officers, soldiers against officers, officers against soldiers, infantry against dragoons, dragoons against infantry, and almost everybody against Cope. At the heart of the matter was the fact that an attack pressed home with cold steel had terrified everyone out of their wits. It had been an unmistakable product of the Highland military culture. In the conventional European warfare of that period, the combat of infantry against infantry had been reduced to a process of attrition, whereby the rival forces faced each other at a range of about 100yds and fired blindly into the smoke. On 21 September 1745 Cope had no reason to suppose that he was dealing with an enemy who would close the distance at a run with raised broadswords. These weapons inflicted gaping, gushing wounds that on the whole were less lethal than those made by bullets, but were endowed with a horror of their own. It was the combination of physical and mental effect that gave the Highland charge its power, and made Prestonpans the pivotal battle that it was – pivotal in the

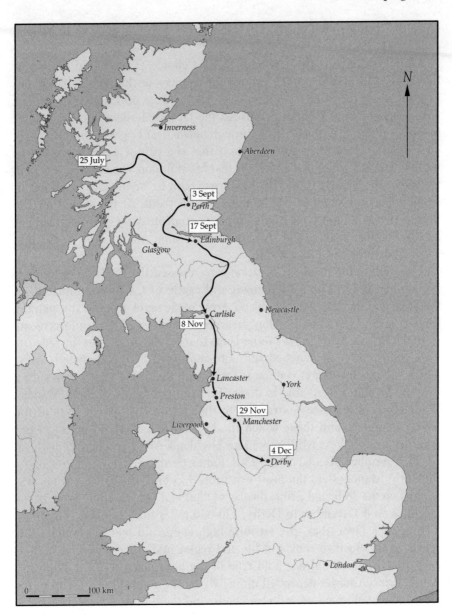

Figure 3. The Jacobite march to Derby, winter 1745.

sense that it imprinted on the Highland Army a potent sense of its tactical superiority.

After Prestonpans the Jacobites faced a choice. They could remain in Scotland and consolidate their grip on the country, or they could march into England along the eastern coast to Newcastle, and cut off London's source of coal. Instead Prince Charles persuaded the Jacobite leaders into the boldest possible option, that of marching through north-west England and ultimately on London. Here lay a contradiction that the prince never managed to resolve. He was 'going for broke', in that his ambition was nothing less than to restore the Stuarts to the British throne, and he hesitated to spell out in detail what provisions he had in mind for Scotland. At the same time the perspective of at least some of his supporters remained not only Scottish, but locally Scottish at that, and their blinkered vision was to work to the disadvantage of the cause as a whole.

The leading troops of the invasion force crossed the English border on 8 November 1745. The walled town and castle of Carlisle submitted on the 15th, and thereafter the Highland Army made rapid progress through the English north-west. The London government summoned up reinforcements from the British Army in the Netherlands to meet the threat, but the redcoats were consistently out-marched and outmanoeuvred by the Highland Army, which was much better at coming to terms with the severe weather. In such a way the Jacobites were able to dodge between the forces of Field Marshal Wade (Cope's successor), stranded to the east on the 'wrong' side of the snowy Pennines, and those which the Duke of Cumberland began to put together in the West Midlands. The Highland Army reached Penrith on 20–21 November, Kendal on the 23rd, Lancaster the next day and Preston on the 26th. Manchester, the most avowedly Jacobite of English towns, was entered on the 28th, and a final display of bluff and fast marching brought the Jacobites on 4 December to Derby, 120-odd miles from London (Figure 3). There, on 5 December, the Jacobite high command met in council. The spirits of the Scottish rank and file and regimental officers were as high as ever, but the same did not hold true in the headquarters of the Highland Army. Prince Charles depended ultimately on the goodwill of a group of the most influential grandees and clan chiefs, and these in turn were inclined to take their lead from Lord George Murray, who remains one of the most enigmatic figures of the '45. Lord George was extraordinarily active, and the author of many brilliant initiatives. He was at the same time moody, vindictive and headstrong to the point of irresponsibility. Prince Charles was almost certainly wrong when he came to believe that Lord George was a traitor, but there was something about the man that undeniably attracted suspicion.

When numbers are measured against time, the rate of recruiting in England compared well enough with that in Scotland, but the English Jacobites had failed to declare themselves in such decisive numbers that Prince Charles could count on a strong English military arm. Meanwhile there was no sign of a French invasion. The forces of Cumberland and Wade were intact, even if they were freezing and exhausted, and a government agent planted a false report that a third army was in the offing. The doubters carried the day, and on 6 December the baffled officers and men of the Highland Army were ordered to turn their noses to the north.

The rights and wrongs of the decision to retreat from Derby will always remain a matter for debate. The Highland Army could almost certainly have reached London, which was only about six days' march distant, and where the Whig citizens were in a state of consternation. On the other hand, King George was resolved to fight for his capital, with the outcome at least in part dependent on how far the government's likely superiority in numbers (about 6,950 troops as against 5,500 Jacobites) would have counteracted the Highland Army's advantage in morale.

The decision to retreat from Derby was not in itself a mortal blow to the cause, for the Highland Army had been neither outmanoeuvred nor outfought, and the spell which had been cast at Prestonpans was as potent as ever. Ultimately the significance of the council's decision on 5 December lay in closing down an important option which had been open to the Jacobites.

The Highland Army disengaged from Derby cleanly, and made its way back through north-west England at such speed that the only forces of the government that came within reach were two flying columns, one from the main army under Cumberland in person, and the other commanded by Major General James Oglethorpe, who, having been detached by Wade, executed a forced march over the Pennines. There were hopes of catching the Scots before they could slip away from England, but on 18 December Lord George Murray fought a creditable rearguard action at Clifton, and two days later the Highland Army crossed the fast-rising Esk and then passed the little River Serk into Scotland (see Blackmore, this volume, for more on Clifton).

In Carlisle, Prince Charles left a garrison of up to 400 troops, including 113 officers and men of the newly raised Manchester Regiment who remained there at their own request. The Duke of Cumberland subjected Carlisle to a siege, and on 30 December he forced the Jacobites to surrender 'at discretion', which left them open to unlimited ill-treatment. Prince Charles was blamed at the time and by critics afterwards, but it had not been unrealistic to think of holding Carlisle as a foothold across the border. The Scottish homeland had meanwhile been contested between the Whigs and redcoats, on the one hand, and on the other by the Jacobites, who were recruiting heavily in the Episcopalian north-east, and had received a very significant accession of strength in the form of a train of artillery and 800 or so regular Scottish and Irish troops who had been shipped from France.

Charles had reasonably enough assumed that he would have this second army at his disposal, but the domineering Lord John Drummond had wrested control from Lord Strathallan, and had refused to bring his men to join the prince in England, despite a request from Charles and the entreaties of a party of his own officers. There was no alternative but to bring together the two groups of forces in the Central Lowlands. Carlisle was left to its fate, and the Highland Army marched by way of a hostile Glasgow to join Drummond outside Stirling on 4 January 1746. The amalgamated forces came to 9,500 men, which gave Prince Charles the best-balanced and largest army he ever commanded. With these resources available the prince laid siege to Stirling Castle, the key to the passage between the Highlands and the Lowlands.

The Duke of Cumberland had abandoned his immediate pursuit, but the redcoats, too, had been massing. The Highland Army had left Edinburgh to the Whigs when it marched into England, and it was here that the much put-upon former army of Cope and Wade gained its third and probably worst commander, Lieutenant General Henry ('Hangman') Hawley. In his own words Hawley was 'resolved to strike while the iron is hot . . . with everything they [the Jacobites] have brought from the north they are now 7,000 men, but that's nothing, they are Scotch, and only so many mouths which must be fed'.[4] Hawley and his generals feared only that the Jacobites might slip away before there was a chance to bring them to battle.

Hawley marched west from Edinburgh on 13 January, and three days later he encamped his 8,000 or so troops outside Falkirk. It was not easy for the Jacobites both to maintain their siege of Stirling Castle and hold the rest of their troops (anything between 6,160 and 8,200 men) in the open air in constant readiness to do battle with Hawley, who was moving rather more slowly than had been expected. Early on 17 January 1746 the Jacobites accordingly struck out from Plean Muir to bring matters to a head. Their march took them across the Carron and Bonny waters and onto the rough pasture of Falkirk Muir, which rose just to the south-west of the town.

Early in the afternoon Hawley awakened to the threat and began to rush forces piecemeal to the high ground. First on the scene were his three regiments of dragoons (the 10th, 13th and 14th) who opened an unsupported attack. They encountered the Jacobite right (southern) wing under the command of Lord George Murray, and were broken by the devastating fire and fierce resistance of the three Clan Donald regiments of the first line, and by the composure of the Lowlanders who made up the second (the Atholl Brigade, regiments of Ogilvy and Gordon). The 14th Dragoons fled back the way they had come, while the 10th and 13th streamed off to the right and received the fire of the whole Jacobite first line in their wild career. Lord George then launched a counter-attack which carried as far as the horrified spectators who had gathered to watch the excitement. It was perhaps typical of him to have no further regard to what was happening to the rest of the army.

The regiments of Hawley's infantry were now coming into action, and not in the best of order, for they were hastening up the slopes in the teeth of a gale of icy rain. On the muir they were met by a furious attack on the part of the Camerons and the Appin Stewarts of the Jacobite left (northern) wing. Altogether, five of Hawley's regiments took to their heels. The disintegration was, however, stayed for a time by the steadfastness of two regiments, Barrell's 4th and Ligonier's 59th, which were sheltered from the onslaught by a ravine, and were able to shoot up the left flank of the Jacobites as they rushed past. One further regiment (Howard's 3rd) and elements of two more (Price's 14th and Battereau's 62nd) were still under command, and Major General Cholmondeley tried to rally the dragoons for a counter-attack. The Jacobite left wing halted amid a spreading panic, and lost contact altogether with Lord George, who had continued his headlong pursuit and was lost to sight.

As the murk of the winter afternoon enveloped the muir, the troops of both sides began to abandon the ground in a less than glorious fashion. The one intact and uncommitted force remaining on the field was that of the Jacobite deep reserve, namely the three picquets of the Irish Brigade and the grenadier company and a fusilier company of the Royal Ecossois, all of them regular troops who had been shipped from France. The Irish Lieutenant Colonel Walter Stapleton brought them into action to decisive effect. Up to 700 of the disordered men of the Jacobite left wing rallied on them, and this final advance induced the redcoats to fall back downhill, many of them in disarray and abandoning their artillery (which had bogged down) to the Jacobites. The day ended with the Jacobites in possession of the enemy camp and Falkirk town, and Hawley's demoralized army in full retreat to Edinburgh.

Some of the government troops had fought better than in any previous action of the '45, but Falkirk had ended in an unequivocal Jacobite victory, being invariably described as such at the time. If the respective casualties are still difficult to establish, the battle had turned to the advantage of the Jacobites by all the criteria then current: ground taken, and the numbers of

Figure 4. Scene from a Jacobite camp. (Contemporary drawing from the Penicuik collection, © Sir Robert Clerk)

prisoners and trophies, the capture of the artillery being particularly significant.

It will perhaps be useful to take stock of what made the Jacobite forces so formidable up to that time. The leadership at all levels was of a high quality, though the importance of setting a personal example could induce even high-ranking officers (such as Lord George Murray) to lose sight of the larger picture. The Jacobite forces were known as the Highland Army, and Highland symbolism, above all the tartan, was sported as a token of solidarity by English, Welsh and Irish Jacobites, as well as by the Scots. It is true that only the clan society of the Highlands could have generated the necessary armed support in the first weeks of the rising, and indeed the Highlanders in the first line of battle remained literally the cutting edge of the cause until its final days. However, it would be misleading to fall in with the London government's representation of the combatant Jacobites as an undisciplined mob of Highland Catholics. In fact Prince Charles structured his forces on the line of a regular army, complete with military law, conventional designation of units and formations, regular pay and a complete hierarchy of ranks. The Jacobites were held under tight discipline, and the celebrated Highland charge was not an expression of blind instinct but something to be conserved and unleashed as the battle-winner that it was.

The Highland Army accommodated a large, growing and ultimately preponderant element of eastern Lowland Scots. In fact the most consistent support for the cause resided not in the Highlands and Islands (most of which remained under Whig control), but in eastern Scotland between the firths of Moray and Tay, where unreconciled Protestant Episcopalians were outraged against the Glorious Revolution, which had violated the divine line of kingship, as invested in the Stuarts, and against the ecclesiastical settlement which had ousted the 'Piskies' in favour of the Presbyterian 'Church of Scotland by law established'.

Prince Charles was a stickler for legal form. According to the usages of civilized war at the time, he was sedulous in the care he took of the enemy wounded and other prisoners, and he released their officers upon their word of honour not to serve against him. In every place of any size which came under his control he had his father proclaimed king in virtue of the authority vested in himself as prince and regent, and he set up an apparatus of civil control, complete with officers and tax collectors. All this effort was designed to build up an impression of credibility for his cause.

Here we have a measure of the task that lay before William Augustus, Duke of Cumberland, who reached Edinburgh on 30 January 1746 to assume command of the beaten army. He brought with him the prestige attached to his birth, as the favourite son of King George II. His objective qualities were another recommendation. While Hawley had tyrannized his troops and led them to defeat, Cumberland was affable to all ranks and attentive to their welfare, and maintained a bluff manner that inspired confidence. Without losing time, the duke set off from Edinburgh on the morning of the 31st to relieve Stirling Castle, which was running short of provisions.

Cumberland's arrival coincided with a crisis in the Jacobite high command. The Highland Army had mounted no proper pursuit of Hawley, and the redcoats were allowed to return to their senses and look forward to the coming of their duke. At the same time, Lord George Murray and the clan chiefs were concerned at what seemed to them to be a runaway desertion among the Highlanders, and on 29 January they presented Prince Charles with an ultimatum demanding a retreat to the Highlands, where they could extend their control, raise fresh men from the lands of the western clans and prepare for a new campaign in the spring. Prince Charles was dumbfounded, for he had been looking forward to the new battle which seemed to be imminent. The weight of opinion was against him, and on 1 February the Jacobites abandoned the siege of Stirling Castle in some confusion, which was a portent of a decline in their hitherto excellent staff work. The leaders came together again at Crieff on 2 February, and Lord George and the chiefs presented a specific plan for a retreat all the way to Inverness, which brought with it the abandonment of the eastern coastlands with their ports and their population of faithful Jacobite Episcopalians. Prince Charles was right to doubt whether his cause would have any future over the long term, for Lord George and his party were writing off a vital base for recruiting and taxation, together with the ports that were the only channel by which French help could still reach the Jacobites on any scale. Charles was overruled. If we consider the history of the rising in terms of the opening or closing of options, then the council at Crieff was of more account than the one at Derby a couple of months before.

Prince Charles and the Highland Division now made for Inverness by an inland path, while Lord George Murray and the Lowland Division followed a route that skirted the coast. Lord George abandoned town after town in his haste, to the extent that his march resembled a flight rather than a retreat. On 27 February a French convoy arrived off Aberdeen with a reinforcement of some 700 regular troops, who would have represented a valuable accession of force, but the ships had to stand off when a party went ashore and discovered that the Jacobites had left the place, and that the enemy army was only a matter of hours away.

Pending the start of the new campaigning season, the Duke of Cumberland established his forces in and about Aberdeen, which he ruled like a conquered city. Prince Charles made his headquarters in Inverness, but the greater part of his men dispersed to gather strength in familiar Highland recruiting grounds, eliminate the isolated garrisons of government troops or act against the Earl of Loudoun, who commanded the forces he had gathered at Inverness from the Campbells and the Whig clans of the far north.

On 18 February 1746 Loudoun had escaped from Inverness to the Black Isle in the face of the Jacobite concentration which was bearing down on him. He then retreated to what he thought was secure refuge, behind the line of the Dornoch Firth and the River Shin and its lochs. Loudoun was not safe even there, for on 20 March the Duke of Perth executed an assault by boats straight across the Firth, an operation which has a claim to be the most accomplished that was staged by either side in the course of the rising. Loudoun's forces scattered, some making for Skye, and the rest for the lands of the Mackays in the far north, where we shall hear of them again.

At Inverness Loudoun had left a garrison in the original Fort George (not to be confused with the later Fort George on Ardersier Point). The Jacobites at once took the place under siege, and on 21 February the garrison surrendered out of fear of being undermined and blown up. This was the first stage in an operation that was intended to secure the strongpoints along the axis of the Great Glen. Fort Augustus at the head of Loch Ness surrendered on 5 March after a Jacobite mortar bomb hit the powder magazine. Fort William at the far end of the Glen proved to be too hard a nut to crack, mainly because the fort could be reinforced and replenished from the sea by way of Loch Linnhe. On 3 April the Jacobites raised the siege, having lost invaluable time and the services of their best gunner, the Irish colonel James Grant, who was incapacitated by a wound and therefore unable to command the artillery at Culloden.

Lord George Murray was typically responsible for the most spectacular of the Jacobite enterprises, namely his raid (16–31 March) into the regality of Atholl. On the first day he broke through the chain of Campbell outposts, and on the 17th he laid siege to Blair Castle, which was held by 300 British regulars under the command of the eccentric old Lieutenant Colonel Sir Andrew Agnew. Lord George had hoped just to raise recruits in his native Atholl, but now he was succeeding beyond his expectations, and even managed to paralyze a corps of 5,000 fine Hessian auxiliary troops, who were deterred from their task of forcing the Pass of Killiecrankie. He asked Prince Charles for reinforcements, but had to obey the command to fall back to the army which was gathering at Inverness.

Skirmishing meanwhile continued east of the Spey between the advance forces of Prince Charles and Cumberland, with no clear advantage to either party. A daring expedition (27 February – 5 March) succeeded in destroying a store of Jacobite arms and ammunition in remote Corgraff Castle, while on the night of 20–21 March a Jacobite raid overcame a Campbell party in Keith.

The Duke of Cumberland was meanwhile building up and training his forces in Aberdeen and the hinterland, where they could be supplied by sea. He grasped that the notion of Highland tactical invincibility had to be broken at both the material and psychological level. He laid solid foundations of staff work and logistics, which not only met the demands of campaigning in the Highlands, but also reinforced his efforts to persuade his troops that he was concerned for their welfare. In the same way he understood that bayonets, unlike broadswords, were effective only when employed by troops working in total concert, and so his celebrated new bayonet drill was designed above all to enhance the solidarity of his men. The army would no longer plunge into action in the style of Cope or Hawley, but move forward in an orderly and cautious manner across reconnoitred ground, supported by a proper train of artillery, and with the flighty cavalry held back until it could intervene to the best effect. Cumberland denied the Jacobites claim to be lawful combatants, but he was now taking them seriously as enemies.

The old Jacobite advantages were falling away. Whether successful or not, the miniature campaigns just described had the effect of dissipating resources which could not be gathered again at full strength for the battle that was sure to come. The high command was as faction-ridden as ever and being eroded by disease, and so the foundation once offered by the Jacobite staff and supply system inevitably began to fall away. The men were literally starving.

For their day-by-day support the Jacobite officers and men depended heavily on their pay, which was now getting into arrears, and the prospects of an improvement were dashed when on 25 February a French sloop, *Le Prince Charles* (formerly HMS *Hazard*), was chased by a British flotilla and had to be beached in the Kyle of Tongue in the far north of Scotland. Captain Talbot and his men managed to get the treasure on shore, but when they struggled to make their way inland they were captured by Mackay clansmen and troops of Lord Loudoun's Regiment (the 64th, refugees from the Dornoch Firth and the Shin). A rescue expedition of 400 men under Lord Cromartie was captured on 15 April at Dunrobin and the Little Ferry, and would in any case have been too late to have fought at Culloden.

The prolonged and severe winter finally released its grip, and Cumberland took the field on 8 April 1746, at a time when Prince Charles was in no position to regroup his forces at full strength. On the 12th Cumberland's army forded the lower Spey just below Fochabers. There was no more than a token resistance, and even much greater numbers than were then available to the Jacobites would have been unlikely to stay the duke's progress, for his officers had identified thirteen practicable passages and could have outflanked any concentration of force.

On 13 April the Duke of Cumberland continued on his cautious way, marching westwards parallel with the coast, and shadowed by a supporting flotilla of the Royal Navy. He passed through Elgin, and camped four miles on the far side on a low rise at Alves.

When news of the passage of the Spey reached the Jacobites at Inverness, 'the town was in a general alarm, and even in confusion. Nothing was heard but the sound of bagpipes, the beating of drums and the clash of arms'.[5] Significant forces had still not reached the prince. The Camerons arrived at Inverness on the 14th, but the MacPhersons and MacGregors were still on their way (and in the event were too late to take part in the final battle). When Cumberland resumed his march that day the only troops that could be spared to stand in his way were a scattering of Fitzjames's Horse and the Hussars, and twenty-eight men of the Irish infantry regiment of Berwick. Skirmishing broke out when Cumberland's advance forces reached Nairn town, and continued for up to five miles on the far side of the Nairn River. The duke was content with his progress, recalled his out-parties and encamped on either side of Nairn, the cavalry on the right (southern) side of the river at

Auldearn, and the infantry on the left side just beyond Nairn town at Balblair.

On the 14th and 15th the Jacobite high command was riven with dissensions as to the best place to fight a battle, and indeed whether it was desirable to stand at all. The rights and wrongs are being argued even now. On the most fundamental issue there was a case to be made for declining immediate combat and instead withdrawing into the Highlands to offer a prolonged resistance there. The instincts of the chief of staff, Colonel John William O'Sullivan, drew him in that direction, but he rejected it when he considered how difficult it would be to maintain any substantial body in the wilds at this difficult season. In any case a campaign in the guerrilla style would have run counter to Prince Charles's constant striving to keep his army in being as a credible conventional force.

With the option of an irregular war put aside for the time being, the arguments revolved around the most suitable ground for combat. The site actually chosen, facing north-east on the comparatively level and open Drumossie Moor, was the one recommended to the prince by O'Sullivan. The choice has since been almost universally condemned, even though there was tactical potential in the enclosures on the two flanks, if exploited properly. Lord George's preferences were superficially more attractive. The first was to array the army above a hollow that reached into the higher ground south of the Nairn–Inverness highway near Dalcross Castle. The next was to fall back across the River Nairn to the formidable heights on the right bank, overlooking the steep valley near Daviot Castle, even at the risk of allowing the enemy a free run to Inverness and its irreplaceable store of oatmeal. Both suggestions made sense in the light of what the Jacobites had seen of the way the enemy had fought at Prestonpans, Clifton and Falkirk. Lord George was not to know how radically the Duke of Cumberland and his master tactician, Major General Humphrey Bland, had transformed the way the army moved and fought. The Duke now approached suspicious passages with elaborate care. Moreover he had with him a new asset in the form of the expert gunners of the Royal Artillery, and they would have found a fine target in an enemy drawn up 'in the shop window' on high ground.

The arguments just described related to a defensive battle, something that was alien to the temperament of the Highland Army. There was therefore an enthusiastic response, when, in the course of 15 April, Lord George Murray came up with the bold and positive proposal to march overnight and attack the enemy in their camp. It was decided that Lord George would take the lead with 1,200 men, while Prince Charles personally accompanied the Duke of Perth with the second division of some 2,400 more. At first the two divisions were to take a common route along the Moor Road (a track corresponding roughly to the axes of the present B9006 and B9091). Lord George was then to turn to the south, cross the Nairn and follow the right bank (the axis of the B9090) and come at the enemy positions from the rear. The second division would continue along the original route and attack frontally from the west. The mile-long column set off at six in the evening of 15 April.

The column became strung out in the darkness and driving rain, and early the next morning Lord George became convinced that the second division had fallen so hopelessly behind that the whole enterprise had failed. Still without crossing the Nairn, he retraced his route for about two miles, then struck north to the Nairn–Inverness highway and followed it back towards Culloden. He must have moved quickly, for the Moor Road was clear when the second division continued on its way, and ultimately came so close to the camp of Cumberland's infantry that the unsuspecting sentries were heard calling to one another in the darkness. Only now did the Duke of Perth learn that Lord George had abandoned the scheme that had brought the Jacobites so close to victory.

Daylight on 16 April found the Jacobites back on Drumossie Moor, exhausted and starving, and their leaders arguing furiously in Culloden House. The dissensions had been exacerbated because Lord George Murray had relegated the Clan Donald from its traditional place of honour, on the right wing of the formal order of battle, and now Cameron of Lochiel was blaming Lord George for the debacle of the overnight march. At quarter past five on the same morning Cumberland's redcoats were on the move, confident, rested, well-fed and well liquored-up, having celebrated their master's birthday in suitable style on the previous evening.

The events of the following hours are related in detail on other pages of the present volume. In essence, Cumberland's army soon came within full view of the Jacobites drawn up on Drumossie Moor. The redcoats then did something they had never done before, namely to wait calmly in their ranks while their artillery exacted a remorseless toll on the Highland Army, and their cavalry began to work around the flanks. Prince Charles saw that his enemy was not going to act according to type, and rather than see his troops continue to absorb punishment to no purpose, he released the army in an attack, relying even now on the spell of Prestonpans. This time the old magic had to contend with a storm of canister and musketry as the distance closed. The Jacobite right centre broke into the enemy array, but it proved impossible to advance further. All the rest of the redcoats were standing their ground, the Jacobite wedge was coming under counter-attack on its right flank, and the precious reserve of 'French' regulars was not at hand, for the

Irish and the Royal Ecossois were committed to ward off the developing threat to the Highland Army's wider flanks.

Before the morning was out, the surviving Jacobites had been beaten from the field and the Duke of Cumberland had begun his remorseless pursuit. It was rare at that period for a victory to be exploited so vigorously, and altogether unknown for the victors to ravage their enemy's homelands, and to proceed over the coming years to destroy the basis of their society.

Chapter 2

The Jacobite Army at Culloden

STUART REID

By friends and enemies alike, both ancient and modern, the last Jacobite army was more often than not referred to as the Highland Army. Strictly speaking this was not an entirely accurate description, for throughout the rising the army was steadily evolving and changing: the men who stood on Culloden Moor on 16 April 1746, willingly or otherwise, belonged to what was in some ways a very different, and certainly much more professional, force than the rather poorly armed Highland host which had charged out of the early morning mist at Prestonpans just seven months before. For a start, a substantial proportion of the army at Culloden came from Lowland Scotland, and it also included a French contingent, itself heterogeneously composed of Scots, Irishmen and Englishmen, as well as native-born subjects of King Louis. There were other Englishmen, Welshmen and Irishmen in the Jacobite ranks besides, and at least one lonely Spaniard, all serving in what was also in many ways a surprisingly conventional eighteenth-century army with cavalry, infantry, artillery, a reasonably competent staff and all the usual supporting elements. Consequently this essay aims to move beyond the popular image of a mere tumultuous mob of Highland swordsmen and so provide a fuller and much more rounded picture of the Jacobite army.

The Highlanders nevertheless remained its single most significant element, accounting for almost all of the front-line regiments, and it will therefore be as well to begin by looking at exactly who was there.

The Regiments at Culloden
That front line originally comprised the following: firstly, three battalions of the Atholl Brigade from Perthshire on the extreme right, totalling about 500 men. The two original battalions/regiments were Lord Nairne's and Lord George Murray's (the latter actually being commanded by Robert Mercer of Aldie), while the third was Archibald Menzies of Shian's; then came Donald

Cameron of Lochiel's 600 Camerons and Charles Stewart of Ardsheal's 200-strong Appin Battalion from Lochaber. Next to them stood Lieutenant Colonel Charles Fraser of Inverallochie's battalion of Lord Lovat's Regiment, mustering about 500 men (the other battalion, commanded by the Master of Lovat, was still hurrying towards the battlefield), and Lady Mackintosh's 700 men under Lieutenant Colonel Alexander McGillivray of Dunmaglas. Both battalions were chiefly raised in the Inverness area, while next to them Francis Farquharson of Monaltrie's 200 men came from Deeside. Then came three more equally small units – a combined battalion of Macleans and Maclachlans under Lachlan Maclachlan of Castle Lachlan and a little newly joined contingent of Chisholms from Strathglas led by Roderick Og, all three of them mustering no more than about 280 men in total. Finally on the left stood the three MacDonald battalions of Keppoch, Clanranald and Glengarry respectively. The first seemingly had about 300 men, and the second 250, while Donald MacDonnell of Lochgarry, who had taken over the third after young Glengarry was killed at Falkirk, had as many as 500 by his own account.[1]

According to these figures, which are largely derived from Thomas Sandby's excellent map (see Figure 18, Chapter 6), there may therefore have been something like a total of 4,000 men in the front line shortly before the battle began. A number of caveats, however, need to be entered. In the first place, Sandby's figures, which appear to have been based on captured Jacobite paperwork, are not only very round but probably followed the usual

Figure 5. Jacobite with targe and broadsword, named as MacDonald of Glengarry. (Contemporary drawing from the Penicuik collection, © Sir Robert Clerk)

eighteenth-century convention of counting only the 'bayonets', for elsewhere on his map he notes there were 1,674 'Volunteers and others'. In other words these figures may be exclusive of officers and non-commissioned officers. Conversely, the second caveat is that all accounts agree that the Jacobite ranks were severely depleted by straggling after the abortive attack on Cumberland's camp the night before and that there may in fact have been several hundred fewer men at the start of the battle, although it is quite impossible to quantify this shortfall in total, far less on a regiment by regiment basis.

Even allowing for both factors, Sandby's overall figures may be about right, for if those 4,000 men were drawn up in the four ranks seemingly adopted by the Jacobites, they will have occupied a frontage of some 1,000m, and by the time the necessary intervals between each battalion are factored in, the whole lot will have fitted very comfortably into the 1,100m gap between the Culwhiniac and Culloden Parks walls where the army first deployed.[2]

They also – and this is all too frequently overlooked – outnumbered the opposing British front line by a factor of nearly 2:1, for it initially numbered just 2,213 rank and file beside officers. Crucially, however, that British line was backed up by another, equally strong, while the Jacobite front line by contrast had very little standing behind it. There was in fact no fully formed second line as such. Instead, and in accordance with French tactical doctrine, the available second-line units were formed together in columns in order to act as a tactical reserve for the front line.

On the extreme right were the regular Royal Ecossois (Royal Scots),[3] commanded by Lord Lewis Drummond and numbering as many as 350 men, posted in the rear of Murray's division. More or less in the centre stood the main 'reserve' under Colonel John Roy Stuart, comprising two battalions of Lord Lewis Gordon's Aberdeenshire Regiment, commanded by John Gordon of Avochie and James Moir of Stonywood respectively, the first being about 300 strong and the latter having around 200 men; then two battalions of Lord Ogilvy's Forfarshire Regiment mustering another 500 men between them; John Roy Stuart's Regiment numbering about 200; Lord Kilmarnock's newly raised Footguards, with another 200;[4] old John Gordon of Glenbucket's Regiment with the same; and the Duke of Perth's Regiment, commanded by the Master of Strathallan with 300 men. Finally, mirroring the deployment of the Royal Ecossois on the right, the left flank of the second line was covered by the regular Irish Picquets commanded by Lieutenant Colonel Walter Stapleton. This composite battalion comprised detachments from the French army's Irish regiments: Dillon, Roth, Lally and Berwick and no doubt some dismounted troopers of the Fitzjames Cavallerie, making a combined total of some 302 men.[5] Once again, however, it has to be stressed that with the exception of the 'French' units, carefully enumerated by the Marquis d'Eguilles, these various figures represent the estimated strength of each unit on 15 April, and that the actual numbers standing on the moor at the outset of the battle next day may have been appreciably less.

However, as related in the narrative essay (Chapter 5), some significant alterations to these dispositions took place before the actual commencement of the battle. In the first place it proved necessary to bring forward three battalions to fill gaps in the front line caused by Lord George Murray's unilateral decision to move the Atholl Brigade forward, throwing the front line askew and stretching it over a longer frontage than it at first had men to fill. Colonel John Roy Stuart's Regiment went to fill a gap in the centre, standing beside others of his name in Ardsheal's Regiment, while Glenbucket's and Perth's were redeployed on the extreme left of the front line. Although O'Sullivan's comment that the MacDonalds 'by this had no more the left, they were almost in the Center' is something of an exaggeration, it is confirmed by Sandby's map.[6] This reinforcement, notionally at least, increased the strength of the front line by another 700 men to something in the order of 4,700 men, while by contrast Cumberland responded by adding just 410 men of the 13th Foot to his own front line.

There were also three bodies of cavalry, posted behind the second line. Firstly there was a composite squadron consisting of Lord Elcho's Life Guards and part of the regular Irish regiment of the Fitzjames Cavallerie on the right, while another combined squadron collectively referred to as the 'Highland Horse' – formed from the Scotch Hussars, Lord Strathallan's Horse and perhaps some of Lord Balmerino's Life Guards – was on the left. Finally, a small escort troop of Life Guards drawn from Balmerino's troop stood with the prince in the centre.[7] The latter group numbered just sixteen men, while the two others seem to have numbered no more than about seventy apiece. All of them, it should be noted, were mounted, however badly. Popular legend notwithstanding, there were no pathetic huddles of dismounted cavalrymen standing aimlessly in the rear. Instead, those individual troopers lacking horses for whatever reason were either incorporated into the ranks of Lord Kilmarnock's Footguards, or else standing in other infantry regiments of their choice.

Nor was the Jacobite artillery at Culloden the ill-assorted assemblage of guns, mismatched ammunition and untrained gunners so often represented by historians. In charge of the artillery for much of the campaign was Colonel James Grant, a well-regarded officer in the French service who organized a little battalion at Edinburgh formed from two companies of the Duke of

Perth's Regiment acting as gunners and a third serving as pioneers. It was originally intended that the latter were to be drawn from those members of the Duke of Perth's who were 'gardeners, carpenters and other workmen to serve as Pioneers and to march at the head of the Artillery',[8] but instead Captain James Johnstone's company appears to have been assigned to the task, together with a detachment from the Manchester Regiment. One of the actual artillery companies, left behind at Carlisle, was commanded by Captain John Burnet of Campfield, who had once 'belonged to the Artillery company at Woolwich'.[9] He was not the only professional gunner, for Grant had brought twelve French gunners with him in October to serve as instructors, and two French artillery officers named d'Andrion and Bodin were among those who surrendered after Culloden, together with an engineer officer named Du Saussey, who had commanded a gun there. The management of the artillery was not therefore quite so amateurish as it is sometimes portrayed, although Grant himself, having earlier been wounded, was not present.

The cannon were mostly British, either obsolete little pieces captured from General Cope's army at Prestonpans or more modern ones taken by the French at Fontenoy and run through the blockade. Over the few short months of its existence the Jacobite army found itself encumbered with a quite surprising variety of pieces. Some swivel guns were landed from the *Le du Teillay* but these lacked carriages of any kind, and although there was a proposal to mount them in 'sleeping batteries' (i.e. simply lay the barrels on the ground) in hopeful anticipation of Cope trying to force the Corrieyairack Pass, it was not until they invaded England that the Jacobites could boast a proper artillery train. According to Colonel Grant, who should have known what he was talking about, this comprised 'thirteen pieces, six whereof were taken from Sir John Cope, six 4-pounders that came from France, [and] one piece that was brought from Blair of Atholl'. Cope's guns were brass 1½-pounder curricle guns, so called because the barrel was mounted on a light flat-bottomed cart or curricle whose shafts doubled as the trail. The 4-pounders confusingly enough were also known as 'Swedish' guns, not because they were Scandinavian in origin but because they were an experimental light iron-barrelled gun, inspired by if not copied from the light artillery employed by Gustavus Adolphus a century before. The last, described as an 'octagon' when it was found abandoned at Carlisle, must have been an old brass piece dating back to the sixteenth century when such octagonal barrels were in vogue.

A number of guns appear to have been left at Carlisle, although the 4-pounders at least were brought back, and in the meantime, on 24 November, the *Le Renommee* landed a small siege train at Montrose comprising two 18-pounders, two 12-pounders and two 9-pounders. In addition another blockade-runner landed a number of British 3-pounders which had earlier been taken at Fontenoy, while another of these useful pieces was subsequently captured at Falkirk. The big guns were subsequently abandoned when the army retreated further north, but there were still twenty-two assorted guns and eight swivels at the end. Inevitably they were of various calibres, but it is clear from John Finlayson's map (Plate 6) that only eleven guns were actually deployed on the moor at the outset, and significantly they correspond to that same number of 3-pounders in the inventory of captured ordnance. Only one other – probably a 'Swedish' 4-pounder – was brought up by the French engineer Du Saussey after the battle had begun, so whatever their failings that day, confusion caused by a multiplicity of calibres was not one of them.

Assessments of what these guns actually achieved tend to be excessively coloured by their perceived poor performance at Culloden, and the fact that they never came into action at all at Falkirk, yet as General Hawley remarked on that occasion, for an army to march without artillery would have been 'silly'.[10]

Organization

Broadly speaking, in so far as it followed any particular pattern, the Jacobite army initially based its organization on that of the British army, although as time went on it betrayed more of a French influence. In the British army of the day (and for many years afterwards) the terms regiment and battalion were interchangeable, since nearly all of its infantry regiments consisted of just a single battalion. The same was true of most Jacobite regiments, which tended to average around 200–300 men and rarely exceeded 500. Some, however, fielded two or more battalions in the French style, but there was little consistency in the practice.

The first to do so was the Duke of Atholl's Regiment which fielded two battalions at Prestonpans and then three single-battalion regiments which were thereafter known as the Atholl Brigade. For the march into England a second rather ad hoc battalion, raised in Aberdeenshire, was also added to the Duke of Perth's Regiment. This was, however, a temporary expedient, and on the regiment's return to Scotland the second battalion was broken up and the survivors transferred to Lord Lewis Gordon's Regiment. Like the Atholl Brigade, this eventually comprised at least three battalions, raised in Aberdeenshire and Banffshire by John Gordon of Avochie, James Moir of Stonywood and Francis Farquharson of Monaltrie respectively, although

Lord Lewis never actually took the field at their head and to all intents and purposes they generally operated as independent units. At Culloden Avochie and Stonywood stood together against Hawley's cavalry near Culchunaig, but Monaltrie's battalion charged with the clans in the front line. Another regiment, Lord Ogilvy's, was originally a single-battalion unit from Forfarshire but, after marching to Derby and back, was joined by a second battalion raised in the meantime by Sir James Kinloch, and thereafter both units operated closely in tandem.

Generally speaking, it was the Lowland regiments that had two battalions, but at least two of the clan regiments had more than one as well; MacDonnell of Glengarry's Regiment at first had a single battalion, which went right through the campaign from beginning to end, but a second one led by Coll MacDonald of Barisdale fought at Falkirk only to miss Culloden through having been sent north in a vain attempt to recover some lost French gold (previously discussed by Duffy). The other regiment, Lovat's, had one battalion at Falkirk and would have been joined by a second on the field at Culloden if the battle had not been lost before they arrived.

Conversely many so-called regiments were wretchedly small and over-officered. The adjutant general, Colonel O'Sullivan, wryly commented that at the outset of the rising:

> All was confused . . . . They must go by tribes; such a chiefe of a tribe had sixty men, another thirty, another twenty, more or lesse; they would not mix nor separate, & wou'd have double officers, [that] is two Captns & two Lts, to each Compagny, strong or weak. That was uselesse . . . but by little and little, they were brought into a certain regulation.[11]

That there were too many officers is indisputable, and the problem was by no means confined to the Highland regiments – for it was particularly acute in the cavalry. 'There were several little people in Banffshire and Buchan, etc.,' commented one observer, 'who raised a few men each, and joined the Lord Lieutenant [Lord Lewis Gordon] and all got commissions of one kind or another, which was by no means hard to be obtained.'[12]

As a rule, under O'Sullivan's influence these smaller units were usually attached to larger ones – both the little contingent which John MacKinnon of MacKinnon brought from Skye and the Glencoe men, for example, were immediately joined to Keppoch's MacDonalds, while both the Glen Urquhart and Glenmoriston men (Grant's for the most part) were attached to Glengarry's Regiment. The Maclachlans, however, were for some reason at first attached not to another clan regiment, but to Lord Nairne's Regiment

Figure 6. Jacobite with targe and broadsword, named as Skiteraluch the Younger. (Contemporary drawing from the Penicuik collection, © Sir Robert Clerk)

in the Atholl Brigade before eventually being formed into a composite regiment with the Macleans shortly before Culloden. In all of these cases it would seem that they retained a fair degree of independence and that, although John Grant of Glenmoriston and Alexander Grant, younger of Shewglie, marched behind Glengarry's banner, they were never fully integrated into his regiment.

In any event, just as in other armies, each regiment was in turn made up of a number of companies of anything up to fifty or sixty men, although usually very much less. Exactly how many companies there actually were varied from unit to unit, but five or six companies seems to have been quite common in Jacobite units rather than the ten normally constituting a regular battalion in the British service or the thirteen fielded by French ones. Interestingly, at least three regiments – Glengarry's, Lochiel's and Lord Ogilvy's – are also known to have had grenadier companies, so presumably some of the others did likewise, although there appears to be no surviving evidence as to how their personnel might have been distinguished as the regiment's elite.

Recruitment

Filling the ranks of these various regiments, battalions and companies was far from easy. In theory the raising of a clan regiment should have been simple enough. The chief first called upon his 'people', that is his tacksmen (those who leased land from him), 'near relations, friends and partakers' to come out and, if they were in agreement, each in turn brought out their own tenants, servants and followers. It was thus possible to quite literally raise a regiment overnight, although arming it properly and keeping the men out sometimes proved a good deal more difficult in the long term.

Even at the very beginning, however, not all of the men came out readily. A fairly typical government intelligence report told how

> upon Thursday the 15th August [1745] Cameron of Kinlochlyon, Cameron of Blairchierr, Cameron of Blairmachult, Cameron of Glenevis, and Cameron alias MacKalonie of Strone, heads of the several tribes of the name of Cameron, came from Lochiel's country and entered Rannoch with a party of servants and followers to the number of about 24 and went from house to house on both sides of Loch Rannoch . . . and intimate to all the Camerons, which are pretty numerous on both sides of the loch, that, if they did not forthwith go with them, that they would that instant proceed to burn all their houses and hough their cattle; whereupon they carried off the Rannoch men, about one hundred, mostly of the name of Cameron.[13]

No fewer than fifty-seven out of eighty-seven men from Glen Urquhart and Glenmoriston, who later surrendered in May 1746, were variously noted to have been 'forced', 'pressed' or in one case 'dragd out'.[14] Similarly the Reverend William Gordon, of Alvie, declared that out of forty-three of his parishioners who were caught up in the rising, only three had gone voluntarily. The rest were forced out by 'burning their houses, carrying off their cattle, and breaking their heads'.[15] Nor was this all, for 'there was an express sent from Alex MacDonald of Keppoch . . . intimating to Alex Macdonald in Drumchastle and Alexander MacDonald of Dalchosney, the informer's father, both in the Duke of Athole's lands of Bunrannoch, that if they did not immediately go and join him, Keppoch, they would be proceeded against with burning and houghing as above'.[16]

Keppoch was evidently a firm believer in employing coercion, and the minister of Lochbroom afterwards testified that on 17 March 1746 Keppoch and some of his men turned up there and unexpectedly surprised the poor people, snatching some of them out of their beds. Others, who thought their old age would excuse them, were dragged from their ploughs . . . while some were taken off the highways. One I did myself see overtaken by speed of foot and when he declared he would rather die than be carried to the rebellion, was knock'd to the ground by the butt of a musket and carried away all bleed.[17]

These claims, obviously enough, were all advanced in mitigation after the rising, when many of these men were facing an uncertain fate. While a healthy degree of scepticism might be called for, it is only to a degree, for there is plenty of other evidence that all too many 'rebels' were forced to enlist. The quality of many of these sometimes reluctant recruits left a lot to be desired, and Captain John Maclean rather blandly recounted how on his march to join the prince's army early in the rising 'we catched a Deserter in a moor in Our Way but after two or three miles travelling with us we let him Goe he being 70 years old only took his Sword for one of our men'.[18] Nevertheless it would be a mistake to assume that all of the men standing in the ranks were pulled unwillingly onto the heather by the arbitrary power of their chiefs or their feudal superiors – or indeed that obedience to their chiefs was the sole determining factor in bringing them 'out'.

What is significant about the Lochbroom incident in particular is that the men in question were not actually Keppoch's clansmen, and most of those being press-ganged by him on this occasion went into the Earl of Cromartie's Regiment rather than his own, for allied to the clan system was the even more widespread and equally archaic concept of vassalage: that is, an ancient obligation on a man to turn out in arms at the behest of his landlord or feudal superior. Thus Alexander McGrowther claimed that as a landholder under the Duke of Perth, 'It was the custom to obey commands', while Peter Maclaren similarly spoke of a 'General notion that they must obey' him as their landlord.[19] If the Jacobite regiments belonging to what was referred to as the Highland Division represented the clans, then those in the so-called Lowland Division were substantially underpinned by vassalage.

Although the regiments belonging to that 'division' were routinely referred to as the Low Country Foot, this was very much an oversimplification. The Duke of Perth's Regiment had both Highland and Lowland companies, and in fact a substantial proportion of the men in many of these supposed Lowland regiments were actually of Highland extraction. This was certainly true of those men raised in the upland areas of Aberdeenshire and Banffshire – in Strathbogie, Strathavan and Speyside by John Gordon of

Avochie and old John Gordon of Glenbucket – and so, surprisingly enough, were the three regiments of the Atholl Brigade, from central Perthshire. All of them were officially accounted part of the Lowland Division. There was, perhaps with good reason, a decided feeling that the Highlanders serving in these particular regiments were a good deal less 'wild' than the ones from the west, but while this might arguably have been the case, the real difference was that they were raised by a combination of vassalage and the personal exertions of their officers rather than simply called or forced out as clan levies.

The Atholl Brigade, standing on the right of the front line at Culloden, was rather uncertainly recruited in this fashion, and in a typical exchange early in the Rising, the Jacobite Duke William[20] wrote to his 'vassals' in the Dunkeld area that, 'As . . . you and the rest of my Vassalls & tenants do not bestir yourselves with that activity that becomes Loyal Subjects . . . I once more require you peremtorely . . . to raise in arms all the men you can, and meet in Pitlochrie.'[21] However, while such orders from a clan chief such as Lochiel – or Keppoch – might have immediately produced the required numbers, whether willing or otherwise, John Stewart of Stenton responded to him a few days later that, 'the whole inhabitants there are quite degenerate from their ancestors, and not one spark of loyalty among them; not one of them will stir without force'.[22] Nor did matters improve thereafter, and in January Duke William was not only still complaining of the 'unspeakable difficulty'[23] he was experiencing in persuading men to enlist, but was also spending far too much time trying to round up those reluctant heroes who had deserted.

It was a similar story elsewhere, and this form of recruiting was not by any means confined to the Atholl Brigade but extended to a number of other areas where local families exercised a traditional influence over their neighbours and tenants – or fondly imagined that they did. In the north-east, for example, the formidable Lady Erroll certainly forced out a number of her tenants to join the regiment of Footguards being raised by her son-in-law, Lord Kilmarnock, to replace his cavalry troop, but otherwise the officers and men following the prince fell into several different categories. While the romantic notion of men cheerfully digging swords and muskets out of the thatch on their cottages on hearing that the Bonnie Prince had come may rightly be discounted, the army could never have been raised in the first place or sustained afterwards without a strong nucleus of willing recruits, although the reasons for volunteering were many and varied.

Factors ranged from a genuine (though not particularly widespread) enthusiasm for the Jacobite cause – or at least a strong objection to the present government, which was not quite the same thing – all the way through to peer pressure or even a sense of adventure. The decision, nevertheless, was rarely taken lightly, and notwithstanding those later claims of being forced or 'dragd' out, the Glen Urquhart men had deliberately committed themselves to the rising after a lengthy and mature debate held one Sunday in Kilmore churchyard, near Drumnadrochit.

One contemporary remarked that at first

> the Rebellion was favoured by almost all the common people. The promise of freeing them from the Malt Tax had a surprising influence upon them, this being a tax the Farmers are especially sensible of . . . . The Rebels therefore hitherto behaving civilly, listing only volunteers, paying freely, taking but some few good horses and arms as they met them, and freeing the country people from the eternal dread they were under of the Malt Gaugers, were looked upon by them as the deliverers of their country.[24]

Otherwise, the single most important reason motivating the volunteers seems to have been a widespread desire to re-establish Scotland's independence. The rising of 1745 was not, of course, strictly speaking a war fought between the Scots and the English, and there were easily as many Scots fighting for King George as were to be found standing in King James's ranks. Yet there is no doubt that in a way it was such a conflict, for many of the Highlanders' imported broadswords were unambiguously inscribed 'Scotland' (or 'Schotlande') and 'no Union', and the Jacobite army was very consciously a Scottish army in both character and appearance. Sir Walter Scott perhaps best captured the truth in his novel *Waverley*, written at a time when memories of the rising were still fresh and some of the actors still living. In Scott's eyes, the majority of those who donned the Jacobite white cockade were certainly very consciously fighting for Scotland, but it was for the old Scotland, and for a king at Holyrood again, rather than for the new outward-looking Scotland and the Union.

Then again, while some joined the rebel ranks from conviction, hope or curiosity, more than a few were simply opportunists suspected of running away from debts and the prospect of bankruptcy. Of James Moir of Stonywood it was said that 'This gentleman very early imbibed the Jacobite principles and was entirely educated that way; his fortune also was greatly embarrassed, so that his going off was no great surprise', and similarly the reason for John Hamilton of Sandstoun's involvement 'was generally imagined to be owing to the disorder of his affairs'.[25] Indeed it was remarked that while several merchants 'of note' had joined in the previous rising of

1715, this time around there were 'none but a few smugglers, and a very few tradesmen'.[26]

Whatever their motivation, some of the volunteers accepted commissions and set about recruiting men of their own, but many came in singly or in groups, perhaps with just a handful of friends and followers, much as two of Grant of Shewglie's sons did, setting off one morning with 'a dozen young fellows'.[27] Others were recruited in more conventional fashion, and John Crawford of the Duke of Perth's Regiment was seen 'with a White Cockade and sergeants halberd, along with a drummer, beating up for recruits for the rebels in Edinburgh',[28] exactly as his regular counterparts might have done.

Nevertheless once the first flush of enthusiasm had passed, recruits – or rather, willing recruits – generally became progressively harder to find and retain, so that in the end not only did the 'forcing' of men into the clan regiments become ever more brutal, but even in Lowland areas, where vassalage was no longer sufficient, the Jacobites resorted to levying men under something akin to the old Scots fencible system.

Utilizing the existing tax records the Jacobite leadership demanded that landowners should supply one able-bodied and properly clothed and equipped man for every £100 (Scots) of valued rent. Unsurprisingly this proved decidedly unpopular, but Lord Lewis Gordon commented in December 1745 that 'Although I have got some volunteers, I assure you that att least two thirds of the men I have raised is by the stipulation att first agreed on, and all those that have not as yet sent in their quotas, have been wrote to in very strong terms.'[29] The tenor of those threats can be imagined from instructions issued to some of his officers, who were to

> require from the heritors, factors, or tenants, as you shall think most proper, an able-bodied man for his Majesty King James's service, with sufficient Highland cloaths, plaid and arms, for each 100£ of their valued rent, or the sum of 5£ sterl. Money for each of the above men, to be paid to J.M. of Stonywood, or his order of Aberdeen: and in case of refusal of the men or money, you are forthwith to burn all the houses, corn and planting upon the foresaid estates.[30]

What was more he meant it, and although it was alleged by some that the Jacobites were more interested in taking the money rather than the recruits, 'the burning of a single house or farm stack in a Parish terrified the whole, so that they would quickly send in their proportion, and by this means, with the few that joined as volunteers, he [Lord Lewis Gordon] raised near 300 men called the Strathboggy Battalion in the country thereabouts'.[31]

How those quotas of men were actually filled is one of the more intriguing aspects of the affair, for when an accounting came to be made afterwards, the lists compiled for the government of those involved in the rising were careful to distinguish between those men who were volunteers, those who were or may have been 'forced' (generally by far the greater number) and those who were 'hired out by the County' or as paid substitutes by individuals.[32]

In Banffshire alone, where a substantial part of the Strathbogie Regiment was recruited, no fewer than one third of those reported to have been with the rebels were recorded as having been 'hired out by the county'.[33] In Forfarshire it seems to have been more common for individuals to hire substitutes to serve in Lord Ogilvy's Regiment. Charles Mather, a ploughman from Montrose, was 'hired by a farmer in his stead', as was James Miller from Glamis and Alexander Robertson from Forfar, but once again other men such as David Scott, also from Forfar, were 'hired by the county'. Surprisingly enough these hired men were rarely treated as real rebels afterwards, or at least they were not considered to be quite as culpable as those who joined in the rising from ideological or other motives, since they had clearly enlisted for money alone. Consequently a quite disproportionate number of them were left undisturbed at home by the authorities, or if they had actually been captured were statistically far more likely to be turned loose – or drafted into the ranks of the British army – rather than transported or brought to trial, since it was evidently not thought worthwhile to prosecute them even by way of example.

The government, or rather the army, was a good deal less lenient, however, when it came to another group – those who had formerly served King George. Collectively they tend to be referred to as deserters, but in reality the majority of British army personnel found serving in the rebel ranks were actually former prisoners of war. Some had once belonged to the Highland independent companies or to Loudoun's newly raised 64th Highlanders, and slipped easily into the Highland ranks alongside their friends and relations – and some of them it has to be said slipped just as easily back again into King George's.

The enlistment of English and Irish regulars was altogether a different matter. Just how many of Sir John Cope's men changed sides after their capture at Prestonpans is hard to assess, although largely anecdotal evidence points to a fairly sizeable number. A witness named Robert Bowey reported that:

On Friday last 27th Sept. he was at Edinburgh and there saw about 200 soldiers with the livery of H.M. King George go down under guard to the Abby, and shortly after saw about 40 carried away under guard . . . and the remainder set at liberty, and this deponent saw many going about at large with white cockades along with the rebels, by reason whereof it was said that they had all initiated the Pretender and were in his service.[34]

Judging by a couple of references in Jacobite orderly books to 'the redcoats of Perths' and John Roy Stuart's, most if not all of them may have ended up in those regiments, and in fact the adjutant of Perth's Regiment, John Christie, was formerly a sergeant in one of Cope's regiments. Few of them seem to have stayed around for very long, however, and of those who enlisted with John Roy Stuart it was commented that 'they mostly all left him'.[35]

Christie was exceptional, and at Culloden most of the former redcoats were not former members of Cope's army, but men who had enlisted into regiments of the French army's Irish Brigade. Some of them were indeed genuine deserters, who had crossed the lines in Flanders months before coming to Scotland with the Irish Picquets or the Royal Ecossois, but the single largest concentration were members of Guise's 6th Foot, who had been captured at either Inverness or Fort Augustus and then press-ganged into the French service. In his accounting of the French forces at Culloden the French 'ambassador' to the rebel forces, the Marquis d'Eguilles, recorded the remarkable figure of 148 prisoners and deserters out of a total of 260 men serving in the Irish Picquets alone – a staggering 60 per cent of their strength.[36] As they were in effect fighting with nooses around their necks (twenty-eight out of eighty-one captured were hanged), it is perhaps little wonder that this particular battalion should have fought so desperately.

The French

The French regiments which these men joined, voluntarily or otherwise, were in Scotland in the first place because on 12 October 1745 a treaty was signed at Fontainebleau formally committing the French government to providing direct military assistance to the rebels.

Origins aside, the French auxiliaries serving with the Jacobite army fell into two basic categories. As might be expected, a number of individual officers acted as military advisers and instructors. The most important, of course, was Colonel John William O'Sullivan, a professionally trained staff officer who served as the army's adjutant-general and quartermaster-general, and notwithstanding a quite undeserved reputation as an incompetent, did so very efficiently. Similarly, Colonel Sir John MacDonald of the Fitzjames

Cavallerie served very usefully as inspector general of the Jacobite cavalry throughout the rising. At a somewhat lower level, perhaps more typical, was the role played by Lieutenant Nicholas Glascoe in the Regiment Dillon, who was appointed major (and chief instructor) of the 2nd Battalion of Lord Ogilvy's Regiment. Inevitably the majority of these military advisers belonged to the Irish Brigade, but other individuals of Irish or Scottish descent included men such as Captain Jean O'Bryen of the Paris Militia, and Captain Charles Guilliame Douglas of the Regiment Languedoc.

Besides these individuals and a small contingent of gunners and engineers, there were also some troops. The first French convoy to run the blockade consisted of three frigates and five Dunkirk privateers carrying two infantry battalions – Lord John Drummond's Royal Ecossois and the famous Irish Picquets. It sailed in mid-November under cover of a gale, and although two of the ships were intercepted by the Royal Navy, the bulk of Drummond's men were landed at Montrose on 26 November, and others at Stonehaven and Peterhead.

The first was a single-battalion regiment formed in 1744 around a cadre drawn from various Irish regiments, although there is some evidence that efforts were made to raise a second battalion while it was in Scotland. The regiment was transported there in full and was lucky to lose only sixty officers and men en route when *L'Esperance* was captured off the Dogger Bank. After the landing at Montrose on 26 November a detachment subsequently fought at Inverurie on 23 December. The grenadier company and a fusilier picquet were at Falkirk, and according to d'Eguilles the regiment was still some 350 strong shortly before Culloden, where it was commanded by Lieutenant Colonel Lord Lewis Drummond of Melfort. Afterwards it surrendered at Inverness on 19 April.

The Irish Picquets, on the other hand, were a composite unit. Initially one picquet or detachment was embarked from each of the six Irish regiments in the French service. According to the 1750 *Regulations*, which reflected established practice, a picquet was a standard-sized unit of company size comprising a captain, lieutenant, two sergeants, a drummer and forty-seven men all to be drawn from the fusilier or line companies of a regiment, although prisoner lists show that those sent to Scotland were double-officered. Unfortunately only three of the picquets, representing the regiments Dillon, Rooth and Lally, actually made it to Scotland, where they were formed into a small provisional battalion, which served at Falkirk, the sieges of Fort Augustus and Fort William and finally at Culloden. On the eve of the battle, d'Eguilles reported that by then they had been reduced to a half, but by recruiting 148 prisoners and deserters, increased their numbers to 260 men, to which should probably be added a further 60 or so dismounted troopers of the Fitzjames Cavallerie and a picquet from the Berwick regiment; the latter landed at Peterhead at the end of February 1746 and served independently of the others until Culloden. According to d'Eguilles there were still forty-two men there but O'Sullivan thought them much weaker, perhaps only twenty-five strong.

Distracted for a time by the possibilities of mounting a full-scale invasion, there were no further attempts to run the blockade until February. This time the entire Fitzjames Cavallerie was embarked at Ostend on 10 February, but only one of the three transports evaded the Royal Navy to land a squadron at Aberdeen on 22 February.

Curiously enough, although designated as Irish and led by officers with Irish surnames, the troopers of this red-coated regiment, also better known as Fitzjames's Horse, were substantially of English extraction and included a surprising number of former merchant seamen. O'Sullivan says that sufficient captured dragoon horses were found for sixty of them, but if so they must have been in very poor condition for both Kilmarnock's and Pitsligo's regiments had to be dismounted in mid-March and their horses turned over. The Marquis d'Eguilles reported they were 131 strong at Culloden but it would appear that no more than half were mounted, so the remainder must have served on foot with the Irish Picquets.

None of these units were very large, but they proved to be an utterly reliable little force which stood firm at Falkirk when everyone else on both sides was running away, and served as a sacrificial rearguard at Culloden. Had all of those shipped actually made it ashore the campaign would have taken on a very different aspect. Even as it was, the arrival of the two little battalions in Scotland had the uncovenanted (and often overlooked) dividend of forcing the withdrawal of a much larger Dutch contingent of ten battalions then serving with the British army. Having earlier been captured at the fall of Tournai they were prevented by the terms of their parole from serving against French troops or their auxiliaries – which the Jacobites had officially become by virtue of that treaty signed at Fontainebleau.

Fighting

The archetypal Jacobite soldier is generally portrayed as a Highland swordsman, carrying not just a basket-hilted broadsword and a round shield or targe, but a firelock musket, a pair of pistols and a dirk besides – all sufficient to inspire that well-worn joke about being as well armed as a modern battleship. Equally traditionally they are also portrayed as fighting in their shirt sleeves, in spite of the fact that the rising of 1745 was essentially a winter campaign culminating in a battle fought on a cold day with occasional showers of sleet.

In reality, both contemporary documentation and illustrations unsurprisingly show them reasonably warmly dressed, with coats and waistcoats above their plaids, and although some 2,000 cheap broadswords were carried from France on the *Le du Teillay*, swords generally appear to have been in surprisingly short supply. One much quoted observer in Edinburgh rather illiterately declared that the men who took the city in September 1745 had

> guns of different syses, and some of innormows length, some with butts turned up lick a heren, some tyed with puck threed to the stock, some withowt locks and some matchlocks, some had swords over ther showlder instead of guns, one or two had pitchforks, and some bits of sythes upon poles with a cleek [hook], some old Lochaber axes.[37]

This sorry picture did not last very long, however – the victory at Prestonpans saw to that.

Most of the clansmen depicted in an important series of eyewitness sketches by an unknown artist from Penicuik, near Edinburgh, are indeed carrying or brandishing their trademark swords (e.g. Figures 5 and 6), and writers of the time on both sides wrote as if all or most had them, it is true. On the other hand, closer investigation reveals a rather different picture. Returns of weapons seized or surrendered in the months after Culloden actually included comparatively few broadswords. When, for example, nineteen men from Glen Urquhart and sixty-eight others from Glenmoriston surrendered to the Laird of Grant at Balmacaan on 5 May 1746, they handed over a total of sixty-nine firelocks, seven bayonets, seven pistols, thirty-four swords, four dirks and one Lochaber axe. Similarly, when a further seventy-seven of Glengarry's men surrendered on 15 May they handed over sixty-five firelocks, but only twenty-six swords and four dirks.[38] It is of course possible that some men were concealing their heirloom swords, but the absence of swords in these and other surrenders is not only consistent but is borne out by the evidence from Culloden itself. The generally accepted estimate is that up to 1,500 Jacobites may have been killed or wounded there, and at least 750 were certainly counted lying dead on the battlefield. Yet when it was cleared afterwards only 190 broadswords were recovered, which means that at best only one in four of those killed or wounded on the moor itself was carrying a broadsword at the time. This would have been sufficient for each of those standing in the front rank – the

Figure 7. Jacobite on sentry duty with musket and bayonet. (Contemporary drawing from the Penicuik collection, © Sir Robert Clerk)

Highland gentlemen – but their followers in consequence must have been relying upon their firelocks and bayonets. This was in fact graphically illustrated not only by the Penicuik sketches, but also by the discovery of a French bayonet in the area where the clans impacted on the British front line at Culloden, during archaeological excavations by a team from Glasgow University in 2005 (see Pollard, this volume).

There may also have been a similar shortage of targes. The named Highland gentlemen, such as Glengarry and Keppoch, depicted in the Penicuik sketches generally carry them, but not the rank and file, and on 30 September the city of Edinburgh was ordered to provide 2,000 'targets' for the army. As most of the Lowland regiments had yet to join the army, this indicates that even the clansmen at Prestonpans were lacking them and that the targes were being ordered to complement those cheap French broadswords brought over by the prince. How many were actually delivered is not known, although Lord Ogilvy ordered 'that all the Officers of his Regiment provide themselves in Targets from the armorers in Edinburgh'.[39] For the most part targes, perhaps like the prince's broadswords, were probably regarded by ordinary Jacobite soldiers as an encumbrance rather than an asset; and in any case even those who did carry targes seem to have thrown most of them away on the night march which preceded the Battle of Culloden.

In fact, all Jacobite soldiers were eventually armed with modern firelocks and usually bayonets as well. The orderly books are full of routine injunctions to officers and non-commissioned officers, requiring them to ensure that their men's arms were 'well fixed' and in good order, and it is clear that their firelocks rather than their swords were regarded as their primary weapons.

As to the preferred type, many no doubt brought a bewildering variety of fowling pieces, blunderbusses and other individually owned guns of all kinds and in all conditions when they first joined the army, but sufficient land pattern firelocks were certainly gleaned from the field of Prestonpans to completely equip Glenbucket's and Lord Ogilvy's newly raised regiments, as well as uncounted individuals. However in October 1745 alone some 2,500–2,600 French muskets were run through the blockade and landed at Montrose and Stonehaven. More followed over the coming months, and a cargo of 2,500 Spanish weapons (which shared the same .69 calibre) was landed in Barra in October or November 1745 and a second in Peterhead in late January 1746. As a result by early 1746 the Jacobites must have been able to standardize their primary weapons to a significant degree, for after Culloden, Ensign Stewart of Lascelles's (58th/47th) Regiment was ordered to draw 'French or Spanish firelocks and bayonets and cartridge boxes' from the train and 'distribute them to the prisoners of our army released here'. Clearly by that time there were not many captured British firelocks among the arms recovered from the battlefield.[40]

The position on cartridge boxes is less clear, however, and those delivered to Ensign Stewart may only have been those taken from the French regulars, for while it cannot be ruled out, there is no actual evidence of their being carried by ordinary Jacobite soldiers. Sometimes ammunition was issued in the form of ready-made cartridges, and there is a single note in the regimental orderly books for Lord Ogilvy's Regiment on 3 November that every man was 'to have 12 shot'[41] (a pretty average ammunition scale for European armies at this period), but ordinarily they may have used powder flasks and carried the shot loose in their pockets – or their sporrans.

General Hawley disparagingly, but not entirely inaccurately, described how the Jacobites 'Commonly form their Front rank of what they call their best men, or True Highlanders, the number of which being always but few, when they form in Battallions they commonly form four deep, & these Highlanders form the front of the four, the rest being lowlanders & arrant scum.'[42] In another frequently quoted passage, James Johnstone summed up Highland fighting methods thus:

Their manner of fighting is well adapted for brave but undisciplined men. They advance with rapidity, discharge their pieces
when within musket-length of the enemy, and then, throwing them
down, draw their swords, and holding a dirk in their left hand with
their target, dart with fury on the enemy through the smoke of their
fire . . . The reason assigned by the Highlanders for their custom of
throwing their muskets on the ground is not without its force. They
say they embarrass them in their operations, even when slung
behind them, and on gaining a battle, they can pick them up again
along with the arms of their enemies; but, if they should be beaten,
they have no [further] occasion for muskets.[43]

However, those following behind the swordsmen could do little more than
swell the numbers and O'Sullivan took a rather less sanguine view in
describing those tactics, writing that:

Any man that served with Highlanders, knows that they fire but
one shot, abandon their firelocks after. If there be any obstruction
that hinders them from going on the enemy, all is lost; they don't
like to be exposed to the enemy's fire, nor can they resist it, not
being trained to charge [i.e. reload] as fast as regular troops,
especially the English, which are the troops in the world that fires
best.[44]

Although Johnstone went on to cheerfully describe just what the front-
rank men did with their broadswords and dirks, actually engaging in
hand-to-hand combat was rare, for the success of a Highland charge
depended on their successfully intimidating the enemy before actually
making contact. It was indeed the Highland gentlemen who won the Battle
of Prestonpans, by brandishing their broadswords menacingly in a headlong
rush which frightened the life out of Cope's raw Scots recruits, brought up
as they had been on folk tales and memories of Highland ferocity. If on the
other hand the defending troops held their nerve and stood firm, the
Highlanders were often reluctant to close with them at all. This is clearly
illustrated by what happened at Culloden.

Owing to a combination of factors, the Jacobite right-wing units became
jammed together in a solid uncontrollable mass which impacted on the
British army's left flank and overran Barrell's 4th Foot through sheer weight
of numbers, but the clansmen were then halted by a counter-attack and
destroyed in a very unequal firefight shoot-out at point-blank range. The
Jacobite left wing on the other hand, slowed by boggy ground, advanced

much more deliberately and then finally came to a halt well short of the British front line. 'They came down three several times within a hundred yards of our men,' wrote one British officer, 'firing their pistols and brandishing their swords; but our brave soldiers appeared as if they took little notice of their bravado.' Baffled by the soldiers' failure to obligingly run away, they hesitated to move further forward. There was nothing unusual in this in so far as most other European soldiers tacitly halted before actually colliding with their opponents, and then commenced firing on each other until one side or the other gave way. The problem, of course, as O'Sullivan pointed out, was that once this happened the Jacobites were simply not well enough trained or equipped to shoot it out on equal terms.

Culloden was by no means the exception to the rule – if anything Prestonpans was the untypical encounter – and when those tactics produced a less than spectacular victory on the rain-soaked hillside at Falkirk four months after Prestonpans, the chiefs were in no doubt about the reason, as Lord George Murray himself explained:

> [T]he best of the Highland officers, whilst they remained at Falkirk after the battle, were absolutely convinced, that, except they could attack the enemy at a very considerable disadvantage, either by surprise or by some strong situation of ground, or a narrow pass, they could not expect any great success, especially if their numbers were no ways equal, and that a body of regular troops was absolutely necessary to support them, when they should at any time go in, sword in hand; for they were sensible, that without more leisure and time to discipline their own men, it would not be possible to make them keep their ranks, or rally soon enough upon any sudden emergency, so that any small number of the enemy, either keeping in a body when they were in confusion, or rallying, would deprive them of a victory.[45]

It would in fact be hard to find a clearer analysis of exactly what went wrong for the Jacobites at Falkirk – or Culloden – and it is interesting to find frequent references to even the clan regiments being drilled and 'disciplined' in the later stages of the campaign.

Although the Irish officers such as Nicholas Glascoe at first bitterly resented being 'forced to discipline the Militia',[46] they quickly found a receptive audience, for the Jacobite army was no mere rabble of Highland swordsmen. In fact there is evidence enough that this had been going on right from the very beginning. Lord Ogilvy, for example, ordered that 'the Serjeants be careful to cause the men keep their arms clean, and qualify themselves for learning the men their Exercise'.[47] Unfortunately it is not at all clear exactly what that exercise was. As it happens one of Ogilvy's men, John Webster from Forfar, was a Chelsea out-pensioner who 'Taught the Rebels the Exercise of the Firelock',[48] which would suggest that initially at least some of them were trained according to the British army's 1727 *Regulations*. On the other hand, Lord George Murray is sometimes credited with devising a simplified drill better suited to Highlanders, but little is known of what it actually comprised, although Johnstone does give an indication of just how rudimentary it was:

> The Highlanders have a very simple manoeuvre . . . well suited to a small army composed of undisciplined men. They formed themselves in line, three deep, and by facing to the right or left, they formed themselves into a column for marching, three men in front; and in the same manner, by facing to right or left, they were instantly in order of battle. It was deemed more advisable to allow them to adhere to their ancient and simple manoeuvre, than to teach them, imperfectly, the more complicated movements of wheeling backwards to form columns of division, sub-division etc. and afterwards to form into line.[49]

It may have been easy, but it was also a very clumsy way of manoeuvring, and the advent of French instructors soon saw the introduction of proper training, not just for the Lowland regiments but for the Highlanders as well. French tactical doctrines, calling for rapid movements in column formation, and an emphasis on shock tactics rather than firepower, were well suited to the Jacobites, as was their practice of firing an initial series of volleys by ranks and then if necessary continuing the fight with a *feu a billebaude*, which essentially meant each man loading and blazing away in his own time. Once again this was something which was far easier to teach raw 'militia' than the complicated platoon firing practised by the British army.

Consequently, the French influence is clearly to be seen in the initial dispositions at Culloden: with the exception of the Atholl Brigade, the front line was at first entirely composed of clan regiments, drawn up not three deep as described by Johnstone, but in four ranks after the French fashion, just as they had been at Falkirk. The difference at Culloden was that the Lowland regiments did not form an extended second line, but were deployed in column formation in the centre under John Roy Stuart, as a powerful reserve ready to move swiftly to wherever they might be needed. These columns were fairly solid tactical formations with a frontage of one or perhaps two companies rather than just three men, and in order to fight they had to be able to deploy from those columns by company or division (paired companies) rather than simply by facing to right or left in some 'ancient' fashion. To do that required proper training.

Unfortunately the effectiveness of that training was never really put to the test, for nearly all of the regiments forming the reserve were steadily bled away before the battle even started, either to fill gaps in the front line or afterwards to form a defensive line in the right rear against an outflanking move by the British cavalry. Consequently, when the Highland charge stalled and the 'emergency' predicted by Murray and the chiefs arose, only two battalions (the Royal Ecossois and Kilmarnock's newly formed Footguards) were left in the reserve, and although they gamely came forward to deliver a token volley, they could do nothing to influence the outcome of the battle.

Chapter 3

The British Army at Culloden

STUART REID

The Battle of Culloden Moor was won by the British army, and while that statement might seem rather self-evident, it is worth emphasizing from the very outset that it was indeed the *British* army and that a partisan tendency in popular literature to wilfully refer to Cumberland's soldiers as Hanoverians glosses over the indisputable fact that the battle was won not by the Germans but by the same British army which not so very much later went on to fight and win less equivocally celebrated victories at Plassey, Minden, Quebec – and Waterloo. Nor, of course, was it the 'English' army, for no fewer than four out of Cumberland's sixteen infantry battalions at Culloden were Scottish ones, and there were plenty of other Scottish officers and soldiers standing in the ranks of what were notionally English regiments. Ironically the only casualty returned by Edward Wolfe's 8th Foot was an Ensign Robert Bruce.

An ever-accelerating process of disbandment and amalgamation has meant that, leaving aside the Footguards and the Parachute Regiment, only one infantry regiment in today's British army – the Royal Welsh – is *not* descended from a battalion that fought at Culloden. As with the Jacobite army therefore it is probably as well to begin by looking at who actually did fight at Culloden.

The Regiments at Culloden

In outline the Battle of Culloden was an uncomplicated affair which appears to have lasted rather less than an hour. The Duke of Cumberland's intentions were clear. He proposed to advance to contact with the Jacobite army and then fight it where it stood. The immediate tactical planning was equally straightforward. The infantry marched across country in three columns abreast which were intended to deploy into three battle-lines stacked one behind the other. Cumberland was aiming, in short, to have sufficient depth

62

to absorb the impact of a Highland charge. However, as his official report relates, it soon became necessary to modify this, and by the time all the preliminary manoeuvring was complete and the first shots exchanged, Cumberland's regular infantry was formed in just two lines at Culloden.

The Culloden regiments appear below as they were organized on the day of the battle in five brigades, each of three battalions of regular infantry, and the unbrigaded Argyllshire men. Ordinarily at this time regiments were referred to simply by the name of their colonel, for the regiment quite literally belonged to him. He approved (or disapproved) all promotions and drew all manner of financial perquisites from it, and the closeness of the interest he took in its welfare ultimately did much to set the regimental 'tone'. Scottish commanding officers, for example, frequently used their patronage to bring in other Scottish officers, and they in turn often brought in Scots recruits to regiments which are now regarded as 'English'. A case in point is Pulteney's 13th Foot, which had a long association with Scotland, and for a long period during the eighteenth century about a third of its officers (including an ancestor of the author) were Scots.

Obviously enough, however, the regiment's title changed with its commanding officer, usually because he had died, which can be confusing in itself. Two regiments at Culloden, for example Dejean's 37th and Conway's 59th, are still usually referred to in most accounts of the battle by the names of their previous commanding officers: Sir Robert Monro, killed at Falkirk, and Francis Ligonier, dead of pleurisy shortly afterwards. Even more confusingly, officers might sometimes be shifted from regiment to regiment, perhaps to take a poor unit in hand or simply to 'promote' an officer to the command of a more prestigious regiment. Thus Lord Sempill once commanded the Black Watch, but by 1746 he had moved on to take command of the more senior 25th (Edinburgh) Regiment – later the King's Own Scottish Borderers.

To avoid the obvious confusion which this sort of thing could lead to (and no doubt assist harassed clerks), numbers were therefore assigned to regiments, supposedly reflecting their seniority within the army, although they would not be ordered to be placed upon regimental colours and drums until 1747 and did not definitely take precedence over the colonel's names until 1751. It should also be noted, however, that like the commanding officers these numbers were not always set in stone. The Black Watch was originally taken into the line as the 43rd Foot, but in 1748 the disbandment of Oglethorpe's 42nd allowed it to assume that number as its own, while similarly the disbandment of ten regiments of marines at the same time saw Conway's 59th become the 48th.

Unlike the Jacobite army it is possible to establish the numbers of men fighting at Culloden quite precisely, although at first sight the evidence can appear confusing since two quite separate, and in some degree contradictory, sets of figures for the number of officers and men serving in each regiment survive.

One is the so-called 'Guildhall List', recording the sums of money distributed to the Culloden regiments from a charitable fund established by London's Guildhall.[1] This does not include the officers, and the figures for the rank and file are generally quite markedly higher than in the second source: Cumberland's morning state for 16 April 1746. The reason quite simply is that the Guildhall fund was distributed between all the men serving in those regiments on that day irrespective of whether they were standing in the ranks, left out of battle back with the baggage, lying sick in hospital or off on detached duties elsewhere. In late March, for example, Major John LaFausille of the 8th Foot was reportedly en route to Aberdeen with as many as 500 recruits and recovered sick men belonging to the Culloden regiments, but he did not catch up with the army before the battle was fought. Others perhaps were indeed present but were still left out of battle for some reason, such as the new recruits and the vestry men (semi-criminal conscripts levied for the duration of the emergency), who were assigned instead to look after the baggage. Since all of these men, whether with Major LaFausille's party or not, were entered on their regiments' books on the day of the action, they qualified for the Guildhall bounty, even though they were not actually standing in the firing line.

The morning state, on the other hand, quite literally lists only those officers and men actually present and fit for duty in each of the fifteen regiments of regular infantry at roll-call on that morning. Unfortunately it does not, for some reason, include any of the men of the Highland Battalion and so we must rely with a certain caution upon the Guildhall List.

First Brigade

Standing on the right of the front line, this brigade was commanded by William Keppel, Earl of Albemarle. In accordance with convention, the most senior regiment within the brigade stood on the right, the next in seniority on the left and the junior regiment in the centre. Thus it was originally deployed with 2/1st (Royal) Regiment on the right, then Cholmondeley's 34th Regiment in the centre and Price's 14th Regiment on the left. Shortly before the battle began, however, Pulteney's 13th Foot was brought forward from the reserve to prolong the battle line by taking up a position on the immediate right of the Royals.

2/1st (Royal) Regiment

Better known as the Royal Scots, this regiment, the oldest in the British army, was unusual in that it had two battalions, of which only the Second Battalion, recalled from garrison duty in Ireland, fought at Falkirk and Culloden, under Lieutenant Colonel John Ramsey.

The Guildhall List evidences thirty sergeants, thirty-seven corporals, twenty-six drummers and 420 privates, but according to the morning state, on the other hand, two field officers, five captains, nineteen subalterns, twenty-nine sergeants, twenty-five drummers and 401 rank and file were actually present and fit for duty. Corporals aside, this represents a discrepancy of one sergeant, one drummer and nineteen men. No casualties were reported afterwards.

Cholmondeley's 34th Regiment

This was another strong regiment, led by Lieutenant Colonel Charles Jeffreys and mustering twenty-two sergeants, twenty-four corporals, fifteen drummers and 433 privates according to the Guildhall List, but only two field officers, seven captains, fifteen subalterns, twenty-one sergeants, fifteen drummers and 399 rank and file in the morning state.

One man was subsequently returned as killed and two were wounded, neither of whom appears in the Chelsea Hospital records. As the regiment was not engaged by Jacobite infantry, all three casualties were presumably the result of artillery fire.

Price's 14th Regiment

Commanded by Lieutenant Colonel Edward Grey, the regiment according to the Guildhall schedule had twenty-two sergeants, twenty-two corporals, twelve drummers and 339 privates, while the morning state evidences two field officers, seven captains, fourteen subalterns, twenty-one sergeants, eleven drummers and 304 rank and file at Culloden.

Only one man was returned as killed – probably Captain Alexander Grossett, who was murdered by a prisoner while serving on the staff – and nine were wounded.

Third Brigade

Forming the left wing of the front line, this brigade, commanded by Brigadier Lord Sempill (of the 25th Foot), mirrored the deployment of the First Brigade, i.e. Barrell's 4th (as the senior regiment) held the left of the whole front line, while Campbell's 21st was on the right of the brigade and Monro's 37th in the centre.

Barrell's 4th Regiment

Led by Lieutenant Colonel Sir Robert Rich, who was to be badly wounded, this regiment is quoted twenty sergeants, twenty-three corporals, ten drummers and 365 privates by the Guildhall List, but according to the morning state it actually paraded two field officers, five captains, thirteen subalterns, eighteen sergeants, ten drummers and 325 rank and file.

Interestingly, in view of the role played by this regiment in the battle, it appears to have had a higher than normal proportion of Scots officers, including Captain Lord Robert Kerr, killed while commanding the grenadier company, and Ensign John Brown, badly wounded while carrying the colours.[2]

Losses were heavy, totalling seventeen officers and men killed and 108 wounded. Moreover, only twenty-nine out of the 103 rank and file returned as wounded survived to be awarded pensions.

Monro's 37th Regiment

Strictly speaking, this regiment was Colonel Dejean's, in succession to Monro, who was killed at Falkirk, but most accounts of the battle still refer to the regiment as Monro's and it was in any case led at Culloden by Lieutenant Colonel William Deane.

The Guildhall figures cite twenty-three sergeants and nineteen drummers, but add twenty-four corporals and quote a figure of 474 privates, but the morning state gives a strength of two field officers, six captains, fifteen subalterns, twenty-three sergeants, nineteen drummers and 426 rank and file, making it the strongest regiment on the field.

Casualties were very heavy, with fourteen men killed on the spot and sixty-eight wounded. Although this represents forty-three fewer casualties than the seventeen killed and 108 wounded reported by Barrell's, all of Monro's casualties were disproportionately concentrated on the grenadiers and the left-flank companies of the regiment. Once again, there was a heavy mortality rate among those initially returned as wounded, and only nineteen of the sixty-eight wounded survived to claim a pension.

Campbell's 21st (Royal Scots Fusiliers) Regiment

Only one field officer (Major Charles Colvill) was present at Culloden, according to the morning state, together with five captains, thirteen subalterns, twenty-one sergeants, fourteen drummers and 358 rank and file. Remarkably the Guildhall figures for once appear to be lower, evidencing twenty-two sergeants, twenty-two corporals, twelve drummers and only 336 privates. It should also be noted that at least one company, under Sir Andrew Agnew, was doing garrison duty at Blair Castle and another was doing likewise at Aberdeen. The reason for this strange discrepancy is therefore unclear.

Seven men were returned as wounded, although only one of them, Mark Whitehead, who had been wounded in the right thigh, later appeared before the board at Chelsea Hospital.

Second Brigade

No brigade commander is identified by map-maker Thomas Sandby (see Woosnam-Savage, this volume), who places the whole of the second line under Major General John ('Daddy') Huske. In keeping with the usual convention, the senior regiment, Howard's 3rd, was initially on the right of the brigade, with Bligh's 20th on the left and Fleming's 36th in the middle. However, like the first line the second was soon extended by bringing Batereau's 62nd forward from the reserve and deploying it immediately to the right of Howard's.

Howard's 3rd Regiment (Buffs)

Named after Lieutenant General Thomas Howard, this battalion was normally commanded by his kinsman Lieutenant Colonel Sir George Howard, but as he was probably acting as brigade commander under Huske, it would actually have been led at Culloden by Major Gerard Elrington.

The Guildhall List gives twenty-four sergeants, twenty-three corporals, sixteen drummers and no fewer than 493 privates, while the morning state evidences two field officers, four captains, ten subalterns, twenty-one sergeants, fourteen drummers and 413 rank and file actually present and fit for duty.

One man was returned as killed and two as wounded, one of whom was Charles Appleton, 30 years old, disabled in the right hand at Culloden.

Fleming's 36th Regiment

This battalion, led by Lieutenant Colonel George Jackson, had twenty-six sergeants, twenty-two corporals, fourteen drummers and 376 privates according to the Guildhall List, while the morning state shows two field officers, six captains, eighteen subalterns, twenty-five sergeants, fourteen drummers and 350 rank and file present on the field.

Six men were returned as wounded, presumably by Jacobite artillery fire, but none of them recovered to appear before a Chelsea board.

Bligh's 20th Regiment

Commanded at Culloden by Lieutenant Colonel Edward Cornwallis, the regiment is credited by the Guildhall List with twenty-three sergeants, twenty-five corporals, fourteen drummers and 464 privates. The morning state on the other hand lists two field officers, five captains, thirteen subalterns, twenty-two sergeants, thirteen drummers and 412 rank and file.

Four men were killed and seventeen wounded.

Fourth Brigade

Forming the left of the second line, this brigade, probably commanded by Colonel Harry Conway, mirrored the deployment of the Second Brigade in that the senior regiment, Wolfe's, was on the extreme left (where it very firmly remained until called upon to counter-attack after the Highlanders overran Barrell's[3]), with Sempill's standing on the right of the brigade and Ligonier's/Conway's in the centre.

Wolfe's 8th Regiment

According to the morning state, the regiment[4] had one field officer (Lieutenant Colonel Edward Martin), seven captains, fourteen subalterns, seventeen sergeants, eleven drummers and 324 rank and file present.

Figure 8. British army troops on campaign in the '45. Note the turned-down brims of the tricorns, which give some idea of how kit was actually worn on campaign.
(Contemporary drawing from the Penicuik collection, © Sir Robert Clerk)

However, nineteen sergeants, twenty-two corporals, eighteen drummers and 387 privates later qualified for a share of the Guildhall fund.

Ensign Robert Bruce, commissioned just two months before being wounded at the battle, was the only recorded casualty.

Ligonier's 59th Regiment

Strictly speaking, this regiment was Harry Conway's Regiment, in succession to Francis Ligonier, who had died of pleurisy shortly after the Battle of Falkirk in January. However, although Conway was actually present at Culloden, the regiment, like the 37th Foot, was still being referred to by the name of its former colonel. Following the disbandment of the original 42nd Regiment (Oglethorpe's) and a number of regiments of army-controlled Marines (44th to 49th Foot), this regiment was re-designated as the 48th Regiment in 1748.

At Culloden it mustered all three field officers, but as Conway commanded the brigade the regiment's immediate commander would have been Lieutenant Colonel George Stanhope. Otherwise, there were five captains, sixteen subalterns, twenty-one sergeants, sixteen drummers and 325 rank and file according to the morning state, and a very similar twenty-one sergeants, twenty-two corporals, sixteen drummers and 342 privates in the Guildhall List.

One man was returned as killed and five wounded, including William Knight, described as disabled in his right foot when he appeared before the Chelsea board.

Sempill's 25th (Edinburgh) Regiment

The morning state reveals this was one of the strongest regiments on the field with all three field officers present (albeit Lord Sempill was actually commanding the Third Brigade and the battalion was therefore led by Lieutenant Colonel Sir David Cunynghame), together with five captains, fifteen subalterns, twenty sergeants, fourteen drummers and 420 rank and file. The Guildhall figures are also high, quoting twenty sergeants, twenty-five corporals, nineteen drummers and 487 privates.

One man was killed and thirteen wounded, but only three of them lived to claim pensions.

Fifth Brigade (Reserve)

The reserve, initially forming the third line, was commanded by Colonel Sir John Mordaunt – not to be confused with his namesake Lieutenant Colonel John Mordaunt commanding the 10th Horse. It was conventionally deployed with Pulteney's 13th on the right, Blakeney's 27th on the left and Batereau's 62nd in the centre. In addition the reserve also included Kingston's 10th Horse, deployed on either side of the Fifth Brigade, but shortly before the battle began both the 13th and 62nd Foot were ordered forward, as described above, to prolong the first and second lines, while Kingston's Horse was also repositioned to cover the right flank of the front line, together with one of the three squadrons of Cobham's 10th Dragoons.

Pulteney's 13th Regiment

The regiment was commanded by Lieutenant Colonel Thomas Cockayne. A total of twenty-three sergeants, twenty-six corporals, eighteen drummers and 479 privates qualified for the Guildhall bounty. The morning state, on the other hand, lists two field officers, six captains, fourteen subalterns, twenty-three sergeants, nineteen drummers and 410 rank and file present.

No casualties were recorded.

Batereau's 62nd Regiment

This unit was disbanded in 1748 and should not be confused with the later 62nd Regiment formed in 1756.

The morning state gives one field officer, seven captains, nineteen subalterns, twenty-four sergeants, eighteen drummers and 354 rank and file present at Culloden, while the Guildhall List also evidences twenty-four sergeants and eighteen drummers, but adds thirty-three corporals and gives the number of privates as 384.

The regiment reported just three wounded: Captain Thomas Carter and Privates William Matthews, wounded in his right side, and Daniel McIntosh, who lost his left leg. All three casualties must have been the result of Jacobite artillery fire.

Blakeney's 27th (Inniskilling) Regiment

The regiment was commanded by Lieutenant Colonel Francis Leighton. The morning state lists two field officers, four captains, fourteen subalterns, twenty-four sergeants, twelve drummers and 300 rank and file, which is reasonably close to the Guildhall's twenty-five sergeants, twenty-two corporals, twelve drummers and 336 privates.

No casualties were reported.

Unbrigaded

The Argyllshire Men

The fourth Scottish unit to fight at Culloden were the Highlanders, usually but not entirely accurately referred to as the Argyle Militia or simply the 'Argyllshire men'. It in fact comprised eight companies rather than the usual ten, of which only four actually belonged to the Argyle Militia. Of the others, three belonged to Loudoun's 64th Highlanders and the last to the 43rd Highlanders. Under the overall command of Lieutenant Colonel John Campbell of the 64th Highlanders,[5] it was divided into two small battalions or wings during the battle, each comprising two companies of regulars and two of militia. One battalion was assigned to help guard the baggage train, while the other served with some distinction in the Culwhiniac enclosures on the left flank of the army. This unit, led by Captain Colin Campbell of Ballimore, included his own company of the 64th Highlanders, one company of the 43rd Highlanders (the Black Watch) under Captain Dugald Campbell of Auchrossan, together with Captain John Campbell of Achnaba's militia company and a second militia company, from Glenorchy, under Captain Duncan Campbell.

The battalion had no recognizable uniform. Campbell of Auchrossan no doubt wore scarlet regimentals with the buff facings of the 43rd, while the 64th officers had white facings. Whether their men were similarly dressed is questionable. Auchrossan commanded an 'additional company' made up of new recruits, and the 64th had similarly been in the process of recruiting when the rising began and all of them, regulars and militia alike, seem to have worn their ordinary Highland clothing, with red or yellow crosses in their bonnets. The significance of the two different colours is unclear, but they may have served to distinguish between the men of the regular companies and the militia.

The 'Argyllshire Men' are not accounted for in the morning state, but according to the Guildhall List there were thirty-two sergeants, thirty corporals, nine drummers and 430 privates in total. It is not entirely certain, however, whether this figure accounts for all of them, as seems likely, or excludes the regulars of the 43rd and 64th Highlanders.[6] In all, nine members of the 64th were killed and wounded, including Ballimore, who was killed, and Dougal McPhail, disabled in the left shoulder and thigh. Only one member of the Argyle Militia was returned as a casualty – Captain John Campbell of Achnaba, who was mortally wounded. None of the Black Watch were returned as casualties.

Cavalry Regiments

For some reason the cavalry are included in neither the morning state nor the Guildhall List, and it is therefore rather more difficult to establish just how many actually fought at Culloden.

Cobham's 10th Dragoons

The regiment was commanded by Major Peter Chaban. According to a parade state dated 28 March 1746, two weeks before the battle, the regiment had 276 men present, and four months later on 1 September it mustered 287 troopers present (including seven new recruits), one man sick and thirteen 'on command', besides officers and non-commissioned officers. As to the latter, there were eighteen sergeants and ten drummers.

Two squadrons of Cobham's served on the left wing in support of Kerr's Dragoons, and one on the right wing with Kingston's 10th Horse, which no doubt accounts for the regiment's light casualties – just one man killed, with four horses killed and five wounded.

Kerr's 11th Dragoons

Originally raised in Scotland in 1715, the regiment still had a high proportion of Scottish officers thirty years later. The 28 March parade state lists 276 soldiers present, including eighteen sick, for a total of 294 men together with 283 horses. A further twenty-six sick men and fifty-four horses had been left behind. By 1 September some of the sick had returned, for the regiment was then reported to have 312 men fit and only sixteen men sick in the charge of a Sergeant Green. In addition to Green, there were a further seventeen sergeants and twelve drummers serving with the regiment at the time.

All three squadrons, commanded by Lieutenant Colonel William, Lord Ancram, fought on the left wing in a brigade commanded by Humphrey Bland. The regiment actually led the assault over the re-entrant to the west of Culchunaig against some Jacobite infantry under Lord Ogilvy and Gordon of Avochie, which no doubt accounts for its relatively heavy casualties, especially in horses.

In all, three men were returned as killed at Culloden with a further three wounded, but four horses were also killed and no fewer than fifteen were wounded.

Kingston's 10th Horse

Historically, regiments of horse were of higher status than dragoons, hence the designation of this provincial regiment raised by the Duke of Kingston specifically for the Jacobite emergency. After the rising it was remustered as the Duke of Cumberland's 15th Dragoons, only to be disbanded in 1748. A well-known painting by David Morier exists, showing a trooper in a red dragoon-style uniform with green facings at this date, but it seems more likely that as provincials they wore blue coats with red facings at Culloden.

It would also appear that the regiment only mustered 211 troopers at Culloden, under Lieutenant Colonel John Mordaunt, which explains why it was deployed in two squadrons of three troops rather than three squadrons of two troops. Only one man was returned as wounded, but two horses were killed and a third was wounded – probably by a volley from the Irish Picquets.

Cumberland's Hussars

Unquestionably the most obscure unit to fight at Culloden, this was a small troop of Germans and Austrians, some sixteen strong, which served as Cumberland's personal bodyguard. They were in effect the only genuine Hanoverian troops present and wore hussar-style uniforms in crimson and green – the duke's livery.

The Royal Artillery

The Royal Artillery prided itself on being the most professional of the services – as indeed it had to be – and by way of demonstrating that, it took its orders from the Board of Ordnance, and its officers and men wore blue coats instead of the traditional red. Its organization was necessarily looser or rather more flexible than that of the infantry, although the basic administrative unit, as in the infantry, was still the company. There was no fixed allocation of guns to a company, and gunners were expected to be able to serve whatever cannon were deemed appropriate, or at least available, for the job in hand. At Culloden, therefore, Captain-Lieutenant John Godwin's company was equipped with light 3-pounders, selected for their mobility on Scotland's notoriously bad roads rather than for their effectiveness on the battlefield. When the men were afterwards redeployed to Flanders, however, they left this particular train of guns in Scotland to be taken over by their successors, while they themselves re-equipped with heavier pieces more suitable to continental warfare.

The numbers of artillerymen present at Culloden are not recorded on the morning state, although the Guildhall List evidences a total of one sergeant, nine bombardiers, fifteen gunners, sixty-seven matrosses and three drummers. Uniquely, however, the muster roll for Captain-Lieutenant John Godwin's Company survives,[7] recording the names of every artilleryman to serve in it during April–June 1746. In total there are two sergeants, twelve bombardiers, twenty-seven gunners, eighty-eight matrosses and three drummers. Allowing for casualties, there are still a total of thirty-one men in excess of the company strength as indicated by the Guildhall List. As they represent a cross-section of all ranks, they are clearly not new recruits and so the additional men must represent a detachment not present at the battle – probably at Aberdeen.

Between them, at any rate, a total of ten cannon were manned, deployed in pairs in the intervals between the six regiments originally forming the front line, and six light coehorn mortars, positioned to fire explosive 'bombs' or shells over the heads of the front-line infantry.

Six gunners were returned as wounded at Culloden, and all six subsequently died of their wounds.

Organization

Each infantry battalion was normally made up of ten companies, one of which was designated as the grenadier company. Originally assault troops, grenadiers were no longer required to throw grenades and nor were they, as popular legend would have it, the tallest and strongest men in the battalion, but rather the older and steadier men who could be relied upon in a crisis. Indeed when a battalion was deployed for action, the grenadiers were split into two platoons and positioned to guard the right and left flanks of the firing line. It was therefore one of the grenadier platoons of Monro's 37th which bore the brunt of that regiment's action, and it is very noticeable that the ages of those of its wounded men appearing before the Chelsea Board are significantly higher than usual.[8]

In wartime it was also common for one or more additional companies to be authorized which were not intended to be combat units, but served as a regimental depot. This did not always work out in practice, since the two companies of the 1st (Royals) captured in the affair at High Bridge in the very first days of the rising were additional companies which had been hastily pressed into service as the only troops available to reinforce Fort William at short notice, and the Black Watch unit that fought at Culloden under Dugald Campbell of Auchrossan was also an additional company.

Each infantry company was normally led by a captain, although three of the regiment's captains also doubled up as what were termed field officers, for example the colonel, lieutenant colonel and major. On a day-to-day basis, therefore, their companies were actually commanded by their lieutenants and in the case of the colonel's company, his frequent absence on other duties meant that his lieutenant was dignified by the curious title of captain-lieutenant and ranked socially as the junior captain rather than the senior lieutenant. Ordinarily the junior officers in each company comprised a lieu-tenant and an ensign, but because the grenadier company was divided into two platoons and posted on either flank of the regiment in action, it had a second lieutenant in place of the ensign. A number of regiments, including the 1st (Royal) Regiment also had additional or second lieutenants serving with the ordinary 'battalion' companies, as a wartime augmentation.

The regimental staff comprised four commissioned officers: the adjutant, quartermaster, surgeon and chaplain. The first acted as an assistant to the major and looked after most routine administration, while the quartermaster was primarily responsible for the battalion's 'quarters', which could be a camp ground, a billet or a garrison. He would also, generally speaking, be responsible for route planning on marches, and looking after the regimental baggage train. He was not, however, at this period, directly responsible for supplies. Both officers might also hold line commissions as ensigns or lieu-tenants in addition to these staff appointments. The regimental surgeon, who also sometimes held a line commission by way of boosting his pay, was of course the battalion's medical officer and was assisted by a mate, who was not a commissioned officer. The fourth staff officer was the chaplain, who did hold the king's commission, but rarely if ever appeared at headquarters, let alone held services.

Cavalry regiments had a very similar command structure, but only mustered six companies – designated as troops – rather than ten, and in action the troops would normally be paired off to form three squadrons, although Kingston's 10th Horse, which may only have mustered about 200 troopers, was formed in just two squadrons at Culloden.

Recruitment

King George's army is all too frequently portrayed as a species of ambulant penal institution comprising the brutal dregs of society – Wellington's 'scum of the earth', enlisted for drink and kept in order only by a savage discipli-nary system. It was, of course, nothing of the sort. What is more, as some remarkable eyewitness sketches by an artist from Penicuik reveal, they were very ordinary British soldiers who, apart from the colour of their shabby red coats, would probably not have looked out of place in the Falklands 250 years later – and this is an impression which is amply confirmed by surviving diaries, letters and official records.

It is certainly true that there were some men at Culloden who would have justified Wellington's epithet. At the height of the emergency in 1745, two acts were rushed through Parliament admonishing magistrates to conscript 'all able-bodied men who do not follow or exercise any lawful calling or employment'.[9] In other words, parish constables were authorized and encouraged to turn over to the army all their drunks, wastrels and petty criminals without the trouble of remanding them to the next assizes. And better yet, for each recruit delivered up they received a bounty of £3 paid into the vestry account, supposedly for the upkeep of any dependants left behind by the reluctant hero. Popular prejudice notwithstanding, the army itself was actually fairly particular about where it found its recruits. 'No strollers, Vagabonds, Tinkers, Chimney Sweepers, Colliers, or Saylors to be Inlisted' was a regular admonition in recruiting instructions, and those issued to recruiting parties for Colonel Samuel Bagshawe's 93rd Foot in 1760, for example, enjoined that they were only to take men who 'were born in the Neighbourhood of the place where they are Inlisted in & of whom you can get and give a good account'.[10] Consequently both officers and soldiers viewed these shabby conscripts with a distinctly jaundiced eye. All of them – just a handful of men in each regiment – were discharged as soon as their services could decently be dispensed with, and in the meantime, being insufficiently trained to fight, they were left with the baggage train and afterwards allotted all the dirty jobs, such as battlefield clearance and burial details, and prisoner handling – with unhappy results.

The majority of soldiers were rather more traditionally found by recruiting parties working markets and hiring fairs up and down the country. Certain regiments – particularly the Scottish ones – had traditional regional affiliations even at this early period, and the Royals, for example, drew a lot of its officers and men from the Highlands in the eighteenth century. For the most part, however, such associations were transient. Although allowed to recruit anywhere within the three kingdoms, it was sensible for units to concentrate their efforts in a particular area at any one time, and for a while their make-up would obviously reflect that, but there was no real continuity. Most of Cope's regiments at Prestonpans, for example, had been largely recruited in Scotland, but within a generation they would be unambiguously English in identity. Nevertheless, Scots still formed a surprisingly high proportion of the army's recruits. Interestingly enough, when the 77th and 78th Highlanders were raised in 1757, a War Office circular required the transfer of eighty Gaelic-speaking non-commissioned officers from nine different regiments to act as instructors,[11] yet only two of the regiments – the 25th and the 26th (Cameronians) – were Scottish units.

Although there were a few king's hard bargains among them and the usual leavening of men running away from petty misdemeanours or pregnant girl-friends, most of those signing on were in reality young and footloose agricultural labourers or tradesmen attracted by the notion of seeing a bit of the world, rather than working themselves to death in the same parish in which they had been born. Peer pressure could also play a part then as now. Weavers and other cloth-workers were common, either because they were thrown out of work by the industry's periodical slumps or else because the sheer boredom of sitting at a loom all day long proved too much for them. Other trades were represented too, but between the two of them, the countrymen and the weavers probably accounted for most of King George's recruits.

As Alice famously remarked to Christopher Robin, a soldier's life was 'terrible hard', but there was no denying its compensations; drill might be strenuous but it was far less so than labouring in fields. Soldiers were properly and regularly clothed and fed, and if their pay was low, at least it was constant – unlike in civilian life. Moreover, when not actually on active service, soldiers were normally allowed to supplement the king's pay by taking on casual work in their surprisingly abundant spare time.

All of them were in theory enlisted for life, but in practice generally found it easy to obtain their discharge, if they wanted it, when most regiments were reduced in strength at the end of a war. Otherwise it normally meant being discharged in their 40s, although at least one soldier at Culloden, Private John Tovey of Monro's 37th Foot, was all of 59 when he had his jaw shot away.[12] In theory there was no pension system unless a man was disabled in the service, since the army, or rather the Treasury, took the robust view that if a man was fit and well at the time of his discharge, he was perfectly capable of earning himself a living without any assistance from the state. Nevertheless, it is remarkable how many of those discharged after twenty years' good service were granted disability pensions on the rather loose grounds of being 'worn out'.

Long-service regulars aside, the army was able to call upon the assistance of a substantial body of loyalists and some other, less enthusiastic levies in 1745. Prior to 1739 the army had policed the Highlands with a number of independent companies, familiarly known as the Black Watch, but in that

Figure 9. Government volunteers learning their exercises. A number of such units were raised in England and Scotland in response to the Jacobite threat. (Contemporary drawing from the Penicuik collection, © Sir Robert Clerk)

year they were converted into the British army's first Highland regiment. Despite a well-publicized mutiny in 1743, the experiment was adjudged a success, and in 1745 the Earl of Loudoun was given letters of service to recruit a second one: the 64th Foot. In one sense, the timing was unfortunate for the rising broke out while the regiment was in the process of being raised, and at least one company, commanded by Cluny MacPherson, defected to the rebels. On the other hand, the other companies, together with three depot companies of the Black Watch, provided a nucleus for what eventually became a substantial body of Highlanders loyal to King George.

The famous Argyle Militia was undoubtedly the most prominent of all the loyalist formations, but active opposition to the 'Jacks' in Scotland was by no means confined to Clan Campbell and its allies. During most of the rebellion, Inverness was held for the Crown by a loyalist army made up of independent companies recruited in the northern and western Highlands – and including the Skye MacDonalds. In combat they generally proved to be as brittle as might be expected of ill-trained and poorly motivated levies, but when stiffened with regulars and properly led, they could be quite effective – and never more so than at Culloden, where Captain Colin Campbell of Ballimore made a substantial contribution to the rebel defeat.

The same, obviously, was true of the various provincial regiments raised in England and the Lowlands. The most important of these was the Earl of Home's Brigade, comprising various Scottish provincial regiments, which successfully defended the Forth crossings late in 1745 and afterwards fought at Falkirk. Even the various ragtag local volunteer militias, such as the Derby Blues or the Aberdeen Militia, were of some use in that they could be employed on rudimentary constabulary duties which would otherwise have had to be performed by regulars. Just as importantly, by their very existence they deterred spontaneous tumults and even uprisings.

Officers and Occasional Gentlemen

Just as the ordinary British soldiers of the eighteenth century are popularly portrayed as some kind of semi-criminal underclass, their officers by contrast are depicted as rich aristocratic dilettantes whose position was wholly dependent on their ability to buy their commissions. There is no doubt that a great many officers, particularly those in the higher ranks, were indeed aristocrats; if not actually titled members of the nobility, they at least belonged to the old landed gentry, which pretty much amounted to the same thing. Overall, however, the aristocrats were actually in the minority. Studies of the origins and social backgrounds of eighteenth-century army officers reveal that no more than a third were found from the aristocracy and the gentry combined, and they were for the most part disproportionately concentrated among the Footguards and the cavalry.

The overwhelming majority of officers were instead drawn from what are rather inadequately referred to as the middle classes – an ill-defined and socially diverse collection of 'private gentlemen', variously drawn from the lesser landed families, and from the families of respectable tradesmen and professional men such as doctors, clergymen, lawyers, 'prosperous farmers' and the like. Some had money with which to purchase their commissions, just as they might otherwise have had to buy their way into a doctor's practice or a legal firm, or at least pay for an apprenticeship or 'articles'; but all too often the money had to be borrowed either from a relative or as a business loan from a banker. Many perforce relied on picking up the many free vacancies, and Captain Robert Bannatyne from Inverness-shire spoke for many when he wrote in 1759 that, 'My father had no great Estate and dying whilst his children were young you may guess whether five of us did not find use for small inheritance.'[13] Both Bannatyne's father and stepfather were clergymen, and neither of them was wealthy. Nevertheless the latter, the same Alexander McBean who successfully interceded with Cumberland for a number of Jacobites taken at Culloden, secured free vacancies for his own son Forbes – who served under Cumberland at Carlisle, commanded a battery at Minden and died a general – and for two of the Bannatyne brothers, of whom Robert died at the storming of Conjeeveram in 1759, and William retired as a lieutenant from Pulteney's 13th Foot to make a modestly fortunate marriage. This sort of success rate seems to have been fairly typical, and goes a long way to explaining why a career in the army was so attractive to the middling sort of people and to Scots in particular.

Surprisingly, some officers, amounting to about 3 per cent of the total, had originally been promoted from the ranks. They included men such as Terry Molloy, a sometime sergeant who successfully held Ruthven Barracks against several hundred Highlanders with just twelve men ('and two of them useless'[14]), while others were posted into newly raised units to provide a leavening of experience among the subalterns.

Even without such men, there was already a strong ethos of profession-alism among the officers. Many were themselves the sons and grandsons of soldiers and belonged to what would become recognized as 'army families', such as the Campbells, Dalrymples, Howards, Urquharts and Wolfes. Far from taking little interest in their duties, many of them were passionate students and influential thinkers. In 1746 the army's official drill-book had been written by the same Humphrey Bland who commanded Cumberland's cavalry, and the much-maligned Henry Hawley was another intelligent theo-retician and practitioner.

Fighting

The well-known illustrations from the 1742 *Cloathing Book* so frequently used to portray the British soldiers at Culloden contribute as much as anything to the impression of them as strange and alien beings, but it is a false picture, for those illustrations were never intended to be more than a schematic identifying all the distinguishing features of each regiment's uniform. The real soldiers of King George can be seen in those scruffy and altogether more convincing figures in the Penicuik sketches.

Notwithstanding the impression given by the *Cloathing Book*, soldiers' clothing and equipment of the time were both practical and comfortable, comprising a red double-breasted greatcoat, worn over a long-skirted waist-coat which was really an under-jacket or tunic, knee breeches, black canvas gaiters to protect the legs from mud and heather – white ones were only worn for show on formal parades – and a tricorn hat trimmed with lace, which metamorphosed on campaign into a broad-brimmed slouch hat. All in all, it was not a bad outfit for a winter campaign in rough country. Their personal equipment included a 46in barrelled Long Land pattern firelock and bayonet, a light sword or hanger (if it had not been 'lost') and all the usual impedimenta of knapsack, haversack and canteen required by all soldiers, rebel or regular.

Cavalrymen were similarly clothed and equipped, with the obvious difference that heavy jacked leather boots were substituted for the gaiters, and broadswords for hangers. The carbines carried by cavalrymen were not noticeably shorter than infantry muskets, since they had a barrel length of 42in and were only slightly smaller in calibre. Other differences included a lack of turned-back lapels on the coats (which were nevertheless cut to be double-breasted) and thin or no lace, and, most strikingly, the wearing of waistcoats and breeches in the regimental facing colour, rather than the plain red ones worn by most infantry units.

Regiments were generally distinguished one from another in two ways. The first was by means of the facing colour used to line the coats. Blue was reserved for royal regiments and most others made do with yellow, buff or green, though there was quite a variation in the exact shade used. Nevertheless, as it was clearly necessary to distinguish between two regiments displaying the same facing colour, a system of decorative lacing had evolved. The lace was actually a worsted tape, almost invariably white, with a pattern of coloured lines, zigzags or other designs unique to the regiment woven into it. This lace was used to edge coats and buttonholes and also appeared on the sleeves, usually in a ladder pattern, although some regiments preferred a herringbone arrangement.

The regiment's grenadier company, made up of the oldest and steadiest men, was also distinguished by the wearing of a pointed mitre cap. This had originally begun as a simple stocking cap but by this period had acquired a stiffened front in the regimental facing colour. Royal regiments, and certain 'old' corps, such as the Royals and Barrell's, were permitted to wear embroidered badges on the front, while less-exalted units made do with the royal cipher.

Ordinarily the British army's tactical system, which officers such as Bland and Hawley had developed and practised so well, simply came down to forming up in a line, three men deep, moving into fairly close proximity to the enemy – 50m or less – then halting and blazing away until fire superiority was achieved and the opposing unit conceded defeat. The conventional view, with a positive wealth of precedent to back it up, was that winning the fire-fight depended on being able to maintain a steady rolling fire, and the chosen method of delivering that fire was 'platooning', as described by Humphrey Bland in his influential *Treatise of Military Discipline* and formally laid down in the official 1728 *Regulations*. This battle drill required a battalion to be divided into a series of ad hoc platoons, each of between twenty and thirty men, who would then fire in a pre-arranged sequence rippling up and down the line. Given sufficient practice and the incentive provided by sheer terror, it was just about possible to loose off four or even five rounds a minute, but under stress soldiers will always fire high, and this rate of fire was not only wasteful but quite unsustainable, since it was common to go into action with as few as twelve rounds. Instead officers and non-commissioned officers were trained to control the firing so that the men remained cool and levelled their firelocks properly, instead of shooting rapidly and wildly. In this regard, individual platoons were obviously much more manageable than complete battalions. Despite its limitations, the tactic of platooning was therefore effective enough in conventional operations – especially against the French, whose fire discipline was notoriously bad – but employing it against Highlanders simply did not work, and worse still, turned out to be downright dangerous. The deliberately paced rate of fire, while well adapted to maintaining a sustained firefight, simply could not kill sufficient numbers of clansmen quickly enough to stop a determined, fast-moving Highland charge, as General Cope's army discovered to its cost at Prestonpans.

Consequently a radical change of tactics was called for, and at Culloden heavy massed battalion volleys would be employed instead. 'The sure way to demolish them', wrote Henry Hawley, just before Falkirk,

> is at 3 deep to fire by ranks diagonally to the Centre where they come, the rear rank first, and even that rank not to fire till they are within 10 or 12 paces but if the fire is given at a distance you probably will be broke for you never get time to load a second Cartridge, & if you give way you may give your foot for dead, for they being without firelock or any load, no man with his arms, accoutrements &c. can escape them, and they give no Quarters.[15]

Hawley of course came to grief himself, but largely through force of circumstances rather than a failure in his tactics, and at Culloden there was a further refinement. There was an obvious danger that if the volley was badly timed and the Highlanders ignored their casualties to press home the charge, the whole battalion might still be reloading as the attack came in. The answer, pioneered by at least some units at Falkirk, was to direct the front rank not to reload after that first volley, but instead to charge their bayonets as soon as they had fired, thus protecting the second and third ranks as *they* reloaded and poured in a succession of volleys at point blank range. In fact Monro's even managed to get off two full volleys at Culloden before charging bayonets.

The cavalry, by contrast, seem to have made little or no attempt to adapt their tactics and arguably failed to perform even their ordinary duties satisfactorily (for a full discussion on the cavalry action at Culloden see Blackmore in this volume). All cavalry regiments comprised six troops – the mounted equivalent of companies – which in battle were paired off into three squadrons, which formed up six men (and horses) deep. In 1746 they were classed either as regiments of horse or dragoons. The former were the more prestigious and reckoned to be true battle or heavy cavalry, while the dragoons were originally mounted infantry and in theory primarily intended to be employed for scouting and outpost duties. Over the years, however, in what was to be a depressingly familiar cycle, this particular role was largely abandoned in favour of charging into battle, locked up knee to knee as heavy cavalrymen. Consequently, although the British army enjoyed an over-whelming numerical superiority in the mounted arm throughout the campaign, its commanders consistently failed to make proper use of that superiority in the all-important scouting and intelligence-gathering role – an omission which is all the more remarkable in that Cope, Wade and Hawley all had a cavalry background. Only some of the provincial and volunteer militia units, most notably perhaps Kingston's 10th Horse (whose title iron-ically enough classed them as heavies), were employed as proper light cavalry and they, for all their later reputation, were usually outclassed as scouts by their rebel counterparts.

In one respect, however, the cavalry performed as it was always intended to – the pursuit after the Highland Army broke. Much has been written about how the dragoons pursued the Highlanders down the Inverness road, ruthlessly cutting down all they met on the way, whether Jacobite soldiers or not. Yet that was precisely what cavalry were supposed to do, and if innocent civilians suffered, that was as much due to the fact that the rebel soldiers were dressed indistinguishably from those going about their lawful occasions, as it was to overexcitement.

The army's behaviour in the aftermath of the battle is indeed a subject which needs to be addressed more broadly here. This letter by Lieutenant Loftus Cliffe of the 37th Foot is fairly well known but has rarely appeared in its entirety, the second paragraph usually being omitted. However, it is very important for the insight it gives into the soldiers' attitudes towards the Jacobites and explains why they felt they 'had ample revenge' for the alleged cold-blooded murder of their colonel and other officers at Falkirk:

> The Hurry I am in going to collect the number of killed and wounded, scarce allows me time to tell you that yesterday we had the bloodiest Battle with the Rebels that ever was fought in the Memory of Man. The same Morning we march'd from Nairn, and met the Gentry about Culloden, the Lord President's House, three

Miles from hence, where we cannonaded each other for some Time; at last the Rebels advanc'd against the Left of our Line where was Barrel's Regiment, and the late Sir Robert Monro's, now Col. De Jean's. Barrels behaved very well, but was obliged to give Way to their Torrent that bore down upon them; Their whole Force then fell upon the Left of ours where I had the Honour to command the Grenadier platoon; our Lads fought more like Devils than Men. In short we laid (to the best of my Judgement) about 1600 dead on the Spot, and finished the Affair without the Help of any other Regiment. You may judge of the Work for I had 18 men killed and wounded in my Platoon. I thank God I escaped free, but my Coat had six balls thro' it. I must now tell you, that in the Midst of the Action the officer that led on the Camerons call'd me to take Quarters; which I refus'd, and bid the Rebel Scoundrel advance, he did, and fir'd at me; but providentially miss'd his Mark: I then shot him dead, and took his Pistol and Dirk, which are extremely neat.

The French have all surrendered Prisoners of War: We have taken their Cannon and Baggage; Lords Kilmarnock and Cromarty are among the Prisoners of Distinction. Our Regiment had ample Revenge for the Loss of our late Colonel, Sir Robert, and the rest of our Officers, whom the Scoundrels murdered in cold blood, but (as I told Lord Kilmarnock) we had ample Revenge in hors. For I can with great Truth assure you, not one that attack'd us escaped alive, for we gave no Quarters nor would accept of any. Our Regiment took three Stand of colours. Our Wounded are Capt. Kinnier and Lieuts. Lort and King, and Ensign Dally kill'd. I now give you Joy of the Day; and be assur'd never was a more compleat Victory gained – Our Goals are full of them and they are brought in by Hundreds.[16]

Two important points stand out. During the battle itself the soldiers were determined to stand and fight, and in the circumstances were taking no prisoners. From their earlier experience at Falkirk they knew that they were in a brutal stand-up fight against a ruthless enemy, who was himself guilty of murdering men in cold blood, having seen there their old colonel first wounded and then finished off as his brother was bandaging him (Dr Monro was killed also), and all those other officers and men either killed where they stood or as they fled. Both the similar experience of other regiments at Falkirk and the stories of how fleeing men were butchered at Prestonpans all contributed to the perception that they were not fighting chivalrous-minded professionals, but murderous thugs and should themselves respond accordingly.

The second important point is Cliffe's closing remark that 'Our Goals are full of them and they are brought in by Hundreds.' It is generally taken as a given fact that hundreds of Jacobite wounded were first left untended and then afterwards murdered where they lay on the moor in the hours and days after the battle, but on closer examination a much more complex picture emerges.

There is no doubt that some wounded Jacobites were finished off as the British army marched across the battlefield on its way to Inverness – Lord Strathallan perhaps was the most prominent victim, but others such as Major James Stewart of the Duke of Perth's Regiment were taken prisoner. It is certainly true that many others were left untended, but the fact of the matter was that, as always, the army itself was overwhelmed by its own wounded and at first had neither the time nor the resources to deal with those of the enemy as well. In his official dispatch announcing the victory, Cumberland reported that he had 50 dead and 259 wounded, which was no doubt true as of that moment, but all too many of the wounded were very badly hurt indeed and the majority would soon be dead. Consequently for days afterwards the buildings at Leanach and other farmsteads were filled not with Jacobite wounded, but with injured and dying redcoats. Only after they were brought into Inverness could the army turn to the surviving Jacobite wounded, and then the gaols began filling up with them. Not all of them made it. Even allowing for the suspect nature of many of the atrocity stories uncritically accepted afterwards, those instances where helpless men appear to have been murdered, such as at Culloden House, seem to have occurred in out-of-the-way places where prisoners were simply an inconvenience. Moreover, those involved were not the regulars quartered in and around Inverness itself, but the despised vestry men set to battlefield clearance and grave-digging and – as later returns reveal – guarding the many prisoners both in gaol and on board the transports which carried so many of them to London.

The British army cannot by any means be totally absolved of what are perceived as war crimes in the aftermath of the battle, but both the true scale and the context need to be appreciated. To borrow an expression from their latter-day descendants, the soldiers' attitude was very much one of 'big boys' games, big boys' rules'.

The Regiments' Successors
At the beginning of this essay I commented on the fact that nearly every infantry regiment in the present British army is descended from a Culloden

battalion. Two of the regiments, Kingston's 10th Horse and Battereau's 62nd Foot, were disbanded shortly afterwards, as were Loudoun's 64th Highlanders and the Argyle Militia, although the Highland Battalion is otherwise represented today, through Auchrossan's Black Watch company, by the Royal Regiment of Scotland.

The Royal Regiment of Scotland is in fact the successor to four Culloden units: 1st (Royal) Regiment, Campbell's 21st (Royal Scots Fusiliers), Sempill's 25th (Edinburgh) Regiment and that company of the 43rd (later 42nd) Regiment – the Black Watch.[17]

The Princess of Wales' Royal Regiment incorporates both Howard's 3rd (Buffs) and Monro's 37th Foot.

The Duke of Lancaster's Regiment incorporates Barrell's 4th Foot, Wolfe's 8th Foot and Cholmondeley's 34th.

Pulteney's 13th Foot is now part of **The Rifles**.

Price's 14th Foot is now part of **The Yorkshire Regiment**.

Bligh's 20th Foot is now represented by the **Royal Regiment of Fusiliers**.

Blakeney's 27th Foot is now part of the **Royal Irish Regiment**.

Fleming's 36th Foot is now part of the **Mercian Regiment**.

Ligonier's 59th (later 48th) Foot is now part of the **Royal Anglian Regiment**.

Both of Cumberland's regular cavalry regiments – Cobham's 10th Dragoons and Kerr's 11th Dragoons – are now part of the **King's Royal Hussars**.

The Royal Artillery of course remains '*Ubique*'.

Chapter 4

Cavalry in the '45

DAVID BLACKMORE

Government Cavalry

The traditional view of the government cavalry in the '45 is of troops who were both incompetent and cowardly or merciless butchers. The Jacobite cavalry is almost invisible. This is simplistic and inaccurate. The Jacobite cavalry was never in a position to challenge the cavalry of George II on the battlefield, but it performed well in the roles of reconnaissance and diversionary manoeuvre. The cavalry of George II put in performances that varied from regiment to regiment, but at Culloden it was the cavalry that sealed the victory.[1]

In early August 1745 Lieutenant General Sir John Cope, the commander of the army in Scotland, received information that a landing by Prince Charles Edward Stuart was imminent. Among the troops available to Cope were two cavalry regiments, the dragoon regiments of Colonel James Gardiner, the 13th Dragoons, and Lieutenant Archibald Hamilton's 14th Dragoons. On 3 August Cope 'gave orders for the dragoon horses to be taken up from grass to be ready for a march'.[2] It was the usual practice for cavalry regiments to put their horses out to graze from early May. This was partly to bring the horses back into condition after the winter months on dry forage, but was also an economy measure.[3] It meant, however, that the horses were not campaigning fit and had not been ridden for three months, and that any recruit horses were completely untrained. Similarly the men would not be riding fit and any recruits were incompletely trained, if they could ride at all. In addition the regiments were dispersed, Gardiner's at Stirling, Linlithgow, Musselburgh, Kelso and Coldstream, and Hamilton's at Haddington, Dunse and surrounding areas.[4] This meant that there would not have been any opportunity for the regiments to practise as a whole regiment, forming individual troops together into squadrons.

In addition to this, both regiments had long been in Ireland, both coming over to the British mainland in 1742.[5] This meant that the establishment of each of the six troops in a regiment had to be increased from twenty-five to fifty-nine men.[6] By 1745 these two regiments were not up to full strength, their combined number of dragoons at Prestonpans being given as 567 instead of the establishment of 708, of whom about half would have been recruits of three years' or less experience.[7] To add to the raw quality of Gardiner's, that regiment had received at least sixty recruit horses in early April.[8]

One of the most telling eyewitness descriptions of Hamilton's Regiment comes from the author of an anonymous history of the rebellion who saw the regiment come through Edinburgh just before the Battle of Prestonpans. The witness describes:

> I saw them ride through the city brandishing their swords; heard them huzza as they past, which was cheerfully answered not only by those in arms, but by the whole crowd; the horses and men, tho' raw and young, looked extremely well, and a person unskilled would have been tempted to put too much trust in them, which I fear many did.[9]

On 16 September they were reviewed by the newly arrived brigadier General Fowke. He later reported:

> I found many of the horses backs not fit to receive the riders, many of the men's and some of the officer's legs so swell'd, that they could not wear boots; and those who really were to be depended upon, in a manner overcome for want of sleep. This being the first time I had ever seen the two dragoon regiments. The same day, before the rebels had advanced with their whole body towards Edinburgh, Colonel Gardiner had acquainted me that from the condition the men and horses were in, and in our situation, it would be extremely right not to wait for night work.[10]

Colonel Gardiner had no illusions about the quality of the dragoons. According to Fowke's brigade major, Captain Singleton, he

> represented to the Brigadier very strongly, and repeated many times ... the bad condition his regiment was in; in particular being harass'd and fatigued for eleven days and eleven nights, little or no provision for the men, or forage for the horses; that many of the men had their legs so swell'd, that they were obliged to cut their boots off; and that if they stay'd another night on that ground, it was to be feared his Majesty would lose two regiments of dragoons.[11]

At Prestonpans, on 21 September 1745, Gardiner's worst fears were realized when the two dragoon regiments broke and ran in the face of the Jacobite

Figure 10. Dragoons and Jacobites. (Contemporary drawing from the Penicuik collection, © Sir Robert Clerk)

attack. According to one writer: 'At the moment they [the Jacobites] raised the shout the young horses on the wings, viz Gairdner's on the right and Hamilton's on the left, affrighted with the noise in the morning, fell a capering, fled off all at once, and disordered the foot; yea, some of them, when their riders were dismounted, ran through the enemy towards Dunbar.'[12]

Between them, the two dragoon regiments lost 114 men captured. Perhaps more significantly both regiments suffered badly with losses among their officers. Colonel Gardiner was killed, Lieutenant Colonel Whitney of Gardiner's was badly wounded and four other officers from this regiment were captured. Hamilton's had Lieutenant Colonel Wright, in command in the absence of Hamilton, Major Bowles and three other officers captured.[13]

Following Prestonpans, Prince Charles led the Jacobite army into England, getting as far as Derby before turning around and heading back to Scotland. On 18 December 1745 the Duke of Cumberland, at the head of a force of cavalry, managed to catch up with the Jacobite rearguard at the village of Clifton, just south of Penrith. Under his command were Major General Humphrey Bland's 3rd Dragoons, commanded by Lieutenant Colonel Honeywood, Field Marshal Viscount Cobham's 10th Dragoons, commanded by Lieutenant Colonel John Jordain, and Lord Mark Kerr's 11th Dragoons, commanded by Lieutenant Colonel Lord Ancram, which were to be the units engaged. In addition there were the Duke of Montagu's 3rd Horse, Field Marshal Wade's 4th Horse, Field Marshal Ligonier's 8th Horse, Lieutenant General St George's 8th Dragoons, the Duke of Montagu's 9th Light Horse and the Duke of Kingston's 10th Light Horse, along with Brigadier Oglethorpe's Georgia Rangers, the Yorkshire Hunters and the Duke of Cumberland's Hussars.

The dragoons and horse were all regular regiments. Montagu's and Kingston's light horse had been raised specifically in response to the rebellion. Oglethorpe's was a unit of mounted infantry actually raised for service in Georgia, but diverted to assist in dealing with the rebellion. Kingston's had already proved its worth in leading the advance of Cumberland's cavalry force, scouting and skirmishing with some success. It was commanded by Lieutenant Colonel Mordaunt, had as captains Lord Robert Manners and Lord Byron, and probably amounted to two squadrons with a strength of a little over 200. The total strength of this force was probably around 2,500. Also with Cumberland were 1,000 volunteer infantry who had been mounted on horses supplied in Staffordshire. However, when Cumberland was faced with the Jacobite rearguard of about 1,000 men holding the enclosures around Clifton, these were still some way behind the cavalry.

The engagement opened with a brief cavalry skirmish between the Jacobites' Hussars and Pitsligo's Horse, who lay in ambush in a farm on the edge of Clifton, and Cumberland's advanced guard of Georgia Rangers and his own Hussars. Cumberland's men were warned of the ambush and drove the Jacobite cavalry off. The main fighting took place after sunset. Three detachments of dragoons, from Bland's, Cobham's and Kerr's, under the command of Lieutenant Colonel Honeywood, advanced on foot against the Jacobite positions. Lord George Murray led a charge that hit the detachment from Bland's and drove them off. Subsequently Murray extracted his men and broke contact with Cumberland. This simple and conventional description, however, does not explain all that is known about this engagement.

Accounts of the strength of the dragoons sent forward vary from 120 from each regiment to 300 in total. Roughly that equates to two troops or one squadron from each dragoon regiment, only a third of their strength, and none were sent forward from St George's Dragoons at all. If this was a serious assault Cumberland could have thrown in over 1,000 dragoons. Furthermore, although dragoons, and indeed horse, were trained and expected to fight on foot as infantry, Cumberland had 1,000 mounted infantry coming up fast who would have been far more suited to an assault on a defended village.

To understand what happened it is necessary to consider the earlier orders that Cumberland had given to Oglethorpe. At about six in the evening on the previous day, the 17th, Oglethorpe had caught up with the Jacobite rearguard at Shap. He had with him about 600 men, and reports of the numbers of

Jacobites in Shap ranged from 300 or 400 up to 1,000. Added to this the terrain was bad, it was dark and raining hard, and his men needed rest and the horses fed. He decided to retire to a nearby village for the night. Cumberland, however, had sent Oglethorpe orders, which he did not receive until the following morning. These were to the effect that if there were under 500 Jacobites in Shap, Oglethorpe should dismount his dragoons and attack. If there were more he was to push in patrols during the night.[14]

With upwards of 1,000 Jacobite infantry in Clifton, the most likely scenario is that Cumberland, eager to attack, was waiting for his infantry to come up. In the meantime, in order to pin the Jacobites in place and in keeping with his earlier orders to Oglethorpe, he sent forward strong patrols of dismounted dragoons to skirmish with them. At the same time he sent Oglethorpe on a flanking march around the right flank and other troops to the left, presumably in an attempt to get behind Clifton and block the Jacobites' line of retreat. Murray's aggressive response was sufficient to allow the Jacobites to withdraw before the trap could be completed.

By the Battle of Falkirk on 17 January, Gardiner's and Hamilton's Dragoons were part of the army under the command of Lieutenant General Hawley. Gardiner's had passed into the command of Colonel Francis Ligonier, who also had the colonelcy of the 48th Foot. He was suffering with pleurisy and in order to take part in the battle left his sick bed in Edinburgh. As the senior dragoon officer, Ligonier was in command of all Hawley's cavalry, which was reinforced on the morning of the battle by the arrival of Cobham's Dragoons.

Cobham's does appear to have been a very different proposition from the other two dragoon regiments. It had been raised at the same time as Gardiner's and Hamilton's, at the time of the Jacobite Rebellion of 1715. Unlike them, it had served continuously in mainland Britain, including a tour of duty in Scotland from 1728 to 1730. In addition, many of the senior officers of the regiment in 1745 had been with the regiment in Scotland, giving them a familiarity with the country and the people. Although it sent a draft to the army in Flanders in 1744 it must have been at or about its full establishment of around 420, all ranks with very few recruits – men or horses.

As with Clifton, the part played by the dragoons at Falkirk is often over-simplified to their charging the Jacobite first line and being driven off after receiving a point-blank volley and engaging in some fierce hand-to-hand fighting with the Jacobite infantry.

When Hawley realized he had been outmanoeuvred by the Jacobites the battle began with a race for the high ground above Falkirk. Hawley's three regiments of dragoons won the race, but were left unsupported by any infantry, and with the first line of Jacobite infantry advancing towards them, eventually they were forced to charge.

Ligonier had placed his strongest regiment, Cobham's, in the centre, with Ligonier's on the left and Hamilton's on the right.[15] Ligonier's and Hamilton's between them numbered 519, while Cobham's numbered about 300.[16] O'Sullivan, Prince Charles's chief of staff, described the attack: 'They detached from the right & left of their horse, about two squadrons in Coloum, while the rest marched in battle.'[17] According to an anonymous account of the battle, the dragoons formed seven squadrons.[18] Ligonier's and Hamilton's, following their losses at Prestonpans, were probably formed in only two squadrons each, while Cobham's formed the more usual three squadrons. It is clear from the several plans of the battle that the dragoons were in two lines. In this case it seems most likely that the two squadrons of Ligonier's and Hamilton's were one behind the other, giving the impression of a column, while Cobham's probably had two squadrons leading with a squadron-wide gap between them covered by the third squadron behind them. Particularly if viewed uphill, Cobham's could well have appeared as a single solid line of battle.

Under the direction of Lord George Murray the Jacobite infantry held their fire until the advancing dragoons were only 10–20yds away. This line had perhaps 2,000 men in it, yet only about 80 dragoons appear to have been hit. The dragoons then spurred their horses forward and into the Jacobite line. Vicious hand-to-hand fighting followed. 'The resistance of the Highlanders was so incredibly obstinate that the English, after having been for some time engaged pell-mell with them in their ranks, were at length repulsed and forced to retire.'[19] First Hamilton's and then Ligonier's broke and retreated. According to an officer in Ligonier's, they broke in part as a result of being hit in the flank by Hamilton's fleeing dragoons.[20] Hamilton's then galloped through and over the Glasgow Regiment in their rear. Ligonier's Regiment left behind their commander, Lieutenant Colonel Shugborough Whitney, killed by the Jacobite volley. Some dragoons, however, had broken through the Jacobite infantry and engaged the Jacobite second line. Given the fate of Gardiner's and Hamilton's it seems most likely that this was Cobham's in the centre of the dragoon line. Ogilvy's were hard pushed to hold them, and it was only the arrival of part of the Atholl Brigade that saved the second line from being broken.[21]

An infantryman in Barrell's Regiment wrote, 'The attack was begun with our three regiments of dragoons, who broke through the enemy, and behaved like bold fellows, and afterwards rallied again.'[22] A dragoon, described as belonging to 'a regiment that behaved extremely well', probably Cobham's, wrote, 'We lost the day for we were all sold to our enemies by treacherous

General Hawley, for we could have got the day if he had done us justice or let us fight like Englishmen as we are.'[23] Another dragoon, Enoch Bradshaw of Cobham's, wrote of 'General Hawley, who does not love us because our regiment spoke truth about Falkirk job'.[24] Even Cumberland himself wrote to the Duke of Newcastle, 'As to the dragoons (who were at Falkirk) people here are much more favourable to them than accounts we had in London seemed to be.' Not that Cumberland was entirely uncritical. In the same letter he continues, 'they are certainly filled with Irish Papists', presumably referring to Ligonier's and Hamilton's from the Irish Establishment, rather than Cobham's. 'In my humble opinion I wish the men could be drafted to Cape Breton, and only the English Sergeants, Corporals, and Drummers kept, and they would by spring, be compleated out of the northern Counties, and till then their horses might be grazed.'[25]

There is little doubt that the dragoons tore a hole in the right flank of the Jacobite army and seriously threatened to break the second line. Had Hawley been quicker off the mark and been able to bring up infantry to exploit that breakthrough, then things might have turned out very differently. There is genuine anger in the letters of Bradshaw and his anonymous comrade at having done their job, at no small cost, but then being let down. Cobham's commander, Lieutenant Colonel John Jordain, had been badly wounded in the stomach.[26] Ligonier's health further deteriorated and he died shortly after the battle. Total losses among the dragoons were possibly as high as 170.[27]

Following Falkirk, Cumberland arrived in Scotland to take command. Pushing forward to Aberdeen he took with him just three regiments of cavalry out of the eleven available to him. These were the dragoon regiments of Cobham and Kerr and Kingston's regiment of light horse. It made sense to take regiments of dragoons rather than horse – they were more flexible, being able to fight dismounted, as demonstrated at Clifton. Their horses were slightly smaller than those of the regiments of horse, a potential disadvantage in cavalry battles where weight mattered, but not in the absence of any significant Jacobite cavalry. More importantly the slightly smaller horses of the dragoons would consume less forage than the larger horses of the horse regiments, a significant factor where the army was heading, and which probably also limited the number of cavalry regiments Cumberland took with him. Two dragoon regiments were sufficient to cover the flanks of the army in battle. Of the dragoon regiments available, Cobham's and Kerr's had performed well at Clifton, and Cobham's appears to have been considered to have done well at Falkirk, where it reformed after its repulse, supported the infantry and covered the retreat of the army. Kingston's horses were smaller even than the dragoons', but the major consideration here was probably the regiment's performance throughout the campaign in scouting; it appears to have been almost constantly the advance guard of Cumberland's army.

As well as their role on the battlefield, cavalry were also largely responsible for protecting the army from being surprised. As part of the official inquiry into Prestonpans, General Cope gave the following evidence about the night before the battle:

> Upon our right a Grand Guard was ordered of 100 dragoons, with a Captain and two Subalterns, near the defile which lies north of the Parks of Preston, and another on our left, from which the Cornet was to advance with 30 dragoons near to Seaton, the Lieutenant with the same number, to support him, posted on the side of the morass, and the Captain and the Quartermaster at the entry of one of the roads leading into the morass, with 40 dragoons to support him.[28]

This is absolutely according to the book, in this case Major General Humphrey Bland's book *Military Discipline*, which tells us exactly the purpose of a Grand Guard and how it worked. First he tells us 'The Grand Guards are to be divided into Captains commands, in each of which there are seldom less than fifty men, or more than a hundred, and each Captain has a lieutenant and Cornet along with him.'

As for where they were to be posted, Bland writes, 'the common rule is to post a Captains command at, or near, each avenue in the front of the army by which the enemy can approach the camp'. Bland further writes, 'When each of these guards consists of 80 or 100 men, they generally post a Lieutenant and 30 troopers, or a Cornet and 20 at a proper distance in their front,' which is exactly what Cope described.[29]

Cope did not tell the inquiry what the duties of the Grand Guard were – the officers of the inquiry would know – but Bland spells it out, telling us in fascinating detail the operational procedures. He tells us that the Grand Guard carried with it forage for the horses, but that the whole guard was not allowed to unbridle to feed at the same time, one rank always being kept mounted at any time. During the night, the Grand Guard also sent frequent patrols around its advanced guards and videts. The videts were pairs of troopers or dragoons posted in front of the Grand Guard. As soon as they saw or heard anything, one would report back to the Grand Guard commander, while one remained to keep watch. If that one was actually attacked or threatened he was to fire a shot and fall back on the Grand Guard. The officer of the Grand Guard in the meantime was to pass on all reports to the field officer of the day. On the night before Prestonpans this was a Major Talbot of the 57th Foot, who Cope described as bringing him frequent intelligence during the night.[30]

Normally Grand Guards were supported by cavalry picquets. These were detachments of men who stayed in camp formed up in their ranks, but dismounted, with the men allowed to lie at their horses' heads. Like Grand Guards they had forage for their horses and so unbridled them. Bland writes that if the enemy were close, one rank was to be kept mounted, being changed every hour. At Prestonpans, however, the whole of the dragoons not posted as Grand Guards were kept 'on standby'.

Whatever happened subsequently, the dragoon Grand Guard at Prestonpans did its job perfectly, detecting the Jacobite attempt to outflank Cope by crossing the morass on his left flank and giving him time to wheel the whole army through 90 degrees to face the threat.

Similarly in the opening moves of the Battle of Falkirk the Jacobite army took a circuitous route, hoping to surprise the army under the command of Lieutenant General Hawley. However, this meant fording the River Carron, and dragoons had been placed at each ford, thus giving Hawley good warning of the approach of the Jacobite army and the route it was taking.

A textbook account of how this would have worked was recorded when the government army occupied Linlithgow in January 1746, and a guard was placed on a bridge over the Avon, which ran between the two armies. 'A subaltern and 20 dragoons took post this night at the bridge, and sent patrols to the other side; 1 Captain, 2 Subalterns and four score dragoons were placed halfway between this post and the gate of Linlithgow from whence perpetual patrols moved the whole night.'[31]

Outpost duty also fell to the lot of cavalry. Humphrey Bland, the British army's leading theoretician and no mean cavalry officer himself, wrote of outposts:

> When a body of men are posted beyond the Grand Guard they are called Outposts, as being without the rounds or limits of the camp. The occasion of their being commanded is generally to prevent the army from being surprized or disturbed in the night by the enemy, or to secure a pass or ford on a river or village, or villages, that may lie between the two armies, as also to keep a communication open with your own garrisons.

He adds, 'When Out Guards are posted in villages they should strengthen themselves in them as much as possible . . . they should likewise strengthen the churchyard or any other part of the village, which they find were proper for their purpose, to retire to when forced from the others, that they may be able to defend themselves till relieved by their army.'[32]

In March 1746 Bland himself established an outpost at Keith consisting of seventy Argyle Militia and thirty of Kingston's Horse. When the Jacobites attacked this outpost on the night of 21 March, the defending militia did indeed fall back on the church and put up a stout resistance before being persuaded to surrender. The men of Kingston's, who were putting up a fierce fight of their own, were then simply overwhelmed.

Jacobite Cavalry

The Jacobite horse was made up of five Scottish units and one regular French unit. The first raised was Strathallan's Perthshire Horse and, about thirty-six strong,[33] was the only Jacobite cavalry at Prestonpans. Later Strathallan's reached a strength of about eighty and other units soon followed – Pitsligo's Horse, which numbered about 130, Elcho's and Balmerino's troops of Life Guards with as many as 160, Kilmarnock's Horse Grenadiers about fifty and the Hussars about eighty. It is unlikely that the total strength of the Jacobite cavalry ever exceeded 500.

As well as by numbers the effectiveness of the Jacobite cavalry was severely handicapped by the quality of the horses. At Prestonpans, once Cope's army had broken, Sir John MacDonald endeavoured to get Strathallan's to follow up the victory, stating, 'The morning light which came quickly, soon showed me the army completely routed. Whereupon I ordered the cavalry to follow me and charge. Lord Strathallan and Mr Gask called to me that I was going too fast, that their horses would not do it.'[34] The Hussars were described as 'having very bad Horses, it occasion'd them to exert all their Vigour in bringing them

Figure 11. Murray of Broughton's Hussars. As a result of indiscipline the unit was later given to the command of an Irish officer, Major John Bagot. (Contemporary drawing from the Penicuik collection, © Sir Robert Clerk)

to a Gallop, tho' very often, the poor Beasts, notwithstanding the Severity used by their Riders, would drop that Speed and take to one more suitable to their Age and Infirmities.'[35]

Mainly because of the efforts of the Royal Navy, very little of the help sent to the Jacobites by France actually arrived. Among the help dispatched was the regular cavalry regiment of Fitzjames. On 23 February 1746, Prince Charles received a letter informing him of the arrival in Aberdeen of a squadron of Fitzjames's with all its horse furniture. Following were another three squadrons and all the regiment's horses. They never arrived, but were captured, leaving the single squadron horseless.[36] It is generally stated that the squadrons of Pitsligo and Kilmarnock had to give up their horses to mount at least some of Fitzjames's. However, the decision to dismount Kilmarnock's and Pitsligo's had already been taken on or just after 18 February 1746 when these units arrived in Elgin after some hard marching in bad weather. 'At the end of this Long march Lord Kilmarnock, Lord Pitsligo and Lord Balmerino's Troops went to nothing, the length of The march had destroyed all Their horses.'[37] Elcho simply says that seventy of Fitzjames's were mounted, and nothing about where those horses came from.[38] O'Sullivan says about the mounting of Fitzjames's 'there were about sixty of the Dragon horses found & given them, it was at least half a squadron mounted, which were very useful'.[39] These dragoon horses were possibly those captured at Prestonpans and which Sir John Macdonald referred to in his account: 'About 50 horses had been taken from the enemy in the battle, and these John Murray had sent to Leith to be kept till the time came for marching, & to be useful to the artillery. The man who had charge of them let them starve.'[40] A French account described Fitzjames's as 'mounted only on crop-tailed horses which we had captured in the two previous battles'.[41]

It is not surprising that O'Sullivan wrote of the Jacobite horse at Falkirk, which were drawn up in the rear of the Jacobite army, 'our horse was not fit to be set in line of Battle, they were not well mounted enough to resist the choc of the enemy's horse'.[42] It would appear, however, that the presence of Fitzjames's began to work an improvement of the Jacobite cavalry generally. After saying that the half squadron of Fitzjames's was very useful, O'Sullivan continues, 'They staid at Elgin & were alwaise apatrouiling, our horse, as well the guardes, as the other began to be formed by them.'[43]

There was, however, a lot that the Jacobite cavalry was fit for. As with the government cavalry there were guard and patrol duties to be undertaken. On 15 December 1745, Pitsligo's were ordered to guard the road out of Kendal towards Lancaster. Their instructions read:

Lord Pitsligo's Horse are to patrol till the break of day with an officer and 30 men on the road that leads to Lancaster. The Body of the Detachment are to be betwixt the Bridge and the Inn called the Cock and Dolphin, where half of them may unbridle and refresh the horses, whilst ten of them will patrol behind the bridge on that same road, unto the second great barn or house on the left hand.[44]

This describes a cavalry Grand Guard, albeit of a somewhat smaller size than recommended by Bland.

Patrolling was carried out by all the Jacobite cavalry, not just the light Hussars who might have been expected to carry the brunt of this sort of work. Orders for the night of 31 December – 1 January 1745–6 read, 'an Officer and 12 of the Perthshire Horse are to patrol this night from Eleven till break of day about two miles from the town on the road of Dumbarton; the Hussars will patrol as usual'.[45] John Daniel of Elcho's Life Guards described a night patrol across the Spey:

Here I had the honour of commanding the last patrolling party that ever crossed the Spey for the Prince's cause. Lord John Drummond having ordered me with ten others to patrol all night towards the enemy, we began our work about seven o'clock and continued it till about five the next morning, being then eight miles from Fochabers and two from the enemy; when we took a man with a Letter from one of Cumberland's Secretaries to the Duchess of Gordon, desiring her to employ all her interest among her vassals in getting down provisions and getting together what forces she could, as the Duke of Cumberland intended to pass the river that day. Having secured the Messenger and Letter, we continued our route, till we came up in a manner to where they were encamped; for as they lay upon the declivity of a hill, and had no guards on the top, we were able to approach very near to them unperceived. But finding them drawn out in order of battle, after seeing all we could see, and some bravadoes and huzzas, we retired with all speed, leaving them to wonder what we meant.[46]

Perhaps the best performance by the Jacobite cavalry came shortly after Cumberland and his army had crossed the Spey and were advancing towards Nairn. Not surprisingly the professionals of Fitzjames's played a major part in this action, and a French report stated, 'its disciplined way of manoeuvring had been copied by the rest of the Prince's cavalry'.[47] Along with the Hussars and Balmerino's Life Guards and supported by the piquet of Berwick's infantry, they carried out a delaying action to slow the advance of Cumberland's army and gain time for the Jacobite infantry to complete their retreat to Nairn. This small body initially formed in a single rank with its left flank resting on the edge of Nairn and facing Cumberland's forces across the River Nairn. It then retreated from Nairn in the face of all eight squadrons of Cumberland's cavalry and four battalions of infantry. According to John Daniel of the Life Guard, 'His grace the Duke of Perth and Colonel O'Sullivan gained immortal honour by their bravery and conduct in bringing us off in good order from under the very nose of the enemy; for notwithstanding all their firing upon our rear, and though we were much inferior in numbers we lost not one man.'[48] O'Sullivan himself described how he 'continued his retraite making volte face from time to time alternatively with the small number of horse he had & those five and twenty men of Berwick's'.[49]

Curiously writers with Cumberland's army describe this great feat of arms in somewhat different terms. James Ray, a volunteer riding with Kingston's, wrote:

> to the left of which, (Nairn) we perceived a Body of the Rebels at a Mile's Distance on which we drew up; but perceiving they did not advance, we fell into marching Order until we came within half a Mile of them, and then observing they did not form but kept in a moving Posture, the Duke of Kingston's Horse, with four companies of the Campbell's were ordered to advance; on this the Rebels fled, and being pursued by some volunteers we had a fine hunting match after them.[50]

Cumberland himself wrote:

> I ordered fifty of the Campbell's who were most advanced, with fifty of Kingston's under Lord Robert Sutton, to push their Rear-Guard which was still at the further end of the town (Nairn). This they immediately did, and drove the Rear-Guard in upon their Main Body, and formed at the other end of the town. In the meantime all the remainder of Campbell's and the cavalry forded the water of Nairn, and pursued them five miles without any loss on our side, and on theirs of eight or ten men killed and three or four taken. In general all the troops that were up behaved well, but Kingston's behaved as well as could be expected from the best old Corps, Lord Robert Sutton having driven more than once with his fifty, a squadron of sixty six of Fitzjames' horse, in upon their Foot.[51]

Cavalry Action at Culloden

When the Jacobite army drew up on Culloden Moor the cavalry, such as there was, was placed on the flanks to the rear. On the left were the Hussars and Strathallan's numbering about seventy. On the right were Fitzjames's squadron and Elcho's troop of Life Guards, also about seventy strong. What was left of Balmerino's troop of Life Guards and Captain Shea and sixteen men of Fitzjames's were escorting Prince Charles.

Initially Cumberland advanced towards Culloden Moor with both dragoon regiments covering the left of the army, save for a small squadron of Cobham's off patrolling to the right. The right flank of the army was covered by marshy ground. Kingston's was in reserve. As the army advanced the marshy ground ended, and Cumberland extended his front by bringing Pulteney's Foot from the rear to the extreme right of the front line of infantry. The front was then further extended to the right by the addition of Kingston's and the squadron of Cobham's that had returned from patrolling. There were thus some 500 dragoons on the left and some 270 horse and dragoons on the right.

The presence of the cavalry on Cumberland's right undoubtedly had an inhibiting effect on the Jacobite infantry who advanced against the battalions of the Royals and Pulteney's. To close with these battalions would have meant exposing their flank to the cavalry. Not surprisingly they hesitated until it was too late and the right flank of the Jacobite infantry was fleeing. At that point, sensing victory, Cumberland rode over to them from his position behind the right of the front line. Approaching Cobham's, 'clapping some of them on the shoulders, [he] call'd out "One Brush, my Lads, for the Honour of Old Cobham"; upon which, rather like Devils than Men they broke through the Enemy's Flank, and a total Rout followed.'[52]

The Jacobite infantry on the left flank were briefly saved from the cavalry by the actions of the regular infantry of the Irish Picquets under Lieutenant Colonel Stapleton. They fired on the dragoons, but then were forced into the walled park on the Jacobite left, where they eventually surrendered. The dragoons and horse rode through the fleeing Jacobites, cutting them down as they went. In the centre of the battlefield they met the cavalry from the left flank.

On the left the advancing regiments of Cobham and Kerr, led by generals Hawley and Bland, found their way blocked by the walls of the Culwhiniac enclosures. In their advance they were supported by three companies of the Argyle Militia and a company of Loudoun's 64th. The militia were instructed to tear down a section of the wall so the cavalry could cross the enclosures. According to Captain Duncan Campbell the breaches made were wide enough for a squadron to march abreast.[53] It is generally accepted that the Jacobites had left the enclosures empty and undefended, although two battalions had been posted outside it to cover that flank. It is clear, however, that the dragoons did not get a completely unopposed crossing of the enclosures, as Ray describes:

> At this instant General Hawley, with four Companies of the brave Campbell's, had broke down the Walls of a Park-Dike, (at which Place we lost two Captains and five private Men of that Party) through which our Dragoons passed, under the Command of Lord Ancram: at the same Time an Officer with a Party of Lord Mark Kerr's Dragoons were sent to dislodge a party of the Rebels that were lurking under the Walls, firing at us, where three Dragoons were killed. We lost but one of Lord Cobham's Men, who was shot close by me at the Rising of the Hill, where we fell upon the Right Flank of the Rebel's second line.[54]

Given that a troop of dragoons in line had a frontage of about 15yds, it would have taken some time to make two passable breaches in the walls of that width. Furthermore, to march ten troops, each in three ranks, across the debris of the walls, across the enclosures and form a line on the other side would have taken time. The precise locations of where the dragoons breached the walls of the Culwhiniac enclosures are uncertain, though see Pollard, Chapter 6. What is clear is that, the enclosures having been crossed, there is only one piece of ground where the dragoons could have formed. That is where the slope up from the River Nairn begins to level off, just above the cairn that lies some 50yds from the enclosures. The six troops of Kerr's Dragoons, who took over the lead from Cobham's, would have had a frontage of some 165yds at a right angle to the wall of the enclosures. The ground above the cairn amply provides the space required. From this position Hawley would also have had a clear view across most of the battlefield.

Behind the buildings of Culchunaig a deep depression runs east–west. Along the far side, Lord George Murray had contrived a defensive line to block the dragoons. This was made up of the cavalry units of Fitzjames and four infantry units. For a short while there appears to have been something of a stand-off.

It has been suggested that this confrontation took place across a stream further to the east.[55] However, for Hawley to have got his dragoons into the position suggested, he would have had to march directly away from the sound of battle, with his flank and rear exposed to attack from around Culchunaig by the Jacobites assembled to block him, and then deliberately place a consider-able obstacle between himself and his enemy. As it is, the maps of Thomas Sandby and Jasper Leigh Jones clearly show the dragoons with their right on the walls of the Culwhiniac enclosures and their left flank beyond the build-ings of Culchunaig. In other words, in advancing, their troops could pass to either side of the buildings.

According to the young James Wolfe, aide-de-camp to Hawley, 'as soon as the Rebels began to give way and the fire of the Foot slacken'd, he [Hawley] ordered Genl. Bland to charge the rest of them with three squadrons, and Cobham to support him with the two. It was done with wonderful spirit and completed the victory with great slaughter.'[56] Quite what happened at this point is not clear, but there does not seem to have been any great mêlée between the dragoons and the Jacobite defensive line. In the entire battle, Kerr's and Cobham's lost only the four men described above by Ray. Rather, the Jacobites opposing the dragoons seem to have drifted away when it became clear that the assault on Cumberland's infantry had been routed. According to an official account:

> The cavalry which charged from the right and left joined in the centre, except 2 squadrons with General Bland, which were then missing, but we soon found they were at the heels of the Rebels. H.R.H. ordered Lord Ancrum with the Cavalry to continue the pursuit as far as possible, which he executed with so much success that a considerable number of the Rebels met their fate in the pursuit.[57]

The two 'missing' squadrons with Bland were probably Cobham's, whose most senior officer present was Major Chaban.

Following the defeat of the Jacobites at Culloden, Cumberland's require-ment for cavalry was not great. On 20 April orders were issued in Inverness for the dragoons to have their horses shod ready for marching, and on 22 April Cobham's were ordered to march the next day.[58] On 11 May, Enoch Bradshaw of Cobham's wrote to his brother, 'And now we have the pleasure of a bed and not hard duty.'[59] On 27 April Cumberland declared, 'The orders against taking anything from the Country people coming to the camp with provisions is again to be read to the men, Especially to the Dragons', but on 29 April Lord Mark Kerr's Dragoons were also ordered away. Kingston's remained with Cumberland, but by late May peacetime activities were already returning when Kingston's were ordered to put their horse out to grass, albeit only during the day.[60]

Chapter 5

The Battle of Culloden:
A Narrative Account

STUART REID

The Battle of Culloden at first sight seems a straightforward affair in which the Highland clans were first pounded by prolonged artillery fire before bravely charging forward to be cut down by the muskets and bayonets of a more numerous and more disciplined foe. Yet probe deeper and a much more complicated story emerges – one in which both sides shifted, turned and manoeuvred, each seeking to gain advantage or counter the moves of the other until in the end the climactic Highland charge was precipitated not by mounting casualties from the Duke of Cumberland's guns, but by the appearance of his cavalry in their rear.

Moreover, in condemning the choice of Culloden Moor itself as a battle-field, critics overlook the fact that the ground which was originally selected by Colonel John O'Sullivan, in his dual capacity as adjutant-general and quartermaster-general to the Jacobite army, was actually a quite different area, some distance to the east. Unfortunately on the morning of 16 April hundreds of stragglers were still missing after the previous night's abortive attempt to surprise the Duke of Cumberland's camp at Nairn. Indeed one account comments that the battle line consisted of scattered groups of men clustered around their colours, and 'as there was no time to march to the ground they were on the day before, they were drawn up a mile further west-ward' – on Culloden Moor.[1]

There the army drew up facing towards the north-east, on an uneven area of what was then rough grass used as a common grazing for the surrounding farms, which were themselves only partially enclosed by stone and turf walls. The left wing rested on the south-eastern corner of a series of dry-stone-walled enclosures known as the Culloden Parks, being part of the mains or home farm attaching to Culloden House, which itself lay at the bottom of the long shallow slope stretching down from the moor towards the main Inverness road and the Moray Firth. These walls provided a secure anchor point for the left flank, but forward of this point the moor was wide open. On the other hand, it was also boggy enough to inhibit movement, especially by horsemen – and in some places soldiers on both sides would find themselves knee-deep in water. The moor was rather drier on the other side, near Culchunaig, where the Jacobite right wing was anchored on the extreme western corner of the stone-walled Culwhiniac Parks. These enclosures stretched (and still do stretch) all the way down to the waters of Nairn, while forward of these particular stone walls a horseshoe-shaped turf-walled enclosure also bulged out onto the moor beside the farm at Leanach.

When Lord George Murray complained to Colonel O'Sullivan that this ground had not been reconnoitred, which was of course hardly surprising in the circumstances, the adjutant-general responded thus:

> here is as good a position as you could desire. You see that Park before you which continues to the river with a wall six foot high, & them houses near it, which you can fill with men, & pierce the walls, that is on your right. You see this Park here is to be our left, & both in a direct line. If there be not ground enough, we'll make use of the Parks & I'll warrant you My Lord . . . the horse won't come to you there.

Murray went off grumbling.[2] He did not, however, follow O'Sullivan's advice to secure his flank, and this may be because, if O'Sullivan is to be believed, this exchange followed directly on from a complaint by Murray that his Athollmen were still standing on the right. At both Prestonpans and Falkirk the MacDonalds had claimed the right wing on the strength of a tradition stretching back to Robert the Bruce's day. However, on 15 April, perhaps stung by aspersions that 'There was not an officer or soldier of them killed or wounded since the beginning of the Campagne,' Lord George Murray had insisted that his own Athollmen should have the right of the front line. 'The McDonnells had the left that day,' complained Donald MacDonnell of Lochgarry, who had commanded Glengarry's Regiment since Falkirk, continuing:

> the Prince . . . agreed to give the right to Ld George and his Atholemen. Upon which Clanranald, Keppoch and I spoke to his RHs upon that subject, and begg'd he wou'd allow us our former right, but he intreated us for his sake we wou'd not dispute it, as he

had already agreed to give it to Lord George and his Atholemen; and I heard HRHs say that he resented it much, and should never doe the like if he had occasion for it.[3]

For some reason, the next day the Athollmen were still standing on the right and were far from demanding that they stay there:

> Lord George comes up and tells Sullivan who had the honr to be near the Prince, that he must change the order of battle, that his Regimt had the right yesterday. 'Gad Sir,' says Lord George swearing, 'it is hard that my Regimt must have the right two days running.'
>
> 'But My Lord,' says Sullivan, 'there was no battle yesterday, besides it is no time to change the order of battle in the enemy's presence . . . for there is nothing more dangerous than to change Regimts from one ground to another in the presence of the enemy.'
>
> The Prince caressed Lord George, prayed him to lead the men, and that he and Sullivan would make them follow in their ranks.[4]

Thus because, as O'Sullivan sensibly pointed out, it would be the height of folly to transfer the battalions on the right of the front line to the left, and bring those on the left to the right while the enemy was fast approaching, they all stayed where they were. As it was, the Jacobite front line originally comprised some thirteen battalions of Highlanders, from Lord George Murray's Athollmen on the right by the Culwhiniac enclosures, to the three MacDonald regiments standing unhappily on the left. In total, if all of them were present, there should have been something like 3,630 men in the front line, besides officers and volunteers, but all the accounts agree that their ranks were severely depleted by straggling and that there may in fact have been several hundred fewer at the start of the battle.

Behind them there was no fully formed second line as such. Instead, drawing on the experience of Falkirk, the Jacobites simply had a number of units grouped in the rear of the first and deployed in column rather than line in order to act as mobile reserves, in accordance with French tactical doctrine. Again working from right to left there were the regular Royal Ecossois, commanded by Lord Lewis Drummond, posted in the rear of Murray's division. Next, more or less in the centre, came the main 'reserve' under Colonel John Roy Stuart, comprising seven of the Lowland battalions, and finally, mirroring the deployment of the Royal Ecossois on the right, the left flank of the second line was covered by the regular Irish Picquets commanded by Lieutenant Colonel Walter Stapleton.

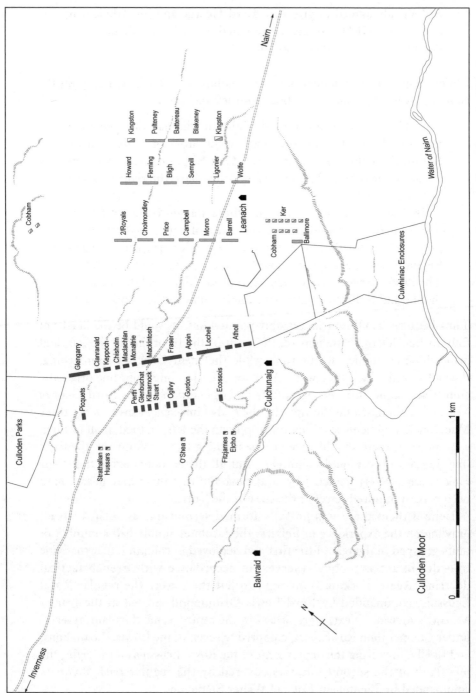

Figure 12. Initial troop dispositions. Ballimore's men begin to break through the enclosure walls to the south. (Based on original by S. Reid, redrawn by G. McSwan, GUARD)

Further back still were three bodies of mounted cavalry, including a small troop of sixteen Life Guards acting as an escort for the Prince, and then two composite squadrons on the right and left respectively – one comprising Lord Elcho's Life Guards and part of the regular Irish regiment the Fitzjames Cavallerie on the right, and the other, collectively referred to as the 'Highland Horse', formed from the Scotch Hussars and Lord Strathallan's Horse.

As the Jacobites gathered up on the moor, the British army advanced steadily towards them and deployed in three lines by the steading at Leanach (Figure 12). Initially Cumberland's front line, commanded by the Earl of Albemarle, comprised the First and Third Brigades: totalling 2,213 rank and file in six battalions from the 1st (Royals) on the right opposite the MacDonalds, to Barrell's 4th Foot on the extreme left just forward of Leanach. Between each of the battalions in the front line was a little Royal Artillery detachment, manning two 3-pound cannon apiece, and there were also two batteries each of three coehorn mortars at the ends of the second line, all under the immediate command of Captain-Lieutenant John Godwin.[5]

Cumberland's second line, commanded by Major General John Huske, was also made up of six battalions, though one, Edward Wolfe's 8th Foot, is frequently depicted standing in a rather improbable position forward of and at a right angle to Barrell's 4th Foot on the left of the front line.[6] In reality they remained in the second line until ordered forward during the decisive counter-attack. The third line, or reserve, comprised Brigadier Mordaunt's Fifth Brigade, flanked by both squadrons of Kingston's 10th Horse.

The rest of the cavalry consisted of two dragoon regiments – Cobham's 10th (less one squadron which was off reconnoitring to the north) and Kerr's 11th under Major General Humphrey Bland – and were posted on the drier ground on the left of the line, together with a half-battalion of Highlanders. Once in contact with the enemy, the Highlanders were under orders to retire to the baggage train in order to avoid any friendly fire incidents, for while some of the regulars belonging to the Black Watch and 64th Highlanders had red jackets, the Argyle Militia had no uniform at all. However, only one wing of the battalion, commanded by Lieutenant Colonel Jack Campbell of Mamore, did so, while the other, led by Captain Colin Campbell of Ballimore, remained with the dragoons. There were just four companies in this half-battalion, a regular company of the 64th Highlanders under Ballimore himself, Captain Dugald Campbell of Auchrossan's Black Watch company and two Argyllshire companies, led by Captain John Campbell of Achnaba and a Captain Duncan Campbell.

Ahead of them were the stone walls of the Culwhiniac Parks, and Major General Bland had a shrewd idea that if he were to get his cavalry brigade through them he ought to be able to turn the rebels' flank. In order to do that, however, he needed infantry support. Cumberland's second in command, Lieutenant General Henry Hawley, agreed, and so Ballimore's Highlanders were sent forward to tear gaps in the walls.

In the meantime Lord George Murray was becoming increasingly concerned about the obstacle offered by the protruding Leanach enclosure, and unilaterally advanced his men down the moor, apparently to a gateway about halfway along the western wall of the Culwhiniac Parks, where he formed the three battalions of the Atholl Brigade into columns in order to better manoeuvre around the Leanach wall when the attack actually began. Although this move was sensible enough in itself, it resulted in considerable dislocation on both sides (see Stephen, this volume, for a contrasting view).

It certainly appears to have taken the Jacobite left wing by surprise, for it was at this time, rather than later, that the MacDonalds famously refused to conform by moving forward. This was hardly surprising since it meant they would give up the security of the park walls and be left with their flank 'in the air'. Consequently the line now stretched along a rather greater frontage, and large gaps now appeared. To his astonishment, Colonel O'Sullivan heard cries of 'Close, close!' and found 'intervals, that he had not seen before'. In the circumstances there was no alternative but to turn to the second line 'for there was no time to be lost, to fill up the vacancy that was left (by Ld George's changement)'.[7] O'Sullivan later recalled that he brought forward Perth's and Strathallan's regiments, but must have been confused by the fact that Perth's Regiment was actually commanded by the Master of Strathallan, for by the time his redeployment was complete it was actually Perth's and Glenbucket's regiments that stood on the extreme left of the front line instead of the MacDonalds, who now 'had no more the left, they were almost in the Center'. John Roy Stuart's Regiment had also been sent forward into the middle of the line to stand beside Stewart of Ardsheal's men.[8]

The move also resulted in some problems for the Jacobite gunners. At the outset of the battle, they had eleven guns just forward of their front line. Most Jacobite maps show them deployed in three batteries on the flanks and centre, but Thomas Sandby, a draughtsman on Cumberland's staff, afterwards depicted a group of four on the right in front of the Atholl Brigade, two in front of John Roy Stuart's Regiment, three in front of Lady Mackintosh's Regiment and the remaining two guns in front of the Macleans and Maclachlans. Clearly they had become scattered when the line moved and shifted during Lord George Murray's 'changement'.

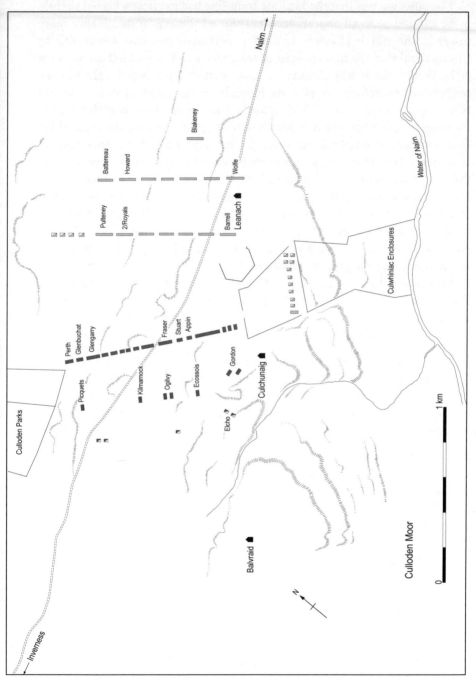

Figure 13. Dispositions following the Jacobite 'changement' and government response; note dragoons are now in the Culwhiniac enclosures. (Based on original by S. Reid, redrawn by G. McSwan, GUARD)

The outcome was that the Jacobite front line had in effect wheeled slightly to its left and so to all appearances had shifted the axis of its advance more towards the north (Figure 13). In practical terms this suggested to Cumberland that the main weight of the rebel attack would fall on his open right flank, which was already to some extent 'outwinged'. He in turn responded, therefore, by posting himself on the right of 2/Royals and bringing forward two of Mordaunt's battalions from the third line, Pulteney's 13th Foot and Battereau's 62nd Foot, to prolong the right of his first and second lines respectively. At the same time, both squadrons of Kingston's 10th Horse were also brought forward from the reserve to cover the right flank, and were then joined there by two troops of Cobham's 10th Dragoons who had earlier been sent reconnoitring towards the north. The end result was that, aside from these cavalrymen, Cumberland's front line now numbered exactly 2,623 bayonets under 461 officers and non-commissioned officers. It was also, it is worth pointing out, still heavily outnumbered by the Jacobite front line.

Meanwhile, General Hawley had begun moving through the Culwhiniac Parks in order to try to outflank the Jacobites. This led to another acrimonious exchange between O'Sullivan and Murray. The former was encouragingly dismissive of the danger at first, but nevertheless recommended that

> as all their horse is at their left, that we shou'd make a breach in this wall, & set in this park Stonywood & the other Regiment [Avochie's] that is in Colloum behind you, who will take their horse in flank, without fearing in the least that they can come upon him.[9]

Predictably, Murray ignored this suggestion, and George Innes reported that, 'Some of Stoniewood's regiment assert, that Colonel Baggot had advised to post them along the outside of that park-dyke, which probably would have prevented a good deal of the mischief these Campbells and dragoons afterwards did; but that Lord George Murray would not hear of it.'[10] Instead O'Sullivan (not Bagot) posted them instead in a 'hollow way' near Culchunaig, after enjoining Stonywood to keep a sentry posted on top to warn of any approaching trouble.

Thus Hawley and his men, complained Murray, were able to traverse the enclosure 'without receiving one shot from the two battalions that were placed to observe their motions'.[11] This was because they had taken up a much more effective position behind that 'hollow way'. This is often identified as the deep hollow bending around the north and east sides of the present Culchunaig steading. Even a cursory examination of the ground, however, will demonstrate that this particular hollow allows a frontage of only about 100m between the steading and the Culwhiniac walls, which is barely enough to accommodate a single squadron of cavalry, let alone the formidable concentration which was building up on both sides.[12] Instead, Captain Duncan Campbell of the Argyles stated that 'The Dragoons went out and formed at a distance, facing the rebels,'[13] while Lord Elcho even more explicitly described the position taken up by his regiment as 'a ditch which Cover'd the right wing'[14] – which clearly establishes it as a much more substantial feature than the hollow by Culchunaig.

As the dragoons cleared the parks, they swung around to deploy into two lines on the open slope below a much longer re-entrant which runs for about 500m more or less in a straight line from west to east on the other side of Culchunaig (Figure 15 below). To all intents and purposes, as James Maxwell of Kirkconnell wrote, Hawley had come 'round the right of the Prince's army and formed in the rear of it!'[15]

It was a stunning development which, far from being a minor sideshow, completely changed the picture of the battlefield. All too aware of the danger, O'Sullivan diverted more units, and by the time Hawley actually closed up to the re-entrant, the crest above was lined by a total of four battalions from Lord Lewis Gordon's and Lord Ogilvy's regiments, as well as the combined squadron of Fitzjames's Horse and Elcho's Life Guards. Unable to see anything of what lay behind the crest, Hawley declined to force a passage across the re-entrant against this battle line, and instead settled down to await events. As they waited, one of Hawley's staff officers, Major James Wolfe – the future conqueror of Quebec – recorded that the firing began at one o'clock in the afternoon.

It was the Jacobites who fired first, almost certainly in response to the threat that had suddenly developed in their rear, and after they had fired just twice in a ripple across their front, Captain Godwin's ten guns replied. Jacobite accounts suggesting that they were fired upon for between twenty and thirty minutes have been accepted by most historians, but the British accounts all record a much shorter bombardment. James Wolfe reckoned it lasted fifteen minutes, but as he was unable to see what was going on, he was relying on sound alone and his estimate must relate to the whole period between the first of the Jacobite guns opening fire and then the last of the British ones ceasing fire because the clans were retreating. Back with the baggage train, Campbell of Airds put its total duration at a very precise nine minutes, while those who were in a position to see what was happening told of an even briefer exchange. One of Cumberland's aides-de-camp, Joseph Yorke, wrote to his father:

> When our cannon had fired about two rounds, I could plainly perceive that the rebels fluctuated extremely, and could not remain long in the position they were then in without running away or coming down upon us; and according as I thought, in two or three minutes they broke from the centre in three large bodies like wedges.[16]

However, as Yorke was speaking only of the British guns, Airds's timing, taken from the moment the Jacobite guns opened the battle, is most likely correct, and during those two or three minutes Godwin's ten light cannon are unlikely to have fired more than thirty rounds between them, most of them at extreme range. It was rare for cannonballs to strike their intended target directly, and gunners usually preferred to drop them short and let them skip along the ground. However, at Culloden the soft ground would have adversely affected that 'grazing' or skipping effect which kept the balls moving just above ground level, while conversely there is ample testimony that a significant number of rounds went flying over the front line. Taking these factors into account, along with statistical analysis of contemporary gunnery tests, it is unlikely that Godwin succeeded in killing or wounding more than an average of one man per shot fired. In other words, no more than twenty to thirty Jacobites can have been killed or wounded by the brief bombardment *before* they charged, rather than the hundreds often claimed.[17]

Similarly there is an equally popular assumption built on this error that, after enduring a prolonged bombardment, the Jacobite attack began spontaneously in response to mounting casualties, and was led by Lady Mackintosh's men in the centre. Once again the actual sequence of events was slightly more complicated. Thanks to Lord George Murray's earlier 'changement', the Jacobite front line was now skewed in such a way that although the right wing was standing some 500m from Cumberland's men, the Duke of Perth's Regiment, standing in the MacDonalds' old position on the extreme left, was still more like 700m away. When Colonel Harry Ker of Graden was sent forward with orders to begin the attack, he rode first to the Duke of Perth on the extreme left and then down the line towards Lord George Murray's position on the right, repeating the orders to each regiment in turn.[18] By starting them off in echelon he no doubt intended that the inadvertent skew would be corrected (Figure 14).

The three regiments of the Atholl Brigade scrambled over the low turf Leanach walls and raced straight towards Barrell's Regiment, but the Camerons were forced against the walls by an involuntary swing to the right by Lady Mackintosh's Regiment and the Frasers next to them. This may have

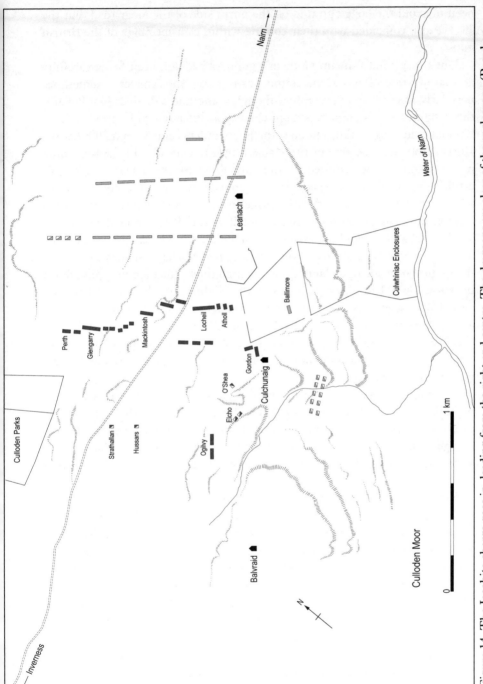

Figure 14. The Jacobite charge goes in, leading from the right and centre. The dragoons are clear of the enclosures. (Based on original by S. Reid, redrawn by G. McSwan, GUARD)

been to avoid the boggy ground on the north side of the moor road, but the swerve also coincided with their coming within canister range of the British guns.

Until that point Captain Godwin's gunners had still been firing carefully at a steady rate of about one round per minute, but canister – sometimes popularly referred to as grapeshot, though grapeshot is distinct (see Pollard, this volume) – was an anti-personnel weapon intended to be fired quickly without troubling to aim, and once the Highlanders came within 300m of the British front line the rate of fire stepped up dramatically. In the remaining ninety seconds or so required for them to close with the redcoats, Godwin's artillerymen could have expected to fire four or even five rounds of canister from each gun, each packed with musket balls. This effectively turned each cannon into a large shotgun and, as small as the little 3-pounders were, a single discharge of double canister might succeed in knocking over as many as eight to ten men. Indeed an eyewitness named Michael Hughes wrote 'that the grapeshot made open lanes quite through them, the men dropping down by wholesale'.[19] Little wonder then that the Highlanders should suddenly shy away from the guns at this point – and it is likely that the Athollmen, Frasers and Camerons received at least five or six discharges of canister from three of the five pairs of guns, which would suggest that in the space of about two minutes they received something in the region of 200 casualties – and worse was about to come.

Whether they were trying to avoid the canister fire or the boggy ground, or both, the immediate result of this sudden swerve was that most of the Jacobite regiments in the centre and right wing became entangled together in a huge mob which rolled right down the road and impacted on Barrell's 4th Foot and Monro's 37th Foot standing on the extreme left of the British front line.

First, however, they had to brave the musketry of at least three front-line regiments: Barrell's, Monro's and Campbell's Royal Scots Fusiliers, mustering some 1,100 men in the firing line. If, as seems likely, Price's 14th Foot also got a volley in, that would increase the full number of muskets to a total of 1,400. A corporal in Monro's afterwards related that 'When we saw them coming towards us in great Haste and Fury, we fired at about 50 Yards Distance, which made hundreds Fall; notwithstanding which, they were so numerous, that they still advanced, and were almost upon us before we had loaden again. We immediately gave them another full fire.'[20]

Gauging the true effectiveness of eighteenth-century musket fire is far from easy. Crude statistical analyses which compare the number of rounds fired in a variety of eighteenth- and nineteenth-century battles with the number of reported casualties tend to demonstrate that only something like 1 per cent of musket balls actually hit anyone. Were that really to be the case here, then the initial British volley would only have dropped about fourteen of the oncoming Jacobites, and no one would have stood around to fire a second one. The truth of the matter is that in most battles a great deal of firing was carried out at ranges much greater than the 50yds quoted above, and was indeed pretty harmless, but at close range it was a very different matter indeed, and even allowing for a universal tendency for soldiers to fire high under stress, the percentage of hits could rise to as high as 10 per cent.

What this means in practical terms at Culloden is that the first volley of musketry may have brought down about seventy or eighty of the attacking clansmen, in addition to those being killed or wounded by canister rounds. Although Price's may not have been in the right place to fire at closer range, the second and much more murderous volley would still have dropped upwards of another 100. Moreover, since all these casualties would have been at the front of a fast-moving and fairly tightly packed mob, they themselves would have buffeted and tripped their comrades as they fell. The very visible effect of both canister and musketry was also vastly encouraging to the British soldiers, and ensured they were not intimidated by the oncoming Highlanders. Thus, contrary to all expectation, neither Barrell's nor Monro's 37th Foot, which was standing next to them, ran away. Instead, after firing that second volley into the Jacobites at point-blank range they stood fast and charged their bayonets:

> Making a dreadful huzza, and even crying 'Run, ye dogs' they [the Jacobites] broke in between the grenadiers of Barrel and Monro; but these had given their fire according to the general direction, and then parried them with their screwed bayonets. The two cannon on that division were so well served, that when within two yards of them they received a full discharge of cartridge shot, which made a dreadful havoc; and those who crowded into the opening received a full fire from the centre of Bligh's regiment, which still increased the number of the slain.[21]

While they had been in winter quarters at Aberdeen, the redcoats are said to have practised a new drill with their bayonets: 'The alteration was mightily little, but of the last consequence,' declared one British officer. 'Before this the bayonet man attacked the sword man right fronting him,' the officer explained, 'now the left hand bayonet attacked the sword man fronting his next right hand man. He was then covered by the enemy's shield where open on his left, and the enemy's right open to him.' In other words, instead of thrusting at the man directly in front of him and having his bayonet parried by the clansman's targe, the soldier was expected to stick his bayonet into the unprotected armpit of the Highlander attacking the man on his immediate right, while trusting the man standing on his left to do the same for him. Although the officer then went on to say that 'This manner made an essential difference, staggered the enemy, who were not prepared to alter their way of fighting, and destroyed them in a manner rather to be conceived than told', it is most unlikely to have worked as smoothly as that in the chaos of battle. What it no doubt did do, however, was give the men the confidence to stand their ground and employ a very different tactic which had proved itself at Falkirk three months before.

Like the best ideas, it was essentially very simple. Ordinarily the British army employed a fire-control technique called platoon firing or platooning. The firing line was broken down into a number of blocks or platoons, which then fired in a pre-arranged sequence so ordered that by the time the last platoons had fired, the first ones had reloaded and were ready to renew the cycle. By this means a ready rolling fire could be maintained for so long as bravery and cartridges lasted, but it had one fatal drawback when facing a Highland charge. The individual platoon volleys – fired by about thirty men apiece – simply could not kill enough of the enemy fast enough to stop them. After Prestonpans, the British army therefore opted to fire massed volleys by complete battalions. The risk then of course was that they might get their timing wrong and the whole lot might still be reloading when the surviving clansmen came close enough to use their broadswords. Rather, the front rank did not make any attempt to reload after the initial volley but instead immediately charged their bayonets to create a hedge of steel behind which the second and third ranks could reload in comparative security.

It is clear that the tactic worked. Cumberland himself expressed his satisfaction with the way Barrell's and Monro's 'fairly beat them with their bayonets'. He declared, 'There was scarce a soldier or officer of Barrell's and that part of Monro's which engaged, who did not kill one or two men each with their bayonets and spontoons.'[22] Nevertheless, they paid a heavy price for their success. In just a few desperate minutes, Barrell's lost seventeen killed and 108 wounded, including their commanding officer, Lieutenant Colonel Robert Rich, out of a total of just 373 officers and men. Unsurprisingly, Barrell's Regiment was burst apart and effectively overrun, temporarily losing one of its colours in the process. Similarly, Monro's afterwards reported fourteen killed and sixty-eight wounded, although proportionately these losses were actually heavier than Barrell's since only a part of the regiment was closely engaged. Nearly all of them were in fact concentrated on the regiment's left wing – and a grenadier officer, identified in a York newspaper as Lieutenant Loftus Cliffe, recorded that he had no fewer than eighteen killed or wounded in his platoon alone, which must have accounted for at least half of them.[23]

This nevertheless was the critical point in the battle, for by this time the rebel command structure had broken down completely, largely because the officers were all out in front and dropping fast. Lieutenant Colonel Charles Fraser of Inverallochie, the Aberdeenshire laird who led Lord Lovat's men, went down; Lieutenant Colonel Alexander McGillivray of Dunmaglas, commanding Lady Mackintosh's Regiment, was first wounded during the charge and then killed in the fighting, as was his second in command, Major Gillies McBean, while Donald Cameron of Lochiel similarly fell well short of the British front line, both ankles broken by canister shot. Right from the beginning, therefore, the three largest regiments were effectively rendered leaderless. Lord George Murray for his part, though notionally a lieutenant general, was now once again behaving, just as he had done at Falkirk, as if he was no more than a brigade commander. Even in this limited role, he failed to exercise any meaningful control or tactical direction of the regiments around him. By his own account he 'lost his horse, his periwig and bonnet . . . had several cuts with broadswords in his coat, and was covered with blood and dirt'.[24] There is no doubting then that he 'behaved . . . with great gallantry', but by getting so involved in the fighting, he completely lost control of his men. Had he instead kept the Athollmen back as a tactical reserve, it might have been possible to widen the gap and exploit the breakthrough.

Instead, more and more Highlanders simply pushed up into the existing penetration rather than attacking the British units immediately to their front. Given a little more time they might still have been able to work their way around the rapidly crumbling flank of Monro's 37th, but the doomed stand by Barrell's 4th Foot had already won precious moments for Major General John Huske, commanding Cumberland's second line, to organize a counter-attack. 'The Regiment [Barrell's] behaved with uncommon resolution,' wrote James Wolfe, who also happened to be a captain in the regiment at the time: 'they were however surrounded by superiority, and would all have been destroyed had not Col. Martin with his Regiment (the left of the 2nd line of Foot) mov'd forward to their assistance, prevented mischief, and by a well timed fire destroyed a great number of them'.[25] It was now, rather than at the outset of the battle, that the regiment took up a position at right angles to the front line, and, moreover, recognizing the desperate urgency of the situation, Huske had ordered forward not just Edward Wolfe's 8th Foot but the rest of

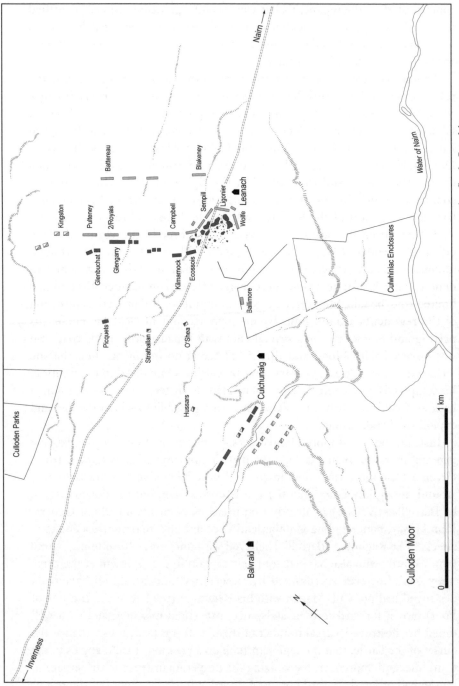

Figure 15. Hand-to-hand fighting on the government left; Wolfe's regiment advance onto the flank. Jacobite reserves are brought forward. Ballimore is positioned behind the north wall of the Culwhiniac enclosures. (Based on original by S. Reid,

Conway's Fourth Brigade, mustering a total of 1,078 bayonets, besides officers and non-commissioned officers (Figure 15).

In order to get into action the brigade first had to move slightly to its left and then clear the Leanach steading, and an early sketch map by Thomas Sandby shows Ligonier's Regiment temporarily dividing into two wings in order to do so. Once past the buildings, however, as Captain-Lieutenant James Ashe Lee of the 8th Foot wrote in a letter home, 'Poor Barrell's regiment were sorely pressed by those desperadoes and outflanked. One stand of their colours was taken; Collonel Riches hand cutt off in their defence . . . . We marched up to the enemy, and our left, outflanking them, wheeled in upon them.'[26] Huske had also sent forward Bligh's 20th Foot from the Second Brigade to plug the gap between Sempill's 25th (Edinburgh) Regiment and the hard-pressed 37th Foot. The result was that all five battalions, and perhaps some determined remnants of Barrell's 4th Foot as well, were soon formed into a large horseshoe-like arc, hemming in the rebels on three sides.

The impetus of their assault having already been blunted, the Jacobite front rank was now brought to a complete halt by Huske's counter-attack, but nevertheless more and more men came still pushing up from the rear until they were all jammed together in one huge immobile mass, flayed by a terrible crossfire at point-blank range. Once again British accounts all relate how after their initial battalion volleys had been fired, their front-rank men stood fast with charged bayonets to protect the second and third ranks as they reloaded and fired time and again. Captain Lee of the 8th Foot reckoned 'the whole then gave them 5 or 6 fires with vast execution, while their front had nothing left to oppose us, but their pistolls and broadswords; and fire from their center and rear (as, by this time, they were 20 or 30 deep) was vastly more fatal to themselves, than us'.[27] This is also confirmed by the corporal of Monro's who stated that 'the Front Rank charged their Bayonets Breast high, and the Center and Rear Ranks kept a continual Firing . . . the Rebels designing to break or flank us; but our fire was so hot, most of us having discharged nine Shot each, that they were disappointed'. Allowing for the two volleys fired as the Highlanders charged towards them and at least one other while Conway's Brigade hurried to their assistance, that would indeed equate to five or six more at this point.

The combined strength of Conway's Brigade together with Bligh's and Monro's regiments amounted to some 1,900 men, exclusive of officers and non-commissioned officers, although enough of Barrell's men may have remained in the fight to make up about 2,000. Conservatively, therefore, and allowing for the front rank of each regiment standing fast with charged bayonets, there were at least 1,200 soldiers firing those five or six volleys. Even if only one in ten of those rounds took effect at this very short distance – and firing over the front rank will have increased the tendency to shoot high – a simple calculation suggests that something in the region of 700 Jacobites were killed or wounded here in the space of just two or three terrible minutes.

By contrast the British army's losses in this phase of the battle were negligible. Bligh's Regiment afterwards returned four men killed and sixteen wounded, while Sempill's Edinburgh Regiment had just one dead and thirteen wounded. Even then some of those casualties were probably men killed or wounded by the earlier Jacobite artillery barrage, for Wolfe's Regiment had just a single officer, the newly commissioned Ensign Robert Bruce, wounded.

Realizing that it was all going badly wrong, Murray tried to get the stalled assault moving again. Knowing that his men would not be able to stand much longer, he managed to make his way out of the press and ran back to hurry forward his own supports. To his dismay there was virtually no one left, for most of the reserves had long since been drawn off either to face the threat posed by Hawley's cavalry on the slope beyond Culchunaig, or to bolster the left wing.

Yet another of the persistent myths which cluster around this battle is the story that the three MacDonald regiments, piqued at being placed on the left wing, refused to charge at all. The story is told with a wealth of circumstantial and outwardly convincing detail, such as the claim that old Alexander MacDonald of Keppoch rushed forward alone, crying that the children of his clan had forsaken him, only to be shot down by the soldiers. He certainly fell, but it is significant that at least three witnesses afterwards testified to finding his body on the ground, as they came running back in retreat and so must have advanced well beyond their fallen chief.

Far from refusing to charge, the MacDonalds, together with Perth's and Glenbucket's men on their left, all started forward at much the same time as the others. However, because the Jacobite front line was skewed in relation to the British one, they had something like 200m further to go than Murray's men on the right, and moreover they also had to cross much boggier ground from the very outset. In fact, Captain James Johnstone, who fought at Culloden as a volunteer in Glengarry's Regiment, afterwards complained that it was not merely boggy but 'covered with water which reached halfway up the leg'.[28]

In the circumstances, it is hardly surprising that the Jacobites' advance on the left wing was so very much slower and ultimately ground to a halt. 'They came running on in their wild manner,' declared Cumberland himself, 'and upon the Right where I had placed Myself, imagining the greatest Push would be there, they came down three several Times within a Hundred Yards of our Men, firing their pistols and brandishing their Swords, but the Royals and Pulteneys hardly took their Firelocks from their shoulders.'[29] The fact of the matter was that the Highlanders were frustrated by the regulars' failure to obligingly run away. 'Our left flinches,' wrote O'Sullivan. 'The Duke of Perth runs to Clanronald's Regiment takes their Collors & tells them from that day forth he'l call himself MacDonel if they gain the day. Lord John [Drummond] & Sullivan brings up the left again.'[30] This time Johnstone thought they got within twenty paces of Cumberland's line and certainly close enough for him to consider it worth discharging his blunderbuss at the redcoats. He even thought that if the Jacobite right wing could have stayed in the fight a few moments longer, he and his MacDonald comrades could still have won the day. It was of course no more than wishful thinking, and all the time the casualties were mounting.

The little units on the MacDonalds' right were faring particularly badly, perhaps because they had become relatively isolated in the centre of the increasingly ragged Jacobite front line. The Chisholms, the combined battalion of Macleans and Maclachlans, and Farquharson of Monaltrie's men all pretty well disintegrated. In fact, all the officers in the small independent company formed by the Chisholms of Strathglas were killed or wounded, while Colonel Lachlan Maclachlan was fatally wounded by a cannon shot – an eyewitness gruesomely described how his 'guts were laid over his horse's neck' – while no fewer than thirteen of Monaltrie's officers fell. Both the Chisholms and Monaltrie's men also lost their colours and, in the circumstances, Maclachlan's may well be one of the unidentified ones. Out on the extreme left flank Perth's and Glenbucket's regiments seem to have advanced with the MacDonalds, but got on the receiving end of at least one volley from Pulteney's and soon retired, leaving Major Robert Stewart pinned beneath his dead horse. As their leaders were shot down one after the other, the MacDonalds too began to give way. Sensing his advantage Cumberland galloped across to the little detachment of Cobham's 10th Dragoons and, according to one, 'clapping some of them on the shoulders, call'd out "One Brush, my Lads, for the Honour of old Cobham"; upon which, rather like Devils than Men they broke through the Enemy's Flank and a total Rout followed'.[31]

It was not quite so dramatic as that, for the dragoons had first to carefully splash their way across the very same boggy ground which had slowed the Jacobite advance and which James Johnstone earlier thought 'well chosen to

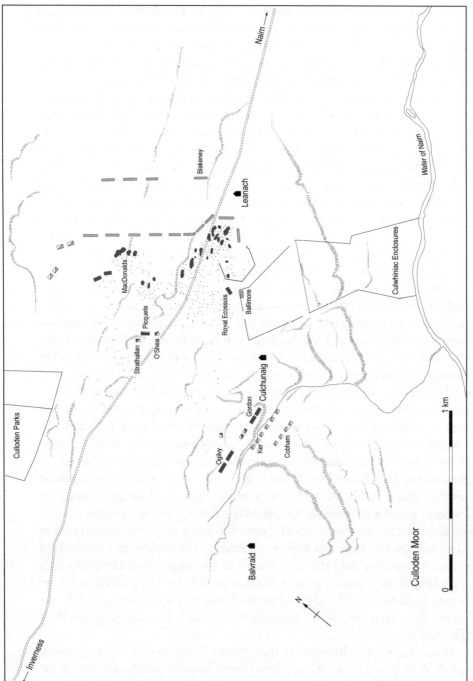

Figure 16. The Jacobite infantry begin to retreat. The Royal Ecossois engage with Ballimore; fighting between the dragoons and Jacobite cavalry is under way. (Based on original by S. Reid, redrawn by G. McSwan, GUARD)

protect us from the cavalry of the enemy'. As a result Perth's and Glenbucket's regiments had certainly disengaged and were well away before the attack came in, and it is also possible that the MacDonalds too were falling back towards the Inverness road before the dragoons got clear of the bog.

To cover their retreat, O'Sullivan brought up the Irish Picquets, who had been one of just three battalions left in reserve at that point, and consequently when Murray came running back in search of support for the collapsing right wing, he found just two battalions still unengaged – the blue-bonneted Royal Ecossois and Lord Kilmarnock's newly raised Footguards. Both regiments followed him forward, but it was already too late. 'I brought up two regiments from our second line, after this, who gave their fire,' said Murray, 'but nothing could be done – all was lost.'[32] As the surviving clansmen dissolved into rout, Kilmarnock's men fired a hasty volley and then ran back with them, and although the Royal Ecossois fell back too, they at least tried to do so with a little more dignity, as befitted their status as regulars. After exchanging token volleys with Campbell's 21st (Royal Scots Fusiliers) they then began to fall back in good order. Sensibly enough, they first moved to their right and then retired along the outside of the Culwhiniac Park wall, where they were masked from artillery fire by the Leanach enclosure. With luck they might have got clean away. Unfortunately they had reckoned without the half-battalion of loyalist Highlanders commanded by Captain Colin Campbell of Ballimore (Figure 16).

After the dragoons cleared the enclosures, Ballimore was ordered to remain there and appears to have initially opened fire at long range on some of the Jacobites – perhaps Lord Ogilvy's men, lining the re-entrant near Culchunaig. This firing was of little more than nuisance value at first, but 'though few were killed by reason of the distance yet many were wounded, especially in the legs and thighs'. Then, as Campbell of Airds gleefully reported, 'Ballimore & his command . . . taking advantage of the Second Dyke as a Breast Work fire Closs on a strong party of the Rebels that then formed the Right, Composed of Lord John Drummond's men being part of the Enemy's second line.'[33] A high concentration of bullets discovered during recent archaeological investigations clearly pinpoints the site of this ambush as being in the otherwise sheltered corner where the Leanach and Culwhiniac enclosures met (see Pollard, this volume). Just how much damage Ballimore's volley inflicted on the Royal Ecossois is unknown, but the regulars fired a withering volley in reply, and as Airds sadly reported afterwards, 'It was in passing a slap [opening] in the second Dyke that Ballimore was Shot Dead, and that Achnaba received his wound of which he Dyed next day.'[34] Six other men in Ballimore's own company of the 64th Highlanders were afterwards returned as dead, and three were wounded in this brief firefight. When their graves were discovered in the following century, it was noted that most had apparently been shot through the head, clearly indicating that they were firing from behind the wall at the time.

Short and sharp though this vicious little exchange proved to be, it was still sufficient to drive Kilmarnock's men and the Royal Ecossois back out onto the open moor and, unwittingly, throw them into the path of Hawley's dragoons.

Up until this point General Hawley had been content to remain passively observing the strong force of Jacobites posted along the crest in front of him. Indeed one of Lord Elcho's officers, Major James Maxwell of Kirkconnell, remembered that 'the ascent was somewhat steep on both sides, so that neither could pass safely in the presence of the other'.[35] Moreover since the Jacobites were above the dragoons, there was of course no way of telling whether they had anything else in reserve. Had Hawley been more aggressive, the battle could easily have been even more of a disaster for the Jacobites and, after revisiting the field five years later, James Wolfe grumbled to his father that 'The actors [Hawley and Bland] shine in the world too high and bright to be eclipsed; but it is plain they don't borrow much of their glory from their performance on that occasion.' Nevertheless, in the circumstances this early caution was understandable, but now, however, as Wolfe related, 'as soon as the Rebels began to give way and the Fire of the Foot slacken'd, he [Hawley] ordered Genl Bland to charge the rest of them with three squadrons, and Cobham to support him with two'.[36]

So far Cobham's, as the senior regiment of the two, had led the advance, but one of its squadrons was of course over on Cumberland's left wing, which meant it was only 180 strong. Therefore Hawley decided to employ the 300-strong Kerr's 11th Dragoons to break through the defensive line on the ridge above. Accordingly, Bland took the six troops through the intervals in Cobham's four, across the re-entrant and on up the slope. The rebels were evidently already beginning to withdraw by this time, but nevertheless unleashed a surprisingly effective volley (Figure 17). Kerr's had three men killed and three others wounded at Culloden, which at first sight appears negligible, but the regiment also reported the loss of no fewer than nineteen horses, so the fight may not have been quite such a walkover after all. This partial check may explain why these particular rebels subsequently got away without further molestation, leading Wolfe to complain to his father that 'You would not have left those ruffians the only possible means of conquest, nor suffer multitudes to go off unhurt with the power to destroy.'

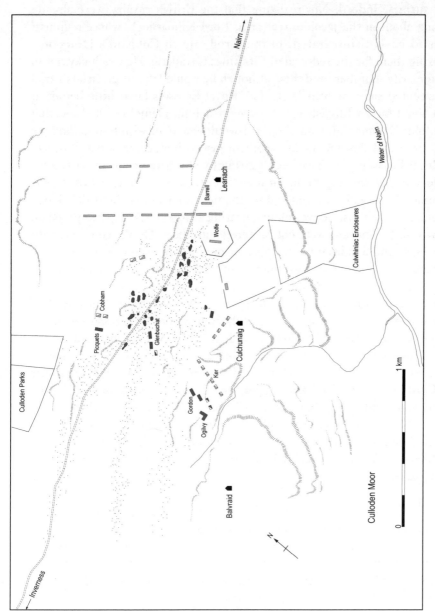

Figure 17. Jacobites stream off the field, with Jacobite cavalry and some infantry still providing a defensive screen against dragoons in the south part of the field. The government infantry begin their advance across the field. (Based on original by S. Reid, redrawn by G. McSwan, GUARD)

Once Kerr's had cleared the way, Cobham's had a much easier time of it and, emerging straight onto the moor, they gave some of the rebels a very nasty surprise indeed. Not realizing that the British cavalry were already roaming about in the Jacobite rear area, Lord Kilmarnock, whose regiment seems to have disintegrated, blithely rode up to Cobham's Dragoons, mistaking them for the red-coated Fitzjames Cavallerie. He was lucky not to be summarily shot there and then, although he would later be given a fair trial and executed some months later. The Royal Ecossois fared little better: at about this time an English volunteer named John Daniel recalled meeting Lord John Drummond, who 'desired I would come off with him, telling me all was over and shewing me his regiment just by him, surrounded'.[37] In fact the Royal Ecossois may have been retiring by alternate wings, or battalions. While part of the regiment, under Lieutenant Colonel Lord Lewis Drummond, certainly surrendered on the field after losing about fifty killed or wounded, their distinctive colours, bearing a large thistle superimposed on the cross of St Andrew, were not captured with them. On the contrary, both the colours and a substantial number of men led by Major Matthew Hale succeeded in getting away with the rest of the low-country regiments which had stood above the re-entrant.

At any event this particular fight may also have given the prince himself precious time to escape. When the artillery bombardment began, many of Godwin's cannonballs were pitched too high and flew over the heads of the men in the front line to cause a certain amount of confusion and dismay in the Jacobite rear. Oddly enough both of the cavalry officers on the Jacobite left, Lord Strathallan and Major Bagot, were badly wounded, presumably by cannon shot, and there is anecdotal evidence that in the centre Balmerino's troop of Life Guards were particularly badly hit, while even Prince Charles had his horse injured by these random shots, and Thomas Ca, a groom standing nearby, was decapitated. According to Robert Strange, one of the Life Guards,

> The Prince, observing this disagreeable position, and without answering any end whatever . . . ordered us down to a covered way, which was a little towards our right, and where we were less annoyed by the Duke's cannon; he himself with his aides-de-camp, rode along the line towards the right, animating the soldiers. The guards had scarce been a minute or two in this position, when the small arms began from the Duke's army, and kept up a constant fire; that instant, as it were, one of the aides-de-camp returned, and desired us to join the Prince.

When the MacDonalds finally broke the prince appears to have been rallying Perth's and Glenbucket's regiments, but seeing Lord George Murray's right wing collapse as well, O'Sullivan immediately rode to Captain O'Shea at the head of the prince's escort squadron and shouted: 'yu see all is going to pot. Yu can be of no great succor, so before a general deroute wch will soon be, Seize upon the Prince & take him off.'[38]

At first the Prince stubbornly refused to retire, 'notwithstanding all that can be told him', but then O'Sullivan spotted Cobham's Dragoons and Kingston's Horse moving forward, and

> seeing this Regiment marching towards our left, as if they were to cut our retrait runs to the Prince, and tells him that he has no time to lose that he'l be surrounded immediately if he does not retir. 'Well,' says the Prince, 'they wont take me alive.' Sullivan prays him to look behind him, & that he's seen the whole moor cover'd with men that were going off & that half the Army was away.[39]

This time O'Shea did his duty and hustled him away safely, accompanied by Perth's and Glenbucket's men.

The retreat, probably unwittingly, was covered both by the Royal Ecossois and by the Irish Picquets, although exactly what happened to the latter is a touch obscure. O'Sullivan simply says that Lieutenant Colonel Walter Stapleton 'makes an evolution or two, fires at the Dragoons & obliges them to retire . . . the Picquets throws themselves into the Park that was on our left, continues there fire'.[40] With them too was a French engineer officer named Du Saussey who had brought up another gun, probably one of the light 'Swedish' 4-pounders, and there they remained in the north-eastern corner of the Culloden Parks for some time, making a thorough nuisance of themselves until Belford and Godwin brought up a number of coehorn mortars to silence Du Saussey's gun, and with Stapleton mortally wounded, the gallant little band at last surrendered.

By that time they were probably the last formed Jacobite unit still on the field. As it broke up, the rebel army effectively divided itself in two. The four Lowland battalions which had been posted above the re-entrant, together with a part of the Royal Ecossois, retained some kind of order and retired southwards, crossed the River Nairn and eventually made their way to Ruthven Barracks. However, with this particular escape route cut almost at once by the dragoons moving up from the south, most of the Highland regiments from the front line were forced to take the understandable but fatal course of running straight back down the road to Inverness. It was just the situation which every cavalryman dreams of: led by Bland, all the dragoons set off after the fugitives and 'gave Quarter to None but about Fifty French Officers and Soldiers He picked up in his Pursuit'.[41]

Although the vigorous and undoubtedly bloody pursuit was afterwards represented in some quarters as tantamount to a war crime, it was in reality nothing out of the ordinary, and indeed the Highlanders themselves had proved themselves equally ruthless when the position was reversed. As James Wolfe, who almost certainly took part in the pursuit himself, remarked, 'The Rebels, besides their natural inclinations, had orders not to give quarter to our men. We had an opportunity of avenging ourselves for that and many other things, and indeed we did not neglect it, as few Highlanders were made prisoners as possible.'[42]

As the first of those fugitives came running down the Inverness road they were met by a battalion of Frasers commanded by their chief's son, Simon Fraser, the Master of Lovat. Popular legend has it that, realizing all was lost, the master promptly faced his men about and marched them straight back to Inverness, with their colours still flying and pipes playing. While there is absolutely no reason to doubt the story, what happened next is far more intriguing. Having safely returned to Inverness, the Frasers then needed to cross the bridge over the River Ness to reach their own country, and there are two different but not inconsistent stories regarding this bridge. One, quite plausibly, has the Master of Lovat proposing to defend it until he was dissuaded by some of the burgesses, who quite understandably wanted to distance the town from the rebels. The other story, much more improbably, has the bridge seized by a party of the Argyle Militia who somehow preceded the dragoons into the town and vainly tried to block the Jacobite retreat. At first sight this particular story seems nonsensical, yet James Johnstone recalled hearing a short but intense burst of firing as he fled past the town, which does point to some kind of a fight. Yet if it was not the Argyles, then the most sensible explanation is to combine the two stories and conclude that the rather slippery Master of Lovat changed sides and that his men tried to block the bridge against their erstwhile colleagues. This might also in turn explain why the master was afterwards treated so leniently by the government, and why he eventually died as a lieutenant general in the British army.

'We had the bloodiest Battle with the Rebels that ever was fought in the Memory of Man,' wrote Lieutenant Cliffe, yet his own and Barrell's Regiment aside, the British army's casualties were on the whole comparatively light. Regimental returns recorded just fifty dead and 259 wounded, although a high proportion of the latter must have died soon afterwards. Lieutenant Dally of Monro's, for example, was officially returned as wounded in Cumberland's dispatch, but had already died by the following day when Lieutenant Cliffe penned his celebrated letter. Similarly, only nineteen out of the sixty-eight rank and file returned by the regiment as wounded afterwards survived to claim pensions from Chelsea, while just twenty-nine out of the 103 rank and file returned as wounded in Barrell's 4th Foot survived. In short, nearly 200 of the wounded appear to have subsequently died, some of them in Inverness.[43]

It was impossible of course to compile accurate returns of rebel casualties, but most estimates reckoned that around 1,500 Jacobites were killed or wounded, besides an initial total of 326 prisoners reported in Cumberland's dispatch. However, on closer examination, it turns out that this figure included 172 of the Earl of Cromartie's men taken prisoner by loyalists in a neat little action at Dunrobin on the day before. The true figures for prisoners actually taken on the day are therefore 154 rebels and 222 'French' officers and soldiers. Afterwards largely unfounded allegations were rife that hundreds of rebel wounded were executed out of hand, although the British army's attitude was summed up by Lieutenant Cliffe, who wrote of the regiment's 'ample revenge for the Loss of our late Colonel'.[44]

Chapter 6

Capturing the Moment:
The Archaeology of Culloden Battlefield

TONY POLLARD

Introduction

This chapter provides a summary and discussion of the findings of archaeo-logical fieldwork carried out on Culloden battlefield in April 2005, though it also integrates earlier work where relevant. This contribution is intended as an interim statement only – a full report on this and other investigations on the site will appear in due course.

Following on from initial work in 2000, as part of the *Two Men in a Trench* television series, Glasgow University Archaeological Research Division (latterly encompassing the Centre for Battlefield Archaeology) was commissioned by the National Trust for Scotland (NTS) to carry out a multifaceted investigation at Culloden battlefield as part of the Culloden Battlefield Memorial Project (CBMP). The main aim of the CBMP was the construction of a new visitor centre, which officially opened in April 2008, and an associated upgrade of the presentation of the battlefield. The results of this fieldwork were in part used to inform the re-display of the battlefield and the interpretation presented to visitors. Metal detector survey, geo-physical survey and limited excavation were combined to pursue a number of research avenues relating to the location, progress and character of the battle and the role of the landscape.

The work discussed below was carried out between 4 and 13 April 2005. Earlier investigations on the site had revealed archaeological evidence indi-cating that pre-2008 interpretations and presentations of the battlefield site were flawed, not least because the battlefield was larger than portrayed.[1] An important objective of the CBMP was therefore to establish as fully as possible the true extent of the battlefield and the location of various elements of the battle as understood from historical accounts and maps of the event.

Most of the April 2005 investigation was focused on areas already touched upon by the 2000 project, largely to clarify and expand upon the results gleaned from what was essentially a rapid evaluation. Since then, several additional areas have been subject to metal detecting, including the footprint of the new centre, but the results of these later surveys are not touched upon here.

The Battlefield Then and Now

Culloden battlefield (OS grid reference NH 7406 4497, centred on cairn monument) is located on reconstituted moorland and grazing land some 6km to the east of Inverness, in the parish of Croy and Dalcross (Plate 8). The site is approximately 160m above sea level, on a rolling terrace largely formed from Old Red Sandstone. Much of the area of the battlefield open to visitors was once occupied by forestry planted in the Victorian era, but this was removed in the 1980s by the NTS in a programme of moorland reclamation and site reconstruction. Extant tree plantations can still be seen to the west of the site, and to the north across the B9006 road, which itself represents a realignment of an earlier road that until the early 1980s ran through the clan cemetery. The core of the battlefield is today occupied by a mosaic of gorse, heather and small birch, with pools of standing water and streams giving some impression of the wet conditions that prevailed on the ground at the time of the battle.

In 2005 a visitor centre, first built in 1970, marked the eastern limit of the site, providing interpretation and orientation displays for visitors to the battlefield. A series of footpaths led from the visitor centre and the partially reconstructed house known as (Old) Leanach Cottage and meandered through the clan cemetery and along the Jacobite line to the west before returning east to the government line.[2] To the south of the clan cemetery are a number of fields, which drop down to the River Nairn. At the time of the battle, at least parts of these would have been enclosed within turf and stone dykes; contemporary battle maps show some of these areas to be cultivated (see Woosnam-Savage, this volume). One of these, partially reconstructed in turf and stone by the NTS in the 1990s, encompassed the ground attached to the farmstead of Leanach, while the larger stone-walled Culwhiniac enclosures sat not far away to the west. The northern limit of the battlefield was defined by the walls of Culloden Parks, attached to Culloden House, the latter over 2km to the north, but like those of Culwhiniac and Leanach these walls were removed in the nineteenth century.

Various elements of the battlefield, including a large tract of the ground over which the Jacobites charged, were presented to the NTS from the 1940s through to the 1960s, and under its auspices the site has become a popular tourist attraction, though it had long before then provided a focus for visitors. From the middle of the nineteenth century onwards a number of monuments were erected on the site, most immediately in the vicinity of the clan graves (see Masson and Harden, this volume).

In addition to these Victorian monuments, there are other built features, the most obvious of which is Leanach Cottage. The contemporary battle maps show a number of buildings in the vicinity of this structure, and after the battle, according to at least one eyewitness account, one of these, described as a barn, was burnt down by government troops while wounded Jacobite soldiers were locked inside it.[3]

Other farmsteads shown on maps of the time were located near Culchunaig, to the south-west of the NTS property. Today, this site is occupied by a later farm complex, and it is uncertain if any remains survive from the original farmstead. Again, according to early maps (see Woosnam-Savage, this volume), a farmstead known as Park House of Urchal was located within the Culwhiniac enclosures, and, although thought at the commencement of this project to be no longer visible, it does appear on the first edition OS map as a ruin.

Prior to the current programme of work, the most thorough archaeological investigation of the site took place in 2000 as part of the BBC television series *Two Men in a Trench*. This project included metal detecting in the Field of the English and adjoining grassed area to the north, and resulted in the recovery of an important assemblage of finds, some of which clearly related to the hand-to-hand fighting between the Jacobite right and the government left. The location of this material also suggested that this contact took place further to the south than suggested by the then current NTS interpretation of the site. Artillery shot (grape and canister) was also recovered from inside the reconstructed Leanach enclosure, which did not marry with most historical accounts of the battle, which imply that the right wing moved around the outside of the enclosure rather than running through it.[4]

The 2000 project also involved the excavation of the rectilinear banked feature attached to the southern gable wall of Leanach Cottage, which was at the time interpreted as the vestigial remains of the so-called 'Red Barn' which was supposedly burned with Jacobites inside it. Excavation revealed this structure to be nothing more than the remains of a walled kitchen-garden dating no further back than the nineteenth century.

Ground-penetrating radar (GPR) survey was also carried out across the burial mounds in the clan cemetery, which is a scheduled area. All of the mounds were found to cover pits, but interestingly further pits, or at least parts of pits, were also suggested beneath the road that until the early 1980s ran through the cemetery (at which point it was simply grassed over).

The objectives of the 2005 fieldwork were:

- to assess the character, extent and condition of buried archaeological remains suggested by geophysical anomalies to the west of Leanach Cottage: this was achieved through the excavation of two trial trenches across the anomalies

- to verify the presence and position of a mass grave related to the burial of government soldiers in the Field of the English: this was attempted through geophysical survey of the area previously subject to radar survey (this element is not discussed here for the sake of brevity)

- to further define the pattern of battle debris in the Field of the English identified during the 2000 project: this was achieved by metal detector survey of the area previously detected (during which only a small sample of artefacts had been excavated).

Results

Topographic Survey: The Road

Although carried out prior to the 2005 work, the results of the topographic survey are worth consideration within the present discussion as they had an important impact on our current understanding of the battle.

Maps of the battlefield appear in most of the many books published on Culloden and tend to portray it as a flat piece of ground, a level playing-field on which the two sides fought to the death. This may also be the impression gleaned by the casual visitor who does not take the time to more fully take in and digest the sometimes subtle changes in topography, which nonetheless may have influenced the battle and its outcome. Many of these were highlighted during a close-grained topographic survey carried out in 2000 and continued in 2005. One of the most important findings was a ridge of high ground which ran diagonally across the field roughly from the centre of the Jacobite line to a point on the left of the government line (Plates 24 and 25). To the north of the spine the ground slopes very gently down toward the modern road and provides a clear line of sight from the centre-right of the government line across to the centre-left of the Jacobite line. The most dramatic manifestation of the southern side of the ridge can be found adjacent to the clan cemetery, where the ground slopes down into a hollow before rising up again to the northern edge of the Field of the English, in the vicinity of the Well of the Dead. This hollow, albeit probably wet, would have been concealed from the view of troops on the government front line positioned anywhere further to the north than Monro's Regiment, to the left of which stood Barrell's, on the left of the entire line.

For the most part, the crest of this ridge corresponds to the route of the old road which crossed the moor and, up until the 1980s, when it was moved further to the north, passed through the clan cemetery. Despite appearing on a number of the contemporary battle maps – it is described as the 'Muir road to Inverness' on Sandby's map (Figure 18) – it has been largely overlooked by historians in their studies of the battle. What has not been overlooked, of course, is that the centre and right of the Jacobite charge clashed with Barrell's and Monro's regiments on the government left. A number of reasons for this veering have been proposed, including a shift to their own right in order to avoid artillery and musket fire from the government centre (see previous chapter); this may have been a factor. Other factors should also be considered, including the road; it is surely no coincidence that its route corresponds to the course of that part of the Jacobite charge which succeeded in reaching the government line. It has been suggested by Woosnam-Savage (this volume) that the modern, pre-1980 road may not have followed the same route, but given the topography and the road's spatial relationship to Leanach Cottage there seems little reason to doubt this. Although it was nothing more than a narrow track, the road would still have provided surer footing than the rough moorland to either side.[5] It is therefore suggested that the road was used to deliver at least part of the Jacobite charge, the rapid headway it allowed having a part to play in the success of the charge from the centre and right.

A further consideration in understanding the bias of the charge toward to the right, and hence to the government left, is the cover which this part of the field may have afforded from government fire. The hollow observed to the south of the clan cemetery, and now more visible on the ground following the recent removal of trees from around the cemetery, would certainly shield some of the charging Jacobites from withering fire delivered from the government centre. It is interesting to note that Morier's famous painting of the battle (Plate 1), which shows the Jacobite assault on Barrell's grenadiers (viewed from the south), depicts the Jacobites in the background being down slope from the action in the foreground, or indeed in a hollow.

By contrast, the Jacobite charge from the left of the line was across open ground covered in places by knee-deep water – it is therefore no wonder that this part of the charge met with little success, being for most of the way in open view of the government right.

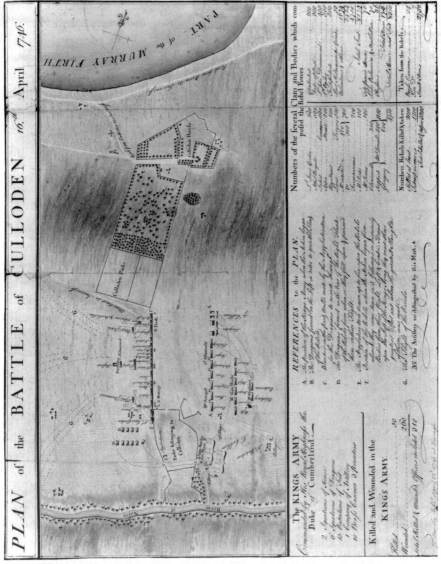

Figure 18. Battle map by Thomas Sandby, 1746. Government lines at the bottom, Jacobite to the top. Note the road crossing between the lines: north is approximately to the right. (The Royal Collection, © Her Majesty The Queen)

The hollow, however, would do little to protect from the fire of the redcoats stationed across its eastern end – those of Monro's and Barrell's regiments. It is also possible that, once in the hollow, the clansmen found it very difficult to get out, and it may have been here that many of them were cut down in the devastating delivery of front and flanking fire described in the previous chapter. It would certainly have been illuminating to have metal detected this area, but it resides within the scheduled boundary of the clan cemetery.

The association of the road and the clan cemetery has been a cause for much consternation over the years, and was finally the reason in the early 1980s for the relocation of this stretch to the north. Before then the motorized visitor, or in earlier times still the carriage-drawn visitor, would have driven through it and seen grave mounds located on either side of the road (Plate 9 is an aerial photograph taken from the west, before the road was moved but after the trees were cut down). Another obvious difference would of course have been the dense stands of trees which covered much of the core of the battlefield prior to their clearance in advance of the road's realignment. The controversy over the road dates back to the 1830s when it was widened by the landowner, Forbes of Culloden (the father of the builder of the monument to the Highlanders). It is a misconception that this date coincided with the construction of the road – it was, after all, there in 1746, albeit in a lesser form. What this widening appears to have done, however, is to disturb the graves on either side of it, as there are stories of bones being disinterred and reburied in a nearby quarry site.[6] These bones may have come from the ends of several of the pits as they were subsumed beneath the widened edges of the newly metalled road. Complaints about this desecration of the cemetery, with the road in some people's eyes being deliberately driven through it, were soon to follow, though it took nearly 150 years for action to be taken.

The truth of the matter is not that the road was driven through the cemetery but that the graves were dug on either side of a pre-existing road. It would make sense for the graves to be dug at a location not far removed from the greatest concentration of bodies (on the left of the government line) but also at a point convenient for the concentration of bodies from other parts of the battlefield (Jacobites were killed as they awaited the charge and at all points during the charge, by either cannon or musket fire). The road would allow bodies to be carried to the gravesite on wagons, at which point they could be transferred to the pits on either side. The issue of who was buried where has been covered in the introductory chapter and so will not be covered again here.

Location of Enclosure Walls

The stone-walled enclosures to the north and south of the battlefield played an important role in the battle, not least because they provided anchor points for the left and right flanks of the Jacobite front line prior to the charge. The north-west corner of the southern of these, known as the Culwhiniac enclosures, was used to anchor the right of this line, though this seems to have moved slightly to the east during Murray's readjustment (see Reid, Chapter 5, but also for a counterview Stephen, both this volume). The northern enclosure, known as Culloden Parks, marked the anchor point of the left flank on the south-eastern corner. In any attempt to reconstruct the battle-field and the original dispositions of the troops, the accurate placement of the enclosures is obviously an important consideration.

Although shown on all of the contemporary battle maps, the last traces of both of the enclosures were previously thought to have disappeared during improvements in the 1840s.[7] An attempt was made by the NTS to reconstruct the north-eastern corner of the Culwhiniac enclosures in 1995, at the same time as the reconstruction of the Leanach enclosure. This effort was based largely on present parish boundary lines, which it was rightly thought coincided with the previous alignments of the enclosures. The remains of various elements of the original Culwhiniac enclosures are, however, still to be seen running along the base of modern fence-lines (Plate 10). This is most obvious in the case of the eastern wall which runs north to south – the alignment of this wall fits perfectly with the location of the reconstructed stone-wall corner and turf-built Leanach enclosure.[8]

Just as striking is the fact that the remains of the buildings which once stood in the stone enclosure, known variously as 'Park', 'Park houses' or 'Park house of Urchal' can still be seen in the field enclosed by these wall remnants. This site appears on only two of the contemporary battle maps, the sketches by Yorke and Elcho (see Woosnam-Savage, this volume; also Figure 19). Today, the structures are almost entirely buried beneath a large mound of clearance stone which has accumulated on the southern edge of the upper part of the Culwhiniac enclosures. On close observation the line of a possible building wall can be distinguished running east to west. It is also suggested that the position of the breach made by the Campbells in the eastern wall of these enclosures is today marked by a gate just to the north of the division between the north and south parts of the enclosures, shown on the contemporary maps and still visible today. The remains of Park House sit against the northern edge of this east–west boundary, and there is an account from Lachlan Forbes, whose father was tenant of Culchunaig Farm the year after the battle, which states that the breach was made 'quite as far or further down than the Park Houses',[9] and this fits well with this location.

Relocating the northern enclosure, known as Culloden Parks, is a more problematic issue, largely due to the fact that most of the original walls seem to have been grubbed out entirely, and in some cases replaced with ditches and gorse hedges. The only surviving segment was found at the junction of four fields (Plates 8 and 11). The very heavily denuded traces of an earlier wall line were observed just to the east of the north-to-south running fence-

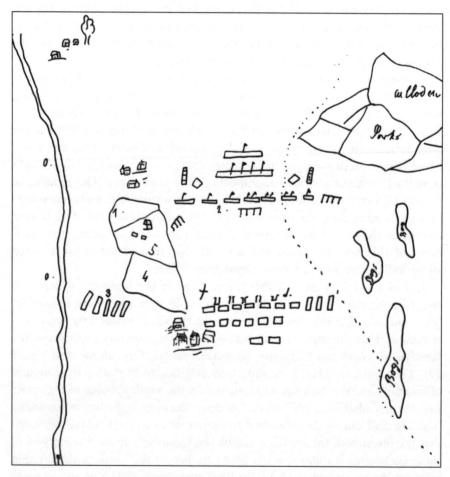

Figure 19. Tracing of sketch map by Colonel Yorke, 1746. Despite its rough, 'back of a napkin' appearance, it is one of the few to show a building in the Culwhiniac enclosures (Yorke would have seen it as he was with the dragoons in this part of the field).

line, aligned at a slight angle to the present line. This may represent the western limit of the northern enclosure. It is unfortunate that no trace of the eastern wall was detected, as it was on the southern corner of this that the left flank of the Jacobite front line was anchored. It should be stressed, however, that given the time constraints related to this element of the work a more intensive search may pay dividends.

Trial Trenching Evaluation

The aim of this element of the project was to establish the character, extent and condition of the geophysical anomaly located to the west of Leanach Cottage. Most of the contemporary maps depicting the battle show the Leanach farmstead consisting of three buildings, one of which may be the present Leanach Cottage (Plates 14 and 15). For many years the banked feature investigated in 2000 was held to represent the remains of the infamous Red Barn. As this feature has been shown to represent nothing more than a nineteenth-century kitchen-garden related to the cottage, the search for the site of other buildings, which may or may not include the torched building, must be focused elsewhere.

A geophysical survey of the Leanach environs revealed an anomaly, some 25m to the west of the cottage. Excavation of this (Figure 20) revealed a linear band of dark brown soil (006) filling a shallow ditch or slot (007) which ran across the trench at a north–south orientation roughly halfway along its length. The feature was around 50cm wide and excavation revealed a depth varying between 10cm at the southern end and 20cm at the northern end. The cut (007) had a curved base, the sides sloping down at a gentle angle from the east but with a slightly steeper face on the western side. The fill (006) was a dark brown sandy loam with some water-rolled stones. The relatively low concentration of stones within the fill is certainly not suggestive of a rubble drain, and if anything, is more likely to represent packing for timber posts.

This last observation is in keeping with what may be a heavily truncated posthole, extending out from the western side of the linear feature. Upon excavation, however, no distinction between the cut (005) and the fill of this feature and those of the linear feature could be distinguished.

Despite the small size of the excavation trenches the archaeological remains encountered provide evidence for a foundation slot, which is therefore suggestive of the former existence of a building on this site. It would not be unreasonable to suggest that it was part of the Leanach farmstead shown on most of the contemporary maps of the battle. The presence of a

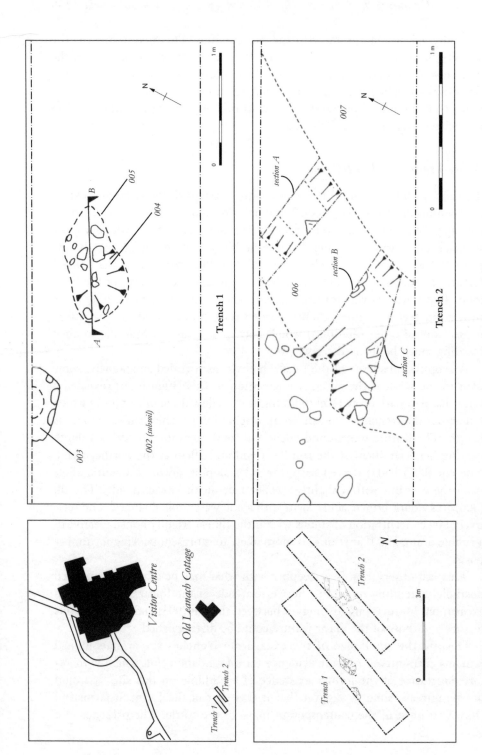

Figure 20. Location and details of the small excavation trenches located above the geophysical anomaly related to the Leanach steading. (© GUARD)

foundation slot does, however, raise a number of issues relating to the nature of both this structure and the building today known as Leanach Cottage.

The cottage was inhabited until 1912 and was partially rebuilt by the Gaelic Society of Inverness and presented to the NTS in 1944. It remains uncertain which features of the cottage, if any, relate to the building that stood on this site in 1746.

A drawing of the cottage made by Peter Anderson and published in 1860[10] certainly shows a slightly different structure, in some respects, to that which stands today (it has not been reproduced here). The view is from the north and shows the hills to the south of the River Nairn in the background. The drawing shows a gable-ended projection running out from the western wall. Today, there is no trace of this feature, which had lost its roof by the time the drawing was made, though the two buttresses pitched against the western wall are still present. The Ordnance Survey Name Book, which contains notes on features made by the map surveyors in 1868, refers to the cottage being ruinous, with the decay apparent in Anderson's earlier drawing having overtaken the entire building. Photographs of the building taken in the 1890s show the refurbished building looking very similar to its present appearance.[11]

Anderson described the building as 'a black clay-built, straw-thatched cottage', which seems rather at odds with what appears to be a largely stone-built structure in the drawing. In today's building the upper part of the gables, within the pitch of the roof, are formed from peat sods and this certainly appears to be the case in Anderson's drawing. There can be little doubt, however, that Anderson, who was a local man, knew a clay-built structure when he saw one, and was not in his description referring to these upper portions only, because in the same volume he describes the buildings at King's Stables as 'built of large stones – the upper portions of the gables of turf'. Interestingly, a catalogue from the sale of articles from Culloden House held in 1897 includes a 'cannon ball, taken out of the Turf Wall of Farm House of Leanach on the battlefield'.[12] Given the roughly north–south orientation of the cottage and the trajectory of the incoming cannon fire, it would be all but impossible for a Jacobite cannonball to lodge in the peat at the gable ends, which again suggests that all the walls were built from turf (this item was purchased by a Dr Allbuth from Leeds for the princely sum of £6, and it is perhaps notable that even in 1897 musket balls from the battle were fetching over £1 apiece).

It is here that the archaeological features encountered in the trial trench may serve to shed more light on the character of the farmstead as it appeared in 1746. Excavation of post-medieval vernacular houses in the Highlands built from stone does not suggest that the digging of a foundation trench was a normal practice before building the wall.[13] Stone walls tend instead to be built directly onto the ground, though crucks to support roofs may rise from holes cut into the ground on the inside of the wall. Timber-laced turf or wattle and daub buildings may, however, require foundation slots as a means of providing support for the upright timber supports, as suggested by the possible truncated posthole in the excavated feature. The excavated evidence may therefore be more in keeping with a turf building than a stone building, and if this is so for one, why not the others? This conclusion should not, however, detract from the historic importance of Leanach Cottage, which probably sits on the site of the original building and incorporates elements from the original structure.

Metal Detector Survey

The most intensive component of the 2005 project was the metal detector survey, which took place over eight days and was carried out by members of the Highland Historical Search Society under the supervision of the author. Most of the survey was carried out within the 'Field of the English' and took in some of the same ground as the 2000 project; it consisted of a wide transect, based on 20×20m squares (covering a total area of some 440×80m). Owing to time constraints of the *Two Men in A Trench* project, a much more limited area had been subject to metal detector survey in 2000.

In order to more fully investigate this part of the site the survey transect (Plate 13) extended from the western boundary of the NTS holding, passed through the reconstructed Leanach enclosure and extended just beyond the point marked by the Well of the Dead, immediately to the north of the survey area. During the 2000 project a sample of around 20 per cent of located finds was removed by excavation (although the bias was toward metal detector signals that were likely to be lead). Additionally, a single metal detector sweep, no matter how intensive, can never hope to identify all of the metal objects in a given area, as signals can vary according to the moisture content of the soil, limitations of detector, skill of operator and orientation of object in the ground. The removal of metal objects can perhaps be compared to a harvest which can take place over several visits – which is why metal detectorists often return to sites they have previously detected. It was therefore felt likely that objects missed during the first survey would come to light during this phase of work.

The 2000 survey in this area recovered evidence related to at least three specific elements of the battle:

1. Grapeshot and canister shot fired into the charging Jacobites by the government artillery. The discovery of both within the Leanach enclosure suggests that the Jacobites charged through this area and did not skirt the enclosure to the north as suggested by most historical accounts and maps. The discovery of grapeshot actually within the scatter of debris associated with hand-to-hand fighting on the left flank of the government line appears to relate to the eyewitness account of a cannon discharged into the 'teeth' of the Jacobites just before they overran the battery.[14]

2. Debris, including buttons, musket and pistol balls and the ball-impacted trigger guard strap from a Brown Bess musket, marking the point of intensive hand-to-hand fighting on the government left, where it was hit by the Jacobite right and centre at the end of its charge across the moor. This location was upwards of 80–100m further to the south than the location of Barrell's Regiment (which was on the far left of the front line) as shown by the NTS display board at the time of the survey (this new position is reflected in the recent re-display of the site).

3. British .75 calibre and French .69 calibre musket balls immediately to the west of the Leanach enclosure, and some of them just inside it, relating to the fire-fight between the Campbells positioned behind the stone walls of the Culwhiniac enclosures and the retiring elements of the Jacobite force. This event is recorded in accounts of the battle with the French muskets suggestive of the Royal Ecossois regiment (Scots in French service). They were brought forward by Lord George Murray to support the failing attack by the Jacobite right, but finding that all was lost they made a disciplined withdrawal, returning fire when they received fire in their flank (see previous chapter). It was the discovery of this scatter in 2000 that clearly demonstrated that the Jacobite line, as delineated by the red flags at the time, was much too far forward (again, this information was used to inform the relocation of the line in the recent re-display of the site).

If the 2000 season of fieldwork gave some suggestion that considerable quantities of battle debris remained buried on the site then this notion was more than confirmed during the April 2005 work (Plate 16). The site was surveyed from south-west to north-east, essentially following the line of the Jacobite charge toward the government line. Metal finds were encountered almost from the very start, with one of the most striking objects coming from the first grid. This was a small ring-headed cross (Plate 17) of typical Celtic form, cast from pewter and possibly modelled on a standing stone cross, even down to the small raised nodules which may take their inspiration from the stone bosses common to these monuments.

The top part of the shaft is perforated by a suspension hole and the lower part of the main shaft appears to have been snapped away. As yet no direct parallels have been identified in museum collections or excavation archives, but there seems little doubt from the handmade nature of the piece and the antiquated appearance of the pewter that it relates to the battle. This was probably a religious amulet worn by a Jacobite soldier, dropped either during the charge, perhaps being tugged from his neck in the mêlée of the advance or ripped from his neck as he was hit by incoming cannon fire.[15]

Personal objects such as the cross were very rare finds, with by far the most common type of battle-related artefact being the lead projectile, with around 260 examples found during the survey. These were of various types but at the most basic level can be categorized as musket shot and artillery shot. The bullets included balls of various calibres, representing a variety of weapons, including pistols, carbines and muskets, while the artillery shot was divided into grapeshot and canister shot. The following section will provide an overview of these categories.

BULLETS

A relatively small number of musket balls (twenty-five) were recovered from the 2000 season of fieldwork. To this modest collection we can add a further 203 bullets of various sizes recovered during the 2005 survey (as a group these should be referred to as shot or bullets, as not all of them are actually musket balls). The study of this artefact type is still in its infancy, especially in the UK, but elsewhere there have been some advances in this field.[16] Before proceeding, however, it should be noted that this is an ongoing programme of analysis and therefore the results reported here should be regarded as preliminary observations only and not absolute statements.

All recovered shot was assessed according to the criteria set out on a specially designed recording sheet. These included: type, lead condition, diagnostic features, deformation, weight and diameter. Size and weight variation suggested that the ammunition related to a variety of different weapons, with the larger examples breaking down into two groups. The larger of these (above 1.68cm diameter) most likely relate to the British Brown Bess musket, which has a calibre of .75 inches, while the smaller examples (below 1.68cm) have been interpreted as belonging to the .69 calibre French muskets used by a number of Jacobite troops, and most definitely by the Irish (Piquets) and Scottish (Royal Ecossois) troops in French service (Plate 18).[17]

Despite some inevitable overlap between the smallest of the large group and the largest of the small group, there is a useful size distinction (and the possibility of intermediate calibres of weapon should not at this stage be written off). A further consideration is that a .75 calibre Brown Bess musket would not have fired a .75 ball but one much closer to .69 calibre, and likewise the .69 calibre French musket would not have fired a .69 calibre ball but one closer to .65 calibre (the weapon's calibre refers to the internal diameter of the barrel, but the ball obviously needs to be slightly smaller than this to fit).

Of the total assemblage of 203 bullets recovered during the survey, sixty-seven were too distorted by impact to allow reliable classification (though most of these seem to be either .69 or .75 musket balls), while nineteen were categorized as pistol or carbine balls, being markedly smaller than the rest. Of the remainder, fifty-eight were judged to be of .69 calibre and fifty-nine of .75 calibre. The equal balance between the two may be a partial result of the analysis (with the incorporation of those lying between the two polar extremes in size creating a median or smoothing out of differences). It seems likely, however, that an imbalance between the two would be discernible if the large proportion of distorted balls were available for categorization – casual observation suggests that the larger of the two sizes are dominant.

On the basis of our present analysis, however, it is not unreasonable to suggest that the Jacobites delivered a high quantity of musketry, which to a degree contradicts the popular perception of the Jacobites delivering a desultory fire while charging and then discarding their muskets in favour of the broadsword. It should not be forgotten that Lord George Murray had issued orders stipulating among other things 'no body to throw away their guns'.[18] The apparently high quantity of Jacobite shot may indicate that, to a degree at least, this command was adhered to. With the foregoing in mind, a further consideration is the use of captured Brown Bess muskets (from Prestonpans and Falkirk) by Jacobite troops, which can only add to the amount of Jacobite musketry represented by the recovered sample.

PISTOL SHOT

Pistol ammunition was clearly much smaller than those bullets categorized as musket shot. During the battle pistols would have been carried by a variety of troops, but most notably by Jacobite officers and the government dragoons. The Scottish pistol, as carried by many Jacobite officers, was part of a distinctive tradition of fire-arms design and manufacture and came in a variety of calibres and sizes, though pistols with a bore of around .50in appear to be very common,[19] while the dragoon pistol was standardized and had a calibre of .63in. In theory, then, it should be possible to differentiate between the two types. As yet, however, no attempt has been made to do this. What does seem likely is that, given the pistol's relatively short range, their find spots indicate areas of close-quarter engagement.

In all, eighteen pistol balls were recovered, and there is a definite concentration of them in the debris scatter where the Jacobite charge hit the government left. These were probably fired during the fiercest of the fighting, most of them by Jacobites. It is highly likely that some pistol balls are also included in the indeterminate group of deformed bullets.

ARTILLERY SHOT

Before any of the firearms discussed above saw action in the battle, the air at Culloden was filled with lead shot fired from the government artillery. The Jacobite artillery, discussed in the previous chapter, fired only iron round shot during the barrage which opened the battle before their guns were silenced. With the enemy artillery out of action the government guns turned on the Jacobite infantry, first sending round shot (iron) into their ranks, but once the charge had begun they switched to two types of lead projectiles (grape and canister). When the charge was well advanced, or even in retreat against the government left, mortars were brought into action. The finds related to these various types of ammunition are discussed below.

GRAPESHOT

Grapeshot (Plate 18) was made up from lead balls with a diameter of around 2.8cm (1.1in, about the size of a squash ball) and a weight of around 100g (3.5oz). Nine pieces of grapeshot were recovered, scattered throughout the length of the transect, with the furthest out being some 340m away from the probable position of the gun that fired it (located between Barrell's and Monro's regiments). The closest piece to this battery was less than 10m away (an explanation for this is presented below).

The fact that the grapeshot was made from lead shows it was Royal Navy issue as opposed to army issue, as the latter was usually made from iron. This should not be too surprising as the army was provisioned by the flotilla of Royal Navy ships which had shadowed its advance up the east coast of Scotland, and by the time of the battle was anchored in the Moray Firth within view of the battlefield. With the 3-pound gun the balls were probably mounted on three-tiered circular wooden platens, with three balls to each, but may equally have been tightly bound in a canvas bag (the name derives from early forms looking like a bunch of grapes). The force exerted by the propelling charge would break open the shroud in the barrel and release the balls into the air pretty much like pellets projected from a shotgun cartridge. Although it just so happened that nine pieces of grapeshot were recovered, it should not be assumed that these all came from the same shot, as several other examples were recovered in 2000.

CANISTER SHOT

Canister shot worked on a similar principle to grapeshot but generally consisted of smaller balls debouched from a tin canister which broke up in the air immediately after leaving the muzzle of the gun. The most common forms simply used musket balls packed into a tin can. Musket balls used as canister shot are readily distinguished from those fired from muskets because they take on a multifaceted polyhedral appearance after being packed together so tightly (which creates slightly concave facets), with this effect perhaps enhanced by the propellant charge adding further pressure to these soft spheres.

Twenty-six pieces of musket-ball-type canister shot were recovered. By another coincidence the piece achieving the longest flight was found almost exactly the same distance away (around 340m) from the proposed gun position as the piece of grapeshot mentioned above.

CANISTER FRAGMENTS

In addition to the lead missiles discharged in a canister, what may be fragments of the canisters themselves were also recovered. The most notable piece was at first thought to be nothing more than the twisted lid of a tin can, which is basically what it is, but closer inspection suggests that it may be the lid from an artillery canister with a diameter of around 2.8in. The Royal Artillery at Culloden used 3-pound guns, with a calibre of around 3in, which, taking windage into account, would make the tin lid an ideal fit for this weapon. Interestingly this piece was found (Plates 19 and 13) not far from where it is assumed the closest battery was situated, having landed on the ground within around 25–30m of being fired. Several smaller fragments of tin may represent canister body sherds.

Coehorn Mortar Fragments

Cannon were the most common form of artillery but the government artillery train also included six coehorn mortars. Unlike the guns, the only contemporary maps which show the mortars deployed on the field are the sketch map by Cumberland's aide-de-camp Cathcart and the map by Royal Artillery fire-officer Jasper Leigh Jones (see Woosnam-Savage, this volume). The former shows all six mortars positioned behind the front line and in front of Howard's and Fleming's regiments on the right flank of the second line. The sketch shows the mortars delivering fire from these positions to all of the Jacobite batteries. Leigh Jones depicts a later stage of the battle where three of the mortars have been brought forward on the right to engage the Jacobite gun concealed behind the stone walls of Culloden Parks (the mortars, with their high trajectory, would obviously be the ideal countermeasure against such protection). Beyond these graphic depictions of the mortars in action it was initially thought that there was no further reference to their role within the battle. It therefore came as something of a surprise to find fragments of exploded mortar shell in the 'Field of the English' and just outside the Leanach enclosure.

Unlike the lead artillery shot discussed above, the mortar discharged an explosive round, more akin to a shell. The projectile was a hollow iron ball packed with powder. When placed into the mortar, a short-barrelled contraption usually mounted on a wooden platform, a fuse fitted into the sphere was ignited, then immediately after that the touch hole on the mortar itself was lit, the propellant charge sending the round, with its fuse burning, up into the air. Depending on the length of the fuse, the shell would either have exploded in the air, sending a deadly shower of angular fragments of iron down onto the heads of the enemy, or hit the ground, bursting up into their faces.

Three iron mortar-shell fragments were recovered (Plate 20). The first two were found very close to the mouth of the Leanach enclosure, one just inside and one just outside, to the south. The largest of these measured around 8×12cm (3×4.7in), with a thickness of 2.5cm (1in) and a weight of 964g (2lb 2.0oz). The second was much smaller, measuring just 4×6cm (1.6×2.4in) and a thickness of 1.5cm (0.6in), with a weight of 178g (6.3oz). A third piece was recovered from the footprint of the new visitor centre, some distance to the east of the main transect. This measured around 6×7cm (2.4×2.8in), with some variation in thickness, going from 1.7cm up to 2.5cm (0.7 to 1in), and weighed 538g (1lb 3.0oz).

It is not possible to say whether all three pieces are fragments from a single spherical shell or from more than one (it seems apparent from the cross-sections that the walls of the hollow iron balls varied in thickness along the circumference – perhaps being thicker at the end where the fuse was located). The presence of a fragment from a location which on the basis of other evidence was clearly behind the government front line (in the area of the new building footprint) may provide some idea of the rather unpredictable trajectory of shells once they had exploded, and as will be discussed below its presence here may be indicative of shells fired at rather closer range than would normally be the case.

NON-PROJECTILE ARTEFACTS

Although bullets and artillery shot represent the most obvious form of debris related to the battle, the assemblage included other classes of objects which also entered the archaeological record on that day. These included pieces of broken weaponry, buttons, buckles and coins, all of which are discussed below.

BROKEN WEAPONRY

Perhaps the most spectacular find made in 2000 was the brass strap from the back of a trigger guard from a 1742-model Brown Bess musket (Plate 21). Recovered from the main debris scatter on the government left, it bore an impact scar from a musket ball, which, after being fired at close range, had passed through the wooden stock, grazed the trigger guard, ripping it off, and then possibly striking the body of the man holding the weapon. It is tempting to regard this man as a government soldier; however, as previously noted, the Jacobites were also using a number of these muskets, captured after previous victories. The size of the scar does, however, suggest a French bullet, and therefore the Brown Bess being carried by government soldier, as does its location on the government left.

Two further fragments of the same type of weapon part were recovered. These were smaller than the previous piece, having been snapped from the terminal end of the strap. The first piece was represented by nothing more than the small spur which would have been inserted into the wood of the stock and in addition to screws helped to keep the fitting in place. The second piece included the spur and also the decorative nodule at the end of the strap, which can be used as a dating characteristic, again pointing to a 1742-model musket.

These pieces should perhaps be considered along with a fourth fragment of the same fitting, this time recovered from the Carse of Stirling during a project geared toward locating the site of the Battle of Bannockburn. This fragment, along with a number of musket balls and several pieces of canister shot, may relate to an otherwise unrecorded skirmish associated with the Jacobite siege of Stirling Castle in 1746.[20] The appearance of no fewer than four pieces from exactly the same part of the musket suggests that this was either a weak point or perhaps more likely a part of the weapon which quite regularly suffered impact during hand-to-hand fighting. Although the bayonet, attached to the muzzle end of the weapon, would be the obvious focus for contact with the enemy, the use of the butt should also not be discounted, with troops in frenzied combat perhaps wielding the musket as a club or using this part of the weapon to parry blows from broadswords.

The largest of these three pieces does appear to have been sheared, perhaps by the downstroke of a sword blade. It should be noted that these manoeuvres are not part of the traditional musket drill, and in requiring some space in which to operate may represent unorthodox fighting techniques once the government line had begun to degenerate into a more disorganized mêlée.

The bayonet, along with the broadsword, has an almost iconic standing in popular perceptions of the Battle of Culloden. It was these two weapons which clashed when the Jacobite charge drove home against Barrell's and Monro's regiments on the left of the government line. The socket from a bayonet (Plate 22) was recovered from just inside the mouth of the re-constructed Leanach enclosure. Some idea of the impact of this fierce fighting on these weapons is to be gleaned from a letter written by a government solider referring to the conduct of Barrell's Regiment: 'After the battle there was not a bayonet in this regiment but was either bloody or bent.'[21] Close examination of this rusted piece of iron does, however, suggest that it is more likely to be a Jacobite rather than a government bayonet, which again moves away from popularist images of the battle, where every Jacobite is armed with broadsword and targe.

There are two characteristic features which point to this interpretation. Firstly, the socket is split, with a join running along its length, whereas on the Brown Bess model the socket has no visible join. Secondly the curved shank which joins the blade to the socket is square in section and does seem exceptionally long for a Brown Bess bayonet (no remnant of the blade itself remains). Brown Bess bayonet shanks were circular in section and usually very short.[22] It is possible that the piece represents a Dutch variation, known as a long-shanked 'Dutch' bayonet, but again these did not have split sockets (the term 'Dutch' was generally used to describe weapons and equipment purchased from a number of continental countries for use by the British army). Taking this into account, it seems far more likely that the bayonet represents a French design for use on the .69 calibre musket, as used by the

1. *An Incident in the Rebellion of 1745*, by David Morier, painted in the late 1740s or early 1750s. The Jacobite right engages with Barrell's grenadiers on the government left. (*The Royal Collection, © Her Majesty The Queen*)

2. The Royal Artillery give fire. (*Re-enactment photo, © Danny Carr*)

3. Pulteney's give fire. *(Re-enactment photo, © Danny Carr)*

4. The Jacobites give fire.
(Re-enactment photo, © Danny Carr)

5. Hand-to-hand fighting on the government left.
(Re-enactment photo, © Danny Carr)

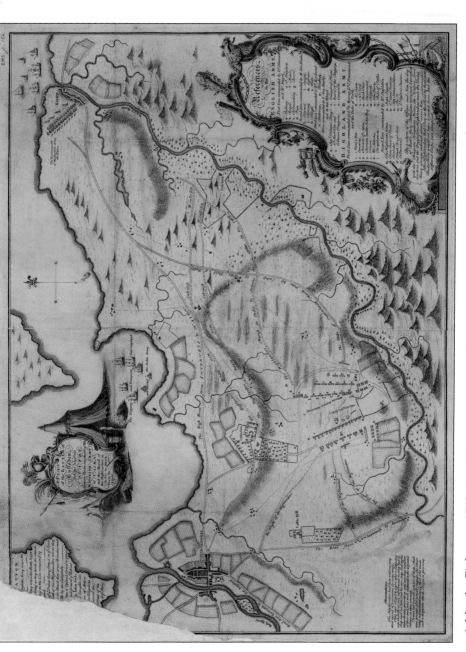

6. Map by Finlayson, 1745. A Jacobite perspective of the battle. *(courtesy the Trustees of the National Map Library)*

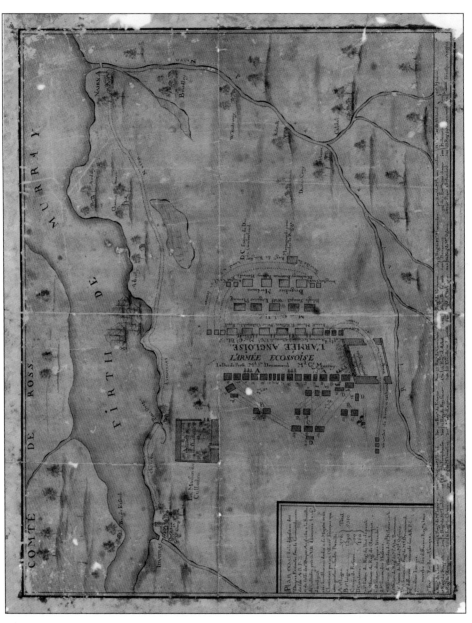

7. French officer's map, 1748. *(courtesy the Trustees of the National Map Library)*

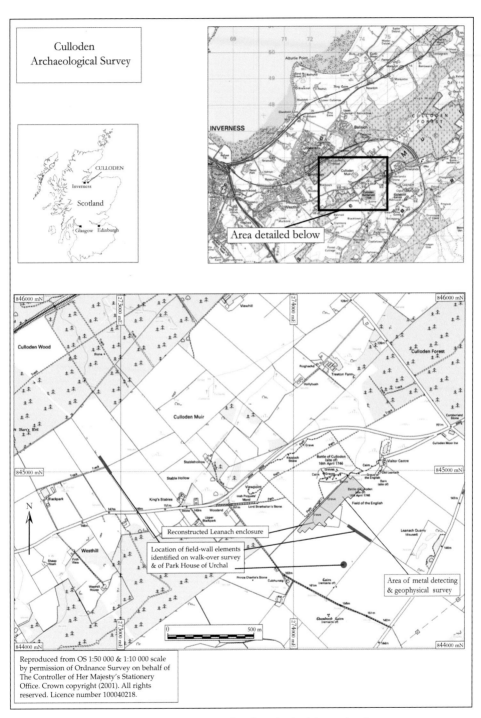

8. Culloden location map showing areas of archaeological investigation.

9. Aerial photograph taken from the west in 1984, showing forestry cleared and road just about to be moved. The 'Field of the English' is the meadow to the right of the frame, with the previous visitor centre sitting above it. (© *National Trust for Scotland*)

10. Remains of the Culwhiniac enclosure wall, taken from the south. (© *Tony Pollard*)

11. Remains of the Culloden Parks wall, from the north. (© *Tony Pollard*)

12. View from the west across the clan cemetery to Leanach Cottage, 2008. The clan monument is to the left and the new visitor centre is just in

13. Survey plan with location of the metal-detector survey finds in the Field of the English. (© *GUARD*)

14. Leanach Cottage in the late nineteenth century. (© *National Trust for Scotland*)

15. Leanach excavation in 2005; Leanach Cottage is in the background. (© *Tony Pollard*)

16. Metal-detector survey to the west of the reconstructed Leanach enclosure; the 'Field of the English' is beyond and the pre-2008 visitor centre is in the background. (© *Tony Pollard*)

17. Jacobite amulet: a pewter cross. (© *Tony Pollard*)

18. Lead projectiles from the battlefield. From left to right: grapeshot, Brown Bess musket ball, French musket ball, heavily impacted musket ball. (© *GUARD*)

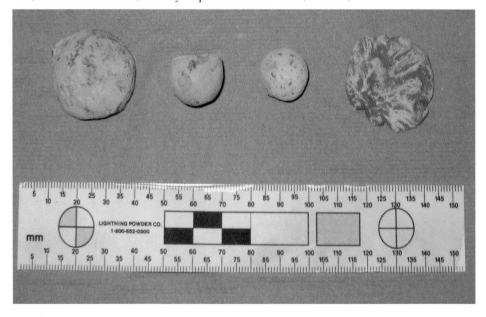

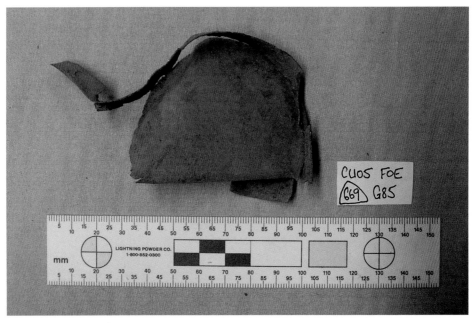

19. Tin lid from 3-pounder canister. (© *GUARD*)

20. Mortar shell fragment from near the mouth of the Leanach enclosure. (© *GUARD*)

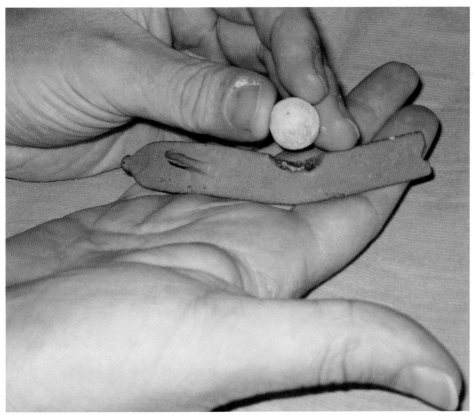

21. Strap from Brown Bess trigger guard with musket-ball impact scar. (© *Tony Pollard*)

22. Socket from French bayonet recovered from near the mouth of the Leanach enclosure. (© *GUARD*)

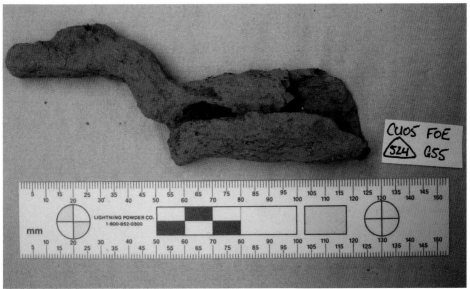

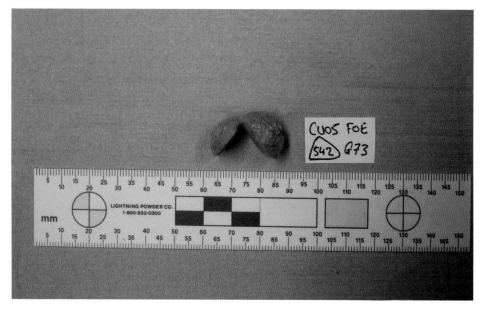

23. Brown Bess musket ball almost cleaved in two. (© *GUARD*)

24. Topographic survey 3D projection from the pre-2008 Jacobite line, looking east toward the government line. (© *GUARD*)

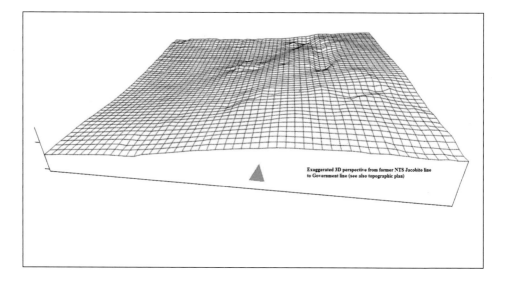

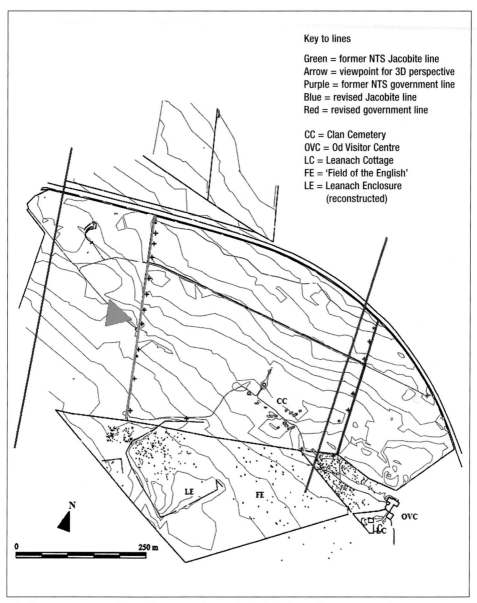

Key to lines

Green = former NTS Jacobite line
Arrow = viewpoint for 3D perspective
Purple = former NTS government line
Blue = revised Jacobite line
Red = revised government line

CC = Clan Cemetery
OVC = Od Visitor Centre
LC = Leanach Cottage
FE = 'Field of the English'
LE = Leanach Enclosure
          (reconstructed)

CC

LE   FE

N

OVC
LC

0   250 m

25. Contour survey plan with pre- and post-2008 Jacobite and government lines. (© *GUARD*)

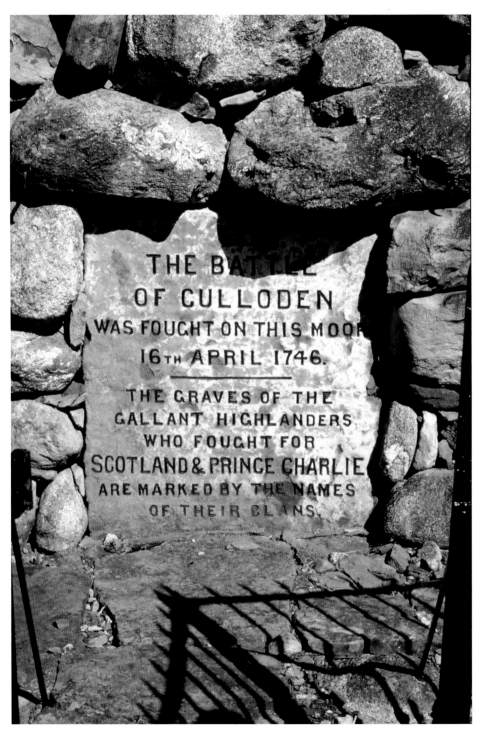

THE BATTLE
OF CULLODEN
WAS FOUGHT ON THIS MOOR
16TH APRIL 1746.

THE GRAVES OF THE
GALLANT HIGHLANDERS
WHO FOUGHT FOR
SCOTLAND & PRINCE CHARLIE
ARE MARKED BY THE NAMES
OF THEIR CLANS.

26. Inscription on the Jacobite monument erected by Duncan Forbes 10th of Culloden in 1881. (© *National Trust for Scotland*)

regular Scottish and Irish regiments in French service. These weapons, which were after all a French invention, had shanks almost as long as the blade itself, which gave the latter something of the appearance of a long narrow spearhead mounted on a shaft. In addition to those used by the French regulars, there were reports that upwards of 4,000 French muskets and an equal number of bayonets and swords were landed in Montrose in 1745 for use by the Jacobite forces.[23]

BUTTONS

A wide selection of button types likely to be related to the battle are represented by twenty-five examples. Buttons can become detached from clothing for a variety of reasons, but most obviously through violent exertion, such as during a charge or hand-to-hand fighting. For this reason buttons were found scattered throughout the transect, but not surprisingly perhaps the greatest number (ten) were found within the debris scatter resulting from hand-to-hand fighting at the eastern end of the transect. Some of these are most likely to be Jacobite, being more ornate and civilian in character than the regimented brass buttons used by the British army at the time. These were of the tombac type, generally in pewter, with both the circular button and centre-mounted suspension loop cast in one piece and commonly used in the eighteenth century as livery or dress buttons. Similar buttons have also been recovered from the site of the first Jacobite battle at Killiecrankie (1689) and the Battle of Sedgemoor in Somerset (1685).

Other buttons do, however, have a more uniform appearance, and two examples of composite brass buttons were recovered. One of these bears an insignia, but unfortunately is in such a poor state of preservation that is not at present possible to discern meaningful detail, while the other is also in poor condition and is broken into several pieces. A composite brass button with a crown motif was discovered in 2000 to the north of the 2005 survey, roughly on the government line.

BUCKLES

A small assemblage of buckles was recovered, including two made from iron and three from copper alloy. The iron examples were of a plain, square type, one with a simple attachment pin passing across the centre of the frame, while the other had a 'T'-shaped swivel bar set into the frame. All of the copper alloy buttons were broken. Two of these are shoe buckles, most probably belonging to Jacobites, while the third is much sturdier and ornate and probably represents a belt or strap buckle, again probably Jacobite.

COINS

Without doubt the most interesting, and probably most important, coin find did not relate to the time of the battle itself but was deposited at least six, and probably more, years after the battle. The small coin is a silver 12 thaler piece dated to 1752 and comes from the Duchy of Mecklenburg-Schwerin, one of the larger German states on the Baltic coast. It bears a bull's-head motif, which along with the griffin was part of the coat of arms of the Dukes of Mecklenburg. It seems highly unlikely that a local ploughman dropped this rather exotic silver coin, but it would not be unusual for soldiers in the British army to be carrying German coins, which were widely used on the continent. Although clearly post-dating the battle by six years, and from the worn condition probably having been in circulation for a number of years beyond then, the coin may represent a visit to the old battlefield by a serving soldier, perhaps one based at nearby Fort George, the main defences of which were completed in 1757.

The location of the coin in the main debris scatter makes even more sense if we consider the possibility that at the time of its deposition the graves of the government dead were marked in some way, perhaps by a mound or mounds similar to those which still cover the Jacobite graves. If a soldier was to visit the battlefield he would undoubtedly pay his respects to his fallen comrades, some of whom he may even have known personally. It is suggested here that the coin was dropped, either by accident or left as a form of offering, at the time of one such visit. If this were the case then this single coin has great importance as it has the potential to mark the location of the government graves.[24]

A number of copper coins (around a dozen) which may be contemporary with the battle were recovered from across the metal detector transect. These are in poor condition and do not appear to retain any trace of surface markings, but this did not prevent several of the detectorists identifying them as Scottish 'turners' (two pence). Some of them at least may represent other low-denomination Scottish coins of the same period, such as bawbees and bodles. These Scottish coins were minted in the second half of the seventeenth century and would still have been in wide circulation by the mid-eighteenth century. Given the makeup of the Jacobite army it is also possible that the French equivalent of the turner, the *tournois*, is also present – examples have been found in other contexts in Scotland.[25] It seems likely that a number of the coins were dropped from Jacobite sporrans or purses during the battle, and it is hoped that closer analysis by a numismatist may cast further light on these objects.

Found after the 2005 survey but certainly worth mentioning here was a silver shilling of King William III, dated to around 1696. The coin, which came from behind the government line, was recognizable through the well-worn silhouette of the king's head on the obverse side, the reverse being worn entirely smooth. There seems little doubt that this was a 'King's shilling' presented to a soldier on his recruitment. Coins of the same type and displaying similar patterns of wear have also been recovered from the Sheriffmuir battlefield (1715) and from fields adjacent to Fort George. These coins clearly remained in circulation for a long time and, rather than being spent by newly recruited soldiers, appear to have been retained as lucky charms or worry pieces, which over time were rubbed between nervous fingers to the point of losing most of their definition.

Interpretation of Artefact Scatter

The metal detector survey resulted in the recovery of a rich and varied assemblage of material related to the battle. This is despite the fact that the battlefield has been picked over by metal detectorists in the past – indeed several recently dug holes were observed on the site in April 2005 (metal detecting on NTS property is illegal without specific permission to carry out archaeological survey). Additionally, although now a grass meadow, the fields were for many years subject to regular ploughing, a process which was probably responsible for the 'disappearance' of the government grave mounds. Very few finds were made in the central part of the battlefield, which up until the early 1980s was covered with conifer plantation. Despite the metal detection of a strip of ground running between the two front lines, not a single relevant artefact was recovered, though heavy musketry had been delivered across this ground. It seems that the deep ploughing relating to tree planting and the presence of the trees themselves, which creates very acid soils, have had a serious impact on the archaeology of the battle. However, this is not to say that material does not exist in these areas, and clearly any future work related to ground breaking or grubbing out of trees should be accompanied by an archaeological presence tasked with identifying up-cast artefacts.

The recovered artefacts provide a unique and visceral insight into the battle and the men who fought it, but they cannot be fully understood without an analysis of their context, that is, where they sat in relation to their neighbours and the surrounding landscape. It is this information which has been missing from battlefield sites when they have been swept by detectorists (metal detector magazines quite regularly carry anecdotal articles about the material removed by detectorists from battlefield sites). This analysis can be used to test elements of the historical accounts of the battle, which in the past have been the only source of information relating to historic conflicts.

Analysis of the transect taken in conjunction with the many historical accounts of the battle has established that the survey has revealed a number of specific phases of the battle which can be teased out from the general spread of material. Such clarity is obviously only possible on a site where there is such a rich body of documentary material, but it may be that sites such as Culloden can provide a means of more fully understanding sites where these accounts are less detailed or altogether absent. The archaeological evidence may also bring some of the historical accounts into question, as they are rarely entirely objective or accurate, either because of partial visibility caused by the 'fog of war' or political and personal agendas which dictate the promotion of one account rather than another. Such bias is probably best summed up in the old axiom that 'history is written by the victors', but at Culloden we benefit also from Jacobite accounts – though it should not be assumed that these are necessarily any less governed by these agendas, including attempts to pass the buck for Jacobite failure in the battle (see Stephen, this volume).

THE CHARGE

Much more so than any other aspect, the Jacobite charge over hundreds of metres of open moorland into the face of grapeshot and massed musket fire is the abiding image of the battle. The most obvious archaeological manifestations of this event are the many finds of artillery and musket shot scattered across the site. It should perhaps be noted that all of the recovered evidence for artillery fire relates to the government guns, as the Jacobites fired only round shot in the opening stages of the battle and this material has thus far remained invisible.

The government batteries fired both grapeshot and canister shot as the Jacobite charge began, and pieces of cannon shot were located as far away as the western side of the Leanach enclosure. This location would place the range across which they were fired at somewhere between 350m and 380m (assuming that the battery was located not far behind the eastern limit of the transect grid).

BULLETS

The recovered bullets also give some idea of the quantity of lead shot thrown at the Jacobites as they advanced on the government line, though, as will be discussed below, only a proportion of this can be regarded as shots fired at the oncoming Jacobites.

Eyewitness accounts from the left flank of the government line, and specifically from Barrell's Regiment, describe a volley delivered at the oncoming charge at a distance of around 50ft followed by a second discharge just before the charge hit home.[26] Evidence for these firings can be seen in the form of musket balls recovered from the transect, which in places can be seen to approximate lines running roughly parallel to the face of the front line. The presence of several apparent lines may be due to some soldiers firing too low or ranks firing slightly one after the other (see the blue triangles representing Brown Bess bullets on Plate 13). The thick white smoke issuing from these black powder weapons would soon obstruct any view of the oncoming enemy, and although the general tendency would be for soldiers to fire high, there were many reports of Jacobites suffering leg and ankle/foot wounds.

Monro's Regiment, positioned to the right of Barrell's, with two cannon in the gap between, appears to have had a slightly different experience, with the regiment able to deliver an almost continuous fire. As an anonymous corporal attests: 'the Front Rank charged their Bayonets Breast high, and the Center and Rear Ranks kept up a continual Firing . . . most of us having discharged nine shot each'.[27]

The majority of lead balls from the transect display no or only slight traces of deformation caused by impact. This is, however, not to say that these did not find a human target. Experimental work has shown that musket balls may pass into or even through the fleshy parts of the human body and be subject to only the slightest change in shape.[28] The picture is, however, very different if the projectile strikes bone or any other hard object, with some of the balls being entirely flattened. Though these are likely to have hit something very hard, such as a stone or metal object, other types of distortion may reflect impact on human targets.

Impact deformation is dictated not only by the hardness of the target and the softness of the bullet but also the range from which the shot was fired – essentially, the closer the target the greater the velocity and the more extreme the distortion, given a hard enough target, of course. Muzzle velocity itself is also subject to a number of variables, including windage and the size of the propellant charge. Both experiment and archaeological finds have established that if fired at close enough range a musket ball will take on the impression of the warp and weft of the clothing worn by the victim of the shot. No such examples have yet been identified at Culloden, but several have been recovered from the site of Sedgemoor (1685) in Somerset.[29] At the other extreme a ball hitting a human body at the limits of the maximum range, as opposed to maximum effective range (for the Brown Bess, the latter is around

100–150yds whereas the former may be upwards of 250yds), would fail to penetrate at all, as the round's momentum will be almost entirely expired (such a round is termed 'wasted').

A relatively common form of distortion is a concave, elongated depression or groove. This was at first thought to be to have been formed by the ball striking a cylindrical object and wrapping around it – hence the term 'wrap' was adopted to describe this feature.[30] Since those preliminary observations, however, a series of experimental firings using replica Brown Bess muskets has established that many of these grooves were created as the ball drove itself into stony ground. Such deformation is therefore more likely to be found on a projectile which has missed its target rather than one which has hit home (similar patterns were visible in the musket ball assemblage from Killiecrankie battlefield).

Another form of deformation, which thus far appears to be unique to Culloden, is the cleaving of the ball almost to the point of breaking in two, but surviving in a hinged state a bit like a clam shell – termed a 'cleave' (Plate 23). It is suggested that these balls have hit against a thin, sharp edge, and given their context it seems reasonable to say that these examples hit the cutting edge of broadsword blades as they were raised in the air during the Jacobite charge. The effect of such impacts on the swords themselves is uncertain, but it would be a very strong blade indeed which remained intact after such a powerful impact. Such an interpretation is strengthened by the fact that cleaves were only found on musket balls situated very close to the government firing line, which suggests that they impacted at close range and high velocity. An alternative explanation has been offered by Alan Birkbeck, who has collaborated on musket experiments with the author. It is possible, he suggests, that differential cooling of lead in gang moulds may provide lines of weakness across which cleavage may occur upon impact (future experimental work will establish which of these hypotheses is the most likely).

THE GOVERNMENT LINE AND THE LEANACH ENCLOSURE

At the time of the survey the position of the government line was marked out by a series of flags and regimental markers which terminated to the east of the 'Well of the Dead'. Field survey in 2000 revealed that the line actually extended further to the south, into the 'Field of the English', with finds such as the Brown Bess trigger guard strap marking points where hand-to-hand fighting had taken place on the government left. The extent of this action was further defined during the current work, with a dense scatter of bullets, musket fittings and other debris marking this point of contact.

On the basis of this material, and its distribution in relation to the landscape, it is apparent that the government line extended across the mouth of the Leanach enclosure, probably in expectation of a Jacobite assault coming through it. The only contemporary maps which show this disposition of troops are those by Daniel Paterson and Sandby – the others show the government left terminating just to the north of the enclosure mouth. That this occurred is clearly indicated by the dense scatter of musket balls, artillery ordnance, dropped coins and so on which were recovered from within the enclosure. Accordingly, there can be little doubt that the enclosure, which is mentioned in very few of the contemporary accounts (in contrast to the stone Culwhiniac enclosures), did not represent a substantial barrier at the time of the battle. Even today the reconstructed turf banks have been heavily denuded by cattle and sheep, and may in places give some idea of the condition of the structure at the time of the battle.

The enclosure's relative invisibility in the written accounts contrasts with the cartographic record, with all of the maps from the time showing the wide-mouthed, horseshoe-shaped structure. This should not really come as a surprise as the maps record features existing in the landscape and were drawn after the battle, whereas the written accounts relate to features only when they played an obvious role in the dispositions and actions of troops during the course of the battle. An exception here may be the description of a suspected dug-in Jacobite battery located on the far right of the line and investigated by Lord Bury at the outset of the battle.[31] It seems likely that these guns were simply placed behind the western bank of the enclosure and therefore looked as though they had been dug in. The fact that the bank was mistaken for earthworks freshly thrown up again points to the enclosure being a less than cohesive feature.

Identifying the location of the hand-to-hand fighting is not quite the same as identifying the position on which the troops of Barrell's and Monro's regiments actually stood prior to the Jacobite attack. Though finds such as the musket fittings clearly suggest close-quarter combat, these are heavily intermixed with musket balls, which were presumably fired over some distance, however short, from the position at which they landed. The corollary of this is that the government musket balls were fired from a position further to the east than the end of the transect, which may mean that the actual line exists just outside the grid. The presence of the musket fittings, however, indicates that the position of the government line ebbed and flowed under the impact of the charge.

The presence of grape and canister shot within this scatter also has implications for our understanding of where the line was situated. Paired batteries of government guns were located in the gaps between the front-line regiments, presumably slightly forward of them. Thus the weapons which fired these pieces of grapeshot were most probably located between Barrell's and Monro's regiments. These guns, under the command of a Sergeant Bristo, were overrun by the Jacobites and the entire crew either killed or mortally wounded (Bristo being among the latter). One very vivid account describes a last shot of cartridge being fired into the teeth of the Jacobites just before they hit,[32] and it seems highly probable that the pieces of grapeshot recovered from this area were from this last shot. It will, however, be noted that the distribution plan shows a quite wide scatter, which may suggest either that the guns were located some distance further to the east to achieve this spread, or that there has been some post-depositional movement of the grapeshot, perhaps by the plough and due to their greater size. The issue of post-depositional movement within the plough horizon should obviously not be overlooked; however, experimental studies do suggest that artefact movement is much more acute in the vertical plain than the horizontal, which can almost be negligible.[33]

FLANKING MUSKETRY

The historical accounts allude to two major episodes of government musket fire, delivered as an enfilade into the side of the Jacobite right flank. The first of these was that delivered by the Campbells from their position behind the northern wall of the stone-built Culwhiniac enclosures, the second by Wolfe's Regiment as it moved around the left flank of Barrell's Regiment to counter the impact of the Jacobite charge (this latter is not discussed further here).

THE CAMPBELLS

Three companies of the Argyle Militia and a company of Loudoun's 64th Highlanders, all under the command of Captain Colin Campbell of Ballimore, were dispatched to knock down the eastern walls of the Culwhiniac enclosures to allow passage for the dragoons posted on the left of the government line in their move to outflank the Jacobite army. Their task accomplished, Ballimore's men moved up to the northern end of the enclosures where they found themselves in a good position to engage with the Jacobite flank. However, by the time the Campbells were in position behind the wall the main charge may have already gone in, having passed across their front. Thus any fire delivered at this point would be at a fairly long range. This situation changed when the French regulars under Lord John Drummond retired from their advance from the second line, having being called up along with Lord Kilmarnock's Footguards by Murray to support the main charge, which by this point was in serious trouble.

Kilmarnock himself wrote that: 'when the second line where I was broke, I was next to Lord John Drummond's regiment, and went with them and the other Low Country Foot along the wall to the south of the Field of Battle which covered us from the Cannon shot of the Duke's army.'[34]

The majority of Kilmarnock's men appear to have left the field at this point, but not so the French regulars, who moved down the field to take shelter in the lee of the northern wall of the stone enclosures – by this time it is likely that the southern battery which covered this zone had in any case been disabled by the charge (but see below with reference to mortars). With a Jacobite unit well and truly now in their sights the militia and Highlanders behind the wall opened fire on the French troops, who wasted no time returning it.

The location of this engagement was detected archaeologically through the presence of French and British musket balls in the vicinity of the north-eastern corner of the Culwhiniac enclosures (like the Leanach enclosure this has been reconstructed by the NTS, and there can be little doubt that it is in the right place). A high proportion of these balls display distortion, which is indicative of their being fired at close range. Some were almost entirely flattened, which suggests that they hit the stone wall of the enclosures themselves. Some writers[35] have suggested that Ballimore's men actually left the shelter of the enclosures to continue the fight, with him being shot dead as he passed a 'slap' or gate. This scenario could be evidenced by the scatter of musket balls, which are spread over a fairly wide area between the northern face of the enclosures and the west end of the Leanach enclosure. The presence of graves traditionally thought to be of Campbell men just inside the northern perimeter of the Leanach enclosure may add some further credence to the more fluid character of this fight. One of the skulls recovered from these graves in the nineteenth century is now on display in the museum in the Royal College of Surgeons in Edinburgh and has been used to suggest that most of the fatalities among this unit were incurred when men popped their heads over the enclosure walls.[36] Indeed, they may have done so while sheltering behind the less substantial turf walls of the Leanach enclosure after leaving the stronghold of the Culwhiniac enclosures, which would certainly make more sense given the location of the graves.

FLANKING ARTILLERY FIRE

A number of the eyewitness accounts make mention of a battery or a single gun being fired into the flank of the Jacobites during the charge. Andrew Lumsden, a Jacobite, wrote, 'Our right was covered by some old park walls that led towards the water of Nairn. The Campbells got behind these walls, pulled them down, and placed a battery of cannon which did great execution on our right.'[37] Another account by an anonymous Jacobite officer (but sometimes attributed to Lord George Murray) reads: 'When the right were within pistol shot it received terrible fire from (the) front and from a side battery supported by the Campbells.'[38] Another anonymous account, this time published in the *Scots Magazine* in April and May 1746, states that 'the rebels were flanked on their left by government cartridge shot, which killed many'.

The gun battery closest to the left was positioned between Barrell's and Monro's regiments and was overrun by the Jacobite charge. However, Murray thought that there might have been a government battery on the second line, and makes mention of the two guns the Jacobites had charged past on the front line. The problem with these accounts is that the government army did not really have any cannon to spare for such a move, with the army's full complement of ten guns already deployed across the front line. The presence of a flanking battery in the enclosures also presupposes that it would have been possible to manoeuvre one through the breach in the enclosure wall in time to bring it into such effective action.

The discovery of coehorn mortar shells in the mouth of the Leanach enclosure may shed some new light on the development of the battle and particularly the role of the artillery. As previously mentioned, these weapons, of which there were six in total, appear on only Cathcart's and Jones's maps, both of which show them located on the right of the government line, in rearward and advanced positions. There is, however, a single eyewitness account which mentions these weapons but with reference to their use on the opposite end of the field, on the government left. Edward Linn, a soldier in Price's Regiment, states: 'Besides two or three of our cannon gave them a closs [*sic*] with grapeshot which galled them very much and so in ane instant they retreated and our cannon and a few Royalls sent them a few small bomb shells and cannon balls to their farewell.'[39] 'Royalls' are coehorn mortars which fired a 5½in shell,[40] and this appears to be the approximate size of the shells represented by the recovered fragments.

It is possible that one of the mortars was carried into the stone enclosure, with its high trajectory making it much better suited to this sort of use than cannon, which would require a breach to fire through. However, placing mortars in the stone enclosure would entail firing them back toward the government line, where the rounds were just as likely to burst among government soldiers as they were among Jacobites. It seems more likely that they were fired from the vicinity of the second government line, from where they arced over the heads of the front line and burst among the Jacobites. Linn's account suggests that they were fired as the Jacobites began to retreat: however, it is also possible that they were fired into the Jacobite charge on its way in, an action which may reflect the seriousness with which the assault was being viewed by government officers. The fact that one of the fragments appears to have flown backward and landed in a rear position may also add credence to this, with the weapon perhaps discharged at closer range than would normally be the case, and the possibility of incurring 'friendly fire' may have been a very real one.

Given that the Jacobites suffered from heavy musketry from the flank, from both the Campbells in the enclosures and from Wolfe's Regiment, which moved around Barrell's left flank, it seems possible that mortar fire from an unobserved position in the rear could readily be mistaken for cannon fire from the flank.

Likewise, massed musketry from the flank may have been so devastatingly effective as also to have been mistaken for cannon fire.

Summing Up

Although the project has done much to further our understanding of the archaeological resource related to the Battle of Culloden and provided a further insight in the nature of the battle itself, these results should by no means be regarded as a definitive statement. Further work is required on both the artefact assemblage, which has thus far undergone only preliminary analysis, and the site itself, which has much potential to reveal further information. What has been established beyond all doubt is that battlefield archaeology can make a valid contribution to our understanding of historic battles, some of which, as is definitely the case at Culloden, do not lack documentary accounts but are none the less distorted by both the fog of war and the sometimes less than impartial attentions of historians.

Acknowledgements

The archaeological team included Amanda Brend (finds officer), Martin Carruthers (excavation supervisor) and Ronnie Scott (surveyor). John Arthur provided able assistance in site set-up, and was also responsible for the processing of the survey data. Jill Harden and Annette Jack provided assistance with the excavation. Many thanks to the Highland Historical Search Society, which, under the leadership of Len Pentecost-Ingram, carried out the metal detector survey – providing a shining example of how archaeologists and metal detectorists can work together. They were: Richard Brand, Patrick Bryant, Jane Crowe, Margaret Douglas, Ross Durance, Gavin Eastwood, Penny Fraser, Alice Glass, Michael Lowdown, Morag MacNeill,

Jim Scott, Sandy Snell, Eric Soanes and Jean Trail. Ian Deveney provided much useful information on the site. Additional thanks to Deirdre Smyth and the staff of the NTS visitor centre at Culloden for their assistance and hospitality. The project was managed for the National Trust for Scotland by Jill Harden and for Jacobs Babtie Ltd by Andrea McNally.

Chapter 7

'To Gather an Image Whole': Some Early Maps and Plans of the Battle of Culloden

Robert C. Woosnam-Savage

Lists of Culloden battle maps and plans and sketches have been created and published before.[1] This short essay attempts to provide a more critical appraisal of some of these vivid resources.[2] For the first time, the handful of maps that are regarded as perhaps the most important are discussed in relation to each other. These are also the works that have been found to be the most helpful in attempting to reconstruct the battle. The type of evidence contained in the maps is considered, from the state of the land in terms of agriculture to the pinpointing of individual artillery pieces and the sites of various actions.[3] The relative dates of the maps are also considered.

Culloden is one of the best-documented of British battles and also one of the most mapped. This is consistent with the development of military cartography in the Age of Reason. Over thirty maps appeared in 1746 alone, of which at least seven or eight were drawn by eyewitnesses to the event.[4] The contemporary and almost contemporary maps and plans of the battle that survive are surprisingly consistent, but some contain what appear to be unique details. Although one may quite correctly discuss the accuracy of these maps and plans, and what is meant by accuracy, their existence has enabled present-day historians and archaeologists to place the various regiments of the opposing armies – and even the whereabouts of certain individuals and actions – on the surviving battlefield with a huge degree of certainty. These battle maps and plans, despite the artificiality of their regimented coloured blocks of 'neat rectangles' and tracks of movement, do attempt to capture the fleeting moment or moments when a particular landscape became engaged as a battle-field.[5] A battle map often does this in a more immediate way than a written account ever could. With a map, one not only sees at a glance a snapshot of the action but also, on the better ones, the fluidity and flow of combat and the lie of the land upon which people stood, moved and died. From the maps of Culloden we see who was facing whom, and where, for instance, the Atholl Brigade under Murray hit the ranks of government troops. In some maps, for a brief moment we might glimpse the movements of Charles Edward Stuart as he crosses the landscape, as well as those of his nemesis, the Duke of Cumberland. To walk a battlefield such as Culloden, with a map in hand made by someone who was there, is the most evocative way of placing oneself in that selfsame landscape, albeit at a different time. And that is the beauty of such maps: although they are only two-dimensional constructs they have the power to deliver a journey through both space and time, often simultaneously representing the beginning, middle and end of a battle. They help us, as the Scottish poet Edwin Muir put it, to 'gather an image whole'.[6]

The first maps and plans were drawn up almost immediately, some perhaps sketched on the battlefield itself, others done at nearby Inverness. Some of these were drawn up by actual participants and are therefore important as eyewitness testimony. Like the written accounts of witnesses of the battle, or of anything else, they too are coloured by time, knowledge and memory and are prone to bias, omission or partisanship. Whatever problems they have, they are the product of those who were present and as such are valuable pieces of evidence. The map by Thomas Sandby, for instance, is an example of this. Although of the greatest importance and apparently topographically accurate, the map is drawn up by the 'official' draughtsman of the victor. Sandby's virtuosity should not blind the viewer to his objectivity, or lack of it. The same is true for maps produced by Jacobites, such as Finlayson. There is no single objective map of the Battle of Culloden.

The contemporary or near-contemporary eyewitness maps provide a riposte to those partisan claims that 'history is written by the victors'. Of the eight maps from Culloden discussed in this essay, five are from government sources (those of Yorke, Cathcart, Sandby, Leigh Jones and Paterson) and three are from the Jacobite side (those of Elcho, the French Officer and Finlayson), including one by a leading Jacobite and another that is often cited as the best map of the battle.

There are still problems between the topography and cartography of the battlefield to be resolved. For instance, the original packhorse track over the moor, shown in many but not all of the surviving contemporary maps, may have been re-routed when it was 'made' in 1835 (see Pollard, as well as Masson and Harden, this volume) and widened in the 1930s. Or it may follow the original line of the old road. Such dilemmas may be resolved by further archaeology. Much of the battlefield was lost to forestry, and many later maps of the nineteenth and twentieth centuries used a great deal of effort – and guesswork – in trying to plot the battlefield on the ground. Some of these worked better than others and gave a remarkably good picture, despite the tree covering of the battlefield.[7] The core area of the clan graves has always been central – and still is – to later plans of the battle. However, other, less accurate, maps, including those in the most popular mid-twentieth century accounts of the battle, are incorrect in many areas.[8] These maps place some of the walls of the various enclosures incorrectly, and also err in the placing and role of Wolfe's Regiment.[9] All contemporary or near-contemporary maps show nothing like the suggested moving of Wolfe's Regiment to behind or in front of certain walls to give fire *en potence* into the Jacobite right flank. This seems to have first appeared in Home's map, published in 1802.[10] The idea appears to derive from both a misunderstanding of various accounts and the *Order of March and Battle*, which states 'Wolf's [*sic*] to be moved upon the flank as the situation requires.'[11] It is quite clear that Wolfe's moved only after the Atholl Brigade had smashed into the government front as part of the counter-attack to this event and for which they were prepared.[12] However, Home's map has for many years been accepted without question and many books use maps clearly based on it, so a fresh look at both the battlefield itself and the maps and other records is crucial.

1. Yorke's Sketch Map, 1746

Very shortly after the battle Colonel Joseph Yorke (c.1723–1792), an aide-de-camp to the Duke of Cumberland, drew a small sketch map in his orderly book (Figure 19).[13] This is probably the earliest surviving plan or map. It formed the basis of another map, which was sent in a letter dated 18 April, with an account of the battle, to his father, the lord chancellor, Lord Hardwicke. The second lacks the finish of Sandby's or Leigh Jones's maps, and it is obvious that Yorke's cartographic skills are somewhat lacking. Apart from the 'Cavalry wth Hawley' and '2 Platoons of the Argyle Militia', no regiments or battalions are identified. However, the basic relevant features such as the cavalry breakthrough in the Culwhiniac enclosures are shown, as is the disposition of artillery. The government artillery is shown made up of ten pieces strung out across the front line, in between the regiments, in five batteries of two. However, the same orderly book also contains a 'schematic' 'Order of Battle [of Culloden]' drawn at Inverness, 2 May 1746, which does show the '10 Cannons and 6 Coehorns'.[14]

Yorke also indicates the 'bogs' on the Jacobite left wing, which may have been part of the same areas that probably impeded its actions to some degree, and was described by Captain James Johnstone of the Duke of Perth's Regiment as 'being marshy and covered with water which reached half-way up the leg'.[15]

More excitingly, as on some fabled treasure map, an 'X' in front of the left of the government lines marks the spot on the battlefield in front of which would have been Barrell's and Monro's regiments. This is 'Where the hottest of the Action was', as Yorke aptly states in the pen-and-ink version of the rough plan. He also shows various steadings on the moor and in particular a house or building within the Culwhiniac enclosures. This must be one of 'the Park houses' mentioned in O'Sullivan's narrative, where he states that he'd 'set fifty men in each of those houses'.[16] Curiously enough, this feature is only noted in one other plan, another 'sketch', that of Lord Elcho.

Yorke also marks the presence of the moor road. However, he is the only one to place it as coming around the southern end of the Culloden House Parks and keeping very much to the north side of the moor, rather than crossing the moor in a long-drawn-out and sinuous 'S' shape upon which the left wing of the government army rested.

2. Cathcart's Sketch Map, 1746

Charles 'Patch' Cathcart, 9th Lord Cathcart (1721–1776), was another aide-de-camp to the Duke of Cumberland. He was wounded during the Battle of Culloden. Although undated, his *Description . . . of the Battle of Culloden*, which includes a written account as well as a map of the battle, provides another important eyewitness source.[17] This map (Figure 21) is comparatively detailed, including the meticulously drawn firing lines of the artillery of both sides, but does not itself name the individual regiments of either opposing army (the names of the government regiments are given in the 'order of March'). It depicts the government infantry lines grouped into five brigades, with the artillery made up of ten cannon in five batteries of two, in the intervals between the front-line regiments. However, it is different from most other maps, as it depicts the most southerly battery ('G') not between Barrell's and Monro's but to the front and left of Barrell's, seemingly in the area (marked on the maps by Sandby, Finlayson and Leigh Jones) of what would be the turf dyke, known as the Leanach enclosure, were it marked on this map. The only other map that features a battery in this position is Paterson's. It is also the only other map (rather than 'schematic'), apart from that of Leigh Jones, to make a distinction regarding the different types of artillery used, as it also indicates the presence and initial location of mortars. The six mortars are shown in one battery placed directly in front of what must be Howard's Regiment and in front of Fleming's, as has been stated by

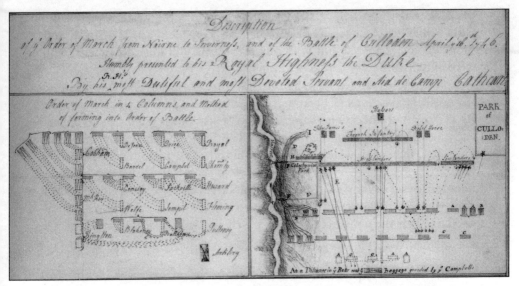

Figure 21. Map by Lord Cathcart, 1746. This is the only map to show all six coehorn mortars on the field. Order of march to left. (The Royal Collection, © Her Majesty The Queen)

Duffy in this volume and elsewhere.[18] Cathcart, by the use of dotted lines to illustrate the trajectories of the bombs, shows that the mortars were used against all the Jacobite artillery positions along the whole length of their line, from the one lone Jacobite cannon in the corner of the Culloden House Parks to the four cannon next to the corner of the 'Colwhyniac Park'.

The Jacobite artillery is of twelve pieces in three batteries, with four pieces in front of the Atholl Brigade, three in the centre of the front line, four on the left wing and the single cannon mentioned above. This differs from the map of Leigh Jones, who places five cannon in front of the right wing. Although Cathcart has few topographical details, he does include the south-eastern corner of the 'PARK of CULLODEN', and the 'Colwhyniac Park' enclosure is shown, although lacking many of the features, such as the dividing wall, found on other maps, such as Sandby's. The front line of the Jacobites is made up of 'Lowlanders' or 'Highlanders', and the same lack of detail is found in the second line and reserves, which includes 'Rebel Horse', 'Hussars', 'French Piquets' and 'FitzJames's'. Actions are noted, such as 'Campbells to throw down the walls FF.' Interestingly, Kerr's and Cobham's Dragoons, on leaving the Culwhiniac enclosures, are shown going past what must be Culchunaig farm before coming up against Fitzjames's.

Cathcart's and Sandby's maps are the only ones to show 'Lowlanders' in the sunken lane, or 'hollow way', running alongside the western wall of the Culwhiniac enclosures. These must be regarded as Avochie's and Stonywood's 'Aberdeen men' from Lord Lewis Gordon's Regiment, who were initially ordered there by O'Sullivan.[19]

An incomplete sketch map, also by Cathcart, curiously does not illustrate any artillery positions.[20] This map contains no landmarks (apart from the River Nairn) or indication of any artillery. It also shows the dragoons apparently moving up between the western wall of the 'Colwhyniac Park' and what must be Culchunaig, which differs from his other map. However, Cathcart's accompanying *Narrative of the Battle of Culloden, April 16 1746* includes detailed descriptions of the Highlanders receiving 'very close fire of grapeshot and musketry in front, and on their left flank'; as 'they could not break in with their Broadswords, they first threw their Durks at Monroe's regt. and then stones'.

3. Sandby's Map, 1746

Thomas Sandby (1721–1798) was appointed draughtsman in the military drawing office at the Tower of London (Board of Ordnance) in 1742. From 1 April 1746 he was employed by the Duke of Cumberland as his 'personal Draughtsman & Designer'.[21] His map, in pen and watercolour, of Culloden is the best known, and arguably the most informative (Figure 18). The *Plan of the Battle of Culloden, 16th April, 1746* also includes an accompanying key.[22] It is highly likely that this map was created for the Duke of Cumberland himself. The map is signed and dated 'April 23d 1746 at Inverness', which means it is one of the earliest known dated maps (only the maps by Yorke can claim to be earlier). Sandby's was produced within a week of the battle and, despite comments to the contrary by certain critics,[23] there is no evidence to suggest that Sandby, even though working in a civilian capacity, was not an eyewitness to the battle.[24]

Sandby's map shows, as do most, Culloden House and its 'Parks' to the north, and the stone-walled fields and enclosures on the south side of the moor, bound east and west by two small streams running down to the River Nairn. These are the 'Parks belonging to Culloden' or 'Culloden Parks' (but which are now more commonly known as the Culwhiniac enclosures). To the north-east of this is an unnamed open-ended turf-walled enclosure now known as the Leanach enclosure.[25] The map also shows a number of apparent farmsteads marked 'village', including what must be Old Leanach Cottage (now replaced by a stone-built cottage constructed in about 1881). The original cottage, or an intermediate rebuild, was still standing in 1867 when it was described as 'a black-clay, straw-thatched cottage' (see Pollard, this volume).[26] The tilled fields to the south around Leanach are also shown. After the battle some became the graves of British soldiers – the 'Field of the English'.[27] Culchunaig farm (the present farm of this name is a nineteenth-century and later rebuild) to the west of Culwhiniac is also shown. Much arable land on the north bank of the River Nairn is shown running from the edge of the moor down to the river. In fact it is quite clear from Sandby, Leigh Jones and Finlayson that Culloden Moor was actually quite heavily cultivated, either tilled or left as rough pasture, and that there were a number of townships or steadings on the moor at the time of the battle, including the most south-eastern, which might be that known as 'Orchal', or later as Urchal.[28] The river is also shown with tree-lined banks. Sandby also includes the road from Nairn to Inverness snaking its way over the moor. It ran over the moor from Leanach to the so-called 'King's Stables'.

The front line of the Jacobite army is shown lined up between the north-western corner of the Culwhiniac enclosures and the south-eastern corner of the 'Culloden Parks' of Culloden House. Gordon's Regiment runs down towards the river, alongside the western wall of the Culwhiniac enclosures, a detail also found in Cathcart's map. Apart from this detail, Sandby's map is in agreement in the most part with those maps of Lord Elcho and Finlayson, although the latter depicts a large gap between the northern end of the Jacobite front line and the corner of the Culloden House Parks. Sandby's Jacobite deployment is that before Lord George Murray's 'changement' and appears to be quite firmly packed between these two points, with only a small gap between the end of the Jacobite left wing and the corner of the walls of Culloden House, in front of which a cannon is placed (as is depicted in Sandby's own panoramic sketch and Cathcart's, Leigh Jones's, Finlayson's and Paterson's maps). This is probably the French, so-called 'Swedish', 4-pound cannon brought up by a French engineer, Captain Du Saussey, during the course of the battle.[29] Although its exact site has still to be pinpointed on the ground, it is possible, using the results of modern satellite and aerial photography, to see that this corner is probably fossilized in the landscape of the present-day field boundaries. This area is at present within private grounds, but sadly this did not stop what was probably much relevant material being removed, literally in 'bucketloads', by metal detectorists.[30]

Sandby's disposition of the Jacobite artillery is a group of four cannon on the extreme right wing of the front line and then a grouping of two, three and two along the line, before the aforementioned single cannon – a total of twelve. This figure accords with a number of written accounts, although the layout is different from that illustrated by Finlayson and others.

The disposition of the government army is clear. Barrell's Regiment is shown abutting the moor road and just in front of a 'village' – the original Leanach Cottage. Sandby also shows how the ten 3-pound cannon were placed in five batteries of two, one between each of the regiments, from left to right. This meant that the two infantry regiments on the far right of the government line, the Royals and Pulteney's, did not have the luxury of artillery protection. This is probably because Pulteney's Regiment (together with Kingston's Horse) was brought up from the third-line reserves to extend the front line when it realized the extent of the Jacobite line after their redeployment. Sandby shows this movement quite clearly by means of a dotted line. The front, as Sandby also shows, was further continued by two squadrons of Cobham's Dragoons. However, Sandby, unlike Leigh Jones and Cathcart, does not indicate the presence or whereabouts of the six coehorn mortars which were also on the battlefield.

Recent reappraisals also confirm Sandby's disposition of Wolfe's Regiment. It was not placed *en potence* beyond Barrell's to flank any attacking Jacobite force, and only moved into such a position after the Highland charge had struck home.[31]

Unlike Leigh Jones or Finlayson, Sandby does not mark the presence of the Royal Navy in the Moray Firth, which gave crucial logistical support to Cumberland.

Sandby clearly shows the cavalry movements on the government left, south of the Leanach enclosure, and how Kerr's and Cobham's Dragoons rode through the Culwhiniac enclosures, through the 'Breaches in the park walls made by the Argyleshiremen', to come through at the 'rear of the Right flank of the Rebels'. The Culwhiniac enclosures are shown divided into two by an east–west-running wall, and, as on all maps, the breakthrough is shown occurring north of this wall, well above the 'kinked' waist of the lower enclosure running down to the river. There is still some debate as to exactly where this breakthrough took place on the physical landscape of today, but it is clear that the government cavalry came out in a hollow or dip on the west side of the enclosures.[32] Sandby also notes that the 'Argyleshire Men' in the Culwhiniac enclosures were 'drawn up to fire upon the Rebels', although he does not indicate the presence of 'Park Houses' or buildings within the upper Culwhiniac enclosure which are mentioned in at least one account.

Sandby is also quite clear about where Charles Edward Stuart, or the 'Pretender', as he called him, was positioned. This was well back behind the Jacobite front line, behind Ogilvy's and Lord Kilmarnock's Footguards (the latter in the same position as in Lord Elcho's map, though Finlayson has him in front of Kilmarnock's). A similar position is noted in the later anonymous French Officer's map, which shows Charles moving around, and places his last position behind a group including Ogilvy's and Kilmarnock's. Sandby also attempts to show the dispersal and 'Flight of the Rebels' in three distinct directions, as does Finlayson in his map. These routes do reflect the directions that many would have taken. One group is obviously heading towards Inverness (for many, no escape at all), another heading southward directly towards the Nairn. Finally, a central group flees in the direction of the road from Inverness to Ruthven. The latter two groups included some of those 1,500 who regrouped at Ruthven Barracks under Lord George Murray, only to disperse on 18 April. They included Charles Edward Stuart, who, crossing the Nairn at the Ford of Fallie, would start that period of his life that would earn him the sobriquet of 'The Prince in the Heather'.

Sandby's Panorama Sketch, 1746

One cannot discuss Thomas Sandby's map without recourse to the watercolour panorama he also produced, *A Sketch of the Field of Battle at Culloden 1746*,[33] which it complements so well (Figure 22). It would seem likely that before he returned to London from Culloden, he made this panoramic sketch of the battle, signed 'T. Sandby 1746'. Full of fascinating detail, it notes various government positions, such as 'Kingston's Regiment'. The depiction of the battle itself appears accurate, although it would seem that the aesthetics of landscape got the better of him, as Sandby cannot resist altering the background – his viewpoint is looking in a generally southerly direction, towards the Culwhiniac enclosures, but rather than depict the rather inconsequential southern bank of the River Nairn he depicts the view north,

Figure 22. Panoramic sketch of the battle, by Thomas Sandby, 1746. Viewed from the north with government lines to the left and Jacobites to the right; artistic licence has been used to show the firth and ships to the south in the background. (The Royal Collection © Her Majesty the Queen)

showing, as he himself notes, the 'Murray Firth' and the hills of Easter Ross, which is much more dramatic. This also enables him to include a couple of vessels in the firth, presumably as an indication of the supporting role of the Royal Navy. He also dramatically placed three Highlanders in the immediate foreground.[34]

Sandby most clearly depicts the south-east corner of the Culloden Parks walls. Although this is sketched in as if complete, on closer inspection there appears to be a gaping hole in it (or at least where one was or was made). This becomes clearer when one recalls the position of the most northerly Jacobite cannon, set at about this corner position. Sandby is probably depicting the damage the wall sustained during the mortar (and cannon) bombardment which took out the lone cannon, an action shown in the maps of others (such as Leigh Jones's and Finlayson's). Alternatively he may be showing how the Jacobites deliberately destroyed parts of these tall walls (possibly up to 1.8m/6ft) to allow the firing of their cannon. There can be, however, no doubt that Sandby is noting this position in particular; if one looks closely one can make out the ghostly outline of a cannon in front of the corner walls, as located in his own maps. Interestingly, Cathcart, Leigh Jones, the French Officer and Finlayson emphatically place the cannon *within* the walls. How much Sandby and Leigh Jones relied upon each other's work, if at all, is not known, but in the end they both appear to be depicting the same incident in their own way. Sandby's attention to this detail indicates that he sketched from life.

The panorama also shows the Jacobite front line stretching from this south-east corner of the wall southwards towards the eastern wall of the Culwhiniac enclosures, together with cannon. A few of the Jacobite left wing are shown moving towards the government line but it is clear that the 'hottest action' (as Yorke called it) is occurring at the other end of the moor, down towards the left of the government line. This is the charge of the Atholl Brigade, which is shown hitting Barrell's and Monro's regiments in front of Leanach Cottage.

Sandby may well have wanted to portray his patron in a spectacular light, but it is known that the Duke of Cumberland, mounted on his horse, The Lizard, moved around the government lines.[35] Cumberland is known to have at one point placed himself upon the right, 'imagining the greatest push would be there', and this is exactly what is seen in the panorama where the 'Duke of Cumberland' is shown in the front line, riding between the Royals and Pulteney's, who Cumberland personally noted 'hardly took their firelocks from their shoulders'.[36] Even allowing for a degree of sycophancy this is probably not far off where Cumberland was, at least at one stage in the battle.

4. Leigh Jones's Map, 1746

Jasper Leigh Jones was, as he called himself on his map, 'Lieutt. Fireworker in the Royl. Train of Artillery' serving under Colonel Belford. The map he 'Survayd' and drew up is *A Plan of the Battle of Colloden between his Maj.s. Forces Under the Command of his Royall Highness the Duke of Cumberland and the Scth. Rebels, April the 16 1746* (Figure 23). It is highly likely that he was an eyewitness to the battle, and, although undated, the map not surprisingly shows with greater detail than any other the disposition of artillery pieces and also their lines of fire, including one with the inscription 'Round Shot'.[37] It also differs in the numbers of pieces and positions. Leigh Jones's interest in the ordnance is only reinforced by his depiction of the government order of 'March' in which he includes the artillery train, labelled 'Cannon' and 'Tumbrells'. In the government army he places the ten cannon in five groups of two, as illustrated in other maps and in various surviving plans of the order of battle in the Royal Collections, in front of and between the regiments of the front line. However, he places one battery between the Royals and Pulteney's, leaving the central gap between Price's and Cholmondeley's without a battery. This is a different disposition from that found in the maps of Yorke and Sandby (who have the gap between the Royals and Pulteney's) and Finlayson and Lord Elcho, who give the government six batteries (twelve cannon), filling all the gaps on the front line, which must be a mistake.

Curiously the mortars, which are known to have been present, are not depicted in their original positions (as perhaps depicted by Cathcart) but in an action substantiated by other maps and sketches. Leigh Jones's map shows only one battery of three 'Cohoorns' (together with four cannon) after they had been moved to a forward position, where they were used to bombard and take out an intransigent Jacobite cannon, which had been set up in the south-east corner of the Culloden Parks. The Sandby sketch shows the cannon just in front of the corner walls, but if this had been the case it would seem unnecessary to bring the mortars up, as cannon alone could have been used if it was in the open. This piece continued firing for some time, and it was probably the last Jacobite artillery position to be silenced in one of the final episodes of the battle itself. Leigh Jones depicts this engagement with apparent scientific accuracy, and depicts the individual trajectories of the mortar bombs as they were being discharged at this sheltered Jacobite position. The further four cannon blasting into this spot, together with the mortars, are shown 'firing from the closest possible range'.[38] One can only presume that these cannon are in fact 'time-lapsed' from the government front-line cannon brought up in this later stage of the battle to support the

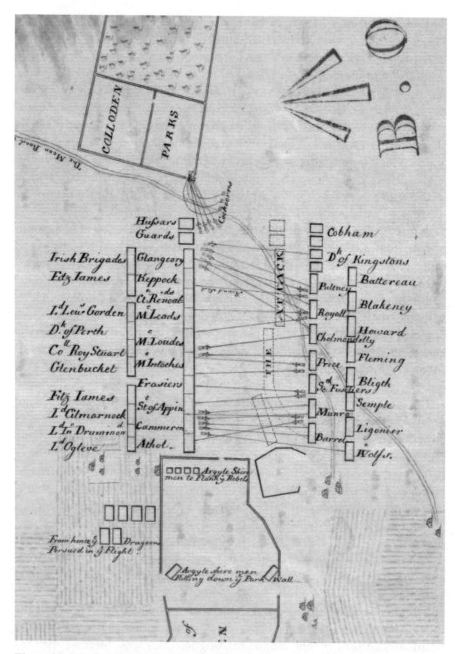

Figure 23. Map by Jasper Leigh Jones, 1746. He was an officer in the Royal Artillery and therefore concentrates on the artillery action. (© National Map Library of Scotland)

mortars. This appears to have been the most heavily bombarded area of the battlefield. Leigh Jones makes no indication of the use of the larger 'Royal' mortars which recent archaeological finds suggest were used in the battle, though these may be one and the same (see Pollard, this volume).

Thirteen pieces of Jacobite artillery are depicted – twelve forward of the front line of the Jacobite regiments. This is the only map to give this figure. Other maps show twelve pieces or less, and it is this number that is generally accepted as correct.[39] Given that Leigh Jones has shown the mortars appearing from nowhere to attack the lone ('thirteenth') cannon, maybe he is again trying to create a time-lapse effect, showing events that happened at different times on the same map, especially as this particular Jacobite cannon had appeared only after the battle had begun. This one piece lodged in the south-east corner of the Culloden Parks, discussed above, is depicted else-where, such as in the Sandby map and panorama. Leigh Jones shows the rest of the artillery in three groups; five are on the Jacobite right, two in the centre and five again on the left. The five on the right in front of the Atholl Brigade (a number also found on Elcho's sketch) reflect a larger grouping (only prob-ably of four, however, as depicted in the maps of Yorke, Sandby, Finlayson and the French Officer) in this immediate area. It has been suggested that they were originally set up in neat batteries of two and it was only after the Jacobite 'changement' that they became more unevenly dispersed.[40]

Leigh Jones also shows where the bulk of the Jacobite charge fell. Two dotted areas between the opposing armies, bearing the legend 'THE ATTACK', show where the Jacobite right fell upon the government left and the regi-ments of Barrell and Monro. The Jacobite left, though gaining the moor track, appears to have faltered before coming into contact with the govern-ment right. What is illustrated here confirms the likelihood of a suggestion[41] that this wing of the Jacobite army (including the MacDonald regiments) did not impotently stand by, as many writers in the past have stated or implied.[42] The left wing played a much more active part in the action than has been generally accepted. In fact one of the most quoted lines regarding the battle, they 'came running upon our front line like troops of hungry wolves', was written by an Alexander Taylor of the Royals, who must have been facing this approaching wing.[43]

The topography is well drawn up, although more 'sketchy' than Sandby's. One sees evidence of the various buildings on the 'Drummossy Moor' as well as 'The Moor Road to Inverness', and areas of tilled ground and trees on the banks of the River Nairn (as in Sandby and Finlayson). The road is shown in more detail on the government side than on any other map. It is shown split-ting into two just on the government front line, in front of Cholmondeley's.

One track continues to Leanach, while the other goes on through both government lines to a second group of buildings, what must be the most south-eastern 'Village' (as Sandby calls it), probably the one named as 'Orchal'.[44] In fact Sandby has this split in the moor road occurring just before Orchal, well behind the government lines. The northern half of the Culwhiniac enclosures is clearly shown, with a gap in the middle of the northern wall (also as in Sandby and Finlayson) but devoid of 'Park Houses' or buildings, which are mentioned in the narrative by O'Sullivan, for example. Leigh Jones is also most clear that it is the 'Argyle Shire men' that are placed behind this northern wall so as 'to Flank the Rebels', as in the map of the French Officer (Wolfe's Regiment is not shown being moved to create a similar effect). Although Leigh Jones shows no other gates or gaps in these enclosure walls, he does show the routes taken by Kerr's and Cobham's Dragoons and their breakthrough of the enclosure walls. They broke through above an east–west dividing wall which divides these enclosure walls into two parts, the lower part with its 'kinked' walls running down to the Nairn, as in the maps of Sandby, Paterson, and Finlayson.

Interestingly, Leigh Jones is also one of the few mappers, along with the French Officer and Finlayson, who bother to depict the Royal Navy flotilla ('The Fleet with Provisions') in the Moray Firth. It has been suggested that Leigh Jones's and Sandby's maps are so similar that one 'is based on the other'.[45] However, they both also contain some major differences and details found in other maps, including those of Jacobites (Finlayson), so this should perhaps be regarded as unlikely.

5. Paterson's Map, about 1746

A map compiled by a Daniel Paterson entitled *A Plan of the Batle of Coullodin moore fought on the 16th aprile 1746*[46] is regarded as contemporary and dated to 1746 (Figure 24).[47] The map has sometimes been associated with the famous map and itinerary compiler who shares the same name. However, this Paterson cannot be the author of the map, as it has been calculated that he was only born in about 1738 and therefore would have been eight in 1746. A much more likely candidate for the authorship of the map is the Daniel Paterson who was an engineer and present at the Battle of Culloden.[48] This Paterson is also known to have made plans and sketches throughout the Highlands in 1746.[49]

Although Paterson includes houses on the moor and even the direction of flow of the River Nairn, the whole general topography appears more sketchy than that of Sandby, Leigh Jones or Finlayson. No moor road from Inverness is shown, and Paterson appears to have lost some details, such as the easterly

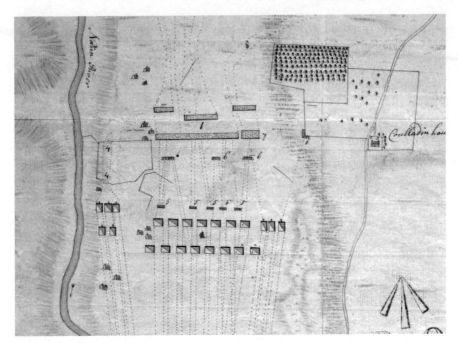

Figure 24. Map by Daniel Paterson, a government engineer, 1746. (© National Map Library of Scotland)

wall running down to the Nairn in the lower Culwhiniac enclosure. His depiction of the Culloden House Parks as an irregular shape is different as well. He has the south-western corner, full of orderly trees, extending out southwards, a feature seen in Elcho's map and another anonymous map.[50] Uniquely, the turf wall of the Leanach enclosure is shown with an extra line running in a south-easterly direction.

All the individual regiments are unnamed, the armies being reduced to blocks of opposing rectangles of various shapes, one 'The Rebells in ordre of Battle' and the other 'The English in Ordre of Battle'. The Jacobite line does not fill the gap between the corner of the Culwhiniac enclosures and the Culloden Parks as in Sandby, but this feature is reflected in Finlayson's map. Paterson also shows what he calls 'a Body of French Cavalry' on the left wing of the Jacobite front line. This again is unlike other maps which tend to place the cavalry in the second line, apart from Leigh Jones, who has 'Hussars' in the same position.

The position of the government army where they 'drew up first' is indicated and, again like Leigh Jones, Paterson attempts to show the lines of fire of the artillery of the two armies. 'The Rebels Canon' are shown in four batteries along the front of the Jacobite line, one in the centre and at each end, together with the fourth battery in the south-eastern corner of the Culloden House Parks, the last as shown in the maps of Sandby, Leigh Jones, Finlayson and the French Officer. The government artillery is shown in five batteries in front of the first line. No mortar positions are shown and the most southerly government battery is shown, as in Cathcart's map, in front of what would be Barrell's and almost within the Leanach enclosure.

Like those of Sandby, Leigh Jones and Finlayson, the Paterson map shows the government cavalry breakthrough in the Culwhiniac enclosures taking place north of a wall that divides the enclosures from east to west. But Paterson shows neither the 'Argyleshire' men, seen in a number of other maps, nor any of the 'Park Houses'. Among buildings he does indicate are the Culwhiniac farm, those buildings that stood before the eastern breach of the Culwhiniac enclosure wall (as does Sandby) and what might be Orchal. The kink in the wall running down to the River Nairn is also depicted and is clearly south of the dividing wall. All the major maps discussed show the cavalry breakthrough above the kinks in these lower walls, and as has been noted above, at least one modern writer[51] places the breakthrough at this narrow kinked waist, where the modern B851 road now runs. This modern interpretation seems attractive but does not appear to match any of the maps.

The 'Rebells retreat', like the maps of Sandby and Finlayson, is broken down into three general directions.

6. Finlayson's Map, 1747–51

It is another Jacobite map (Plate 6) that has been called 'the most detailed and probably the most accurate plan of the battle'[52] and 'acknowledged by contemporaries as the best plan of the encounter'.[53] The engraved map entitled *A Plan of the Battle of Culloden and the Adjacent country Shewing the Incampment of the English Army at Nairn, and the March of the Highlanders in Order to Attack Them by Night*[54] is almost certainly correctly attributed to Captain John Finlayson.[55] Finlayson, a 'mathematical instrument-maker'[56] at Edinburgh, acted as commander of the Jacobite artillery at Culloden after Colonel James Grant (who would also produce maps of the Jacobite campaign himself[57]) had been struck by a ball at the siege of Fort William in March. The map has been described as 'precise and intricate', which given Finlayson's occupation is not at all surprising.[58] Many details were integrated into later maps. Interestingly a version of the map was possibly even taken from Finlayson himself, as one version bears the handwritten note 'January the 18th 1753 Siez'd upon John Finllayson By me N. Carrington'.[59] The map was originally printed at a time before this, probably some time between 1747 and 1751. Detailed troop dispositions are given, as well as the marching order of the government army as it approached Culloden. It even includes the route of the disastrous Jacobite night march towards Nairn the night before the battle. As Finlayson was another person on the field, it is possible that his first hand-drawn map, which does not appear to have survived, was made shortly after the battle.

Not surprisingly, given Finlayson's work on 16 April, the disposition of the Jacobite artillery is detailed. A battery of five pieces are shown in front of the right wing of the Jacobite army (as in Leigh Jones and Elcho) with another one of two in the centre, along with another at the northern end of the Jacobite line. One more cannon at 'F' (as in Cathcart, Sandby and Leigh Jones) is depicted in the south-east corner of the Culloden House Parks. This was 'A Cannon not brought into the Field in time of Action, which play'd on Kingstons Horse & favour'd the Retreat of the Left Wing.' This, however, only gives a total of nine pieces (like Elcho), whereas most maps and accounts agree on twelve pieces (as in Yorke and Sandby). Finlayson gives the government army twelve pieces of artillery, in six batteries of two, in front of and between all the front-line regiments (again as in Elcho, but unlike most others who give only ten, such as Yorke, Cathcart, Sandby, Leigh Jones and the French Officer). He does not indicate the presence of government mortars.

What is different, and is more difficult to explain, is the gap shown between the corner of the Culloden House Parks walls and the beginning of the Jacobite front line. Most other maps, such as those of Sandby, show this line tightly packed between this corner and the north-west corner of the Culwhiniac enclosures. This gap features in at least two other maps, one by Paterson and another which may be based upon Finlayson's map, in part in any case.[60] A smallish gap is shown in Leigh Jones's map but is not on the apparent scale of Finlayson's.

The government cavalry are shown in their original disposition and then their various movements around the battlefield. Kerr's and Cobham's Dragoons break through the Culwhiniac enclosures north of an east–west dividing wall (as in Yorke, Sandby, Leigh Jones and Paterson), to come out facing the rear of the Jacobites. Kingston's Horse and the squadron of Cobham's Dragoons are shown moving to the north from where they will eventually pursue the retreating Jacobites. Finlayson's version of the Culwhiniac enclosures agrees in general outline with other representations, and, like Sandby's map and that of Leigh Jones, it shows an apparent gap or gate in the northern wall. This gap is possibly the spot where Captain Colin

Campbell of Ballimore was shot in the head while 'passing a slap [opening]' to face the Royal Ecossois.[61] Also, like Sandby and the French Officer, Finlayson places the Argyllshire men definitely within the walls of the upper Culwhiniac enclosure. Finlayson also shows another small gate in the eastern wall of the northern enclosure, a feature not noted elsewhere, north of the government army breakthrough point.

Finlayson's map, like Sandby's and Leigh Jones's, shows the battlefield as containing areas of boggy ground as well as areas of tilled or cultivated ground, probably using the runrig system, particularly on the northern slopes of the bank of the River Nairn. Various steadings are dotted around the moor, indicating that the area was not the 'blasted heath' so beloved of romantic fiction. This was a landscape of rough pasture which people inhabited and worked. Culloden House itself and its surrounding parks are clearly delineated, as are the trees within these parks, among which some of the tired Jacobite army must have rested following the aborted night march: 'The men were scattered among the woods of Culloden, the greatest part asleep.'[62] The track leading up from Inverness onto the moor, which appears to cut across the battlefield on a south-easterly line to head towards Leanach, is clearly shown. Barrell's Regiment is clearly shown on the track, as in Sandby. However, Barrell's is shown well in front of the Leanach Cottage, in line with the Leanach enclosure, as in Leigh Jones, and not just in front of it as Sandby portrays it. Whatever the actual placement, Finlayson, like Yorke, shows the point of contact between Barrell's and the right of the Jacobite army.

An interesting feature of the map is the inclusion of the ships of the Royal Navy under Commodore Smith. 'The Shipping and Transports that supplied and attended the Duke's Army' are shown in a strip-cartoon or time-lapse manner in the Moray Firth. This naval presence is shown only by Finlayson, Leigh Jones and the French Officer. Finlayson shows the ships first at the mouth of the River Nairn, where they had dropped anchor at about 6pm on 15 April, supporting 'The Encampment of the English Army' of the Duke of Cumberland, just south-west of Nairn at Balblair, which was set up on the evening of 14 April, the day before his twenty-fifth birthday.[63] The ships are next shown having sailed westwards and taken up a position off Alturlie Point, from where they could have witnessed the battle to some degree. The navy's close support of the army is an often ignored feature of the battle, presumably because all the most immediate action took place on land between two armies.

Finlayson does not locate the Duke of Cumberland, but does place Charles Edward Stuart, '23. The Pr.', behind the front line, behind Farquharson's and in front of Kilmarnock's (Elcho places him behind).

Just as Sandby had done, Finlayson also depicts the 'Flight of the Highlanders' occurring in three general directions. Before the ford over the Nairn at Fallie, two of these routes joined 'The Road from Inverness to Ruthven'.

Finlayson's map is often quoted as being 'contemporary' or of '1746',[64] but even this must be treated with some caution for internal evidence in the surviving printed maps points to a later date. Clearly shown on the tip of Ardersier Point, stretching out into the Moray Firth, is the outline of a fortified structure. At the time of the battle this area was a barren sandy point, save for a little 'fisherman's hut',[65] and this feature can only be the outline of the new Fort George, designed in 1747 and not completed until 1767. This suggestion of Fort George must reflect the fact that the idea to build this fort was known about. So although the original map may have been drawn up in 1746, it was only being reproduced some time after the decision to build the new fort in 1747.[66] This would help confirm the date of 1751 given for at least one of Finlayson's maps, particularly as he was imprisoned in this year.[67]

Finlayson appears to have been captured immediately after the battle, as a 24-year-old 'John Findlason, Engineer, Artillery, [of] Edinburgh' is listed in 'A Return of the Rebel Officers and soldiers now Prisoners in Inverness, 19th April 1746' in the Cumberland Papers at Windsor Castle.[68] He was transported on board the *Jane of Alloway* to Tilbury Fort but was released and back at home by August 1747.[69] However, Finlayson was in custody again in 1751 'for treason displayed in his Jacobite geographical work'.[70] While in prison Finlayson petitioned the Duke of Newcastle for the plates of his maps to be returned to him. His attempts to disguise his loyalties, using the term 'Pr.' (Prince or Pretender?) for Charles Edward Stuart on his maps was never going to fool anyone, particularly as it can have been no great secret that at Culloden he had been firing cannon in the general direction of the Duke of Cumberland. It is therefore unlikely that the plates were ever returned. However, he was released again after which, in 1753, a copy of this map was seemingly seized from him.[71]

7. Lord Elcho's Sketch Map, between 1747 and 1754

The map *The Battle of Culloden fought on Wednesday 16 of April 1746* was drawn up by David Wemyss, 6th Earl of Wemyss (1721–1787), better known as Lord Elcho. Although only published at a much later date (1907), it appears to have all the immediacy of a contemporary or near-contemporary sketch and has been dated to 1747,[72] but despite 'his astounding memory',[73] it should be borne in mind that the narrative in which the map appears was 'written about 1754'.[74] Lord Elcho commanded his regiment, Lord Elcho's

Life Guards, in the rear of the Jacobite lines around Culchunaig, and fought in the action against the government cavalry that had broken through the Culwhiniac enclosures. The diagrammatic plan included in his memoirs is more of an annotated sketch than a map.[75] The best that can be said of land-marks such as Culloden House is that they are generally in the right place if not of the correct shape. Elcho does not show the moor road but does show Culloden House Parks as split into two defined areas. More interestingly, he is one of the few (like Yorke) to show what must be one of the houses in the Culwhiniac enclosures. However, although Elcho's positioning of the Jacobite regiments is pretty good, the numbers in the regiments are often at variance with other sources, such as Sandby. Glenbucket's men are placed in the front line (unlike Finlayson, who places them in the second line but shows them moving forward).[76] This apparent discrepancy is simply explained by the fact that Glenbucket was moved to the front during Murray's 'changement', or even that the Jacobite positions are based on the orders of 15 April, not those on the day of battle.[77] Elcho is obviously even less sure of the government army, giving the numbers of men in each regi-ment as a strangely uniform 500 (the three cavalry regiments are each divided into two blocks of 150).

Twelve cannon are shown on the government artillery lines between the front-line regiments, and two batteries of two more pieces (presumably the mortars) between the regiments of Wolfe and Conway (Ligonier's) and Blakeney and Battereau. This formation is not shown elsewhere. Ligonier's Regiment was renamed Conway's and the names of other regiments, such as Dejean's (formerly Monro's) and Sackville's (formerly Bligh's), for instance, also altered in the time after Culloden, and so perhaps reflect the slightly later date Elcho made this map.

Elcho shows the Jacobite artillery as only nine pieces, five in front of the Atholl Brigade and four on the extreme left wing. There are no cannon shown centrally. This is at odds with other maps, and only Leigh Jones shows five cannon on the right wing, but he also shows a centrally positioned battery as well. No lone gun in the Culloden House Parks is depicted.

Charles Edward Stuart is depicted as being in the rear centre, behind Kilmarnock's, as in Sandby's maps. Elcho also shows Kerr's Dragoons being the most easterly and ahead of Cobham's, as is shown on other maps such as Sandby's. Elcho's map is only one of two which shows the small regiment of Sir Alexander Bannerman, the other being that of the French Officer.

8. French Officer's Map, about 1748

Another map only came to light in 1996.[78] This map is a hand-drawn and coloured map which was drawn up about 1748 (Plate 7). It is written in a French hand and entitled *Plan exact de la disposition des Troupes Ecossoises sous le Commandement des son A.R.P.C. et de Celle des Troupes Angloises ala Bataille de Culloden*. The letters 'A.R.P.C.' stand for Prince Charles Edward Stuart, and the map is dedicated to 'Sa Majeste tres Chretienne' (Louis XV) by 'un Officier François qui etoit present a la dite Bataille'. Sadly the compiler did not go as far as naming himself or his regiment and so remains anonymous, and we can only hazard a guess as to which contingent of the Jacobite army he served in. However, the map shows greater detail in the centre rear, so the compiler may well have been in the Royal Ecossois or Irish Picquets.

Surprisingly this map has not received as much attention as it merits, being only mentioned in passing.[79] There are presumably a number of reasons for this, including the fact that it is undated and anonymous. The geography is also fairly imprecise in places: it is even suggested that the map-maker's interpretation of the coastline of the Moray Firth owes more to the Firth of Forth and that he may 'have used an existing map of the Battle of Prestonpans as his topographical source'.[80] However, details on the map include some fascinating and unique ones, which seem to imply that it is not just a copy of existing versions of the battle.

Charles Edward Stuart is shown no fewer than three times, by the use of a five-pointed white star to indicate the 'different stations' he occupied during the course of the battle. He is first ('1.e') shown in front of the 'Regt. De Roy Stuart' on the right wing of the Jacobite army. John Roy Stuart and his men were only brought up to the front line from the second line after the 'changement', so this gives us an idea of the particular moment this map is showing. The second ('2.e') position is behind the front line, on the left wing, behind the regiments of Keppoch and Glengarry. The third ('3.e') position is behind Bannerman's ('Benerman') and Ogilvy's regiments (similar to the position shown in Sandby), which are both shown, by means of dotted lines, as having moved up again during the 'changement', to their '2.e. station' behind the front line. Mention of Alexander Bannerman's small battalion, here numbered 90, is interesting, as Lord Elcho's is the only other map to include it (which he numbers as 150). It has been stated that the regiment was probably subsumed by another regiment or was 'in the left rear of the army'[81] (where Elcho places it), though this map would appear to contradict that and suggest that it was in the right rear, at least at one point.

These movements of Charles are fascinating and could show his response to the government cannonade, which kept him moving around the lines. Of course how valid these positions are is unknown, as no other known map contains such precise details. Even the ones that do attempt to place Charles (such as Sandby, Elcho and Finlayson) usually place him at a fixed point in the centre or at the rear. The number of positions for Charles and their centrality give him a more dynamic role on the landscape of battle than that with which he is usually credited. As a recent writer has said, 'Charles Edward was not at that moment standing far in the rear but was actually in the centre.'[82] This map does give us a unique glimpse of events on the battle-field concerning the Stuart prince.

The Jacobite artillery is shown as made up of twelve cannon, one group of four in front of the Atholl men, and the remaining eight in two batteries of three along the Jacobite front line, with one battery of two guns set in the south-east corner of the Culloden House Parks. The larger grouping is to be found in other maps (Yorke, Sandby and Finlayson), but everyone else who notes the artillery position in the corner walls only places one piece, and so the French Officer must be mistaken on this point.

The government artillery is depicted as numbering ten pieces, placed in batteries of two between the front-line regiments, and although this map-maker shows some movement, such as Kingston's horse, he does not show Pulteney's being moved forward.

Although depicted in a more schematic form than in many of the other maps, the 'Campbells du party Anglois' are particularly highlighted by their sheer mass, tightly packed up along the northern wall of the Culwhiniac enclosures and blasting into the left flank of the Jacobites. The French Officer seems to have been particularly impressed with their contribution to the battle, including much smoke from their muskets.

Interestingly this French map, perhaps because of the frequent naval engagements between Britain and France, does show the naval 'Transports Anglois' (as do Leigh Jones and Finlayson).

Conclusion

These early maps appear to have provided the basis for the explosion of maps which followed. However, none of the later maps add much to the information given in these previously drawn, painted and published maps and plans.

As Lord George Murray said of the Battle of Falkirk in 1745, 'It is not an easy task to describe a battle.'[83] The early maps and plans of Culloden show this to be true. Some are surprisingly in accordance with each other and others not so. This appraisal has shown that several of the maps may be of a later date than were previously thought, and this should be borne in mind when treating them as primary eyewitness evidence. Generally the maps tend to agree; the major differences are in the disposition of artillery and the absence or presence of the Royal Navy. The exact positioning of the lone Jacobite cannon, within or without the corner wall, is also a moot point. Cathcart's and Paterson's placing of a battery of government guns within the Leanach enclosure could be extremely significant, as it means the Atholl Brigade would have charged straight onto it. More importantly some maps show Charles Edward Stuart moving about the battlefield, giving him back a role denied him by many writers. Alongside the archaeological work that has been carried out (see Pollard, this volume) and the reappraisal of contemporary written accounts, this analysis of the early maps shows that they are crucial in creating one of the best-interpreted battlefields of the modern western world. They give us a chance to picture that snapshot of time when Culloden Moor became a bloody killing ground for a battle fought in a very real and physical landscape.

Finally, like all good history, even the mapping of the Battle of Culloden produces at least one puzzle. In his *Great Map* of Scotland made between 1747 and 1755, William Roy detailed various battles of the Jacobite risings and rebellions, such as Killiecrankie (1689), Glenshiel (1719), and Falkirk (1745). However, when it came to Culloden something happened. The area is depicted in all its topographic detail, including the River Nairn, Culloden House, the park walls, and the tilled fields and enclosures. But of the battle there is no sign. As has been asked, 'now how did that get past Cumberland?'[84] One detail alone appears, but only on Roy's sketch map for this area – a solitary dotted line shows the 'Track of Artillery'.[85] It does not show how the artillery was used or disposed. It shows no other relevant military detail, no troop placements, nothing. It is not known when Roy drew this sketch, but presumably the track of 'deep ruts cut into the boggy terrain' was still visible.[86] Apart from this the Battle of Culloden might as well never have happened. So what is happening here? Why has Roy, a military man and certainly 'fascinated by depicting battles and campaigns',[87] deliberately not marked the site of the Duke of Cumberland's most glorious victory over the Jacobites? Did Roy have Jacobite sympathies?[88] We do not know, but it does illustrate what maps choose to show or not. Even battles can mysteriously vanish from the landscape.

Acknowledgements

The author would like to thank various people for their help and support: Dr David Brown of the National Archives of Scotland, Dr David Caldwell of the National Museums of Scotland, Dr Christopher Duffy, Chris Fleet of the

Map Library (National Library of Scotland), Olive Geddes at the NLS, Antonia Lovelace, the late Ross Mackenzie, Fiona Marwick, former curator of the West Highland Museum, Dr Tony Pollard, Stuart Reid, Deirdre Smyth of the National Trust for Scotland and Rhian Wong, Royal Library, Windsor Castle. A special thank you and mention must go to Carolyn Anderson, AHRC research student at the University of Edinburgh and the Map Library (NLS).

Chapter 8

Irish Intriguers and Scottish Councils: Post-Culloden Narratives and Their Recriminations

JEFFREY STEPHEN

In his *Journal of a Tour to the Hebrides, with Samuel Johnson,* James Boswell recalled a conversation in Edinburgh between Johnson, Lord Elibank and Sir William Forbes. The conversation turned to the topic of the Jacobite rebellion of 1745, a subject that had very much interested Johnson during his tour, a particular highlight of which had been meeting the 'celebrated Miss Flora Macdonald'. As MacDonald recounted the story of her role in helping the prince escape from Benbecula to Skye, Johnson had listened to her with 'placid attention' before remarking that her story 'should be written down'.[1] Back in Edinburgh, the subject of the 'rash attempt' of 1745 was raised and Johnson agreed with Boswell's observation 'that it would make a fine piece of History'. Johnson expressed the opinion that 'A man, by talking with those of different sides, who were actors in it, and putting down all that he hears, may in time collect the materials of a good narrative.' Lord Elibank doubted if 'any man of this age could give it impartially'. Nevertheless, it was suggested that the time was ripe to make such a collection, 'for many of the people who were then in arms, were dropping off; and both Whigs and Jacobites were now come to talk with moderation'.[2]

In the twenty-seven years that had elapsed since Culloden, much had already been written and considerable efforts made to record the testimonies of participants. Histories published in the aftermath of the rebellion tended to be written by those loyal to the government, some having been volunteers in its army. Michael Hughes and James Ray, who were volunteers from London and Whitehaven, and an anonymous writer all published lengthy narratives of their experiences.[3] From a Jacobite perspective, exiles recorded

187

their experiences in narratives that would remain unpublished for many years. In the immediate aftermath of Culloden, Robert Forbes, later Bishop of Ross and Caithness, began compiling a collection of speeches, letters, journals, narratives, poems and other material about and by those who had taken part in or witnessed events.[4] Indeed, the first of Flora MacDonald's two accounts of her adventure with the prince had already been recorded, and by the time Johnson had expressed his desire for a collection of material, it had already become to some extent a reality.[5]

If the material collected by men such as Forbes was not always noted for impartiality, Forbes himself was scrupulous in demanding accuracy and attention to detail. Outlining his methods, he wrote, 'I never chuse to take matters of fact at second-hand if I can by any means have them from those who were immediately interested in them.' Those working for him were instructed to pay particular attention to names, places and dates. Forbes insisted he was only interested in telling the truth, 'I love a precise nicety in all narratives of facts, as indeed one cannot observe too much exactness in these things . . . I love truth, let who will be either justified or condemned by it . . . I would not wish to advance a falsehood upon any subject.'[6] Forbes's collection, which he named *The Lyon in Mourning*, was eventually purchased by Robert Chambers, who published some of the material in a volume of *Jacobite Memoirs* as well as using it as a source for his *History*.[7]

Nothing of the nature of the *Lyon* was ever produced in relation to those who served the government. One contemporary and anonymous manuscript was written after conversations with many of those who had taken part.[8] Furthermore, John Home, divinity student turned playwright, came about as close to an impartial account as any contemporary was likely to get. Home had been a member of the volunteers that tried in vain to save Edinburgh and had been present at the Battle of Falkirk, where he was taken prisoner. He began collecting material for a history of the rebellion in 1746 but concentrated more fully on the work from the late 1770s; as he put it, he had 'taken no small pains for many years to procure authentic information of what I did not see'. Home collected accounts of each battle and visited battlefields with individuals who had been present, 'and sometimes principally concerned'. Unlike previous histories, Home sought a Jacobite perspective and wrote to the prince and former Jacobites, asking specific questions about certain events in which they were involved.[9]

Attempting to collect and collate individual accounts is one thing; making sense of them all is another altogether. It would be unrealistic to expect eyewitness accounts to harmoniously fit together like pieces of a jigsaw. Despite their common experience, there are discrepancies attributable to a number of factors. The most obvious difference between Jacobite accounts and those by government soldiers was the time elapsed between the battle and when the account was written. Accounts by government soldiers were predominately written as letters to friends and family in the days immediately following the battle when the action was still fresh in the mind and recollection vivid.[10] The letters were written by men still elated at having just won a famous victory. Richmond Webb's response was typical when he bragged that the Highlanders had 'not had such a thrashing since the days of old Noll'.[11] While they gloried in their victory they could afford to be magnanimous and acknowledged the bravery of their defeated enemy. According to Alexander Taylor, the Jacobites 'came running up our front line like troops of hungry wolves and fought with intrepidity', and Hugh Ross told his wife, 'to do them justice, they fought with courage and gave us a very faire battle'.[12]

Nevertheless, willing as these soldiers were to acknowledge the bravery of their opponents, they were unwilling to show them any mercy. While British army casualties were slight, Jacobite casualties were very high.[13] Letters and narratives made no attempt to hide the brutality, and emphasized the nature and extent of the slaughter. Charles Whitefoord's graphic recollection was fairly typical. 'Those in front were spitted with the Bayonets; those in the Flank were tore in pieces by the musquetry and grape shot.'[14] Few were spared, and cutting down retreating rebels was regarded as something of a sport: as James Ray's macabre description put it, there was 'much knapping of noddles'.[15] The sources attributed the bloodletting by government troops to a number of factors. Many of the men at Culloden had fought at Falkirk. They had unfinished business to settle and there was a strong desire for revenge and for an opportunity to wipe away the stain of their humiliation. There was the small matter of Prestonpans, where the rebels had cut down retreating redcoats and mercilessly slaughtered men trapped in the walled gardens of Preston House. James Wolfe acknowledged that the battle offered them the opportunity to avenge themselves of many things 'and indeed we did not neglect it, as few Highlanders were made prisoner as possible'.[16] However, the determination of British forces to inflict such a bloody and brutal defeat upon their enemy can be attributed primarily to their widespread belief that the prince had ordered his men to give no quarter. Captain Thomas Davis wrote of their determination to capture the prince in order to exact 'revenge for the unnatural orders he gave out in the morning before the action not to give a man of us quarter, which written orders have been found upon them'.[17]

Jacobite accounts were written much later – escaping was a higher priority. However, having reached the safety of the continent, they took the view expressed by James Maxwell of Kirkconnell and recorded their experiences while still fresh in the memory. Some years after the event, the prince asked Sir John MacDonald, one of his closest and most trusted advisers, to write a narrative of his experiences. MacDonald had written nothing down and defended himself against possible charges of partiality by attributing errors in his narrative to the defects of memory rather than 'any hatred or envy against any one named therein'.[18] Tricks of the memory, plain forgetfulness or confusion caused by the heat of battle, or even the position occupied on the field, were all factors capable of affecting a narrative. They help explain differences on issues such as the time the battle started, the duration of the cannonade, the duration of the battle, the sizes of the respective armies and the amount of Jacobite casualties.[19]

While accounts of government soldiers are a straightforward narrative of events celebrating their heroic and comprehensive victory, significant Jacobite narratives are coloured by the bitter recriminations that followed so comprehensive a defeat. Mistakes had been made; there was blame to be apportioned and old scores to settle. Writing one's own account of events was an effective exercise in self-justification, as well as an opportunity to dish the dirt on erstwhile colleagues. In that respect the accounts of the major figures tended to mirror the divisions that emerged within the Jacobite camp during the rebellion. Understanding those divisions helps to make sense of the conflicting accounts of events. Bitter personal rivalries and jealousies had emerged during the campaign, leading to a total breakdown in relations between the prince and his Scottish council. This breakdown in relations had a greater impact on the outcome of the battle than Cumberland's army. For those at the heart of the divisions, subsequent narratives served to perpetuate their bitter war of words. A great deal had been ventured and lost by many, and if blame for the fiasco was to be apportioned each side knew where to place it. Right from the start this raised questions about reliability. Of the narrative written by William O'Sullivan, adjutant-general and quartermaster general in the prince's army and one of the original party that accompanied him from France to Scotland, James Stuart wrote to Charles that 'It were a pity that an account of your unfortunate expedition should not be put in writing and by a good hand, but such a paper should be composed with nice regard to truth and prudence, so as not to disgust, much less wrong, particular persons who appeared for you on that unhappy occasion.'[20]

One of those 'particular persons' and the principal target of O'Sullivan's narrative was Lord George Murray. Long before Culloden, Murray had become the *bête noire* of the prince and the close circle of associates he increasingly relied upon for advice, namely, O'Sullivan, Sir Thomas Sheridan and Sir John MacDonald. However, this dispute should not be seen as one between Murray and the prince, or Murray and O'Sullivan. It was a dispute between the prince and his closest associates, on one side, and his Scottish council, on the other. There was no love lost between the factions. Robert Strange referred to the clique surrounding the prince as the 'Irish intriguers'. James Johnstone claimed that the 'Irishmen' governed the prince 'at their will', and that their influence was most injurious to his interests.[21] Donald Cameron of Lochiel (nineteenth chief of the clan Cameron), Murray and Maxwell were all critical of the undue influence that men such as Sheridan and O'Sullivan had over the prince. The contempt with which the Scots held these men was summed up in the words of Master-Muster Henry Patullo, who, in answer to a query by John Home about an account of the expedition at the Scots College, said there was none 'but some injudicious lying catchpenny pamphlet published by some of the French Irish officers who had been on the expedition'.[22] David Wemyss, Lord Elcho, colonel of the Life Guards, complained that what annoyed the Scots the most was 'the preference that the Prince gave on every occasion to the Irish . . . As they knew that we disliked them, they had inspired the Prince with a hatred towards Lord George Murray.'[23] Murray bore the brunt of the acrimonious breakdown in relations between the prince and his council, primarily because his character, tactics and loyalty had been the subject of constant clandestine whispers by the 'Irish intriguers' to such an extent that the prince no longer trusted him.

As the campaign progressed, differences between the two groups intensified over strategy and goals, but in particular over the decision-making process by which these issues were addressed. The Scots finally moved to tackle the problem on 6 January 1746 when they presented a memorial to the prince just after leaving Glasgow. They complained about the prince's secrecy, his abandonment of councils, his lack of consultation with the chiefs and his reliance on Secretary Murray, John Hay and Irish officers such as O'Sullivan. Unhappy about the way decisions were being made and their exclusion from the process, the Scots wanted a greater say and demanded more frequent councils.[24] The memorial argued for discretionary power to be given to individuals in command during a particular crisis such as a skirmish. Such powers had already been used by Murray at Clifton, when advancing up Falside Hill before Prestonpans, and would be used by Murray to justify the return to Culloden during the night march.[25] The prince regarded the memorial as a demand for him to relinquish the authority he had received from his father, and bitterly rejected it by insisting that 'my authority may be taken from me by violence, but I shall never resign it like an Idiot'.[26] It was a highly significant moment that helps explain the subsequent lack of council meetings and why none were held at Culloden. The prince would not suffer a council to overrule him.[27]

Murray became the focal point for the hostility of the prince and his associates because, as the leading officer, he was the spokesman for the council, and because he was so highly regarded by its members. The strained relations between the prince and his council proved to be an ideal scenario for Murray's enemies to portray him as disloyal. Brooding over his defeat while on the run in the Highlands, the prince became convinced that those he had trusted had betrayed him, principally Murray, who was blamed 'as being the only instrument in loseing the battle'.[28] Back in France, the prince 'talk'd very ill' of Murray, and when Murray went to Rome in 1747 to see James, Charles urged his father to detain him until he had explained his conduct, in which the prince believed were several acts of disobedience, insolence and attempts to create dissension. The prince would have preferred the 'Divill' secured in a castle unable to escape and without pen or paper.

Later that year in Paris, the prince refused to see Murray and asked him to leave the city, which he did.[29] English volunteer John Daniel shared the intense dislike of Murray of his patron, the Duke of Perth, and attributed Murray's actions during the night march to treachery.[30] Sir John MacDonald held Murray in similar contempt.[31] It is no coincidence that the prince's hostility towards Murray should be reflected in the narratives of O'Sullivan and MacDonald, both of which were written at the prince's request. Neither narrative was published at the time, but it is clear that their substance was being circulated among Jacobite exiles and that the 'clandestine whispers' against Murray during the campaign continued after it. O'Sullivan's narrative was the product of the prince's desire to inform his father of events in Scotland. He was sent to Rome in February 1747 with authority 'to declare openly and without the least reserve to the King, everything that has come to his knowledge, either in France or in Scotland in relation to my affairs'.[32]

However, if Murray had his detractors, he also had defenders. Referring to the criticism of Murray, Colonel Henry Ker of Graden stated,

> The publick has been no ways favourable to Lord George Murray, but if they had been witness of his zeal and activity from the time he joined in that affair to the last of it, his exposing his person wherever an occasion offered, and in particular at the battle of Culloden, where he went on with the first and came not off till last, they would have done him more justice.[33]

Lochiel, whose narrative was written in April 1747, said of Murray, 'that nobleman had distinguished himself up till then on every occasion that offered itself, just as he did subsequently, bearing himself always with the utmost prudence and resolution so that he has won the esteem and trust of the whole nation'.[34] According to James Maxwell, 'If Lord George Murray's opinion had greater influence in the council than the Duke of Perth's, the Secretary's or O'Sullivan's, it was only because those that composed the council had a better opinion of Lord George's understanding and skill.'[35] Maxwell had been a major in Lord Elcho's Life Guards and escaped with Elcho to France. He lived for five or six years at St Germain outside Paris, and it was just after he arrived there that he began writing his narrative, as he put it, to satisfy the curiosity of many and to explain why the expedition was undertaken, how it was conducted, 'and by what mismanagement or misfortune all was irrecoverably ruined at Culloden'.[36] As an eyewitness, Maxwell believed he was in as good a position as anyone to undertake such a task. His commanding officer, Lord Elcho, had also written an account and both appeared to have done so with a view to publication. Almost 100 years passed before Maxwell's narrative was published, and another sixty years before Elcho's was published.[37]

As one would expect, Murray was capable of defending himself. In fact he fired the first shot in the post-Culloden war of words. In a scathing letter to the prince the day after the battle, he attacked Charles for undertaking his expedition without positive assurances of significant assistance from France. Murray also questioned the competence of O'Sullivan and John Hay of Restalrig, both of whom had become so 'odious to all the army' that, had there been time before the battle, he and the leading officers intended applying to the prince for some kind of redress. Articulating what was a widespread view among the council and officers, Murray insisted that O'Sullivan had been unfit for the tasks to which he had been assigned, and that he had 'committed gross blunders on many occasions'. Murray highlighted two in particular. The first was O'Sullivan's choice of ground, of which Murray complained, 'never was more improper ground for highlanders than that where we fought'. The second was O'Sullivan's 'fatal error yesterday to allow the enemy those walls upon their left which made it impossible for us to break them'. Turning on John Hay, who had responsibility for feeding the army, Murray argued that had Hay done his duty their ruin might have been prevented. In the critical days prior to the battle 'our army was starved'. Their starvation was the reason for the failure of the night march and the disorganized state of the army on the day of the battle. Murray insisted that, with a well-provisioned army and a better choice of ground, 'in all Human probability we would have done by the Enemy as they have unhappily done to us'.[38]

Less than a month later Murray wrote a letter in response to accusations that the Highland army had not behaved as bravely as usual, and that the principal officers had 'not done their duty', the latter phrase being code for betrayal and treachery. Of course, Murray was also writing in his own defence. While his anger had mellowed somewhat since Ruthven, he nevertheless returned to the same key issues. It was not intended for publication but having left a copy at the Scots College in Paris, Murray clearly wanted others to read it.[39] Murray wrote subsequent accounts in response to the criticisms of him mentioned by Ker. One developed in detail the issues raised in his letter of 10 May. Another was in response to a question from William Hamilton of Bangor, who wanted to know if Murray was in favour of the night attack and, if so, in what way did he think it ought to have been conducted. Hamilton believed the controversy surrounding the march and Murray's role in it needed to be 'cleared up'. Murray agreed, 'for doing so will satisfy others, as well as do me justice'.[40] Murray also provided an account of his role in the rebellion for a history Hamilton had planned to write. Hamilton never wrote a history, but Murray's narrative *Marches of the Highland Army* was published by Robert Chambers, who had purchased the *Lyon in Mourning*. Chambers reminded readers that Murray pressed his own services upon their attention because he was conscious when he wrote of 'many false imputations being urged against him'.[41] The recriminations focused on three key disputed decisions: the decision to fight, the choice of ground and the decision to undertake a night attack. With Cumberland advancing steadily towards him, the prince as commander-in-chief was determined to stand and fight without waiting for reinforcements. The decision was his and it was made with the support and advice of his close advisers, but in opposition to the advice and wishes of Lord George and other leading officers, particularly Lochiel.[42] Murray, the chiefs and leading officers were unhappy about the decision to fight while the army was physically debilitated by hunger and fatigue, and while under-strength. They wanted to wait until the rest of the army had arrived. Lord Cromarty and his men were still in the north and, unknown to the prince, captured later that day. Cluny MacPherson and his men were still in Badenoch, and Simon Fraser was marching to Inverness from the west. The army was boosted later on the 15th by the arrival of Alexander MacDonald of Keppoch and his regiment. Nevertheless, the prince was unmoved, and any suggestion of a retreat or of waiting for the reinforcements was rejected.[43]

The prince's recollection of the decision was that on the morning before the action he had 'used all his rhetorick, and eloquence against fighting, yet my Lord George out-reasoned him, till at last he yielded for fear to raise a dissension among the army'.[44] John Daniel also blamed Murray for the decision to fight that day and said that it was the prince who wanted to retire.[45] Given Daniel's adoration of his Christ-like prince, the only possible explanation for such a catastrophic decision was that it must have been Murray's. However, the Marquis d'Eguilles recalled that on the morning of the battle he had pleaded with the prince to take alternative action but found 'him immovable in the resolve he had taken to fight at any cost'.[46] The suggestion that it was Murray who persuaded a reluctant prince to fight flies in the face of overwhelming evidence that points to Murray as the leading advocate of taking alternative action.

Initially, the alternative action suggested by the Scots had been to retreat into the Highlands and regroup before resuming the campaign. There were variations of this theme, such as breaking up the army and holding the passes into the Highlands, from where they could launch occasional raids into the Lowlands for provisions and supplies, or simply quickly regrouping north of Inverness before confronting Cumberland in a couple of weeks.[47] Such suggestions have generally been dismissed despite being seriously promoted as a realistic and achievable, albeit last resort, alternative by leading officers and the French ambassador.[48] With Cumberland's arrival imminent, it was suggested that they take up a position on more suitable ground while awaiting reinforcements. There was considerable disquiet about the ground chosen by O'Sullivan for battle. According to Dougal Graham, O'Sullivan's plan was to allow Cumberland to advance towards them unhindered:

> But lead him to some ugly ground,
> Where cannon and horse were useless found:
> So pitched upon Culloden place,
> Where dykes and bogs might vex his grace.[49]

Murray also claimed that O'Sullivan insisted 'that the moor was so Interspersed with moss and deep ground that the Enemy's horse and cannon could be of little advantage to them'.[50] O'Sullivan stoutly defended his choice of ground, but the officers objected on the grounds that it was unsuitable to the military style and tactics of the Highlanders and not likely to pose any problems for Cumberland.[51]

As far as Murray and the chiefs were concerned, they faced the worst possible scenario – having to fight while unready and unfit, and on the worst choice of ground. With these concerns in mind, Lieutenant Colonel Walter Stapleton and Colonel Henry Ker were dispatched to reconnoitre ground to the south on the other side of the River Nairn. They reported that it was better ground for their army, being both steep and difficult, 'so that the enemy's cannon and horse could be of no great use to them there'.[52] There was a general consensus among the officers that they should make their stand on the other side of the river where the terrain would assist rather than hinder their style of combat. The prince rejected Murray's suggestion on the grounds that it appeared as though they were avoiding the enemy. It also left the road to Inverness open, and the prince was determined not to lose the town because of the ammunition and baggage there.[53] While Murray had been searching for an appropriate alternative strategy, Cumberland's non-appearance had prompted the prince to suggest a night attack on the camp at Nairn. He had been unsuccessful in canvassing the support of the chiefs and officers, but they reluctantly acquiesced when their proposal of retiring to a more favourable position south of the River Nairn was rejected.[54] When contrasted with fighting on unsuitable ground without waiting for reinforcements, a night attack appeared to be the lesser of two evils.[55]

The bitter fall-out from the failed night march hardened attitudes on the part of the prince and his associates, who refused to countenance the suggestions of the council.[56] However, enclosure walls between which the Jacobite army had formed, further complicated the dispute about the ground. Cumberland's sudden arrival forced a rapid deployment on ground half a mile nearer to Inverness.[57] In their new position they now had the Culwhiniac enclosure walls on their immediate right and the walls of the Leanach enclosure directly in front of the regiments on the Jacobite right flank. This was not an issue the previous day as the enclosures had been behind the Jacobite lines. The decision to line up between the walls had been O'Sullivan's, who believed they would compensate for the shortage of men because they would afford protection to their flanks. O'Sullivan insisted that the ground, with park walls on either side, was as good as they could desire.

However, the presence of the walls and enclosures fatally undermined the Jacobite cause that day. The decision was not, as has been suggested, the best of a bad job, but the worst of the available scenarios. It was a major miscalculation.[58] The position and the rationale behind choosing it only served to vindicate the Scots' argument that the choice of ground was a poor one, and that the best course of action was to have crossed the river to better ground and await reinforcements. Any sense of security offered by the walls quickly evaporated when two regiments of dragoons and about 140 of the Argyle Militia under the command of Lieutenant General Henry Hawley and Major General Humphrey Bland decided to flank the Jacobite right by passing through the parks.[59] O'Sullivan insisted that the horse would not come through the parks and that they could not come between Murray and the river unless they broke down the walls. He believed that rather than break down the walls, Cumberland's left would be placed against them just as their own right was. Rather than a liability, he claimed that the parks and the 6ft high walls would offer protection, and suggested to Murray that he should fill the houses at Culchunaig with men and pierce the walls of the house in order to fire at the enemy from that position. He added that if Murray and the men on the right did not have enough ground they could make use of the parks. O'Sullivan later claimed that in response to Murray's continued concern for his flank, he told him that he could prevent a flanking move by the enemy by breaking the wall and ordering Stonywood's Regiment and another regiment inside the park. According to O'Sullivan, the enemy horse would break in the face of their fire.[60]

Murray rejected O'Sullivan's suggestion because Cumberland's men had already broken into the enclosures at the time of the discussion; it was clearly too late to put men into the enclosures. Furthermore, in the event of being overwhelmed, the enclosures would have become a prison and men picked off as they tried to escape through the gaps.[61] Typically, O'Sullivan's recollection of events differed from the others. He claimed that he recommended Stonywood's and Avochie's for the role and that he led them down by a 'hollow way'[62] so that their movements could not be seen, and told them not to reveal themselves. They were to have one sentry to watch and inform the rest of what was happening.[63] However, the other sources agree that Murray ordered two regiments to form opposite the dragoons upon the 'brink of a hollow way',[64] in a position where they could watch their enemy and be seen. Their visibility was designed to act as a deterrent.[65] This holding operation was relatively successful in that Cumberland's dragoons were kept at bay for the duration of the attack and did not engage until the Jacobites were in disorderly retreat. However, the Campbells had occupied the enclosures and taken up a position behind the walls that would allow them to attack the Jacobite right flank as it attacked. Murray recognized this, and it is possible that his delayed attack was because he hoped Cumberland's men would continue to advance along the enclosure and thus negate some of the danger. They did not, and the rest is, as they say, history.

The anger evident in Murray's letter from Ruthven is therefore understandable. Having insisted that the ground would hinder rather than help them, his assessment was justified by events, although it was hardly the vindication he was looking for. The ground proved to be no obstacle to Cumberland's artillery, horse or infantry, all of whom played their part in turning Culloden into a killing field. Furthermore, the problems caused by the enclosure walls proved particularly costly for Murray's Regiment, many of whom died as a result of the deadly crossfire from the Campbells who had taken up a position behind the walls.[66] There is also strong evidence to suggest that Cumberland's men managed to get at least one piece of artillery into the enclosures that targeted the Jacobite flank with grapeshot. According to Andrew Lumsden, 'Our right was covered by some old park walls that led towards the water of Nairn. The Campbells got behind these walls, pulled them down, and placed a battery of cannon, which did great execution on our right.'[67] Murray, James Maxwell, Robert Strange, James Johnstone, John Wedderburn, an anonymous Whig historian who based his account on testimonials from combatants, and Charles Whitefoord's narrative and map of the battle all corroborate Lumsden's testimony. These sources are quite clear that the Jacobite right was hit in the flanks by grapeshot, and all of the Jacobites with the exception of Johnstone were on the right and in a good position to know (but see Pollard, this volume, p. 161).[68]

This heavy cost was all the harder to take in light of the fact that the Scots had insisted that it was not too late to redeploy, and that by crossing the river, a confrontation would have been delayed long enough for their reinforcements to arrive. With more men on better ground, they believed they had a chance.[69] We will never know what might have happened, but could the outcome have been any worse? More importantly, those who were present, officers privy to the debate, agree with Murray's assessment. Elcho insisted that affairs in the Jacobite camp in the days leading up to the battle were characterized by a 'great disorder'.[70] Taking into account all of the circumstances of that day, he was persuaded that the only appropriate course of action open to them was to cross the River Nairn, where he believed the Duke would not follow. They could wait until night and then attack.[71] James Maxwell agreed. The avoidance of action at that point would have enabled the exhausted men to recover and allowed reinforcements to arrive, and 'Nothing was easier than to avoid an action for several days.' The prince could have retired beyond Inverness, 'but he thought either of these would be an argument of fear, an acknowledgement of the Duke of Cumberland's superiority and discourage the army'.[72]

Robert Strange perfectly summed up the feelings of many when he wrote that the army had for weeks been on a short allowance of bread that had enfeebled their bodies. The prince's funds were spent. The men had received little money and were owed considerable arrears. They had spent the previous night under arms and performed a long and strength-sapping march. They were worn out with fatigue, were hungry, had no food nor time to rest, and were outnumbered two to one by their enemy. What, he asked, could justify the 'deliberate folly and madness of fighting under such circumstances?' Of course, the answer was nothing could justify fighting, and the implication of Strange's statement was that the prince was guilty of folly and madness. Nevertheless Strange continued, with a heavy sense of fatalism, 'our time was come. We were at variance within ourselves: Irish intriguers and French politics were too predominant in our councils.'[73] Consequently, Murray's reservations about the choice of ground and his suggestions about crossing the river were rejected. The prince instead chose to follow the advice of O'Sullivan, Sheridan and the others, as Henry Patullo explained:

> proposals were made to retire over the river Nairne and avoid fighting at so great a disadvantage which might have been done with great facility. But Sir Thomas Sheridan and others from France, having lost all patience, and hoping, no doubt for a miracle, in which light most of them had considered both the victory at Preston, and that at Falkirk, insisted upon a battle, and prevailed, without reflecting that many were absent, and those on the spot spent and discouraged by a forced march, during a long dark night, whereas upon the other two occasions, the men were in full vigour and spirits.[74]

Lochiel also blamed the prince's decision to fight upon the advice of Sir Thomas Sheridan, 'whose only conception of war was to fight at every opportunity, wanted the Prince to await the enemy and fight'.[75] According to Murray, the prince's closest advisers urged an immediate battle because they did not want to endure a summer campaign. He believed the prince could endure it but wrote, 'it's true Sir Thomas Sheridan &c. could not have undergone it; so we were obliged to be undone for their ease'.[76]

Undone they certainly were. Events demonstrated that Murray and his colleagues had been right to question the choice of ground, right to question the decision to fight and right to argue in favour of what was regarded as a more suitable alternative. O'Sullivan's narrative and its unrelenting denigration of Murray must be seen in this light. His account of the night march and battle consists of a series of semi-fictional cameos in which he contrasts his loyalty, industry and bravery with Murray's obstructionism, disloyalty and cowardice. It is a version of events that clashes not just with Murray's but also with other accounts that collectively question O'Sullivan's reliability as a witness. Bearing as he did a large share of the responsibility for those fatal decisions, the tactically inept and negligent O'Sullivan used his narrative to defend his actions and shift the blame for the fiasco onto Murray. According to O'Sullivan, it was not the lack of men, their poor condition or the unsuitable ground chosen for battle, but Murray's cowardice that was responsible for the ineffectiveness of the Jacobite attack. O'Sullivan claimed that the Jacobite left, where he was stationed, received the heaviest fire. While he led his men forward in the face of that fire he saw Murray 'going off' with the right wing. MacDonald also blamed Murray, who was said to have 'fled at the very beginning with his men'.[77]

Not even a bad memory could excuse MacDonald's version of events. It is true that Murray and the right retreated, and once they began their retreat, the rest of the line followed. However, they only retreated after they had been involved in an incredibly fierce and brave conflict which they could not sustain because of their lack of men, heavy casualties and the failure of the charge at other parts of the line to make an impact, particularly the left. The bravery and action of the right was well known and generally acknowledged by both sides, but completely ignored by MacDonald and O'Sullivan. Both men were guilty of the sin of omission. They knew what happened on the right but deliberately omitted everything except the retreat, in order to give the impression that Murray the coward had run off with the rest of the right wing and was responsible for the defeat.[78]

According to O'Sullivan, Murray's culpability extended beyond his precipitous retreat to responsibility for disrupting the line prior to the attack. O'Sullivan claimed that Murray's Regiment and those beside him changed their formation from three to six deep, effectively halving their breadth and doubling their depth. According to O'Sullivan this created gaps in the line that he rushed to fill up before battle commenced, and that as a consequence, the MacDonalds were almost in the centre rather than on the left. O'Sullivan is the only source to mention this change. Turning the regiments on the right into columns and moving them forward to such a degree that resulted in considerable dislocation would be a highly significant action. Yet no one else mentions it. The silence of the sources is surely significant. Sources such as Ker and Maxwell do mention the fact that the lines were not parallel and the consequences, but do not attribute this to actions of Murray. However, unlike O'Sullivan, the sources are unanimous in placing the MacDonalds on the left when the line charged and not in the centre (see the opposing view proposed by Reid, this volume).

If Murray did make the change, and some historians have suggested that it made sense because it would have enabled him to better negotiate the Leanach enclosure that stood in front of him,[79] then to close the gaps created would have been a mistake because they would have closed naturally as a result of negotiating the Leanach (see Pollard, this volume, for an archaeological response to these suggestions). The incident has been given added significance due to an historical interpretation that argues that it led to a dislocation because the changes pushed the right wing forward by a considerable distance. This dislocation was responsible for the fact that the Jacobite line was not parallel to Cumberland's.[80] There is no documentary evidence whatsoever, not even from O'Sullivan, to suggest that Murray moved the right wing forward in this way. Quite the opposite: MacDonald, who surely would have mentioned it had Murray done it, stated that their right rested on a house and as the enemy advanced 'our line never moved'. Maxwell likewise pointed out that when the prince was ordering Murray to attack, the Campbells had already occupied the enclosures and taken a position behind the walls, and at this point Murray still had the farmhouse on his immediate right. He was clearly not halfway down the enclosures, but still in his original position from which, according to Maxwell, he was very reluctant to advance when ordered to do so because of the danger posed by the Campbells.[81] Indeed, had the right been as far advanced as has been claimed it would have been a very easy target for the Campbells even before the attack.

The fact that the Jacobite line was not parallel with Cumberland's had nothing to do with Murray's supposed changes. It was the result of the position taken by the government line, which was ultimately determined by the nature of the terrain. The Jacobites were already in position as Cumberland advanced. While his left advanced to a position on firm ground at the other end of the enclosures, his right was unable to advance as far because of the boggy ground.[82] By the time Cumberland's army had taken its final position, there was a greater distance between his right and the Jacobite left than there was between his left and the Jacobite right. The Jacobites attempted but failed to resolve the problem by having their left advance first.[83]

At the heart of the dispute was the question of whether or not Culloden should have taken place at all. The principal officers in the Jacobite army present at Culloden opposed fighting on that moor on that day. Because of the nature of the ground they were expected to fight upon and the state of the army, they wanted to retire either across the River Nairn or towards Inverness and wait for the reinforcements they soon expected to arrive. They did not want to avoid a fight but only to delay it long enough to enable them to fight on the best possible terms. Bearing in mind what happened at Falkirk, the ease with which Cumberland achieved his victory can be attributed largely to the series of foolish and fatal decisions taken by the prince and his close advisers. Those decisions were taken because of the prince's breakdown in relations with his Scottish council. His unwillingness to listen to any advice they offered lies at the heart of the explanation as to why an army that was victorious at Falkirk was so easily disposed of at Culloden. While primary responsibility for the debacle rests with the prince, he was aided and abetted in his decision-making by Sheridan, MacDonald and principally O'Sullivan. The Scots rather generously tended to absolve the prince of responsibility and blamed the 'Irish intriguers' for the fiasco.

Chapter 9

Drumossie Moor: Memorialization, Development and Restoration in an Evolving Historic Landscape

ELSPETH MASSON AND JILL HARDEN

Today Drumossie Moor is a landscape of fields, farm buildings and houses, as well as roads, areas of forestry and heather moorland. It was not so varied some 250 years ago when Jacobite forces supporting the Stuart royal lineage met the army of the Hanoverian King of Great Britain on 16 April 1746. Since the Battle of Culloden the changes seen across the area have been considerable. Some have even been quite controversial in the minds of those who were and are passionate about this iconic, windswept moor.[1]

The Battlefield Landscape, 1746–1846

Certain contemporary Jacobite sources relate the unsuitability of the ground at Drumossie Moor for the battle in general and the Highland charge in particular.[2] It was a bleak, heather moorland – boggy, open and dreary. But the wider plans and maps of the area, such as those drawn at the time by Finlayson and Sandby,[3] indicate a much more varied landscape (Plate 6 and Figure 18). The maps show that most of the battlefield was open land, presumably used as hill-grazing for cattle, criss-crossed by tracks between farmsteads. However, to the south the slopes were cultivated as rigs or open fields. In addition there were a couple of large enclosures known as Parks of Culloden (the western of these being better known as the Culwhiniac enclosures), defined by stone and/or turf dykes, possibly used for winter grazing and manuring. Similarly the slopes to the north-west had been enclosed, creating the Culloden Parks, and planted with conifers.[4] Agricultural improvements had obviously begun in the area, funded by Duncan Forbes of

203

Culloden, the Lord Advocate of Scotland and Lord President of the Court of Session at the time of the rising.

It is unclear whether the investment in the estate continued under his son John Forbes, but expansive plans were certainly implemented during the last two decades of the eighteenth century by the Lord Advocate's grandson.[5] Arthur John Forbes was responsible for the demolition of the old family home and construction of the extant classical mansion that is still known as Culloden House, along with its new home farm buildings. He encouraged further enclosure of the land across the well-drained soils of the slopes immediately south and north of the battlefield. 'Bullets and fragments of armour that are picked up by people in the neighbourhood (presumably after ploughing the new fields) are anxiously sought after and preserved by the virtuosi as curiosities and valuable relics.'[6] But it is clear that the moorland that characterized the Drumossie ridge was neither drained nor enclosed at this time, as 'Strangers still visit the field of battle, though there is little to be seen on it, excepting the graves of those that fell in the action, which are discerned by the green surface, while the rest of the ground is covered in black heath.'[7]

As with so many other Highland estates, the first four decades of the nineteenth century were a period of decline for Culloden. Arthur's son Duncan George ran up huge debts with an excessive lifestyle.[8] This resulted in the estate being entailed. Independent trustees were appointed to control its management, or rather its dilapidation. It is possible that this apparent lack of interest was a factor in the desecration of some of the clan graves when the new macadam road was created between Inverness and Croy in the 1830s: 'It was a brutal act to drive this road through the graves. It was done in the absence of the proprietor, and we are glad to rest in ignorance of the wretch who planned it. James Macdonald, however, who lived in the old house of Leanach and saw the work done, said the bones had been reinterred.'[9]

After Duncan died in 1840 his son Arthur attempted to breathe new life into the estate. He renovated the farm steadings and seems to have encouraged agricultural improvements across his tenancies. He must have been responsible for the forestry plantings that were established across much of the field of conflict,[10] as well as the associated land divisions, presumably created at much the same time. However, all of these works overextended the Forbeses' finances and there was a lengthy hiatus after the mid-1840s until 'he was able to return . . . interesting himself in the improvements of his estate, and in every useful measure in the district'.[11] It was during this period of financial stringencies that others initiated a scheme that would further change the battlefield forever.

The Culloden Memorials

For the hundred years following April 1746, while Culloden and its after-math were remembered in art, in story and in song, there was no sign on the moor itself to indicate where the battle had been fought. According to one observer:

> There being no tumulus or obelisk on the heath to mark the spot where the contest took place . . . visitors often experience some difficulty finding it; and we must therefore endeavour to assist them. The battle was fought on a ridge of the moor . . . [the graves] consist of two or three grass-covered mounds, rising slightly above the adjoining heath, at the distance of about 200 or 300 yards from a small patch of corn land and a cluster of cottages, between which and them a marshy hollow also intervenes.[12]

It may have been difficult for tourists to identify the site but the descendants of those who had fought and died there never lost sight of the place of slaughter. On the centenary of the battle:

> The pleasantness of the day drew vast crowds of persons to the field of Culloden. Most of the teachers in town indulged their pupils with a holiday and groups of the little wanderers might be seen in all directions, spreading over the moor or sitting by the graves of the slain, listening to tales of the battle and the position of the rival armies . . . aged men and women related the exploits of their fathers and grandfathers, not a few of whom had fought and bled at Culloden. Parties in carriages, gigs and carts were frequently arriving; and altogether there could scarcely be less in the middle of the day, than three thousand persons on the moor.[13]

The ceremonies on the battlefield that day were followed by a select dinner in the Caledonian Hotel in Inverness, chaired by Mackintosh of Mackintosh, during which the suggestion that a memorial cairn should be commissioned was considered. 'The long-meditated project of erecting some memorial to the dead at Culloden was again revived,' the *Inverness Courier* reported:

> proposing a simple, but massive, cairn as the most touching and the noblest memorial of the nation's admiration and respect. In this the company universally agreed, at the same time concurring in the propriety of consulting Mr Forbes of Culloden for permission to

erect the cairn and to enclose the green mounds of the dead. A subscription for carrying out these objects in a suitable manner was instantly commenced.[14]

Over the hundred years since the fighting took place, the desire for a commemoration on the field of battle had grown, although it seems that the importance of identifying the site for visitors was at least as great a consideration as that of raising a lasting memorial to the clansmen who had fallen. Certainly in 1847 it was reported that:

> Strangers are often at a loss to find the exact place on which the battle was fought; but, to remedy this, Mr. Patrick Park, an eminent sculptor has very handsomely offered to cut a statue of a Highlander, placed on a suitable pedestal, to be erected on a particular spot of the moor, for the guidance of future visitors.[15]

Why this offer was rejected is unclear – perhaps neither the reporters nor the sculptor had been aware of the proposal to construct a memorial cairn.

One part of the original scheme was soon completed, though – the area of the clan graves was enclosed within a turf and stone dyke. But the proposed memorial cairn scheme was moving more slowly, and it was not until June 1848 that it was announced that the Elgin architect Thomas Mackenzie had drawn up plans for an impressively imposing structure.

The foundation stone of the Culloden monument was laid on Wednesday, 19 September, the following year. Clearly it was a day to be remembered:

> the day was held by most of the citizens as a holiday, the greater number of the shops in Inverness being closed. The procession mustered in the Academy Park . . . The banners and flags were numerous and handsome . . . The large number of individuals attired in holiday guise gave the field a gay and lively appearance, and the numerous attendance of the wealth and fashion of the district showed the sense they entertained of the truly national character of the proposed monument . . . [T]he large crowd . . . assembled on the moor . . . could not have been fewer than 5000 individuals . . . horses and vehicles of every description, from the dairyman's cart to the family carriage so thronged the road.[16]

Other sources record that:

> Sir Robert Peel had been asked to perform the ceremony, but declined, although he expressed appreciation of the proffered honour and had previously sent a donation of £5 to the funds.

There was a procession from Inverness, led by a band of music, and including six Incorporated Trades and Masonic deputations. The stone was laid by Sir William Anderson, R.W.M. of St. John's Operative Mason Lodge of Forres. The monument which was designed by Mr. Mackenzie, Elgin, was intended to be a gigantic cairn, with flights of rustic steps leading to the top. It was hoped that tablets and memorials to clans and individuals would occupy places in it; also a group of statuary would be placed in front.[17]

The *Illustrated London News* also carried the story and included an engraving of the proposed monument (Figure 25).[18]

This grandiose edifice, with its tombstone-shaped tablets and statuary of a weeping widow and her child, would have been not only an extraordinary memorial to the fallen, but also a fine example of how Victorians sought to honour the dead. However, it was never built. Despite appeals at home and abroad, the sum required to complete the monument could not be raised. In February 1850 it was reported that 'Further progress is temporarily impeded

Figure 25. The original monument proposed in 1849, taken from the *Illustrated London News*, 29 September 1849.

by the exhaustion of the funds . . . It is calculated that an additional sum of £100 will still be required to bring the monument to the proposed height of thirty feet. Of course this sum does not include the price of the statuary which may afterwards be erected.'[19]

There was no further work on the cairn and through time the foundations fell into disrepair. However, there is a suggestion that Arthur Forbes of Culloden had plans for an obelisk in 1858, and that it was for this that the 'E.P. fecit' stone, which is incorporated in the present cairn, was intended. An entry dated 1858 in the Ordnance Survey Name Book refers to a memorial having been 'commissioned by Mr. Forbes' which 'was abandoned before it had reached six foot above the foundation'.[20] While the Ordnance Survey map of 1871 shows that a square foundation had been laid, it is clear that no work was ever carried out upon it, and in 1872 *The Sixpenny Guide to Inverness and Vicinity* informed its readers that 'The great collection of stones within the clearance in the wood was intended for a commemorative monument, but the proposal was abandoned.'

While the Ninth Forbes of Culloden had been unsuccessful in his attempt to raise a memorial to the fallen, he had certainly introduced marked changes to the battlefield landscape. No longer was the centre of the field of conflict open, barren and bleak – it had been planted with trees to such an extent that in 1872 the site of the memorial was referred to as 'The great collection of stones within the clearance in the wood'.[21] The land to the north and south had also changed and had become farm fields, bounded by stone dykes. Most of the irregular-shaped old enclosures had been removed[22] so that the land could be cultivated efficiently. These developments reflect an active approach to estate management, even though the property was still entailed, implying that the financial position of the Forbes family had markedly improved by the time Arthur died in 1879.

His brother Duncan followed in his footsteps on the estate and at the battlefield. It was at his behest that the present memorials were raised in 1881. These included the gravestones at the head of the grass-covered mounds in the clan cemetery, each of which was inscribed with the name of the clan believed to be associated with the grave (this association certainly pre-dates this event, as the graves are named in the same way on the Ordnance Survey map, first published in 1871 – see the introduction to this volume). Oddly, in view of repeated calls for a battlefield memorial over the previous fifty years and in contrast to the ceremonials that had attended the laying of the 1849 foundations, the completion of the cairn and placing of the gravestones appear to have passed without notice. Nor was there any mention of the other inscribed stones Duncan had set up, such as that by

King's Stables Cottage, or the fact that he seems to have repaired Leanach Cottage.[23] As far as can be ascertained, there is no mention of the work in either the *Inverness Courier* or *Advertiser*. It is probably impossible to establish conclusively why this should have been so, but several theories have seemed worthy of investigation.

In terms of both local and national politics, 1881 was not a good time to draw attention to an uprising that had, in effect, been a civil war. During the second half of the nineteenth century Gaels were becoming increasingly accepted within society. This was in stark contrast to the sense of separateness between Gael and Lowland Scot that had been apparent for over four centuries, and which had been exacerbated by the Jacobite risings. At the annual dinner of the Gaelic Society in January 1882, there was reference to a 'request to parliament for the repeal of [the] anti-kilt act following Culloden' and to the 'prejudice and ignorance of "word battle" between Gael and anti-Gael during [the] last century. [However] Gaels can now claim cousinship and kindred with the best races in Europe.'[24] It is perhaps significant that, although Duncan Forbes was himself a member of the Gaelic Society, his part in raising the cairn and gravestones is not mentioned in any minute of their meetings that year. At a time when many Gaels were happy to be assimilated into national and international society, it was perhaps thought inexpedient to mark the creation of memorials to honour the dead of a rebel 'Highland' army.

It is reasonable to presume, moreover, that a landowner such as Duncan Forbes of Culloden would not have wanted to raise the spectre of past uprisings when there was again political unrest in the Highlands. The issue at this time was land reform. Charles Withers writes that 'the passing of the Irish Land Act in 1881 . . . was important in further raising the consciousness of Highlanders on matters of agitation and opposition to the authority of landlords'.[25] Referring to the period, Ewan Cameron writes of the increasing assertiveness of the Highlander, apparent in 'journalism, politics and the creation of Highland pressure groups', influencing government policy at this time.[26]

However, it is also possible that Freemasonry was an issue. The foundation stones had been laid in 1849 with full Masonic ceremony. There is no evidence that Duncan Forbes of Culloden was a Freemason. Perhaps he did not wish either to involve or cause offence to the Lodge.

None of these suggestions, however, seems to satisfactorily explain why Duncan Forbes's work in raising the gravestones and the long-awaited cairn was, apparently, ignored by both press and public. Perhaps the answer lies in an understanding of the man himself. As Deputy Lieutenant and Justice of the Peace, as well being chairman of a number of organizations that included the Board of the Royal Academy and the Inverness Farmers' Society, Duncan Forbes clearly took an active interest in the community of which he was a leading member. He regularly attended the General Assembly of the Free Church in Edinburgh. However, his apologies were often tendered to social occasions in Inverness and all the evidence seems to point to an unassuming man who lived quietly with his widowed sister-in-law at Culloden House.

It seems that Forbes not only had a general interest in preserving evidence of the past on his estate, giving 'a good example to other proprietors, in having a clause inserted in his leases binding the tenants to preserve all . . . monuments of antiquity',[27] but, like his late brother and his sister-in-law, he was sympathetic to the Jacobite cause. In proposing the vote of thanks, following a visit to Culloden House in July 1886, the secretary of the Inverness Scientific Society and Field Club mentioned that 'Mr Forbes had taken much interest in all matters connected with Culloden Battlefield, and had erected stones marking the graves of the dead, as well as a suitable monument of undressed stones.'[28] At the time of his death in April 1897, *The Inverness Courier* reported that 'unlike his ancestor, President Forbes, [the late Duncan Forbes] had a leaning to the lost Jacobite cause; at all events he honoured the memory of it. This was shown in his graceful act in erecting a great cairn on the Moor of Culloden to mark the graves of the gallant Highlanders who fought for Scotland and Prince Charlie.'[29]

The position taken by President Forbes in 1745 and 1746 is probably significant. Undoubtedly the most eminent member of the House of Forbes, the Lord President of the Court of Session had been a staunch supporter of the government. George Menary records that, 'His real work lay . . . in his attempt to save from themselves some of the Highland leaders who wished to espouse the Stewart cause.'[30] Entrusted with the task of raising twenty Independent Companies, he met the expense of so doing largely from his own pocket: 'The President spent £1500; the Treasury repaid him £500.'[31] It is recorded that 'The Lord President nearly ruined in this cause his ample fortune and left his affairs in great perplexity and decay', and writing to his nephew, Will Forbes, the President expressed regret at the 'restricted patrimony' he was leaving his son.[32]

As far as can be ascertained, there is no reference in any minute of the trustees' meetings of the entailed Culloden estate to funds having been allocated to the cost of the erection of the cairn and gravestones. The present Duncan Forbes of Culloden believes that his ancestor probably raised the memorials himself, meeting the expense from a small personal income which he would have received from the trustees. The expense would not have been great; both the cairn and the gravestones are of local stone and Duncan Forbes would have had estate workers who could well have carried out the manual work. Only the engraving would have required the services of a skilled craftsman (Plate 26).

While the political climate may have been significant, perhaps the most likely reason for there having been no recorded ceremony or public acclaim when the memorials were raised in 1881 was that Forbes of Culloden chose to have it that way. His eminent ancestor, driven by his own deeply held political convictions, had opposed the Jacobite cause at great personal and financial cost. This Duncan Forbes wished to honour the clansmen who had fallen. It is in keeping with what is known of him that he should have done so at his own expense and with little fuss. He would undoubtedly have known of the Masonic involvement in laying the 1849 foundations and this may have been a factor in his decision. In the absence of further evidence, there is no way of being sure but it can probably be assumed that, in accordance with the wishes of Duncan Forbes, when the work to raise the cairn and gravestones was complete, with no ceremony and no press report, the workmen simply packed their tools and went home.

Developments on the Battlefield, 1897–1937

Drumossie Moor appears to have undergone little further change before the First World War. It remained a farmed and afforested landscape peppered with small farmsteads and cottages (Plate 14), crossed by the minor road from Inverness to Croy. The only permanent intrusion was into the setting of the battlefield, with the construction of the new railway from Inverness to Aviemore immediately to the north and east.

However, developments in the subsequent decades did impact upon the field of conflict to a greater or lesser extent. The Culloden estate began to be broken up in the 1920s with the sale of certain farms and forests. Parcels of land were then sold for private house-building and, later, the impact of some of these new developments proved to be quite controversial.[33] It was not just the buildings that alarmed those with a passion for what the Culloden battle-field represented. There was also outrage regarding the lack of respect that some people were showing while visiting the clan graves area. A contemporary guidebook to the area includes the plea, 'It is particularly requested that parties visiting the field of battle will not in any way destroy or dig up the graves. Too much of this has [already] been done.'[34] Whatever the case, the Gaelic Society of Inverness became particularly active in attempting to protect and preserve particular structures on the battlefield. The society railed against vandalism and litter–louts around the memorial cairn.[35] It argued against the regular improvement and widening of the road through the clan graves area, for the works could not avoid disturbing the burial mounds.[36] The society even suggested that the road should be moved away from the core of the battlefield.[37] It also regularly raised funds to ensure that both Leanach Cottage and King's Stables Cottage were repaired and re-thatched as necessary, now that they were unoccupied.[38] But its greatest campaign, supported by many others, related to the building of a bungalow – 'Achnacarry' in 1934–5, close to the area of the clan graves.[39]

Today it seems inconceivable that any non-agricultural development was deemed appropriate in the area that was known to have seen the most hand-to-hand fighting of the battle and thus the greatest carnage. Even more controversial was the fact that the building was not just a home like 'Raasay Cottage' a few hundred metres further east. For at least the first five years 'Achnacarry' also served as a tearoom with, for a while, petrol pumps. An indication of the furore this development engendered can be gauged from the newspapers of the time. The then Forbes of Culloden wrote to the *Inverness Courier* when 'Achnacarry' was first built to disassociate himself from the development: 'The buildings to which objection is being taken are upon land which ceased to be part of the Culloden estate a good many years ago, and however much I may share the objectors' feelings I am powerless in the matter.'[40] The subsequent erection of the petrol pumps in 1936 caused much discussion in various committee meetings of Inverness County Council:

> Lochiel . . . Chief of Clan Cameron . . . said he had visited the battlefield the other day and was perfectly horrified to see a teahouse built in that field [of the English]. He was informed no legal objection could be taken to the house being built there but as regards pumps, he strongly objected to them . . . [because] space for tanks was being dug underneath the pumps which meant digging into a burial-ground.[41]

A response from Alexander Monro, the owner of Leanach Farm who had enabled the building of the bungalow and petrol pumps, was equally robust:

> the present commotion is scarcely justified . . . I cannot think that it is desired to convert the whole reputed battlefield into a park. These three acres which are reserved as a memorial of the battle and graveyard of the dead are enough for sentimental purposes. If

every battlefield were for ever to be reserved as such there would be today a very limited number of buildings in Flanders.[42]

The Daily Record & Mail was not convinced: 'Sacred Ground Invaded . . . Petrol pumps on famous field must go!'[43]

It was during this outcry that the National Trust for Scotland first became publicly involved with issues pertaining to Culloden battlefield. Since its establishment in 1931, the Trust has aimed to be the conservation charity that protects and promotes Scotland's natural and cultural heritage for present and future generations to enjoy. Invited by the Gaelic Society of Inverness to investigate the contentious issue that was 'Achnacarry', the Trust formally objected to the retrospective planning application for the petrol pumps. This followed a site visit by Sir John Sutherland, representing the charity, who used the opportunity to take a range of photographs of this and the other tearoom development at the Leanach crossroads around 400m further east.[44] Although the planning application was refused, a compromise was reached regarding the re-siting of the petrol tanks (potentially resulting in yet more damage to the battlefield). It is ironic that within the decade 'Achnacarry' had been sold and ceased its commercial trading. But the tearoom further east proved to be very successful. Even in the mid-1930s it served in excess of 8,000 teas a year – so tourism was having a major impact on the vicinity in general and the small area around the memorial cairn in particular (the latter being the only part of the much larger battlefield that was easily accessible to members of the public).

Restoration and Conservation of the Battlefield: The Work of the National Trust for Scotland

The 'Achnacarry' debacle had certainly raised awareness of the importance of Culloden battlefield among members of the Trust. It had also increased the understanding of landowners as to potential roles for the charity. And so, although there had been a certain frostiness between individuals and the Trust in the preceding years, from 1937–45 Leanach Cottage, the memorial cairn with the clan graves area, an access route from one to the other, King's Stables Cottage, and the Cumberland Stone were all gifted to the organiza-tion.[45] But the vast majority of the battlefield remained in the hands of others, including individual farmers and the Forestry Commission (which had purchased the afforested portions of the Culloden estate in the mid-1920s). The field of conflict therefore continued to be both largely inaccessible and potentially subject to inappropriate developments.

Initially issues arose because of the rise in visitor numbers to the clan graves area and the lack of facilities for them. After the Second World War people came by bus and, increasingly, by car to this clearing within the forestry. They stopped on the roadside (so they were often actually parked on the grave mounds), dropped litter and occasionally added graffiti to the memorial stones.[46] Within ten years or so, the two organizational landowners recognized that they had to start to address the problems, and the early 1960s saw much activity at the site, largely related to visitor management rather than conservation. To discourage parking on the verges and the graves, the Trust created a car park about 200m east of the memorial cairn. At the same time the Trust opened an exhibition in Leanach Cottage and established a footpath between it, the car park and the graves area. Signage proliferated. Meanwhile the Forestry Commission opened up two forestry rides and put regimental markers in place to give an indication of the deployment of the two armies, based on the research by the Trust's representative, Iain Cameron Taylor. Visitor numbers exploded – for 1966 they were recorded as 83,256. Working in partnership with others, the Trust therefore began an ambitious programme for change. Although hardly any additional land was acquired, a purpose-built information centre was opened by the car park in 1970. But tourists could still only access the clan graves area, the forestry rides and Leanach Cottage. There was little opportunity for visitors to grasp the size of the battlefield, stretching as it did from the farm fields in the south, across the public road and the forestry plantations, to other farm fields in the north and from Leanach Cottage in the east to Culchunaig Farm in the west.

While the area of the clan graves and Leanach Cottage were subject to significant visitor pressures, the Trust was also aware of other impacts on the battlefield as a whole. Before the Second World War the Gaelic Society had urged the County Council to move the public road away from the battlefield, stating, 'The desecration of an historic site and graveyard is an outrage on all decency, and . . . all right-minded people resent it . . . the Battlefield [should be] restored as it was formerly and, if possible, the road should be diverted.'[47] The physical impact of road-widening from single track to two-way, the routing of water supplies and telephone lines along the roadside, and the noise and safety issues associated with the public road passing across the centre of the battlefield continued to erode the integrity of the site. In 1960 the principle of moving the road was once again discussed, but in this instance, while the county surveyor agreed with the Trust regarding the veracity of the proposal to re-route it to the south, it was deemed not a priority.[48] Nevertheless, in 1962 a first step was taken in the restoration of the battlefield. The Trust had argued the case for the undergrounding of the overhead phone wires, and this was done.[49] While the vision of re-routing the road to the south was not forgotten, it took over twenty years to reach fruition. In the early 1970s the County Council was approached twice by the Trust to consider the proposal, but on neither occasion was the concept given a high priority.[50] However, it was partially successful a decade later. While it proved impossible to re-route the road southwards, beyond the area of the battlefield, a route that passed to the north of the clan graves area was deemed acceptable (Plate 9).[51] Today, the Trust aspires to a further re-routing of the road, so that it no longer crosses the field of conflict at all.[52]

'Achnacarry' continued to be a thorn in the side for many. Although after the Second World War it became a private home, its impact on the setting of the clan graves and Leanach Cottage was significant. Visitors walking to or from the memorial cairn passed the bungalow and must have wondered at the inscribed stone by the roadside in front of the building indicating 'Field of the English – they were buried here.' When the property was advertised for sale in 1971 the Trust stepped in and purchased it. 'Achnacarry' was demolished the following year and the restoration of the battlefield took another step forward.

However, there were still development threats to the site. Inverness was expanding and pressure to sell land for housing around the battlefield was strong. Today, this has by no means diminished – indeed it has grown exponentially. In the late 1960s one conservation solution was thought to lie in the local authority's designation of the area as a Conservation Area,[53] but it is clear that the limited controls have not been altogether successful. Another solution was for the Trust to purchase fields to limit development opportunities. For this reason, in 1989 the option was taken to purchase the so-called 'Field of the English' and other land to the south of the battlefield. It is something of a paradox that recent archaeological research has proved that some of this land is actually part of the field of conflict. But even now the Trust cares for less than 50 per cent of the area that constituted the battlefield. Further decisions about land acquisition may therefore have to be taken in the future, funds permitting, because there is increasing concern about how to maintain the integrity of the area. The Trust recognizes that other solutions also need to be discussed, agreed upon and implemented to protect this significant site and its setting, not the least being the introduction of legal protection for this battlefield and others across Scotland.[54]

For many, the greatest step in the restoration of the battlefield began with the acquisition in 1981 and 1983 of areas of forestry from the Forestry Commission, in advance of the re-routing of the public road. As part of these works the forestry plantation immediately north and south of the old road was felled. Suddenly the battlefield was transformed. However, the removal of the trees in 1983 left rough ground that proved to be a rich seedbed for birch and gorse, juniper and young conifers. They were not welcome but have twice taken hold of the area. Felling in the mid-1990s was followed a few years later by an inspired scheme to control any subsequent regeneration by grazing the area using Hebridean sheep.[55] The battlefield had to be divided into manageable grazing units and so it was criss-crossed with post-and-wire fences. But the sheep failed to hold back nature, while the fencing impacted on the setting of the field of conflict and visitors' experiences. Today a more intensive regime of scrub control, using mechanical heather-cutting machinery, has had to be introduced to fulfil the Trust's aim of returning much of the battlefield to a semblance of how it was at the time of the battle. But palaeo-environmental research is still required to confirm the nature of the vegetation across the area in the early and mid-eighteenth century. Then it will be possible to ascertain exactly what the Trust should be trying to re-establish on Drumossie Moor.

While there is still an opportunity to be seized regarding environmental studies, the Trust's research into other facets of the landscape across the battlefield has produced some very positive results. Using various archive sources[56] it proved possible to locate, in principle, the enclosure dykes at the south side of the field of conflict that had been removed in the nineteenth century. Their ghosts were buried in the parish boundaries, a fact recognized in the first instance in the 1860s.[57] It was decided to recreate those parts of the Leanach and Culwhiniac enclosures that were originally on Trust land. It was only possible to build short lengths of the drystone dyke that constituted the Culwhiniac enclosures because of the proximity of the Trust's property boundary. The Leanach enclosure, however, was an altogether different task. Staff and volunteers spent hundreds of work-days constructing its 450m long stone-and-turf dyke, using locally sourced materials. Today, these recently constructed features are integral to the visitor experience of the battlefield.

Conservation and appropriate restoration continue to be at the heart of the Trust's philosophy for Culloden battlefield. Most recently the Culloden Battlefield Memorial Project has brought together archaeological and histor-ical research to ensure that a fresh interpretive approach could be adopted across the battlefield, as well as within a new visitor centre (see Pollard, this volume). Having recognized that the 1970s information centre could no longer cope with visitors' expectations,[58] it was then realized that the infor-mation centre had been built across the southernmost part of the second line of the government army. Following extensive archaeological work in 2004 and 2005, a new site, south of the government lines, was chosen for a modern visitor centre created by Gareth Hoskins Architects with Ralph Applebaum exhibition designers, and built by Morrison Construction plc.[59] Access to a wider area of the battlefield has been formalized through a revised framework of footpaths (see Plate 12), and conservation principles have been adopted to ensure that the memorial cairn and other features will be conserved for the future. However, as with the previous information centre, this is not the end of the story. As noted above the Trust still has the aspiration to move the main road even further away from the battlefield, re-establishing open access to the northern half of the field. There is also the realization that archaeological research still has much to offer in developing an understanding of the events on the day. And there is the need to ensure that the setting of the battlefield is not compromised any more than it has been to date, for it is people's perceptions – their emotional responses to a place – that can be so easily spoiled by inappropriate changes.

The Battle of Culloden has passed into the national consciousness of the Scottish people. The tens of thousands who now visit the battlefield annually do so for a complex variety of reasons. For some it is part of the tourist trail, for others it is an important historical site, for yet others it is a place of pilgrimage where they may feel the haunting pathos of this place of slaughter. The Trust recognizes that the preservation and promotion of Culloden battlefield for present and future generations is never-ending – an apt memorial to those who fell in the last, decisive battle of this civil war.

Chapter 10

The Significance of Culloden

Daniel Szechi

Historical events are never isolated phenomena. To understand why an event such as Culloden happened, what followed afterwards and how it touched the lives of so many, the battle has to be connected to its context. On 16 April 1746 millions of human beings all across the British Isles were getting on with their lives much as they always had done. The European great powers were scheming against and fighting each other long before and long after that fateful day. Secret Jacobites in Scotland, England, Ireland and Europe were hoping and dreaming of final victory and the vindication of their cause. All of these elements in the great mosaic of human affairs were touched by what happened on Drumossie Moor that bleak spring morning.

What follows below is a brief exploration of the big picture surrounding the battle. Culloden manifestly did not come out of nowhere, and though we should never neglect or ignore the role of the individual in shaping great events, individuals are also to a very great extent prisoners of their times and circumstances. Historians, then, always have to be aware of the ebb and flow of abstract influences on human behaviour. We usually describe these influences under the heading of 'social and political forces'. And the social and political forces that made the '45 happen, and brought it to a field outside Inverness, were deep, multi-layered and diverse.

One of the key movers of events was undoubtedly the struggle between the European great powers that is usually encapsulated in the catch-all term 'the War of the Austrian Succession'. The war was a long one by modern standards, lasting between eight and nine years depending on where the starting point is set, and from a grand strategic perspective the '45 was just one theatre of that much larger, global conflict, and Culloden was just one moment (albeit a decisive one) in that particular regional struggle. Hence it is appropriate to look at the significance of the '45 (rather than Culloden alone) within that larger context first. The battle was, though, of special

218

importance to the peoples of the British Isles, and important events like it tend, at least for a while, to change the dynamics and shape of political affairs. So the battle's impact on the workings of British politics will be the next area explored. Of all the communities of the British Isles and beyond, however, there was one for whom Culloden had a very special significance: the Jacobites. The final part of this examination of the meaning of the bloodshed on 16 April will, then, look at what Culloden meant for the Jacobite movement as a whole.

The '45 and the War of the Austrian Succession

The great European war of which the '45 was a small part was not a single big conflict such as the Napoleonic Wars or the First World War. Rather, it was a set of parallel wars that periodically merged, and sometimes separated, before finally petering out in a general peace founded on mutual exhaustion in 1748. Thus Britain was continuously at war from October 1739, but technically only at war with France from March 1744, and Prussia was at war, but only with the Habsburgs, from December 1740 to October 1741 and then again (officially) from August 1744 to December 1745 – which means the conflict has no hard and fast starting point. The fighting began and ended for different states at different times. As far as the British were concerned, the war started as an entirely distinct and unique conflict with Spain in October 1739.[1] From 1741 this Spanish-British war began to merge with the more general European war precipitated by Frederick II (the Great), King of Prussia, in December 1740, when he invaded and conquered most of the rich Habsburg province of Silesia.[2] The Habsburg dynasty ruled a conglomeration of regions and peoples, under multifarious titles (in some places the Habsburgs ruled as dukes or counts, in others they were recognized as kings or emperors), stretching from modern-day Belgium (known at this time as the Austrian Netherlands) through northern Italy on into lands now part of modern Slovakia, Hungary and Croatia. Of all its possessions, however, Austria was the most important, which is why the dynasty is generally termed the House of Austria, its polyglot army described itself as 'Austrian', and the war Frederick set off is known as the War of the Austrian Succession.[3]

The succession element in the name given to the war refers to the dynastic crisis with which the Habsburg Empire was confronted in October 1740 when the emperor Charles VI died. His heir was his oldest daughter, Maria-Theresa; the crisis arose from the fact that female inheritance was not allowed under many of the diverse legal codes through which the Habsburgs ruled their scattered and jealously distinct territories. Frederick's invasion was calculated to exploit this problem. He hoped that it would take some time for Maria-Theresa to consolidate her authority and adequately muster the military resources of her empire in such a fashion as to be able to oppose his seizure of Silesia, and that she might even accept it as a *fait accompli*. But Frederick had not taken sufficient account of either Maria-Theresa's character and determination or of the likelihood that his invasion would set off a pan-European war. France and Spain both saw the setback to Habsburg power and authority delivered by Frederick as an invitation to wrest territory from a rival and extend their own spheres of power and influence.[4] They accordingly widened the war, France by allying itself with Bavaria and Prussia and commencing operations in Germany, and Spain by invading Italy.[5]

The British were left in a quandary by these developments. The British government of George II was heartily glad that there was now a possibility of bringing Britain's traditional ally, the Habsburgs, into the British war against Spain, but they did not want to get involved in an internal German conflict such as Frederick's Silesian war. British reasoning was straightforward: fighting in Germany would divert Habsburg military resources away from fighting Spain and France, the powers the British regarded as their main enemies. Aiding the Habsburgs against Prussia would also lay open George II's beloved German possession of Hanover to Prussian attack. The British therefore had to try to walk a diplomatic tightrope: convincing the Habsburgs that they really did support their ambition of regaining Silesia, yet not provoking Frederick into attacking Hanover.[6] At the same time they had to try to coax the Habsburgs into committing their armies to the defence of the Austrian Netherlands – a part of her empire which Maria-Theresa regarded as expendable if that was what it took to regain Silesia[7] – so as to prevent a French conquest.

French control of the Low Countries was something successive rulers and governments in England had desperately opposed since the sixteenth century. In the end, the only way to defend this Habsburg territory turned out to be the negotiation in 1743 of a grand European alliance in support of the Habsburgs. Known as the Pragmatic Alliance (the 'pragmatic' element refers to its commitment to restoring Maria-Theresa to her rightful authority throughout her inheritance despite the fact she was a woman), this united Britain, the Netherlands, the Habsburgs, Savoy-Piedmont and a number of lesser German princes against the Bourbon powers of France and Spain. It specifically did not commit Britain and the other allies of the Habsburgs to fighting the Prussians, and thus in a sense it was always an unsatisfactory pact as far as the key player, Maria-Theresa, was concerned. Nonetheless, it involved the full scale commitment of the British army to the Low Countries, plus the payment of large British war subsidies to the Habsburgs, the Dutch, Savoy-Piedmont and sundry lesser German princes. In return, these engaged to commit as many troops as possible to the fighting in their vicinity.[8] Each of the allies, though, naturally pursued its own interests within the alliance. Thus the Habsburgs sent as few troops as they could get away with to the Low Countries, the better to boost their forces in Bohemia and Italy; the Dutch tried to fight the war in as low-key a fashion as possible so as to avoid disrupting their trading relations with the Bourbon powers, and Savoy-Piedmont refused to undertake any military activity that was not in its direct interests, regardless of its obligations to its allies.[9]

The upshot was that by the summer of 1745 Britain had became far more deeply engaged in warfare in various places on the continent and the world beyond than it had ever envisaged in 1739. There was fighting going on against French and Spanish forces in North America and the Caribbean, and in 1746 the conflict spread as far as India, where the British and French East India Companies had hitherto maintained a pact not to participate in the wars of their respective home countries.[10] Because a hostile power in control of the Low Countries could easily use them as a base for an invasion of the British Isles, the most important theatre of the war from the British point of view, however, always remained the Low Countries, and for Britain it was always there that the war would be won or lost.[11] The wholesale commitment of the British army to the war there, indeed, corresponded to a very stark reality: the government of George II believed that without it the Austrian Netherlands would be conquered by the French, who could then force Britain to commit the bulk of its relatively small army to home defence. This would have locked up the bulk of Britain's military assets uselessly holding position in southern England to ward off an invasion, allowing France the strategic initiative elsewhere in Europe and the world more generally. And precisely because they realized the importance of the Low Countries to the British, Louis XV and his ministers threw the bulk of their troops and their best generals into the war there.[12]

The two opposed commanders whose skills and armies would decide the fate of the region were, on the British and allied side, William Augustus, Duke of Cumberland, and, on the French side, Maurice, Comte de Saxe. The two were an essay in contrasts. Cumberland was a young man who owed his rapid promotion to the fact that he was the favourite younger son of George II. He was an eager student of the art of war, but never showed any ability at it beyond a good competence. Compared with other generals of the era, he was reasonably solicitous of the welfare of his men, and generally administered his army efficiently enough to make sure that they usually had ample food and sufficient equipment to do their job. Cumberland, though, soon developed a reputation for being a strict, and rather brutal, disciplinarian, and though this may well have been exaggerated it did not endear him to his men. On the battlefield he tended to be quite aggressive and stubborn, which when added to his, at best, average tactical and strategic sense meant that he tended to order attack after attack even when at a disadvantage, and when fighting against unfavourable odds. His army correspondingly tended to take a lot of casualties whenever he fought a battle, which also probably did not endear him to his men.[13]

Maurice, Comte de Saxe, was a very different kind of soldier. Born one of over 300 illegitimate children credited to Augustus the Strong, Elector of Saxony and King of Poland, he was in his late forties when he took the field against Cumberland in 1745, with a long military career behind him stretching back to the age of twelve. He was a professional soldier to his fingertips, in 1732 had written a radically innovative and insightful treatise on the art of war, and already had a very well-deserved reputation for being a cunning and subtle commander. When France went to war in 1741 it was de Saxe who was assigned the most demanding tasks, and, despite his growing invalidity (the consequence of years of hardship on campaign and enthusiastic dissipation whenever he was not) he fully justified Louis XV's confidence in him. In 1742 he captured Prague in Bohemia, and when given the task of conquering the Low Countries and penetrating the great fortress belt built up there by the Dutch to keep the French out of the Netherlands, he systematically accomplished it. De Saxe did so by carefully prepared, swift moves designed to wrong-foot his opponents. In general, he deliberately did not seek battles, instead using his skills to manoeuvre his opponents into positions from which they were unlikely to succeed if they were so foolhardy as to attack him. Unlike Cumberland he was not a believer in draconian discipline, yet he easily persuaded his troops to do their best for him. Indeed, he may well have been the most popular commander on either side during the war.[14]

Cumberland and de Saxe fought two battles between 1745 and 1747; de Saxe won them both, and another against Field-Marshal John Ligonier besides, and in between times punched his way through the fortress belt to reach the Netherlands in early 1747.[15] The most hard-fought of these battles was Fontenoy in 1745, and its course and outcome is very representative of the two generals' abilities and what happened when they encountered each other on campaign. At Fontenoy, de Saxe effectively dared Cumberland to march into a crossfire between his entrenched artillery and light troops if he wanted to attack de Saxe's main body of infantry. Cumberland, aggressive as ever, obligingly marched into the trap, and despite sundry heroics on their part, his precious corps of British infantry was badly shot up and forced to retreat. Cumberland was only able to extricate himself successfully (shedding bitter tears as he did so) because de Saxe literally collapsed with physical strain and illness as the battle was won. And the final charge that gave the French victory was provided by none other than the elite Irish brigade.[16]

Which brings us back to the Jacobites and the '45. The Irish brigade was at this time composed of first- and second-generation Irish immigrants to France, who enlisted, in part at least, in the hope of serving the exiled Stuarts.[17] France had long been the patron and sponsor of the Stuart cause, and it was generally believed among the Jacobites that of all the European great powers, France was the likeliest to commit itself to restoring the exiled dynasty. Nor was their trust entirely misplaced. Restoring a grateful, and dependent, Stuart monarch to the thrones of the British Isles could have served France's interests very well, and for that reason successive French kings and regents and their ministers had quietly subsidized the Jacobite government in exile, and occasionally encouraged it by taking a polite interest in its plots and schemes.[18] When war loomed between Britain and France the French government immediately activated its Jacobite connection, and at the end of 1743 brought Charles Edward Stuart, the Jacobite Prince of Wales, to France to participate in an invasion of England, to be commanded by de Saxe, planned for February 1744. This went awry as a result of cold feet and consequent delays on the part of the English Jacobites, which led to the British government learning of the project and rounding up suspected Jacobites, and a terrible storm that badly damaged the French invasion fleet.[19] Assuming an invasion now had no hope of success, de Saxe led off the army assigned the task to reinforce the French invasion of the Low Countries. This was a consummate success, and rapidly conquered maritime Flanders.[20] Meanwhile Charles Edward was simply kept on the back burner, bored, albeit comfortable, in a borrowed chateau in rural France, to be re-activated in the event of further need or opportunity. He was, of course, not at all happy with this role, and accordingly plotted and carried out his own invasion of Scotland in 1745.[21] At the time he did so, in the summer of 1745, de Saxe was following up his victory at Fontenoy. City after city fell to him, and there was virtually nothing the allies could do about it. Indeed, the pace of de Saxe's advance was accelerated by the withdrawal of more and more British troops back to the British Isles, first to guard against another French invasion attempt and then to oppose Charles Edward's newly mustered, hard-marching and successful little Jacobite army.[22]

For the rest of the '45 de Saxe continued to take every opportunity to exploit the distraction created by Charles Edward, despite the desperate efforts of the French government to throw together another invasion attempt in support of the Jacobite prince in December 1745 and January 1746, sharply diminishing the troops and munitions available to him.[23] In January 1746, for example, de Saxe broke with convention by launching a lightning strike against Brussels in the dead of winter, and swiftly forced the surrender of the city. In March he began the siege of Antwerp, and before Cumberland and his troops in Scotland could be transferred back to the continent, cracked that exceedingly tough nut in June, when the city finally capitulated. By the end of the campaigning season he had added Mons, Charleroi and Namur to these impressive conquests.[24] The allies were left little choice but to try to stem the French advance by forcing a major battle. They dithered about doing this, however, and so set themselves up in a very poor tactical position that instead allowed de Saxe to attack them at advantage at Rocoux on 11 October 1746. As was his custom, de Saxe managed the battle carefully, bending all his efforts towards chewing up the British troops, who were still the best the allied army had, and, once again, succeeded very well indeed. The allied army retreated in confusion, and de Saxe calmly retired into winter quarters.[25]

Coming into the campaigning season of 1747, the allied situation had apparently improved, in that Cumberland was back in the Low Countries at the head of a large allied army, but in fact the allied cause was in serious trouble. Though the Scottish Jacobites had by then effectively been beaten into sullen submission, the British government was now alert to what the Jacobites could very quickly achieve if given the opportunity. Consequently it remained nervous about the possibility of a new Jacobite rising and held troops back from the war in the Netherlands to safeguard Britain's domestic security, thus weakening allied chances of turning the war around there.[26] The Dutch were also economically exhausted, intensely war-weary, and alarmed at the seemingly inexorable advance of de Saxe and the armies of France towards their frontier.[27] In the circumstances it was clear that only a decisive victory could rescue the alliance's fortunes. De Saxe urbanely sought to prevent them even getting close by denying them the opportunity to force a battle on him at any kind of advantage. And another fruitless campaigning season, spiced with a few more French captures of key fortresses, might well have brought an end to the war. As it turned out, however, Louis XV became impatient with de Saxe's Fabian strategy. De Saxe duly manoeuvred himself into an excellent position at Laffeldt on 2 July 1747, and would probably have crushed the allied army had it not been for Field Marshal Ligonier, whose good advice and personal initiative enabled Cumberland to make a much better fight of it than would otherwise have been the case. Even so, the allied army was defeated, and lost Ligonier when he was captured by the French while leading a desperately heroic cavalry charge to cover its retreat. The French rounded off another successful campaigning season by capturing the great Dutch fortress of Bergen-op-Zoom, which had hitherto been thought to be impregnable.[28]

The onset of the '45 also had an indirect impact on the general disposition of the war across the continent. In central Europe in 1745 the Habsburgs and their German allies were once again engaged with Frederick the Great, who in 1744 had recommenced military operations against Saxony and Bohemia in response to allied successes in 1743 (notably the defeat of a French army by a 'Pragmatic Army' commanded by George II at the Battle of Dettingen). Frederick found himself in more difficulties than he had anticipated in fighting against a revitalized Habsburg army, and was only able to retrieve his fortunes by hard-fought victories at Hohenfriedeburg and Soor in 1745.[29] These setbacks, along with other defeats in Italy at the hands of the Spanish, and the possibility that Britain might be knocked out of the war by a Jacobite capture of London, persuaded the Habsburgs to make a hurried and unsatisfactory peace with Frederick at Dresden in December 1745.[30] In turn, this paradoxically helped retrieve allied fortunes in another theatre. Because the peace of Dresden opened the prospect of a Habsburg rally in northern Italy when they transferred their troops there from central Europe, it encouraged Charles-Emmanuel, the King of Savoy-Piedmont, not to abandon the Pragmatic Alliance. Habsburg defeats in Italy and the possibility that Britain might be forced out of the war by a Jacobite revolution had earlier led him to contemplate the possibility of a separate peace or even a change of sides. Instead, Dresden and British government successes against the Jacobites prompted the cunning Savoyard to launch a counter-offensive. Charles-Emmanuel first carefully lulled the French and Spanish into inactivity by opening bogus peace negotiations, and then sent their armies in northern Italy reeling back in pell-mell retreat by a surprise attack.[31]

So what was the impact of the '45 on the War of the Austrian Succession? It clearly influenced the course of events in the Low Countries. The absence of Cumberland and large numbers of British troops in late 1745 and early 1746 certainly helped de Saxe methodically advance France's military frontier northwards towards the Netherlands. Indeed, the fall of Brussels and Antwerp is probably directly attributable to the '45. De Saxe was, of course, doing just fine before the Jacobite rebellion, and defeated substantial British forces twice more (at Rocoux and Laffeldt) after it was over, before the treaty of Aix-la-Chapelle concluded the war in 1748. Nonetheless, the '45 accelerated the pace of his conquest of the Low Countries. This in turn offset allied successes in Italy late in the war, notably their victory at Piacenza. This was as locally decisive as Culloden, and might have been exploited to force France at least to make a hasty peace.[32] The potential, as opposed to actual, impact of the '45 also influenced the outcome of the war. The Austrians terminated their separate war with Prussia by permanently ceding Silesia to Frederick the Great, in part because they no longer felt sure of the stability of the Whig regime in the British Isles. The British government held back troops in Britain for fear of another Jacobite rising. The result was that the '45 speeded up the process through which all parties to the war reached the conclusion that it was best brought to an end, which concomitantly helped the French limp home in better shape than they otherwise would have done – in strategic terms an excellent return on the small investment France made in the rebellion.

Culloden and British Politics

With respect to the politics of the British Isles, Culloden itself was a profoundly important event. The battle was not quite the end of a political epoch, but it certainly accelerated political changes that, in time, profoundly altered the structure and dynamics of politics in all three kingdoms. England and Wales, Scotland and Ireland each, however, possessed a unique political chemistry and so we must look at each one separately.

In England and Wales in 1740 the basic political division was between Whigs and Tories. These are usually described as political parties, and they certainly had many of the features that we associate with modern political parties: recognized leaders, a common agenda, zealous local organizers and an identifiable constituency in the political nation (i.e. those entitled to vote at some time during their lives – at this time only around 15 per cent of the adult male population).[33] Their mode of operation, though, was very different because of the way the constitution and the electoral system worked in the eighteenth century. There were, of course, two houses of Parliament, the Lords and the Commons. They were not fully equal in power, because the constitutional convention that only the Commons could initiate taxation had been established in the late seventeenth century, which meant that the Commons had the final edge in disputes with the upper house. Nonetheless, the Lords retained full veto power on any legislation arising in the Commons, acted as the final court of appeal in legal cases and was generally regarded as the nation's constitutional fire brigade. Because the peers in the Lords also disposed of great estates, they were also very influential in deciding the composition of the Commons, so that for all its supposed constitutional superiority, the Commons was often de facto manipulated by members of the upper chamber.[34]

The peers' great estates gave them this power over the Commons because the electoral system was gloriously full of jealously maintained, local medieval leftovers that rendered almost every constituency's politics unique. There was, for example, absolutely no uniformity in the size and voting qualifications of the electorate. The counties were a partial exception in that they all had the same qualifications for voting: a voter had to own or lease land worth 40 shillings a year in rent. But the electorate in each county varied from tens of thousands in Yorkshire to a few hundred in Rutland. Alongside the counties there were also a scattering of enfranchised boroughs, entitled by their royal charters to return one or (much more commonly) two MPs to Parliament. The number of MPs returned by the boroughs far outnumbered those from the counties, though the county seats were reckoned more prestigious, and the regulation of the franchise in each one was peculiar to that borough. Hence in some boroughs a local oligarchy centred on the municipal authorities returned the MP, in others ratepayers of various kinds and values had the vote, in a few owning a share in the local salt mine made you a voter and in still others twenty-four hours' residence enfranchised a man. The net effect of these eccentricities was to make elections in the boroughs regularly manipulable by local landowners through patronage and judicious pressure on their tenants and other economic dependants, and the greatest and most powerful landowners in any locality tended to be the peerage.[35]

That is to say that the peerage, and landowners more generally, thus had a great deal of practical political power, and dominated both political parties. Nevertheless, the parties' social leaders certainly shared certain basic political principles with their plebeian followers. The Tories saw themselves first and foremost as the defenders of the Church of England and its overwhelming legal dominance of religious affairs in England and Wales against the perceived threat to its ascendancy from Dissenters and Catholics. The Tories also believed themselves to be the defenders of traditional English values (including the ascendancy of land-ownership versus other forms of property) and the heirs of the Cavaliers who had fought for Charles I during the great civil war of the mid-seventeenth century. They were also supposed to be the party of the monarchy, but by the early eighteenth century the Tories were far more concerned with upholding the Church of England and the traditional order in the countryside than with unconditional support for the monarchy, the more so because, as far as many, if not most, Tories were concerned, the monarchy had been seriously compromised.[36] The principal occasion for this was that the Hanoverian dynasty, which inherited the throne in 1714, decisively favoured the Tories' Whig rivals for at least the next forty-six years. This stemmed in large part from the ideological position taken by the Whigs, which centred on a general defence of the Protestant cause (i.e. they equated and subsumed both Anglicans and Dissenters) in the British Isles and, to a certain extent, beyond it. The Whigs were also more committed than the Tories to advancing commercial interests located in the cities and sustaining the powers of the monarchy, so long as it was appropriately Whiggish and thoroughly Protestant in its outlook. Because they had been in power for over a generation by the 1740s, the Whig party also saw itself as the natural, indeed only, party of government.[37]

The Tories had initially been estranged from the Hanoverians by the smears and calumnies which their Whig rivals heaped upon them, and by their own intrinsic coolness towards a foreign, originally Lutheran, German dynasty following on the reign of their beloved, piously Anglican Queen Anne.[38] Some sections of the Tory party followed this up by secretly opening negotiations with James Stuart, son of the exiled James II, with a view to exploring the possibility of restoring the Stuart line by a foreign invasion or domestic uprising. Their plotting eventually helped precipitate the 1715 Jacobite rebellion in Scotland and northern England, but just as significantly in the long term, provoked George I and George II to commit the government of the British Isles wholly to the Whigs.[39] From 1716 to 1760 the Tories were proscribed from all national and almost all local government office. There were a few occasions when both the first two Hanoverian kings considered the possibility of readmitting selected Tories to power, but these proved abortive. The net result was that by the 1740s a significant section of the Tory party had become crypto-Jacobite, and those who were not so inclined still tended to be permanently politically opposed to the government of George II.[40]

This all changed as a direct consequence of the Battle of Culloden. Despite all their plotting and pre-rebellion blustering, the English Tories conspicuously failed to support the Jacobite army when it marched into England in 1745.[41] In part this was because many Tories were no more pro-Stuart than they were pro-Hanoverian, and in part it was because Charles Edward had failed to fulfil the basic condition the English Tory-Jacobite plotters had always insisted on being met before they would rise: that the French invade with a regular military force. Because both groups of Tories thus acted merely as spectators in the struggle between Whigs and Jacobites, the Tory party in England emerged intact from the '45.[42] The disaster at Culloden, though, effectively discredited the Stuart option and the section of the party associated with it. A dwindling minority of hard-core Tory Jacobites continued to talk about and plot for a Stuart restoration into the early 1750s, but, even more than in the past, it was all sound and fury signifying nothing.[43] When Charles Edward secretly visited London in 1750 the Tory Jacobites were more anxious to get him out of the city and back to the continent than they were to do anything for him.[44] After 1750, too, the party as a whole also began to find the piously Anglican, serious-minded and utterly respectable George, Prince of Wales (the future George III), much more attractive and hopeful than Charles Edward, who was fast becoming a choleric, drunken womanizer with very little in the way of attachment to any religion.[45] In effect the Tory party was finally warming to the Hanoverian dynasty, or at least its reversionary interest. They were thus set up to embrace the new monarch, who proclaimed that he 'gloried in the name of Britain', when the Prince of Wales became George III in 1760. And, ironically enough, the new king proceeded to kill the Tory party by kindness. Readmitted to court and public office by a king they genuinely liked, and with their Jacobite wing moribund if not dead, the Tories had nothing to hold them together and the party disintegrated in the early 1760s.[46]

Scotland was part of the same polity as England, and had been since 1707, yet Culloden had a much greater impact there than south of the old border. This was not reflected on the surface of Scottish politics. Since 1715 Scotland's representation at Westminster had been split between two rival Whig groups: the Squadrone, a loose coalition of aristocrats, lairds and bourgeoisie that first emerged in the pre-Union Scottish Parliament, and the Argathelians, who were the friends, clients and followers of the greatest Whig magnate in Scotland, the Duke of Argyll. Neither Whig faction was ever able completely to oust its rival from power, and their deadly hostility to each other had effectively enabled the Scottish Tories, who were virtually all Jacobites to a greater or lesser extent, to survive as the hidden kingmakers of Scottish politics. Neither the Squadrone nor the Argathelians were willing to allow more than one or two Tory candidates, and those usually in Whig clothing, to represent any of Scotland's seats, or serve as one of the sixteen representative peers returned to the Lords each election, but both Whig factions needed the Tories' votes and political influence on the electorate, and were willing to shelter their allies from legislation designed to strike at them.[47] The '45 comprehensively smashed these cosy political arrangements. As it happened, the Squadrone had managed to gain a brief ascendancy over the Argathelians in the early 1740s, so it was on their watch that many of their former political allies, the Scottish Tories, came out in rebellion. Responsibility for the initial rout of the Whig regime in Scotland was also assiduously laid at the Squadrone's door by the Argathelians. The government in London was accordingly displeased with the Squadrone, and they were soon displaced from office and power in the aftermath of the rebellion. This led, surprisingly quickly, to the disintegration of the Squadrone as an effective political force. The Argathelians duly inherited the earth, or at least 'North Britain'. They no longer even had to butter up the Tories. Those who had turned out in the rebellion were either dead or on the run; those who had stayed at home were actively trying to avoid attracting government attention, and so they either quietly and apolitically tended their own affairs or threw in their lot with the Argathelians. The '45, by discrediting the Squadrone, and the defeat at Culloden, by physically removing one section of the Tory party and driving the other into political withdrawal or submission, delivered Scotland into the hands of the House of Argyll for the next fifteen years.[48]

Ireland's politics were very different from those prevailing in the rest of the British Isles. The Irish Parliament was a dependent legislature, barred from even considering legislation that had not been submitted to, and approved by, the Privy Council in London. Landowners in Ireland enjoyed equivalent intrinsic power to that wielded by their English and Scottish counterparts, but many Irish landowners were not primarily engaged with Irish politics. Because the wealthiest among them also owned estates in England and Wales, they tended to concentrate their political energies on Westminster rather than the biannual assembly in Dublin. The Irish Parliament was also, deliberately, only representative of a very small part of the Irish population. All Catholics were prohibited from voting or any other participation in the political process, and the last loopholes in this legislation were removed in the 1720s. This meant that in practice 75 per cent of the Irish population was automatically excluded from legal political activity. Of the 25 per cent of the population who were Protestant, many were disenfranchised because of their relative poverty or the quirks of the electoral system in their area, and most lived in small communities which were easily controlled by local landowners engaged with Irish politics. The upshot of this was that the tone and trend of Irish political life was set by the rise and fall of parties and politicians at Westminster, and the electoral process was dominated by landowners and their interests.[49]

The Irish Tory party was basically killed by English and Scottish Tory involvement in the '15. It was, in any event, unlikely that the Tories would have endured, given that Irish politics always tended to move so emphatically in favour of whichever party was in the ascendant at Westminster, but any connection between a party and the possibility of a Catholic Stuart restoration was liable to have a doubly negative impact in Ireland. And so the Irish

Tory party rapidly went into terminal decline and effectively vanished from the scene by the early 1720s. Irish politics then became the exclusive preserve of various Whig factions, which sought to advance themselves into power and office by alliances with other Whig factions at Westminster. This was the 'undertaker' system, so-called because leading Irish Whig politicians would undertake to run Ireland in such a fashion that Irish affairs would not trouble political business in London, and yet provide a sizeable chunk of patronage, in the form of sinecures and pensions, that their Westminster allies could use to bolster their supporters' loyalty. In return, the undertakers and their followers gained office (with all its associated emoluments) and power in Ireland.[50] This was not entirely to Ireland's disadvantage. Keeping the kingdom off the political agenda at Westminster was probably for the best as far as the mass of ordinary Irish men and women were concerned, given the purchase that anti-Catholic gesture politics still had in England and Scotland. The Irish Parliament was also left with not much else to do with its time other than tend to Ireland's economic interests, and this it did relatively well. Compared with the catastrophic seventeenth century and the bitter strife of the late 1790s, the era from the mid-1720s to the 1740s was thus a quiet period in Irish history, during which the foundations of the economic prosperity of the later eighteenth century were laid, notwithstanding the dreadful famine of 1740–41.[51]

This was also a period when the old assumptions and verities of Irish politics began quietly to fray. Already by the 1730s a few politicians began to separate themselves from the undertaker factions in Dublin. These were the self-proclaimed 'Patriots', and undoubtedly some of them adopted this position only so they could cause trouble enough to persuade the undertakers to buy them off with offices or pensions. Others, however, were palpably sincere, and while there were never great numbers of Patriots, real and otherwise, in the Irish Parliament, they silently forced an adjustment of the tone of politics in Dublin. These men, who were of course all Protestants, consciously identified themselves with Ireland's culture and history, opposed political interference from Westminster, insisted that Ireland's best economic interests should be consulted regardless of how it affected Britain and sought to ease the legal restrictions on the Catholics.[52]

In terms of practical political impact, though, the Patriots were decidedly ineffective – until the late 1740s. The key patriotic issue was necessarily the situation of the Catholic community in Ireland. This had been, on the surface, pretty much quiescent for over fifty years after the Williamite conquest of Ireland in the 1690s, and as a consequence the fear of another Catholic uprising that cemented the Protestant community's solidarity began to decay after 1720. In particular, the fact that the Irish Catholics remained quiet during both the '15 and the '45 prompted Patriot politicians increasingly to criticize the legal discrimination the Catholics had to endure, and to argue that the Catholics were no longer a threat to Ireland's security. By the end of the decade, and in direct response to the disaster suffered by the Jacobite cause at Culloden, populist Patriot politicians such as Charles Lucas were even publicly advocating the readmission of the Catholics to public life.[53] Ironically, this rhetoric was actually or wilfully oblivious of an open secret with respect to the Catholic community: the fact that a great many, if not most, Irish Catholics were still emotionally committed to the Stuart cause. They expressed this commitment symbolically through their poetry, songs and stories, all of which were part of a vibrant oral culture which still had a central role in the cultural life of a primarily rural community. They also, though, expressed their support for the Stuart cause physically, just not (for the most part) in Ireland. Every year up to the 1740s hundreds of young Irishmen quietly slipped out of Ireland to enlist in the Irish regiments that were part of the regular French and Spanish armies. In total, tens of thousands followed this path. A major incentive to join these military formations was the promise whispered by recruiting sergeants and well understood within the Catholic community, that one day, some time soon, the Irish regiments would return, restore the exiled Stuarts, vanquish the Catholics' Protestant oppressors and restore the Catholics to their rightful position in Irish society.[54] Of course, this never happened, and the little stream of Irish recruits into the French and Spanish armies was probably diminishing by the 1740s.[55] Culloden and the defeat of the '45, therefore, simply accelerated the process. It also enhanced the credibility of members of the surviving Catholic elite who claimed that the Catholic community was no longer a standing threat to the Hanoverian dynasty and the Revolution settlement on which it rested. By the 1750s the small minority of surviving elite Catholics were cautiously beginning to sound out the possibility of seeking redress and an end to discrimination on the basis of their loyalty to the existing order, and were being increasingly taken up by the Patriot politicians.[56] In many ways, then, Culloden and the '45 indirectly helped bring on the beginning of the end of the Protestant ascendancy in Ireland.

The '45 and the Jacobite Cause

If the '45 was vastly more significant for the peoples of the British Isles than it was for the rest of Europe, it was still more important and transformative for the political and social group most directly concerned: the Jacobites. There were effectively three Jacobite communities, one each in England and

Wales, Scotland and Ireland. All were profoundly, and adversely, affected by the '45.

The most dramatically hit was, naturally enough, the Scottish Jacobites. They were obviously the mainstay of the entire rebellion, and they suffered accordingly when it was defeated. Probably more than 3,000 Scottish Jacobites were killed in the course of the fighting, the subsequent harrying of the Highlands and the executions which followed its suppression. Thousands (it is impossible to be sure of the exact number) more were wounded and/or incarcerated in various prisons (many died as a consequence of the foul conditions they were kept in) and another 1,000–2,000 were transported to the Americas. Still thousands more were obliged to move from their homes either to elsewhere in the British Isles or overseas to save themselves from harassment or retribution on the part of the authorities and their Whig partisans.[57] After the 1747 Act of Indemnity some of these were eventually able quietly to resume their former lives; probably most were not. Even when they did, they found life in the Highlands at least irrevocably changed. From 1747 to 1748 a series of measures specifically designed forever to remove the Jacobite threat in the Highlands passed at Westminster. The Highlands were disarmed, wearing Highland dress was prohibited, and the traditional legal powers of many chieftains and Highland noblemen were abolished.[58] The net impact of this series of blows on the coherence of the Jacobite community in Scotland was severe.

It did not, though, immediately kill Scottish Jacobitism among the social elite who were the directors and controllers of Scottish society in this very hierarchical age. Inspired, directed and sometimes led by these men, small-scale violent and non-violent resistance to government forces stationed in the Highlands and elsewhere in Scotland continued on into 1747.[59] There were, too, continued contacts between those Jacobites among the elite who had escaped into exile and those Jacobites who remained in Scotland, and new plans for another uprising were propounded by veterans of the '45 clear up to 1759.[60] None of them, however, came near to fruition. The only result was to give Jacobitism its last Scottish martyr when Dr Archibald Cameron, a Jacobite agent working to prepare a new rising, possibly with Prussian support, was arrested and executed in 1753.[61] Because of the distrust Charles Edward had developed of many of his senior officers during the later stages of the rebellion, and his increasing conviction that capturing England was the sole and ultimate key to victory, the new 'action' party that developed around the prince in the 1750s also did not put a high priority on either repairing the Scottish community or raising a new rebellion in Scotland.[62] The elite Jacobite Scots exiles, and by transference those still at home, accordingly became alienated and embittered. They had given their all, as far as they were concerned, and many now felt that they were receiving neither respect nor consideration within the Jacobite movement in its aftermath.[63]

Of course, this perception of the dynamics of the Jacobite movement was not fair. James Stuart and Charles Edward helped particular Scottish leaders, such as Lord George Murray and Donald Cameron of Lochiel respectively, try to remake their lives on the continent (however, see Stephen p.192, this volume, for an idea of Charles Edward's feelings about Murray following the '45), and there remained a good number of Scots, such as Ewen MacPherson of Cluny and Dr Cameron, actively engaged in plotting and planning for the next uprising.[64] Nonetheless, the focus of Jacobite activity had undoubtedly shifted away from Scotland, and at source there were practical reasons for this. Not only was the Scottish Jacobite community in disarray, it was also the most comprehensively disarmed and the most subject to official surveillance. De facto the Scots Jacobites had been at the heart of the Jacobite cause since 1707 because they were the most committed to its success. Only a Stuart restoration could fulfil their objectives of a revolution in the Kirk and the end of the Union with England they so hated. Now the Scottish Jacobites were effectively broken. A great many Jacobite sympathizers in Scotland had refused to come out during the '45; they were certain to be even more cautious in the event of another rebellion, while the activists who had made the rebellion happen were now effectively removed from the scene.[65] Even when some of these former activists returned home, Scottish Jacobitism did not revive. The main avenue home was provided by the mediation of friends and kinfolk who were absolutely uninvolved in the rebellion, many of whom were Whigs of various stripes. They, in effect, stood surety to provide their Jacobite kith and kin a way back. To have betrayed their trust by rebelling again would have been downright dishonourable, and few of the elite Scots Jacobites who returned home in this fashion were willing to incur such a stain on their honour.[66] Many of the Scottish Jacobites, and particularly the social elite among them, felt they had done enough for the Stuarts.[67] It was someone else's turn. And, as is the way of these things, submission to the prevailing order matured over time into acceptance and finally engagement. By the time of the American Revolution the most striking thing about the Scottish elite was its unquestioning loyalism.[68]

English and Welsh Jacobitism followed very much the same path. Not that the English Jacobites had turned out in any significant numbers at either the elite or lower levels of society, but they too were daunted by the outcome of the '45.[69] The wave of Jacobite rioting that swept the west Midlands in 1750 may have been planned as a precursor to a Jacobite rising there. But when it came time to buckle on their swords and rally their plebeian followers, the Jacobite gentry who were supposed to lead it predictably lacked the courage to do so.[70] As we have already seen, the English Tories' Jacobite wing was effectively discredited by the rebellion. Up to 1746 they could always plausibly argue that there was an alternative to the sterile, hopeless politics of constitutional opposition to the Whig regime; after Culloden it was increasingly hard to do so. In any event, the Scottish Jacobites were always more numerous as a proportion of the Scottish population than their English counterparts, and were generally better armed. In the Jacobite Highland clans they also had a set of ready-made military formations (though the military aspect of the clan system was in sharp decline in the eighteenth century).[71] The Anglo-Welsh Jacobite elite had never enjoyed these advantages in the more regionally fragmented, more socially polarized atmosphere of England and Wales, and the great majority of the general population was completely unarmed, which is one of the reasons the English and Welsh Jacobites were always looking for outside military intervention to achieve a Stuart restoration.[72]

For all practical purposes, as opposed to the internal political dynamics of the Jacobite movement, where English influence tended to be predominant, English and Welsh Jacobitism depended on a strong Scottish Jacobite movement to sustain its credibility.[73] Moreover, 'credibility' in this case applies not only to the impression of Jacobite strength in the British Isles held by foreign powers, but to the Anglo-Welsh Jacobites' belief in their own chances of success. If the Scots, with all their apparent advantages, could not overthrow the Whig regime, what chance did the far smaller (as a proportion of the population) Anglo-Welsh Jacobite community have? Hence by the early 1750s only a few diehards were still actively plotting an English uprising, and even if there was anything more substantive underlying their activity than was the case in previous plots – which is doubtful – they lost heart in the mid-1750s when Charles Edward contemptuously spurned their pleas for him to clean up his private life. By then the prince was a hopeless, bitter alcoholic with an all-too-public propensity for beating up his mistresses, and the remaining English and Welsh Jacobites essentially lost faith in him and ceased actively to work for the Stuart cause.[74]

Because of Ireland's complex of religious, social and political antagonisms, it ultimately became the last bastion of Jacobitism in the British Isles. For a great many Irish Catholics Jacobitism was intrinsically woven into their personal identity. Given their circumstances in Ireland and the British Isles more generally, they had nowhere else to go for political redemption. And since Irish involvement in the '45 primarily took the form of small contingents of Irish troops in French service being thrown piecemeal into the fighting in Scotland in order for the French government to show willing, despite its inability to mount a serious invasion of England, Irish Jacobite losses (in human and political terms) were, despite their heroic conduct and heavy casualties at Culloden, proportionately very much less than those of the Scots.[75]

Irish Jacobitism was, however, unusual in that unlike the other nations in the British Isles, Irish Jacobite soldiers overseas played a profoundly important role in the Irish Jacobite community. Since the 1690s Catholic Ireland had provided a steady stream of recruits for ethnically Irish regular military formations overseas. The Irish brigade in French service was still primarily composed of first- or second-generation Irish immigrants. These units thereby markedly affected the disposition of the Irish Jacobite community. Once again, it was the conduct of the social elite that was crucial. Because many elite, and dispossessed elite, Catholic Irish families with Jacobite sympathies sent their sons into honourable (and remunerative) military service in France and Spain, as a way of striking back against their oppression in Ireland and promoting the possibility of a Stuart restoration that would redeem them permanently, they effectively weakened the impact of Irish Jacobitism at home. The presence in France and Spain of these brisk young scions of the Catholic Irish elite commanding Irish units that regularly declared, and publicly displayed, their loyalty to the exiled Stuarts, and otherwise embodied the hopes and aspirations of the Irish Catholic community, naturally prompted restless and adventurous young Irishmen from humbler backgrounds to emigrate and enlist.[76] The Irish brigade and the Spanish regiments were thus composed of some of the best military material available in Ireland. The net effect was to remove precisely that component of the Irish Jacobite community that would have been at the heart of any rebellion in Ireland itself. So the very presence, and even more, the success of the Irish troops on the continent in the service of France and Spain meant that the likelihood of a Jacobite rising back home was silently diminished.

This helps explain why the most oppressed, most hopeful Jacobite community, the Irish, never again rebelled in the British Isles after 1692.[77] In one sense, by throwing in their lot with Britain's enemies, thousands of Catholic Ireland's young men were effectively in rebellion in every generation until the late eighteenth century, but because they were so successful as soldiers on the continent, this benefited the community they sprang from little if at all. Perversely, this was precisely because of what made the army of Catholic Ireland overseas so formidable and so promising for the Catholic community back home: they were regular soldiers in the French and Spanish armies. This meant that unless their employers agreed to commit them to an invasion attempt they were not about to go near the British Isles. And though this constraint was a serious problem for the Irish Jacobite community before the 1740s, the problem was greatly compounded by the failure of the '45.

In any event, France and Spain were only going to back an invasion when they considered it in their own best interests.[78] By removing the serious possibility of a Scottish rising, it made an invasion elsewhere in the British Isles centred around these Irish troops a much more chancy prospect. France and Spain accordingly became even more cautious and sceptical about the prospects of Jacobite success than they had generally been since the 1690s.[79] This meant in practice that the Irish Jacobites' hopes of an invasion by the army of Ireland overseas were likely only to be realized in unpropitious circumstances. The Irish regiments in French and Spanish service were first-line, crack troops, to be conserved and used where they could be most effective in fulfilling their employer's agenda, hence after 1746 the only time that France or Spain would consider throwing them into such a desperate venture as an invasion of the British Isles was when France and Spain were in grave danger of defeat in a wider war. Which, of course, meant they would only be committed to an invasion during a war against Britain when they were least likely to succeed, as was precisely the case with the last Jacobite-centred French invasion attempt on the British Isles in 1759. The French government agreed to back the invasion only when it was in the most terrible straits in virtually every theatre of the Seven Years' War. Consequently the Royal Navy was ready and able to thwart the attempt at the Battle of Quiberon Bay.[80] Thus despite the fact that significant elements of the Irish Catholic population may have remained secretly attached (however in-coherently) to the Stuarts until the 1790s, after 1746 the Irish Jacobite community was effectively hamstrung by its own success in creating a powerful Irish and Jacobite military force beyond the British Isles.

The '45 was truly a turning point in European and British history. In the context of the never-ending struggle for ascendancy of the European great powers, the Jacobites' successes allowed France to exit the War of the Austrian Succession on substantially better terms than might otherwise have been the case. Napoleon is alleged to have said that winning Fontenoy alone ensured the survival of the monarchy in France for another thirty years, and Fontenoy's significance lies in the fact that it allowed France's armies to roll on to further conquests in the Low Countries – something to which the '45 also made no small contribution.[81] If the emperor was correct, the '45 may well have helped postpone the French Revolution.

In the context of the British Isles as a whole, the defeat of the '45 eviscerated Scottish Jacobitism and enfeebled the English Tory party. Both languished and ultimately died as a consequence. Only Irish Jacobitism remained vital, and because of great-power politics it was unable to capitalize on its own success. It too waned and died after the Seven Years' War. The net effect was to transform the politics of the British Isles. From the 1760s onwards there was no longer a dynastic threat lurking overseas, nor a Jacobite underground plotting and dreaming at home to keep the Whig hegemony united. A new politics, of reform and radicalism, that was eventually to shatter the old Whig ascendancy, moved to the fore. Culloden, it seems, was more than just the death knell of the Jacobite cause.

Notes

Tony Pollard: Introduction

1. From the Gaelic 'Cùil Lodair'. At the time, the moor was also known as Drumossie, but the place's association with Culloden House, home of the lord president, and its estate were to give it preference when it came to giving the battle a name.

2. Thanks to their role in the American Revolution in the 1770s the Hessians have earned something of a reputation as the 'boot boys' of the British state. Washington Irving's story *The Legend of Sleepy Hollow* (1820) indicates how these troops, one of whom was the spectral headless horseman, had become bogey-men of American folklore. It is now, however, little remembered that during the '45 the commander of the Hessian contingent in Scotland, Prince Friedrich, son and heir of the Friedrich who hired the troops out to George II, was himself a Jacobite sympathizer, and was later exposed as a Catholic.

3. Tony Pollard and Neil Oliver, *Two Men in a Trench: Battlefield Archaeology, the Key to Unlocking the Past* (Michael Joseph/Penguin, 2002).

4. John Prebble, *Culloden* (Secker and Warburg, 1961), and Katherine Tomasson and Francis Buist, *Battles of the '45* (BT Batsford, 1962). The former shows the line sitting at the junction of two enclosures, one of which is presumably meant to be the Leanach enclosure, though it is rectangular, while the latter has the Jacobite right anchored on the turf dyke of the Leanach enclosure. These versions, and indeed the late nineteenth/early twentieth century map by Cameron, may have their antecedent in the map provided by Home in his 1802 *History of the Jacobite Rebellions* and on which the Jacobite right is anchored very close to the north-eastern corner of the Culwhiniac enclosures, there being no trace of the Leanach enclosure.

5. Mackay was to be in command of the government army which suffered defeat at the hands of the Jacobites under Dundee at the Battle of Killiecrankie in 1689. He was killed in 1692 at the Battle of Steenkerque.

6. The departure of James was viewed as an abdication, and as such was used for political gain; the Scottish Parliament ruled that in leaving the country he had forfeited his right to the crown.

7. One only has to look at the numerous websites devoted to tartan and clans to see the various opinions expressed. Those associated with clans and heritage may prefer to promote the long and noble history of clan-affiliated tartans, whereas those with a commercial interest may prefer a more egalitarian, 'anyone can wear a kilt' attitude.

8. James Ray was an English volunteer from Whitehaven who served in Cobham's Dragoons. He wrote of his experiences in *A Compleat History of the Rebellion from Its First Rise in 1745, to Its Total Suppression in the Glorious Battle of Culloden, in April 1746* (1754).

9. Martin Martin, *A Description of the Western Islands of Scotland, circa 1695* (Edinburgh: Birlinn, 1994).

10. Frank Adam, *The Clans, Septs and Regiments of the Scottish Highlands* (first published 1908; 8th edn, 1970, rev. Sir Thomas Innes of Learney).

11. Robert Forbes, *The Lyon in Mourning, or, A Collection of Speeches, Letters, Journals etc. Relative to the Affairs of Prince Charles Edward Stuart by the Rev. Robert Forbes, A.M. Bishop of Ross and Caithness, 1746–1775*, edited with a preface by Henry Paton (Edinburgh University Press, 1896). In earlier battles, such as Killiecrankie in 1689 and Sheriffmuir in 1715, the plaid was removed at least by some prior to going into battle so as to provide more freedom of movement. At Culloden, however, Murray ordered 'The Highlanders to be in kilts', and there are certainly no accounts to support disrobing prior to the battle.

12. Reminiscences of a visitor to Culloden published in the *Inverness Courier* on 22 January 1840 (reproduced in *Bloody Culloden*, edited by John MacDonald, *The Inverness Courier*, 1995): 'As we sat on the greensward of these battle-graves, we observed that in many places the turf had been broken up by digging; and our young guide told us that scarcely a party came there but was desirous to carry away the fragment of a bone as a relic.'

13. In the author's experience there appears to have been an increase in recent years of the appearance of cremated human bones around the base of the gravestones in the clan cemetery.

14. Allan I. Macinnes, *Clanship, Commerce and the House of Stuart, 1603–1788* (East Linton, 1996), pp. 211, 215. Also, 'The Aftermath of the '45', in Robert Woosnam-Savage, *Charles Edward Stuart and the Jacobites* (Glasgow Museums, 1995). The term 'ethnic cleansing' was also recently used by programme presenter Paul Murton to describe the brutal treatment of the Armstrong clan in the Scottish borders meted out by James V in the 1530s, in response to their 'reiving' activities (*Scotland's Clans*, BBC2, 6 October 2008).

15. Stuart Reid describes such claims as 'fashionable but silly' in the back-cover blurb for the recent reappraisal of Cumberland in *Sweet William or the Butcher: The Duke of Cumberland and the '45* by Jonathan Oates (Barnsley: Pen and Sword, 2008). Similar sentiments are expressed within the book's covers. The Agincourt claims were well reported in the British press in October 2008 and related to a conference in Agincourt at which French academics discussed the issue.

16. Although the Geneva Convention was a more recent development a number of works on the rules of war were published in the 18th century. Among the most influential was Emerich de Vattel's *The Law of Nations*: though not published until 1758 it built on earlier works such as those by Wolff and Vitoria, and among other issues related to the idea of Just War stated that although the women and children

of an opposing nation could be defined as the enemy, it was not lawful for them to play an active part and likewise it was not lawful to kill them as one would an enemy combatant (reference from Peter Silver, *Our Savage Neighbours: How Indian War Transformed Early America*. Norton: New York, 2008, p. 58). Over 3,400 Jacobites were taken prisoner in the days and weeks following Culloden. Of these, 120 were executed, forty as deserters from the government army who had gone over to the enemy. It has been suggested that about 750 prisoners died in captivity – the official figure is around eighty, with the same fate suspected of another 684 who cannot be accounted for. Many perished on the hulks transporting them to trial in London (A.W. Speck, *The Butcher: The Duke of Cumberland and the Suppression of the '45*, Welsh Academic Press, 1995). Eventually 1,287 were released, most of the remainder being transported to the colonies.

17. Oates, *Sweet William*.
18. Some of these claims of 'forcing' can of course be disregarded as attempts by captured Jacobites trying to lay the blame for participation in the rising on their superiors, but evidence for what elsewhere would be defined as tyrannical over-lordship is not wanting. Stuart Reid discusses the issue in the present volume and refers to a number of examples in *The Scottish Jacobite Army, 1745-46* (Osprey, 2006). Examples include threats issued to the MacDonalds of Bunrannoch by Alex MacDonald of Keppoch, the 15th. In the 1715 rising none other than the Earl of Mar had also reverted to menace, and Szechi quotes William Touch, who wrote that Mar sent parties to the homes of reluctant tenants, 'who did sett fire to their houses, and corn yards'. Szechi also recounts the story of Allan MacDonald, Captain of Clanranald, who, according to clan tradition, was shot in the back by his own men on the field at Sheriffmuir ('fragged', in modern parlance) in revenge for being dragged into the rising against their will. Daniel Szechi, *1715: The Great Jacobite Rebellion* (Yale University Press, 2006), pp. 124–5.
19. Eric Roberts, *The Highland Clearances: People, Landlords and Rural Turmoil* (Edinburgh: Birlinn, 2000).
20. Hawley in a letter to the Duke of Richmond, quoted in Speck, *Butcher*, p. 166.
21. Many of these men were Scots, and some of them Highlanders. Cumberland had seen fit to limit the latter to subservient roles at Culloden, keeping most of them back with the baggage, but he felt no such compunction in having them take a lead role in the punitive operations which followed.
22. These or similar sentiments are commonly expressed, though often in not such polite terms, in the readers' comments sections of the websites of newspapers such as the *Herald* and the *Scotsman* whenever they run a Culloden-related story, which is not infrequently.
23. Robert Burns, 'Such a Parcel of Rogues in a Nation' (1791).
24. Christopher A. Whatley, *The Scots and the Union* (Edinburgh University Press, 2006).

25. The expression of quite virulent anti-English sentiment is not unusual in the readers' comments referred to in note 22, some of it coming from foreign nationals with Scottish ancestry.

26. This process was also reflected in the titles of military units: for instance the Scots Fusiliers, renamed as such in 1685 after being originally raised in 1678 as the Earl of Mar's Regiment of Foot, were renamed as the North British Fusiliers in 1707, the year of Union.

Chapter 1. Christopher Duffy: The '45 Campaign

1. Marquess of Tullibardine, Sir John MacDonald, Aeneas MacDonald, Colonel Strickland, Sir Thomas Sheridan, Captain O'Sullivan and George Kelly.

2. Patrick Crichton, *The Woodhouselee Ms* (London, 1907), p. 38.

3. Alexander Duncan, 'Journal of the Rev. Alexander Duncan', 1745, private collection.

4. Lieutenant General Henry Hawley, Hawley to the Duke of Cumberland, 15 January 1746, Cumberland Papers 9/81, Royal Archives, Windsor Castle. Quoted by gracious permission of HM the Queen.

5. *Memoirs of Sir Robert Strange . . . and of his Brother-in-Law Andrew Lumisden*, 2 vols (London 1855), vol. 1, p. 55.

Chapter 2. Stuart Reid: The Jacobite Army at Culloden

1. It is difficult to find any consistency in the maps, both ancient and modern, purporting to show the Jacobite deployment, and the question is certainly hindered by use of Lord Elcho's map based on the deployments of the day before. The dispositions as discussed here are primarily based on Thomas Sandby's maps and in particular the one completed at Inverness on 23 April 1746, and on the equally detailed map by the Jacobite engineer John Finlayson (see Woosnam-Savage, this volume, for detailed discussion of these).

2. In calculating the area occupied by a body of troops it is necessary to allow 1m of frontage per man, subdivided by the number of men in the ranks. Thus 200 men drawn up in four ranks will occupy a frontage of 50m. The late John Prebble quoted a Napoleonic-era drill-book to allow just 22in – just over half a metre – per man, but mid-eighteenth-century drill-books were more generous, and in any case (a) what holds good on a gravel parade ground does not work too well on a rough moorland, and (b) Prebble's figure makes no allowance for the greater space required to load and fire muskets or for the intervals within units between platoons. A similar empirical calculation can be made for cavalry units, allowing 2m for each horseman in the front rank.

3. This is the modern title used in preference to the contemporary 'Royal Ecossais'.

4. Sandby credits this unit as being just fifty strong, which corresponds with the last muster as a troop of cavalry on 16 March 1746 (State Papers Domestic, 82–142), but since that time Kilmarnock had absorbed Crichton of Auchengoul's

little corps and acquired some fresh recruits. Both Elcho and Johnstone state it was 200–300 strong at Culloden.

5. W.B. Blaikie, *Origins of the Forty-Five* (Scottish History Society, 1916), p. 178.

6. A. Tayler and H. Tayler, *1745 and After* (London, 1938), pp. 160–1.

7. Blaikie, *Origins of the Forty-Five*, p. 214. Some modern sources, relying on O'Sullivan's statement that he instructed Captain Shea of Fitzjames's Horse to get the prince off the field at the end, assume the escort was found by that regiment. However, John Daniel, of Balmerino's, states unequivocally that his troop formed the escort.

8. 'Orderly Book of Lord Ogilvy's Regiment', special number of *Journal of the Society of Army Historical Research*, 2 (1923), p. 13.

9. A. Tayler and H. Tayler, *Jacobites of Aberdeenshire and Banffshire in the Forty-Five* (1928), p. 129.

10. Quoted in Katherine Tomasson and Francis Buist, *Battles of the '45* (1967), p. 107.

11. Tayler and Tayler, *1745 and After*, pp. 60–61.

12. 'Memoirs of the Rebellion in Aberdeen and Banff', in Blaikie, *Origins of the '45*, p. 130.

13. Sir Bruce Gordon Seton and Jean Arnot, *Prisoners of the '45* (Scottish History Society, 1928–9), vol. 1, pp. 270–71.

14. Rev. William Gordon of Alvie, vol. 1.

15. State Papers Domestic, pp. 83–391.

16. Seton and Arnot, *Prisoners of the '45*, vol. 1.

17. State Papers Domestic, pp. 94–241.

18. I.G. Brown and H. Cheape, *Witness to Rebellion* (East Linton, 1996), p. 21.

19. Seton and Arnot, *Prisoners of the '45*, vol. 1, section on Atholl Brigade.

20. Confusingly there were two Dukes of Atholl above ground at the same time. Duke William was an attainted Jacobite who returned from exile with the prince and is better known as the Marquis of Tullibardine. His younger brother, Duke John, was a supporter of the government but prudently took himself off to Bath until all was over. Both were older brothers of Lord George Murray.

21. Seton and Arnot, *Prisoners of the '45*, vol. 1, p. 305.

22. Ibid., p. 306.

23. Seton and Arnot, *Prisoners of the '45*, vol. 1, section on Atholl Brigade.

24. Blaikie, *Origins of the Forty-Five*, p. 122.

25. Ibid., pp. 116, 119.

26. 'Memoirs of the Rebellion in Aberdeen and Banff', p. 131.

27. Wm. Fraser, *Chiefs of Grant* (1883), vol. 2, p. 56. The report, by the Laird of Grant's factor, named two of their followers but dismissed the rest as 'only servants to some of the tenants'.

28. State Papers Domestic, 89/272.

29. Tayler and Tayler, *Jacobites*, p. 31.

30. 'Memoirs of the Rebellion in Aberdeen and Banff', p. 129.

31. Tayler and Tayler, *Jacobites*, pp. 31–2.
32. Lord Rosebery and W. Mcleod, *List of Persons concerned in the Present Rebellion* (Scottish History Society, 1890).
33. Ibid.
34. Seton and Arnot, *Prisoners of the '45*, vol. 1, pp. 274–5.
35. Ibid., vol. 1.
36. Blaikie, *Origins of the Forty-Five*, p. 178.
37. Patrick Crichton, *The Woodhouselee Ms*, ed. Archibald Francis Steuart (London, 1907), p. 25.
38. Seton and Arnot, *Prisoners of the '45*, vol. 1, pp. 288–90.
39. 'Orderly Book of Lord Ogilvy's Regiment', p. 2.
40. Seton and Arnot, *Prisoners of the '45*, vol. 1, p. 290.
41. 'Orderly Book of Lord Ogilvy's Regiment', p. 13.
42. Quoted in Tomasson and Buist, *Battles of the '45*, pp. 105–06.
43. James Johnstone, *A Memoir of the Forty-Five* (London, 1958), pp. 82–3.
44. Tayler and Tayler, *1745 and After*, pp. 150–53.
45. Blaikie, *Origins of the Forty-Five*, p. 202.
46. James Allardyce (ed.), *Historical Papers Relating to the Jacobite Period* (Aberdeen, 1895), vol. 2, pp. 418–24.
47. 'Orderly Book of Lord Ogilvy's Regiment', p. 7.
48. Rosebery and W. Mcleod, *List of Persons*, p. 192.
49. Seton and Arnot, *Prisoners of the '45*, vol. 1.

Chapter 3. Stuart Reid: The British Army at Culloden

1. W.B. Blaikie, *Origins of the Forty-Five* (Scottish History Society, 1916), p. 432.
2. Or so it may be inferred from the fact that the 1 September return noted that he was recovering from his wounds in Edinburgh.
3. Maps depicting the regiment rather improbably deployed forward of and *en potence* (at right angles) to Barrell's are perpetuating an error in John Home's 1802 *History of the Rebellion*.
4. The regiment's colonel was Major General Edward Wolfe, the father of James Wolfe, the future conqueror of Quebec – who was present as an officer on General Hawley's staff.
5. He became the 5th Duke of Argyll in 1770 and died a field marshal in 1806.
6. The figure of 430 men looks about right and if so should be devalued by about 10 per cent in line with the other regiments to get the numbers actually present. It is just possible, however, that the figure does not include the regular companies for some reason, but may include Argyle Militia companies not present, for example serving in Perthshire. On balance, however, it is probably best to accept it at face value.
7. The National Archives, WO 10, 28–34.
8. WO 120.
9. 18 Geo II c12.

10. A.J. Guy, *Colonel Samuel Bagshawe and the Army of George II* (London, 1985), p. 210. Colliers, chimney sweeps and sailors were to be avoided not because of any assumed character defects but rather because they were considered particularly susceptible to tuberculosis and other respiratory diseases.
11. WO 4/53, 25 January 1757.
12. WO 120.
13. Letter attached as codicil to his will, July 1759, Register of Madras Mayoral Court, vol. 61, p. 7.
14. *The Report of the Proceedings and Opinion of the Board of Officers on the Examination into the Conduct, Behaviour and Proceedings of Lieutenant General Sir John Cope, Col. Peregrine Lascelles, and Brig. Gen. Thomas Fowke from the time of the Breaking Out of the Rebellion in North Britain in the Year 1745 til the Action at Prestonpans*, p. 155.
15. Quoted in Katherine Tomasson and Francis Buist, *Battles of the '45* (1967), pp. 105–06.
16. *Newcastle Journal*.
17. Strictly speaking, the Argyll and Sutherland Highlanders (5RRS) might claim to be descended from the Argyle Militia, but if so then the Highlanders (4RRS) could equally well claim descent from the Jacobite army, much as some US National Guard units are affiliated to regiments of the Confederate Army. The story is indeed told of a now forgotten proposal to amalgamate the Black Watch and the Gordons being hastily abandoned when it was pointed out to the War Office that the two regiments hated each other as they had fought on opposing sides at Culloden.

Chapter 4. David Blackmore: Cavalry in the '45

1. The research for this paper was supported by the A.V.B. Norman Research Trust.
2. *The Report of the Proceedings and Opinions of the Board of General Officers on Their Examination into the Conduct, Behaviour and Proceedings of Lieutenant General Sir John Cope, Knight of the Bath, Colonel Peregrine Lascelles and Brigadier General Thomas Fowke* (London, 1749), p. 6.
3. J.A. Houlding, *Fit for Service* (Oxford, 1981), pp. 292–3.
4. *Report of the Proceedings*, p. 5.
5. C.R.B. Barrett, *History of the XIII Hussars* (Edinburgh and London, 1911), p. 33; Colonel Henry Blackburne Hamilton, *Historical record of the 14th (King's) Hussars* (London, 1901), p. 12.
6. Barrett, *History*, p. 32; Houlding, *Fit for Service*, pp. 415–22.
7. S. Reid, *1745: A Military History* (Staplehurst, 1996), p. 32.
8. Barrett, *History*, p. 35.
9. Anonymous, *The History of the Rebellion in 1745 and 1746* (n.p., n.d.), p. 54.
10. *Report of the Proceedings*, p. 71.
11. Ibid., p. 75.

12. Anon., *History of the Rebellion*, pp. 74–5.
13. *The Gentleman's Magazine*, vol. 15, October 1745, p. 518.
14. F.J. McLynn, *The Jacobite Army in England, 1745* (Edinburgh, 1998), pp. 180–86.
15. *The History of the Rebellion in 1745 and 1746, Extracted from the Scots Magazine* (Aberdeen, 1755), p. 126.
16. Reid, *1745*, pp. 99–100.
17. A. Tayler and H. Tayler, *1745 and After* (London, 1938), p. 118.
18. Lt. H.N. Edwards, 'The Battle of Falkirk,' *Journal of Army Historical Research*, vol. 4 (1925), pp. 129–30.
19. James de Johnstone, *A Memoir of the Forty-Five* (London, 1958), p. 88.
20. E. Dunbar Dunbar, *Social Life in Former Days* (Edinburgh, 1865), p. 352.
21. G.B. Bailey, *Falkirk or Paradise* (Edinburgh, 1996), p. 118.
22. John Marchant, *The History of the Present Rebellion* (London, 1746), p. 314.
23. *Report on the Manuscripts of the Late Reginald Rawdon Hastings of the Manor House, Ashby De La Zouch*, vol. 3, *1724–1817*, HMC (1934), p. 54.
24. Rev. R. Forbes, *The Lyon in Mourning* (1896), vol. 1, p. 381.
25. Capt. G.T. Williams, *The Historical Records of the Eleventh Hussars* (London, 1908), p. 37.
26. Bailey, *Falkirk or Paradise*, p. 118.
27. Andrew Henderson, *The History of the Rebellion* (London, 1753), p. 268.
28. *Report of the Proceedings*, p. 39.
29. Major General Humphrey Bland, *A Treatise of Military Discipline*, 7th edn (London, 1753), pp. 227ff.
30. *Report of the Proceedings*, p. 39.
31. Edwards, 'Battle of Falkirk', p. 128.
32. Bland, *Treatise*, pp. 232–3.
33. David Lord Elcho, *A Short Account of the Affairs of Scotland in the Years 1744, 1745, 1746 by David Lord Elcho* (Edinburgh, 1907), p. 253.
34. Tayler and Tayler, *1745 and After*, p. 81.
35. James Ray, *A Compleat History of the Rebellion* (Bristol, 1750), p. 127.
36. Elcho, *Short Account*, pp. 395–8.
37. Ibid., p. 393.
38. Ibid., p. 398.
39. Tayler and Tayler, *1745 and After*, p. 146.
40. Ibid., pp. 90ff.
41. Service Historique de l'Armée de Terre, A1 3153, Campagne d'Ecosse, quoted in C. Duffy, *The '45* (London, 2004), p. 499.
42. Tayler and Tayler, *1745 and After*, p. 117.
43. Ibid., p. 146.
44. Major A. McKenzie Annand, 'Lord Pitsligo's Horse in the Army of Prince Charles Edward, 1745–6', *Journal of the Society for Army Historical Research*, vol. 60 (1982), p. 232.

45. Major A. McKenzie Annand, 'Lord Strathallan's Horse, or the Perthshire Squadron in the Army of Prince Charles Edward', *Journal of the Society for Army Historical Research*, vol. 57 (1979), p. 230.
46. W.B. Blaikie, *Origins of the Forty-Five* (Edinburgh, 1975), p. 209.
47. Service Historique, quoted in Duffy, *The '45*, p. 499.
48. Blaikie, *Origins of the Forty-Five*, p. 210.
49. Tayler and Tayler, *1745 and After*, p. 153.
50. Ray, *Compleat History*, p. 330.
51. Williams, *Historical Records*, p. 43.
52. Reid, *1745*, p. 168.
53. Ibid., p. 149.
54. Ray, *Compleat History*, p. 339.
55. Reid, *1745*, p. 151.
56. R. Reilly, *The Rest to Fortune: The Life of Major-General James Wolfe* (London, 1960), p. 52.
57. East Sussex Record Office, ASH 3503.
58. Military Orders by His Royal Highness the Duke of Cumberland, Nottingham University, Hallward Library, Galway Collection, Ga 12835.
59. Forbes, *Lyon in Mourning*, vol. 1, p. 381.
60. Military Orders.

Chapter 5. Stuart Reid: The Battle of Culloden

1. Ker of Graden, in R. Chambers, *Jacobite Memoirs of the Rebellion of 1745* (Edinburgh, 1834), pp. 138–9.
2. O'Sullivan, in A. Tayler and H. Tayler, *1745 and After* (London, 1938), p. 163.
3. W.B. Blaikie, *Itinerary of Prince Charles Edward Stuart*, pp. 120–21.
4. O'Sullivan, in Tayler and Tayler, *1745 and After*, pp. 160–61. It is hard to avoid the impression he may have been deliberately needling Murray at this point.
5. Lieutenant Colonel William Belford, the man normally credited with commanding Cumberland's gunners, actually held a staff appointment as Commander Royal Artillery (CRA), and as such was primarily responsible for the administration of the artillery train and the army's ammunition columns, rather than the immediate tactical control of the guns.
6. This originates in an error in John Home's *History of the Rebellion* published in 1802 and has been blindly perpetrated ever since.
7. O'Sullivan, in Tayler and Tayler, *1745 and After*.
8. This is confirmed by both Sandby's and Finlayson's contemporary plans, as well as a rather rougher sketch drawn by Lieutenant Colonel Whitefoord.
9. O'Sullivan, in Tayler and Tayler, *1745 and After*, p. 163.
10. Rev. R. Forbes, *The Lyon in Mourning*, pp. 86–7.
11. Ker of Graden, p. 140.
12. Sandby, it is true, certainly appears to depict the dragoons partly facing a cluster of buildings obviously intended to represent Culchunaig, but he seems to suggest

on both his maps and an ink wash sketch he produced of the battle that the majority of them were positioned to the west of the steading.

13. Campbell's account can be found, with those of other officers serving with the Argyles, in the National Library of Scotland, NLS 3733–5.

14. David Wemyss, Lord Elcho, *A Short Account of the Affairs of Scotland in the Years 1744, 1745, 1746*, ed. Hon. Evan Charteris (Edinburgh, 1907).

15. James Maxwell of Kirkconnell, *Narrative of Charles Prince of Wales' Expedition to Scotland in the Year 1745* (Maitland Club, 1841), p. 151. Kirkconnell's account is particularly valuable as he was the second in command of Elcho's Life Guards and took part in the defensive action now unfolding – it will be noted that he explicitly declares Hawley was now in the rear of the Jacobite army, rather than hanging on its flank.

16. Quoted in J. Black, *Culloden and the '45* (Stroud, 1990), p. 170.

17. It is perhaps worth emphasizing the point that the cannon used by both sides at Culloden were very much smaller and less effective than the 9-pounders and 12-pounders routinely used by armies in the Napoleonic Wars – and indeed in the American Civil War.

18. Ker of Graden, in Chambers, *Jacobite Memoirs*, p. 142; 'As the right was further advanced than the left, Colonel Ker went to the left, and ordered the Duke of Perth, who commanded there, to begin the attack, and rode along the line till he came to the right, where Lord George Murray was, who attacked at the head of the Atholl men.'

19. Michael Hughes, in K. Tomasson and F. Buist, *Battles of the '45* (London, 1976), p. 181.

20. *Newcastle Journal*, 1746.

21. Hughes, in Tomasson and Buist, *Battles of the '45*, p. 181.

22. Cumberland to Newcastle, Account of the Battle of Culloden, 18 April 1746, TNA, PRO, SP 54/30/21A.

23. See the letter quoted in Chapter 3 (pp. 83–4).

24. Murray, letter of 16 May, in George Charles, *History of the Transactions in Scotland in the Years, 1745-46* (Leith, 1817), p. 317.

25. Beckles Willson, *Life and Letters of James Wolfe* (London, 1909), pp. 62–5.

26. J. O'Callaghan, *History of the Irish Brigades in the Service of France* (Glasgow, 1870), p. 450. NB: O'Callaghan refers to him as Thomas Ashe Lee, but the Commission Register (WO 25) clearly gives his Christian name as James.

27. O'Callaghan, *History of the Irish Brigades*.

28. James Johnstone, *Memoirs of the Rebellion in Scotland* (1970), p. 122.

29. Cumberland to Newcastle, Account of the Battle of Culloden, 18 April 1746, PRO, SP 54/30/21A.

30. O'Sullivan, in Tayler and Tayler, *1745 and After*, pp. 163–4.

31. *Newcastle Journal*.

32. Murray, Letter of 16 May, p. 317.

33. Donald Campbell of Airds, letter to Archibald Campbell of Stonefield, National Library of Scotland (NLS), MS 3735.
34. Ibid.
35. Maxwell of Kirkconnell, *Narrative*, p. 151.
36. Willson, *Life and Letters*, p. 63.
37. 'A True Account of Mr John Daniel's Progress with Prince Charles', in Walter B. Blaikie, ed., *Origins of the Forty-Five, and Other Papers Relating to That Rising* (Edinburgh: Scottish History Society, 1916), p. 215.
38. O'Sullivan, in Tayler and Tayler, *1745 and After*, pp. 163–4.
39. Ibid.
40. Ibid.
41. Cumberland to Newcastle, Account of the Battle of Culloden, 18 April 1746, PRO, SP 54/30/21A.
42. Willson, *Life and Letters*.
43. The Chelsea Hospital Registers (TNA, WO 120) record the names and other details of all the wounded who survived long enough to appear before a board in 1748. The mortality rate among the wounded was clearly very high, and it is notable, for instance, that all six Royal Artillery casualties initially returned as wounded died within a relatively short time.
44. *Newcastle Journal*, 1746.

Chapter 6. Tony Pollard: Capturing the Moment

1. Tony Pollard and Neil Oliver, *Two Men in a Trench: Battlefield Archaeology, the Key to Unlocking the Past* (Michael Joseph/Penguin, 2002).
2. These footpaths have been realigned as part of the recent re-display of the site and new footpaths have also been created, perhaps most notably passing through the Leanach enclosure.
3. Robert Forbes, *The Lyon in Mourning*, ed. Henry Paton (Edinburgh University Press for the Scottish History Society, 1895–6), p. 12.
4. It was at first thought that this indicated the enclosure was in the wrong place, but there now seems little doubt, following a second map-based exercise using the contemporary maps and verification on the ground of the position of the neighbouring stone enclosure.
5. This area of the moor was outfield at the time of the battle, and would have been grazed by cattle. The vegetation would therefore have been nowhere near as dense as it is today. The gorse and other vegetation largely reflects the colonization of the acid soils created by the long-time presence of coniferous trees.
6. Iain Cameron Taylor, *Culloden: A Guidebook to the Battlefield with the Story of the Battle, the Events Leading to It and the Aftermath* (Inverness: NTS, 1965), p. 10.
7. Kenneth Aitchison, 'Culloden Dykes: Documentary Research', unpublished report for the National Trust for Scotland, December 1994.
8. The fact that the stone Culwhiniac enclosures kink around the earth and stone

Leanach enclosure indicates that they were built later – which again suggests that the latter was old and perhaps partially dilapidated in 1746.

9. Stuart Reid, *Like Hungry Wolves: Culloden Moor, 16 April 1746* (London: Windrow and Greene, 1994), p. 87.

10. A.P.K. Wright, *The Culloden Battlefield Memorial Project: Heritage Impact Assessment* (Forres, 2004).

11. Duncan Forbes, 'Purchasers' catalogue of the valuable contents of Culloden House which were sold by auction, by Messrs A Fraser and Co, Inverness, on 21 July 1897, and following days', printed in the *Northern Chronicle*, 1897.

12. Ibid.

13. Olivia Lelong, personal communication.

14. Reid, *Like Hungry Wolves*, p. 100.

15. Further evidence for the use of charms or amulets by soldiers came in the form of a silver shilling of William III found in the metal detector survey of the visitor-centre footprint. The obverse showed the heavily worn head of the king but the reverse had been worn entirely flat. There seems little doubt that this was a 'king's shilling' presented to a soldier on recruitment and retained as a lucky piece thereafter – good fortune to be brought on through the act of rubbing. A very similar piece was recovered from the 1715 battlefield of Sheriffmuir.

16. For research into musket ball morphology in the USA, see Daniel M. Sivilich, 'What the Musket Ball Can Tell: Monmouth Battlefield State Park, New Jersey', in *Fields of Conflict: Battlefield Archaeology from the Roman Empire to the Korean War* (Westport, CT: Praeger Security International), pp. 84–102.

17. Caution must be exercised in the application of this distinction, as there is some quite considerable, if small-scale, variation in the size and weight of musket balls across the board – which should not be unexpected in the pre-industrial production of ammunition. Before firm conclusions can be drawn it will be very useful to assess assemblages of ammunition known to have originated from each of the two weapon types – preferably from curated unused stocks rather than archaeologically recovered examples.

18. Reid, *Like Hungry Wolves*, p. 58.

19. Martin Kelvin, *The Scottish Pistol: Its History, Design and Manufacture* (London: Cygnus Arts, 1996).

20. Pollard and Oliver, *Two Men in a Trench*.

21. Reid, *Like Hungry Wolves*, p. 99.

22. Erik Goldstein, *The Socket Bayonet in the British Army, 1687–1783* (Rhode Island: Andrew Mowbray, 2000), p. 84.

23. Christopher Duffy, *The '45* (Cassell, 2003), pp. 206–07.

24. The location of the coin coincides with a geophysical anomaly which would certainly merit investigation in the search for the government graves.

25. N. Holmes, *Scottish Coins: A History of Small Change in Scotland* (Edinburgh: National Museum of Scotland Publishing, 1998).

26. Reid, *Like Hungry Wolves*, p. 98.

27. Ibid., p. 100.

28. Carried out as part of *Two Men in a Trench* and more recently as part of student research within the Centre for Battlefield Archaeology, University of Glasgow.

29. Recovered by Jon Pettet during his metal detector survey of the battlefield.

30. Tony Pollard, *Culloden Battlefield: Report on the Archaeological Investigation*, GUARD Report 1981 (University of Glasgow, 2006).

31. Reid, *Like Hungry Wolves*, p. 109. Samuel Boyse describes Lord Bury going forward to inspect what looked like a 'grand battery' in his memoir *An Impartial History of the Late Rebellion in 1745* (Dublin, 1748), p. 148.

32. Reid, *Like Hungry Wolves*, p. 97.

33. Colin Haslegrove, 'Inference from Ploughsoil Artefact Samples', in Colin Haslegrove, Martin Millett and Ian Smith, eds, *Archaeology from the Ploughsoil* (Dept of Archaeology and Prehistory, University of Sheffield, 1985).

34. Reid, *Like Hungry Wolves*, p. 109.

35. E.g. op. cit., p. 111.

36. Ibid., p. 109.

37. Lumsden, quoted in Walter B. Blaikie, ed., *Origins of the Forty-Five, and Other Papers Relating to That Rising* (Edinburgh: Scottish History Society, 1916).

38. 'A Particular Account of the Battle of Culloden April 16, 1746', in *A Letter from an Officer of the Highland Army to His Friend at London* (London, 1746).

39. Linn, quoted in W.H. Anderson, 'The Battle of Culloden, 1746, as Described in a Letter from a Soldier of the Royal Army', *Journal of the Society of Army Historical Research*, 1 (1921).

40. W.L. Ruffell, *The Coehorn Mortar*, 1999, http://riv.co.nz/rnza/hist/mortar/mort2.htm.

Chapter 7. Robert Woosnam-Savage: 'To Gather an Image Whole'

1. Peter Anderson, *Culloden: The Story of the Battle* (Stirling: Eneas Mackay, 1920), pp. 173–5; Donald G. Moir, ed., *The Early Maps of Scotland to 1850* (Edinburgh: Royal Scottish Geographical Society, 1983), vol. 2, pp. 145–8; K.R. Aitchison, 'Culloden Dykes: Documentary Research', unpublished report for the National Trust for Scotland, December 1994, pp. 11–15.

2. Some maps are discussed in various books or anthologies, such as the map, probably by Finlayson, which not only has been attributed to 'an unknown soldier', but is also misdated to 1745 in one book (Lez Smart, *Maps That Made History: The Influential, the Eccentric and the Sublime*, Richmond: The National Archives, 2004, p. 123). It appears again, this time correctly attributed, in a short chapter entitled 'The Last Battle: Culloden 1746' in Peter Barber, ed., *The Map Book* (London: Weidenfeld & Nicolson, 2005), pp. 200–1. Other short accounts of some of the maps include, for instance, the short summary of three 'Contemporary maps' in Walter Biggie Blaikie, *Itinerary of Prince Charles Edward Stuart* (Edinburgh: Scottish History Society, 1897), pp. 103–8; a discussion in Iain Cameron Taylor, *On Telling the Culloden Story* (Stirling: A. Learmonth,

1969), pp. 4–9; a very short note on, again, three maps in Iain Cameron Taylor, *Culloden*, 5th rev. edn (Edinburgh: National Trust for Scotland, 1972), pp. 30–31; and an anonymous article, 'This Day in History: The Battle of Culloden, 16th April 1746 and the Jacobite Rebellions', *Map Forum*, no. 5 (spring 2005), pp. 36–40. A study was commissioned by the National Trust for Scotland to determine the position of the stone walls and other structures on the landscape and this used a number of contemporary and later maps. The unpublished report includes a list of maps 'more extensive than any published' (Aitchison, 'Culloden Dykes', p. 1), and, although perhaps somewhat limited (the author did not manage to examine all the maps and was looking at them from a landscape perspective only), is the most useful work on the subject.

3. Many other, mostly anonymous, maps, plans and orders of march and battle drawn up by Board of Ordnance staff exist in most of the major collections of manuscripts and maps in the United Kingdom, such as those in the Royal Archives, Windsor Castle (Cumberland Collection 730017, 730018 and 730019, for instance). Although contemporary, and containing useful information, many are merely diagrammatic. They also suffer from the fact many are undateable, as pieces were copied as part of the training of BO draughtsmen, so many are later copies of copies. Two plans by Colonel Charles Whitefoord (Add. MS 36592) and the coloured plan of the battle by John Elphinstone (K.Top.XLVIII.22) are both in the British Library, London, and should be noted. A slightly later plan (of about 1750) appears in Major General Richard Bendyshe's manuscript note-book (C.T. Atkinson, 'Culloden', *Journal of the Society for Army Historical Research*, vol. 35, 1957, pp. 18–22). Space sadly precludes discussion of all these maps.

4. The first widely available published maps and plans appeared within only three or four weeks of the battle happening: *A Plan of the Disposition of both Army's in the ever memorable battle and defeat of the rebels by His RH the Duke of Cumberland. Ap 16 1746 near Collodon House* was published by J. Dubois on 7 May 1746 (National Map Library, National Library of Scotland, Edinburgh, EMS. s.157, 157a) and 'The Order of Battle on Culloden Moor' appeared in the *Scots Magazine*, vol. 8, May 1746, p. 217. The latter is worth noting on these grounds alone but is of limited value. It is all the more surprising therefore to find it used as the one contemporary 'map' of the battle in a recent book on the rebellion: Michael Hook and Walter Ross, *The '45: The Last Jacobite Rebellion* (Edinburgh, HMSO, 1995), p. 106. It was called 'quite untrustworthy' as long ago as 1897 (Blaikie, *Itinerary*, p. 97). Numerous copies of this magazine exist, such as that in the National Library of Scotland, Edinburgh (Nf.Sp.Ser.1).

5. Tony Pollard and Neil Oliver, *Two Men in a Trench* (London: Michael Joseph, 2002), p. 276.

6. From *Reading in Wartime* in *The Collected Poems of Edwin Muir*, 1960. Used with permission of Faber & Faber Ltd. The same quote was also used in the title of

the book *The '45: To Gather an Image Whole*, ed. Lesley Scott-Moncrieff (Edinburgh: The Mercat Press, 1988).

7. Anderson, *Culloden*, p. 48, for example.

8. Katherine Tomasson and Francis Buist, *Battles of the '45* (London: Batsford, 1962), p. 169; John Prebble, *Culloden* (Harmondsworth: Penguin, 1976), p. 63. The map in the latter has been reproduced in comparatively recent books on the subject (Hook and Ross, *The '45*, p. 100).

9. Stuart Reid, *Like Hungry Wolves: Culloden Moor, 16 April 1746* (London: Windrow & Greene, 1994), p. 101.

10. John Home, *The History of the Rebellion in the Year 1745* (London: Cadell and Davies, 1802), p. 227.

11. Cumberland Collection, 730018, Royal Archives, Windsor Castle.

12. Stuart Reid, *1745: A Military History of the Last Jacobite Rising* (Staplehurst: Spellmount, 1996), pp. 163–4.

13. There are in fact four sketch maps associated with Yorke in the British Library, London. One (BL, Add. MS 35354, f.222) is a rough sketch by Yorke drawn on the field of battle and sent to his father, the Earl of Hardwicke, on 18 April 1746. The second is in Yorke's Orderly Book, 1746 (BL, Add. MS 36257, f.75) and is an undated and unfinished rough sketch. The Hardwicke Papers has a map (BL, Add. MS 35889, f.107) accompanying a copy of a letter to the Earl of Hardwicke, again written on 18 April 1746. It bears an 'X' but this is not explained. The final map in the Hardwicke Papers (BL, Add. MS 35889, f.111–12) is dated 22 April 1746.This is from Lord Hardwicke to the King 'with Acctr. Plans of the Action at Culloden received from Col. Yorke'. This is a pen and ink copy of Add. MS 35354, f.222, mentioned above with an explanation.

14. Hardwicke Papers: Yorke's Orderly Book, 1746 (BL, Add. MS 36257, f.100). I am grateful to Carolyn Anderson for this reference.

15. Chevalier de Johnstone, *A Memoir of the 'Forty-Five*, ed. Brian Rawson, 2nd rev. edn (London: Folio Society, 1970), p. 122.

16. Tomasson and Buist, *Battles of the '45*, p. 156; Alastair Tayler and Henrietta Tayler, eds, *1745 and After* (London: Thomas Nelson, 1938), p. 162.

17. The Royal Archives, Windsor Castle (Cumberland Papers, Main/14/4, 1746, 16 April – 13 May). This map is mentioned only infrequently, if at all, and then only as 'Hist. MSS. Comm. Rep. ii, 27' (Anderson, *Culloden*, p. 173, and Aitchison, 'Culloden Dykes', p. 15). The possible importance of this map has only been recognized once before: Christopher Duffy, *The '45: Bonnie Prince Charlie and the Untold Story of the Jacobite Rising* (London: Cassell, 2003), pp. 514, 517.

18. Duffy, *The '45*, p. 514.

19. Reid, *Like Hungry Wolves*, p. 88; Tayler and Tayler, *1745 and After*, p. 163.

20. Cathcart MSS, Acc. 12686/50, National Library of Scotland, Edinburgh.

21. Yolande Hodson, 'William Roy and the Military Survey of Scotland', in William Roy, *The Great Map: The Military Survey of Scotland, 1747–55* (Edinburgh: Birlinn, 2007), p. 10 and n. 11.

22. Adolph Paul Oppé, *The Drawings of Paul and Thomas Sandby in the Collection of His Majesty the King at Windsor Castle* (Oxford: Phaidon, 1947), p. 150; Royal Collection, Print Room, Windsor Castle, no. 17177.

23. Oppé, *Drawings*, p. 46.

24. What has not yet been satisfactorily explained is the relationship between the Sandby map and a similar one in the Cumberland Collection (Windsor Castle, no. 730026) made by a 'Dug[ald]. Campbell', one of 'the Engineers with the Duke' at Culloden, who may have been an eyewitness (Whitworth Porter, *History of the Corps of Royal Engineers*, London: Longman, Green, 1889, p. 161). A very similar map (Cumberland Collection, Windsor Castle, no. 730025, reproduced in Evan Charteris, *William Augustus, the Duke of Cumberland: His Early Life and Times (1721–1748)*, London: Edward Arnold, 1913, opposite p. 266), probably by another engineer (Shultz?), has seemingly been incorrectly discussed as a sketch by Sandby (Stuart Reid, *Culloden, 1746: Battlefield Guide*, Barnsley: Pen & Sword, 2005, p. 72). Another printed version of Campbell's map is to be found in the Royal Library, Windsor Castle (no. 730027). I am grateful to Carolyn Anderson for this reference. The complex relationship between the Culloden maps of Sandby, Campbell and Shultz is still to be resolved.

25. The drawing and cartographic skills of Sandby are so good that some details, such as various outlines of the field boundaries, particularly in the enclosures towards the River Nairn shown in this map, are still clearly recognizable on present-day Ordnance Survey maps.

26. Anderson, *Culloden*, p. 37.

27. Pollard and Oliver, *Two Men in a Trench*, pp. 271–3.

28. Home, *History of the Rebellion*, p. 227.

29. Reid, *Culloden, 1746*, pp. 70, 106. This cannon arrived late 'coming up the hill' and 'was mounted on its own by a large flat stone at the south east corner of the Culloden enclosure . . . A stone, traditionally marking its site, can be seen in the field just north of King's Stables Cottage' (Cameron Taylor, *Culloden*, p. 38). If this is correct, then the puzzle of the exact location, as discussed by other authors (Reid, *Culloden, 1746*, p. 144), of the south-east corner of the Culloden Parks is resolved. Certainly a modern map shows the place of the cannon, and therefore presumably the stone (Cameron Taylor, op. cit., p. 29).

30. Pollard and Oliver, *Two Men in a Trench*, p. 278.

31. Reid, *Like Hungry Wolves*, p. 101; Reid, *Culloden, 1746*, p. 66.

32. Oppé, *Drawings*, p. 151. It has been proposed that the breaches in the walls are on the line of the present B851 road (Reid, *Culloden, 1746*, p. 148), but this may be too far down. Perhaps it occurred higher up, even as far up as the wall that still runs on this east–west line.

33. Royal Collection, Print Room, Windsor Castle, no. 14722.

34. Oppé obviously has doubts about where this sketch was drawn: 'a loose and rapid sketch . . . if any part of it were made on the spot' (*Drawings*, p. 46).

35. William Allen Speck, *The Butcher: The Duke of Cumberland and the Suppression of the 45* (Caernarfon: Welsh Academic Press, 1995), p. 139.
36. Ibid., p. 143; Rex Whitworth, *Duke of Cumberland: A Life* (London: Leo Cooper, 1992), p. 85.
37. National Map Library, National Library of Scotland, Edinburgh, MS 1648 Z 03/30b.
38. Duffy, *The '45*, p. 523.
39. Reid, *Like Hungry Wolves*, p. 84.
40. Reid, *Culloden, 1746*, p. 70.
41. Ibid., pp. 94–8.
42. Prebble, *Culloden*, p. 103.
43. J.C. Leask and H.M. McCance, *The Regimental Records of the Royal Scots (The First or the Royal Regiment of Foot)* (Dublin: Alexander Thom, 1915), p. 150.
44. Home, *History of the Rebellion*, p. 227.
45. Aitchison, 'Culloden Dykes', p. 2.
46. National Map Library, National Library of Scotland, Edinburgh, MS 1648 Z.03/30a. He also made another, later but of 1746 (which ignores the moor road), and also compiled one entitled *The March of the Royal Army from Fochabers to Inverness with one exact Plan of the Battle of Culloden April 16 1746*. Another copy of the Paterson map in the National Archives, Kew (TNA, PRO, MR 1/491), is given the date '? 1746'.
47. Aitchison, 'Culloden Dykes', p. 14: another version of the Paterson map in the Royal Library, Windsor (no. RCIN 730023).
48. Porter, *History*, p. 161. I am grateful to Carolyn Anderson for this reference.
49. Pieces by him include a plan of the ruinous Fort Augustus after the Jacobite siege dated 2 June 1746 (BL, K.Top.L.15) and another of 'the roads from Fort Augustus to Bernera' dated 21 June 1746 (BL, K.Top.XLVIII.63).
50. Ashley Baynton-Williams and Miles Baynton-Williams, *Maps of War* (London: Quercus, 2007), p. 132.
51. Reid, *Like Hungry Wolves*, p. 87.
52. Blaikie, *Itinerary*, p. 97. The sentiment is also shared by others, such as those that describe Finlayson's map as 'possibly the best' (Moir, *The Early Maps of Scotland*, vol. 2, p. 145).
53. Barber, *Map Book*, p. 200.
54. Richard Sharp, *The Engraved Record of the Jacobite Movement* (Aldershot: Scolar, 1996), p. 225, no. 756. Copies of this map exist in a number of collections: the British Library, London (BL, Maps *9115 (3)), the National Archives, Kew (TNA, PRO, MPF 1/1), the National Library of Scotland, Edinburgh (EMS.s.156), the National Museums of Scotland, Edinburgh (P.1983.102), and the Royal Library, Windsor Castle (no. 730031), to mention but five examples.
55. Listed as 'Ensign' (Alastair Livingstone, Christian W.H. Aikman and Betty Stuart Hart, eds, *No Quarter Given: The Muster Roll of Prince Charles Edward Stuart's Army, 1745–46*, Glasgow: Neil Wilson, 2001, p. 137), he is also described

as 'Captain' and made at least two maps including *A General Map of Great Britain*. For more detail about Finlayson and his maps see Blaikie, *Itinerary*, pp. 107–8. As the map is unsigned even the National Library of Scotland only attribute it to John Finlayson.

56. Robert Forbes, *The Lyon in Mourning*, ed. Henry Paton, 3 vols (Edinburgh: Scottish Historical Society, 1895–6), vol. 1, pp. 156–7.

57. Grant (or Grante) was a 'member of staff of the French Royal Observatory' (Charles Sanford Terry, ed., *The Forty-Five: A Narrative of the Last Jacobite Rising*, Cambridge: Cambridge University Press, 1922, p. 192) and became 'Colonel of the Artillery to the Pr. in Scotland'. He was not in charge of the artillery at Culloden, having been incapacitated when struck by a spent cannonball during the siege of Fort William, not 'killed' as some writers state (Hook and Ross, *The '45*, p. 100). He escaped (Livingstone et al., *No Quarter Given*, p. 137) and his map of 1747 was originally published in Paris (Sharp, *Engraved Record*, p. 224, no. 752). It was made up of nine sheets. Copies exist in various collections, such as the National Map Library, the National Library of Scotland, Edinburgh (EMGB.s.3).

58. Smart, *Maps*, p. 124.

59. The National Archives, Kew, PRO, MPF 1/1.

60. Baynton-Williams, *Maps of War*, p. 132. The anonymous map, ex Gulston Collection, is described as 'Anon, Edinburgh, c.1746, copperplate engraving' (op. cit., p. 133), though the same map is also given a London provenance elsewhere (Anon., 'This Day in History', pp. 36–7, 39). The same map seems to belong to the 'Finlayson family' of maps: the Jacobite cannon are depicted in three groups, one in the front centre with two others at the left and right wings, together with the lone cannon in the Culloden House Parks.

61. Sir James Fergusson, *Argyll in the Forty-five* (London: Faber and Faber, 1951), p. 172; Reid, *1745*, p. 169.

62. James Maxwell of Kirkconnell, *Narrative of Charles Prince of Wales' Expedition to Scotland in the Year 1745* (Edinburgh: Maitland Club, 1841), p. 148.

63. Reid, *Like Hungry Wolves*, p. 59, and Duffy, *The '45*, p. 505.

64. Aitchison, 'Culloden Dykes', p. 14; Anderson, *Culloden*, p. 173.

65. Iain McIvor, *Fort George* (Edinburgh: HMSO, 1988), p. 6.

66. Chris Tabraham and Doreen Grove, *Fortress Scotland and the Jacobites* (London: Batsford/Historic Scotland, 1995), p. 94.

67. Blaikie, *Itinerary*, p. 107. The one in the British Library, London (BL, Maps *9115(3)), is dated to '1752'. Finlayson also drew up a much larger map: *A General Map of Great Britain; wherein are delineated the military operations in that Island during the years 1745 and 1746 and even the secret Routs of the Pr– after the Battle of Culloden until his escape to France*. Copies of this map can be found in a number of collections, such as the National Map Library, the National Library of Scotland, Edinburgh (EMS. s.91). This Finlayson 'General Map' has, confusingly, also been attributed to Grant (Sharp, *Engraved Record*, pp. 224–5, no. 753).

Another copy (on linen) in the National Museums of Scotland, Edinburgh (NT 168) is reproduced in George Dalgleish and Dallas Mechan, *'I am Come Home':* *Treasures of Prince Charles Edward Stuart* (Edinburgh: National Museum of Antiquities, 1985), pp. 19–20, 22.

68. James Allardyce, ed., *Historical Papers Relating to the Jacobite Period, 1699–1750,* 2 vols (Aberdeen: New Spalding Club, 1895–6), vol. 2, p. 611.

69. Sir Bruce G. Seton and Jean G. Arnot, *The Prisoners of the '45* (Edinburgh: Scottish History Society, 1928–9), pp. 192–3.

70. Blaikie, *Itinerary*, p. 107.

71. Livingstone et al., *No Quarter Given*, p. 137.

72. Aitchison, 'Culloden Dykes', p. 14.

73. Alice Wemyss, *Elcho of the '45* (Edinburgh: Saltire Society, 2003), p. i.

74. Ibid., p. ii.

75. David, Lord Elcho, *A Short Account of the Affairs of Scotland in the Years 1744,* *1745, 1746*, ed. Evan Charteris (Edinburgh: David Douglas, 1907), between pp. 432 and 433.

76. Ibid., p. 424.

77. Reid, *Like Hungry Wolves*, p. 128.

78. Margaret Wilkes, 'Culloden: The Jacobite View', *Scottish Records Association Newsletter*, spring 1996, p. 2; National Library of Scotland, National Map Library, Edinburgh, Acc. 11323. The map was only revealed when it was presented to the Library during the year of the 250th anniversary of the Battle of Culloden in 1996.

79. David Clark, *Battlefield Walks: Scotland* (Stroud: Sutton, 1996), p. 137.

80. Wilkes, 'Culloden', p. 2.

81. Reid, *Like Hungry Wolves*, pp. 83–4.

82. Ibid., p. 107.

83. Robert Chambers, *Jacobite Memoirs of the Rebellion of 1745* (Edinburgh, 1834), p. 82.

84. Chris Tabraham, 'The Military Context of the Military Survey', in William Roy, *The Great Map: The Military Survey of Scotland, 1747–55* (Edinburgh: Birlinn, 2007), p. 35.

85. British Library, London (BL, K.Top.L.44–1).

86. Hodson, 'William Roy', p. 12.

87. Ibid., p. 18.

88. It has been very tentatively suggested, by Yolande Hodson, that this Roy could be the same William Roy that was taken prisoner at Culloden ('Return of the Map', *The Scotsman*, 15 January 2008). Coincidentally what has not been commented on before is that this William Roy, aged 24, from Lanark and taken prisoner in June 1746, was sent to Tilbury on the *Jane of Alloway* – the very same ship that one John Finlayson appears to have been on (Seton and Arnot, *Prisoners of the '45*, p. 292).

Chapter 8. Jeffrey Stephen: Irish Intriguers and Scottish Councils

1. James Boswell, *The Journal of a Tour to the Highlands with Samuel Johnson*, ed. R.W. Chapman (Oxford, 1970), p. 282.
2. Ibid., p. 426.
3. Michael Hughes, *A Plain Narrative or Journal of the Late Rebellion Begun in 1745* (London, 1746); James Ray, *A Compleat History of the Rebellion from Its First Rise in 1745, to Its Total Suppression in the Glorious Battle of Culloden, in April 1746* (1747); *A Journey through Part of England and Scotland along with the Army under the Command of His Royal Highness the Duke of Cumberland* (London, 1746). Accounts by those not involved included *The History of the Rise, Progress, and Extinction of the Rebellion in Scotland in the Years 1745 and 1746* (London, n.d., c.1750); Andrew Henderson, *The History of the Rebellion, MDCCXLV and MDCCXLVI* (Edinburgh, 1748); *The History of the Rebellion in 1745 and 1746, Extracted from the Scots Magazine: With an Appendix containing an Account of the Trials of the Rebels; the Pretender and his Son's Declarations &c* (Aberdeen, 1755); *The history of the rise, progress and extinction of the rebellion in Scotland, in the years 1745 and 1746, with a particular account of the hardships the Young Pretender suffered after the Battle of Culloden until he landed in France on 10th October 1746* (London, 1746); James MacPherson, *The history of the present rebellion in Scotland, from the departure of the Pretender's son from Rome down to the present time, taken from the relation of Mr James MacPherson* (London, 1745); John Marchant, *The History of the Present Rebellion* (London, 1746). For some Jacobite accounts see John Burton, *A Genuine and True Journal of the Most Miraculous Escape of the Young Chevalier from the Battle of Culloden to his Landing in France* (London, 1749); Robert Forbes, *A plain, authentic and faithful narrative of the several passages of the Young Chevalier &c from the Battle of Culloden to his embarkation for France to which are added poems &c wrote on that occasion* (London, 1765).
4. Robert Forbes, *The Lyon in Mourning, or, A Collection of Speeches, Letters, Journals, etc Relative to the Affairs of Prince Charles Edward Stuart*, ed. Henry Paton, 3 vols (Edinburgh: Scottish History Society, 1895–6).
5. The second account, written in 1789, is published in Henrietta Tayler, ed., *A Jacobite Miscellany: Eight Original Papers on the Rising of 1745–1746* (Oxford: Roxburghe Club, 1948).
6. Forbes, *Lyon in Mourning*, vol. 1, p. xv; vol. 2, p. 256.
7. Robert Chambers, ed., *Jacobite Memoirs of the Rebellion of 1745* (Edinburgh, 1834); Robert Chambers, *History of the Rebellion of 1745–46* (Edinburgh, 1869).
8. Henrietta Tayler, ed., *The History of the Rebellion in the Years 1745 and 1746: From a Manuscript Now in the Possession of Lord James Stewart-Murray* (Oxford: Roxburghe Club, 1944).
9. See John Home, *The History of the Rebellion in Scotland in 1745* (London, 1802), pp. 2–3, 329–30 and 337–40; NAS, GD1.53.86, Questionnaire sent out by John Home.

10. For example, Northumberland Record Office, ZAN.M12/C39/55, Hugh Ross to his wife; NRO, ZRI/27/4/66, Richmond Webb; NRO ZRI/27/4/65, Captain Thomas Davis; National Archives of Scotland, GD 18/3260, John Clerk to his uncle Sir John Clerk of Penicuick; Earl of Ilchester, ed., *Letters to Henry Fox* (London: Roxburghe Club, 1915), pp. 10–12; W.H. Anderson, 'The Battle of Culloden, 1746, as Described in a Letter from a Soldier of the Royal Army', *Journal of the Society of Army Historical Research*, 1 (London, 1921), pp. 21–3, Edward Linn to his wife; Forbes, *Lyon in Mourning*, vol. 1, pp. 380–82, Enoch Bradshaw to his brother; Beckles Willson, *The Life and Letters of James Wolfe* (London, 1909), pp. 62–3; P.C. Yorke, *The Life and Correspondence of Philip Yorke, Earle of Hardwicke, Lord High Chancellor of Great Britain*, 3 vols (Cambridge, 1913), pp. 522–4, Joseph Yorke to his father.

11. NRO, ZRI/27/4/66; NRO, ZAN.M12/C39/55; W.A.S. Hewins, ed., *The Whitefoord Papers, Being the Correspondence and Other Manuscripts of Colonel Charles Whitefoord and Caleb Whitefoord from 1739 to 1810* (Oxford: Clarendon, 1898); Forbes, *Lyon in Mourning*, vol. 1, pp. 380–82.

12. NRO, ZAN.M12/C39/55.

13. British casualties were recorded as fifty dead and 250 wounded. Exact numbers of Jacobite casualties are unknown, and this is reflected in the range of guesses from the 1,500 estimated by James Wolfe, 1,600 by Thomas Ashe Lee, 1,800 by John Clerk, 2,000 by Cumberland, 3,000 by Charles Whitefoord and 3,800 by Hugh Ross. The Jacobites did not contest the figures and made no attempt to 'lessen their losses'. In fact, one account reported that rebel prisoners had claimed that they had lost over 4,000 men, which is the highest estimate of all.

14. Hewins, *Whitefoord Papers*, p. 78.

15. Ray, *Compleat History*, p. 337.

16. Willson, *Life and Letters*, pp. 62–3.

17. NRO, ZRI/27/4/65. See also ZAN.M12/C39/55; Forbes, *Lyon in Mourning*, vol. 1, pp. 380–82.

18. Alistair Tayler and Henrietta Tayler, eds, *1745 and After* (London, 1938), p. 28.

19. There were differences about when the battle began. George Stanhope wrote that the Jacobite cannon began at 2pm, whereas Hugh Ross wrote that the battle began about 1pm and was finished by 2pm. Edward Linn wrote that the battle began a little after 12 and was over by 1pm. Similar contradictions exist on the Jacobite side. Andrew Lumsden said the battle began at 2pm and Robert Strange said 1pm, and Captain Felix O'Neill said it began between 12 and 1. Regarding the duration of the cannonade before battle commenced, only accounts from government soldiers give specific times. Alexander Taylor wrote that the cannonading lasted half an hour, Edward Linn three-quarters of an hour. They probably mean the total length of time the artillery fired, as opposed to the time between it starting and the Jacobites charging. Of the other accounts that give specific times, Joseph Yorke stated that the rebels charged after 2–3 minutes of artillery fire; Donald Campbell of Airds, 9 minutes; Henry Seymour Conway, 10

minutes; James Wolfe, 15 minutes. George Stanhope wrote that the small-arms fire began about 15 minutes after the cannonading. With regard to the size of the respective armies, Jacobite accounts tended to emphasize how reduced in numbers they were, and lacking in regiments, and that as many as 1,000 men who had been on the night march were asleep when battle began. Lumsden gave Jacobite figures at 6,000 and 120 horse, while Cumberland's was 12,000 and 1,200 horse. Robert Strange claimed the Jacobites were outnumbered two to one. John Daniel claimed that about one third of the prince's army of 12,000 was at Culloden, while the government force was at 12,000. On the other hand, those on the government side tended to put the rebel numbers higher. Charles Whitefoord wrote, 'The number of the enemy very much exceeded ours in the morning but was considerably reduced before sunset.' George Stanhope thought the rebel army to be 9,000 strong. Hugh Ross wrote that the government had 6,400 effective men and the rebels had 8,000. An anonymous account in the *Scots Magazine* put the rebels at 9,000 and the government force at 7,000. Clearly government forces outnumbered the Jacobites, even if Hugh Ross does not agree. The defeated Jacobites wanted to emphasize that they were depleted and overwhelmed in numbers. The government forces raised the numbers of rebels because it attached greater glory to their victory.

20. Tayler and Tayler, *1745 and After*, p. 27.
21. Charles Winchester, ed., *Memoirs of the Chevalier Johnstone*, 3 vols (Aberdeen, 1870–71), vol. 1, pp. 10 and 104.
22. Home, *History*, pp. 329–30.
23. 'A Portion of the Diary of David Lord Elcho 1721–1787', in Tayler, *Jacobite Miscellany*, p. 160.
24. William B. Blaikie, *Itinerary of Prince Charles Edward Stuart from his Landing in Scotland, July 1745, to His Departure in September 1746: Compiled from the Lyon in Mourning, supplemented and corrected from other contemporary sources* (Edinburgh: Scottish History Society, 1897), pp. 73–4.
25. Ibid., pp. 73–4.
26. Ibid., pp. 74–5.
27. Blair Castle Archives, JAC. A I. 12.
28. 'Neil Maceachain's Narrative of the Wanderings of Prince Charles in the Hebrides', in Walter B. Blaikie, ed., *Origins of the Forty-Five, and Other Papers Relating to that Rising* (Edinburgh: Scottish History Society, 1916).
29. David Wemyss, Lord Elcho, *A Short Account of the Affairs of Scotland in the Years 1744, 1745, 1746*, ed. Hon. Evan Charteris (Edinburgh, 1907), p. 446; Blaikie, *Itinerary*, pp. 81–2.
30. 'A True Account of Mr John Daniel's Progress with Prince Charles', in Blaikie, *Origins of the Forty-Five*, p. 212.
31. Sir John MacDonald's narrative is included in Tayler and Tayler, *1745 and After*, pp. 157 and 162.
32. Tayler and Tayler, *1745 and After*, pp. 26–8.

33. Forbes, *Lyon in Mourning*, vol. 2, pp. 363–4.

34. 'Memoire d'un Ecossais', in John S. Gibson, *Lochiel of the '45: The Jacobite Chief and the Prince* (Edinburgh, 1994), p. 180.

35. James Maxwell of Kirkconnell, *Narrative of Charles Prince of Wales' Expedition to Scotland in the Year 1745* (Edinburgh: Maitland Club, 1841), p. 157.

36. Ibid., p. 2.

37. Ibid., preface; 'A Portion of the Diary of David Lord Elcho', p. 127. Sir Walter Scott, when writing *Tales of a Grandfather*, used both extensively.

38. Blaikie, *Itinerary*, pp. 79–80. The letter was not written at a point at which the cause was considered to be lost. Murray and a large body of men had gathered at Ruthven and were awaiting instructions, assuming there would be a counter to the events of the previous day. They only dispersed when ordered to do so by the prince.

39. It was eventually published in London in 1749: [Lord George Murray], *A Particular Account of the Battle of Culloden April 16, 1746: In a Letter from an Officer of the Highland Army to His Friend at London.* Copies of the account found their way around leading Jacobites. Papers in the National Archives of Scotland, attributed to Francis Farquharson of Monaltrie and Alexander Forbes, Lord Pitsligo, are in fact manuscript copies of Murray's account. See NAS, GD1/53/81/1, Account of the Battle of Culloden on the 16 April 1746 from an original manuscript in the handwriting of Francis Farquharson of Monaltrie; TD 2004/34 Account of the Battle of Culloden 16 April 1746.

40. Home, *History*, p. 361.

41. Blair Castle Archives, JAC A I. 12, Some remarks upon a letter wrote the 10 May 1746; Home, *History*, pp. 359–68; 'Marches of the Highland Army', in Chambers, *Jacobite Memoirs*, p. 130.

42. Forbes, *Lyon in Mourning*, vol. 1, p. 86; Home, *History*, p. 361, Murray to William Hamilton, 5 August 1749.

43. 'A Portion of the Diary of David Lord Elcho', p. 161.

44. 'Neil Maceachain's Narrative', p. 240.

45. 'A True Account of Mr John Daniel's Progress', p. 212.

46. Blaikie, *Origins of the Forty-Five*, pp. lxix–lxx.

47. Home, *History*, pp. 359–69, Lord George Murray's letter to William Hamilton, 5 August 1749; 'Memoire d'un Ecossais', pp. 180–81; Blaikie, *Origins of the Forty-Five*, pp. lxix–lxx.

48. C. Duffy, *The '45* (London, 2003), p. 502; Winchester, *Memoirs of the Chevalier Johnstone*, p. 117. Johnstone believed that a prolonged campaign in the Highlands was a last resort, but a retreat into the Highlands would have enabled them to regroup and take on Cumberland within a couple of weeks; Blaikie, *Origins of the Forty-Five*, pp. lxix–lxx.

49. *The Collected Writings of Dougal Graham*, ed. George MacGregor (Glasgow, 1883), p. 159.

50. *The Chronicles of Atholl and Tullibardine Families*, 5 vols (Edinburgh, 1908), vol. 3, p. 280.

51. Tayler and Tayler, *1745 and After*, pp. 161–3; *A Particular Account of the Battle of Culloden*, p. 5; *Chronicles of Atholl and Tullibardine*, vol. 3, p. 278.

52. *Chronicles of Atholl and Tullibardine*, vol. 2, p. 278.

53. Home, *History*, pp. 361–2; Duffy, *The '45*, p. 504. Duffy argues that Murray did not explain how he was going to fight his battle on his chosen ground and that he may well have been thinking of a holding action that would win time to enable the army to break free. This is unlikely – Murray seems to have believed the ground offered the best chance of actually winning a battle.

54. Home, *History*, pp. 361–2, Lord George Murray's letter to William Hamilton, 5 August 1749.

55. *Particular Account of the Battle of Culloden*, p. 9.

56. Maxwell, *Narrative*, pp. 147 and 155.

57. 'A Short Account of the Battles of Preston, Falkirk and Culloden; by a Gentleman who was in these actions', in Blaikie, *Origins of the Forty-Five*, p. 417; Tayler and Tayler, *1745 and After*, p. 160. See also 'Memoire d'un Ecossais', pp. 180–81; Forbes, *Lyon in Mourning*, vol. 1, p. 86, and vol. 2, p. 361.

58. Stuart Reid, *Culloden, 1746: Battlefield Guide* (Pen & Sword, 2005), p. 55.

59. John Cameron recorded that Murray had initially viewed the walls as beneficial. However, it is clear that after observing Cumberland's move, he quickly changed his mind about the supposed security offered by the walls. He sent O'Sullivan, Henry Ker and John Roy Stuart to reconnoitre the park down to the water of Nairn. They reported that it was impossible for the cavalry to come that way and get between them and the river without throwing down the walls. Furthermore, the walls went down to the riverside and the banks of the river were too high for horse to negotiate. According to Cameron, Murray was apparently on the left with the Duke of Perth when he was warned by Lochiel of the potential dangers of a flanking move on the right. Forbes, *Lyon in Mourning*, vol. 1, p. 86, and vol. 2, p. 361; Tayler and Tayler, *1745 and After*, pp. 161–2; Hewins, *Whitefoord Papers*, pp. 76–80. According to James Wolfe, who was with Hawley, the dragoons had moved through the enclosures and were posted at the rear of the Jacobites before the infantry fire began. See Willson, *Life and Letters*, pp. 62–3.

60. Tayler and Tayler, *1745 and After*, pp. 161–2. Charles, also realizing the threat posed by government troops breaking into the enclosures, sent orders to Murray on a number of occasions to enter and take the enclosures, but Murray apparently 'paid no attention to it'. Winchester, *Memoirs of the Chevalier Johnstone*, p. 107. A number of officers favoured lining the walls with men, and a member of Stonywood's Regiment reported that 'Colonel Baggot had advised to post them along the outside of that park dyke, which probably would have prevented a good deal of the mischief these Campbells and dragoons afterwards did.' Forbes, *Lyon in Mourning*, vol. 1, p. 86, and vol. 2, p. 278.

61. A suggestion to line the walls was rejected because of a lack of men. The Whig

historian believed that had the wall been lined with men, 'neither the dragoons nor the Campbels could have approach'd it without great loss'. His assessment was based on the assumption that Murray had 800 men available to line the wall, which he did not. See Tayler, *History of the Rebellion in the Years 1745 and 1746*, p. 218.

62. Tayler and Tayler, *1745 and After*, p. 163.

63. Ibid.

64. Maxwell, *Narrative*, p. 151.

65. Henry Ker stated they were placed facing outwards, covering the right of the two lines, and they were to observe the motions of the enemy. John Cameron stated that Murray ordered Ogilvy's to cover the flank. Elcho stated that Murray ordered Avochie and Elcho's and Fitzjames's Horse to face them, thus preventing them from passing a ditch that covered the right wing. James Maxwell stated that Murray ordered Avochie to advance towards the Campbells, but they had already broken into an enclosure towards the river and made a passage for the dragoons to go round the right of the Jacobite line and form at the rear of it. Murray then ordered Elcho's Life Guards and Fitzjames's Horse to form opposite the dragoons upon the 'brink of a hollow way'. They were not, as O'Sullivan claimed, down in the hollow way out of sight, but on its brink. According to Maxwell, 'the ascent was somewhat steep on both sides, so that neither could pass safely in the presence of the other'. Furthermore, the Campbells advanced no further and Avochie was ordered to watch their motions. Elcho, *Short Account*, p. 430. Maxwell, *Narrative*, p. 151. Forbes, *Lyon in Mourning*, vol. 2, p. 362.

66. NAS, GD1/93/15. John Wedderburn, Master of Blackness and a Captain in the 1st Battalion of Ogilvy's Regiment, wrote that the Atholl men suffered greatly from grapeshot and from the Campbells firing at them from behind the park walls. 'A body of men supposed to be Campbells certainly fired over the dyke upon the flank of the Atholmen which must have been the cause of so great a slaughter. Stewart of Killiehassie commanded the flank company consisting of 34 privates and he himself and three of them only came off.'

67. Blaikie, *Origins of the Forty-Five*, p. 418.

68. Hewins, *Whitefoord Papers*, p. 78; NAS, GD1/93/15; Maxwell, *Narrative*, pp. 152–3; *Memoirs of Sir Robert Strange and Andrew Lumisden*, ed. James Dennistoun, 2 vols (London, 1855), p. 64; Blaikie, *Origins of the Forty-Five*, p. 418; Murray, *Particular Account*, p. 16; Winchester, *Memoirs of the Chevalier Johnstone*, p. 107.

69. 'A Portion of the Diary of David Lord Elcho', p. 161.

70. *Chronicles of Atholl and Tullibardine*, III; Elcho, *Short Account*, p. 430.

71. Elcho, *Short Account*, p. 430; 'A Portion of the Diary of David Lord Elcho', p. 161.

72. Maxwell, *Narrative*, p. 147.

73. *Memoirs of Sir Robert Strange*, p. 60.

74. Home, *History*, pp. 332–3.
75. 'Memoire d'un Ecossais', p. 181.
76. Home, *History*, p. 368; Blair Castle Archives, JAC A I. 12, Some remarks upon a letter wrote the 10 May 1746. Johnstone likewise argued that the prince should have taken action to avoid an immediate conflict, 'above all, the delay would have given time for all those absent on leave to return to the army'. Winchester, *Memoirs of the Chevalier Johnstone*, pp. 106 and 117.
77. Tayler and Tayler, *1745 and After*, p. 162.
78. Ibid., p. 164.
79. Reid, *Culloden, 1746*, p. 67; Tayler and Tayler, *1745 and After*, p. 163.
80. Reid, *Culloden, 1746*, p. 67. According to Reid the move was sensible enough but carried out without prior consultation, and led to dislocation on both sides.
81. Maxwell, *Narrative*, pp. 151–2.
82. Hughes, *Plain Narrative*.
83. Forbes, *Lyon in Mourning*, vol. 2, p. 363. Henry Ker went to the left and ordered the Duke of Perth to begin the attack in order to rectify the line.

Chapter 9. Elspeth Masson and Jill Harden: Drumossie Moor

1. National Trust for Scotland, *Cuil Lodair/Culloden* (2007).
2. C. Duffy, *The '45* (2005), pp. 502–4.
3. J. Finlayson, 'A Plan of the Battle of Culloden' (1746), in the National Library of Scotland, EMS.s.156; T. Sandby, 'Plan of the Battle of Culloden' (1746), in the Royal Library, Windsor. A full list of contemporary and near contemporary plans of the battle is to be found in D.G. Moir, ed., *The Early Maps of Scotland to 1850* (1983), vol. 2, pp. 145–8. See also Blackmore (this volume).
4. A. Simmons, ed., *Burt's Letters from the North of Scotland as Related by Edmund Burt* (1998; first published 1754), pp. 131–2.
5. J. Mitchell, *Reminiscences of My Life in the Highlands*, vol. 1 (1971; first published 1883), p. 62.
6. *Old Statistical Account of Scotland*, vol. 11 (1794), p. 561.
7. Ibid.
8. Mitchell, *Reminiscences*, pp. 63–4.
9. M.A. Macdougall-Heasman, 'Culloden Moor, 1746 to the Present', unpublished master's dissertation, University of St Andrews, 1992, p. 13.
10. The afforested land was recorded by James Fraser for Peter Anderson's publication produced in 1867, *Guide to Culloden Moor & Story of the Battle*, p. 34, as well as by the Ordnance Survey in 1870 during their survey for the first edition 1:10,560 maps of the area.
11. Mitchell, *Reminiscences*, p. 65.
12. G. Anderson and P. Anderson, *Guide to the Highlands and Islands of Scotland* (1834), pp. 107–8.
13. *Inverness Courier*, 22 April 1846.
14. Ibid.

15. K. Douglas, J. Smith and D. Fraser, *A History and Description of the Town of Inverness* (1847), pp. 147–8.
16. *Inverness Advertiser*, 25 September 1849.
17. *Inverness Courier*, 20 September 1849.
18. *Illustrated London News*, 29 September 1849.
19. *Inverness Advertiser*, 26 February 1850.
20. Ordnance Survey Name Book, Parish of Daviot and Dunlichity (1858).
21. Anon., *The Sixpenny Guide to Inverness and Vicinity* (1872), p. 23.
22. Anderson, *Guide to Culloden Moor*, pp. 33–8.
23. By associating these buildings with the battle, Duncan Forbes had recognized their traditional importance, but whether today's structures actually date back to 1746 is not known.
24. 'Report of the 10th Annual Dinner 1881', *Transactions of the Gaelic Society of Inverness*, vol. 10, pp. 84–109.
25. C.J. Withers, *Gaelic Scotland: The Transformation of a Culture Region* (1988).
26. E.A. Cameron, 'Embracing the Past', in D. Broun, R.J. Finlay and M. Lynch, *Image and Identity: The Making and Re-making of Scotland through the Ages* (1998), pp. 195–219.
27. A biography of the Forbeses of Culloden was written as a preface to the sale particulars of the contents of Culloden House, produced as *Purchasers' Catalogue: The Valuable Contents of Culloden House which were Sold by Auction by Messrs A Fraser & Co Inverness on 21 July 1897 and Following Days*. This quote is taken from page 9.
28. 'Meeting of the Societies at Inverness 30 July 1886', *Transactions of the Inverness Scientific Society and Field Club*, vol. 3, p. 190.
29. *Inverness Courier*, 9 April 1897.
30. G. Menary, *The Life and Letters of Duncan Forbes of Culloden, 1685–1747* (1936).
31. C. de B. Murray, *Duncan Forbes of Culloden* (1936), p. 183.
32. Menary, *Life and Letters*.
33. For example, see the correspondence columns in the *Inverness Courier* for 27 and 30 August 1935, as well as 6 and 10 September 1935.
34. Anderson, *Guide to Culloden Moor*, p. 89.
35. Transactions of the Gaelic Society of Inverness [TGSI], *Report of the Annual Meeting 27 January 1933*, vol. 36, p. 411; *Report of the Annual Business Meeting 29 January 1937*, vol. 38, p. 6.
36. MacDougall-Heasman, 'Culloden Moor', pp. 37–8.
37. TGSI, *Report of the Anniversary of Culloden 16 April 1936*, vol. 37, p. 367.
38. A.P.K. Wright, 'The Culloden Battlefield Memorial Project Heritage Impact Assessment', unpublished report for the National Trust for Scotland, 2004, pp. 16–17.
39. TGSI, *Report of the Annual Business Meeting 31 January 1936*, vol. 37, p. 291.
40. 'Correspondence', *Inverness Courier*, 29 October 1935.
41. 'Lochiel's Protest', *Inverness Courier*, 3 April 1936.

42. 'Editor's Post Bag', *Northern Chronicle*, 29 April 1936.

43. 'Sacred Ground Invaded', *Daily Record and Mail*, 3 April 1936.

44. National Trust for Scotland, Archives, Culloden, JD 0150 C.26, packet.

45. National Trust for Scotland, *Culloden Management Plan, 1993–98* (1993), p. 2.

46. National Trust for Scotland, Archives, Culloden, JD 0151 C.12 1951–2 and C.11 1954, correspondence.

47. TGSI, *Report of the Anniversary of Culloden 16 April 1936*, vol. 37, p. 367.

48. Wright, 'Culloden Battlefield', p. 17.

49. Ibid., p. 18.

50. National Trust for Scotland, Archives, Culloden, JD 0152 C.10i–ii 1971 and 1972, correspondence, as well as Inverness County Council & Committees, 1974, *Minutes*, p. 1121.

51. Highland Regional Council, *Minutes of Meetings* (1983), pp. 1047, 1332 and 1346, and National Trust for Scotland Archives, Culloden, JD 0156, correspondence, and JD 0157, Culloden bypass papers.

52. National Trust for Scotland, Culloden Property Statements, 2008–2011, p. 9.

53. Inverness-shire County Council Planning Papers: Conservation Areas (1968).

54. National Trust for Scotland, Culloden Property Statements, 2008–2011, p. 17.

55. Dalcairn Consultants, 'Culloden: The Field of the English: The Battlefield – Ecological Management Proposals, 1999–2004', unpublished report for the National Trust for Scotland, 1998.

56. K. Aitchison, 'Culloden Dykes: Documentary Research', unpublished report for the National Trust for Scotland, 1994.

57. Anderson, *Guide to Culloden Moor*, pp. 20–21.

58. As discussed in Wright, 'Culloden Battlefield', as well as by Gaia Group, 'Culloden Battlefield: A Vision and a Strategy for the Management of the Property and the Future of the Visitor Facilities on the Site' (1998), and in D. Bryden, 'Culloden Visitor Management System: Process and Plan', unpublished reports for the National Trust for Scotland, 2003.

59. The new information centre has had extensive media coverage since December 2007, for example *The Saturday Telegraph*, travel section, 23 February 2008. A new site guidebook has been published: see note 1.

Chapter 10. Daniel Szechi: The Significance of Culloden

1. Jeremy Black, *Britain as a Military Power, 1688–1815* (UCL Press, 1999), pp. 125–8.

2. Reed Browning, *The War of the Austrian Succession* (New York: St Martin's, 1993), pp. 42–3.

3. Christopher Duffy, *The Army of Maria Theresa: The Armed Forces of Imperial Austria, 1740–1780* (New York: Hippocrene, 1977), p. 17.

4. Michael Hochedlinger, *Austria's Wars of Emergence: War, State and Society in the Habsburg Monarchy, 1683–1797* (Longman, 2003), pp. 248–9; Jeremy Black, *Eighteenth Century Europe, 1700–1789* (New York: St Martin's, 1990), p. 290.

5. Browning, *War of the Austrian Succession*, pp. 55–8, 66, 80.
6. Paul Langford, *Modern British Foreign Policy: The Eighteenth Century, 1688–1815* (Adam and Charles Black, 1976), p. 120.
7. Browning, *War of the Austrian Succession*, pp. 68–9.
8. Ibid., pp. 101, 109–10, 142–8.
9. Duffy, *Army of Maria Theresa*, p. 156; Browning, *War of the Austrian Succession*, pp. 61–2, 113, 118, 134, 172, 173–4.
10. Black, *Britain as a Military Power*, pp. 125–31; John Keay, *The Honourable Company: A History of the English East India Company* (Harper Collins, 1993), pp. 274–9.
11. Langford, *Modern British Foreign Policy*, p. 18.
12. Black, *Britain as a Military Power*, pp. 63, 69; Browning, *War of the Austrian Succession*, pp. 130, 170–72, 194.
13. W.A. Speck, 'William Augustus, Prince, duke of Cumberland (1721–1765)', *Oxford Dictionary of National Biography* (Oxford University Press, 2004; online edn [http://www.oxforddnb.com/view/article/29455, accessed 3 March 2007]). William A. Speck is also the author of the best biography of Cumberland: *The Butcher: The Duke of Cumberland and the Suppression of the '45* (Oxford: Basil Blackwell, 1981).
14. 'Saxe, (Hermann-) Maurice, comte de', *Encyclopædia Britannica Online* [http://search.eb.com/eb/article-9065972, accessed 3 March 2007]; Browning, *War of the Austrian Succession*, pp. 77–8; André Corvisier, ed., *A Dictionary of Military History and the Art of War*, English edition, ed. John Childs, trans. Chris Turner (Oxford: Basil Blackwell, 1994), p. 727. There is no modern English language biography of de Saxe.
15. Browning, *War of the Austrian Succession*, pp. 206–13, 219, 259–60, 269, 282–6, 313–17, 319–20, 352–3.
16. Armstrong Starkey, *War in the Age of Enlightenment, 1700–1789* (Praeger, 2003), pp. 107–25.
17. Harman Murtagh, 'Irish Soldiers Abroad, 1600–1800', in Thomas Bartlett and Keith Jeffery, eds, *A Military History of Ireland* (Cambridge: Cambridge University Press, 1996), pp. 307–12; Éamonn Ó Ciardha, *Ireland and the Jacobite Cause, 1685–1766: A Fatal Attachment* (Dublin: Four Courts, 2002), pp. 34, 180, 205, 258–9.
18. Daniel Szechi, *The Jacobites: Britain and Europe 1688–1788* (Manchester: Manchester University Press, 1994), pp. 87–94.
19. Ibid., pp. 95–6; Eveline Cruickshanks, *Political Untouchables: The Tories and the '45* (Duckworth, 1979), pp. 36–78.
20. Browning, *War of the Austrian Succession*, p. 158.
22. Frank J. McLynn, *Charles Edward Stuart: A Tragedy in Many Acts* (Routledge, 1988), pp. 92–126.
22. Jeremy Black, *Culloden and the '45* (Stroud: Sutton, 1990), pp. 163–6.

23. Frank J. McLynn, *France and the Jacobite Rising of 1745* (Edinburgh: Edinburgh University Press, 1981), pp. 75–163.

24. Browning, *War of the Austrian Succession*, p. 269; Black, *Britain as a Military Power*, p. 68.

25. Browning, *War of the Austrian Succession*, pp. 284–5.

26. Black, *Culloden*, pp. 196–8.

27. Browning, *War of the Austrian Succession*, p. 306.

28. Ibid., pp. 314–16, 319–20.

29. Hochedlinger, *Austria's Wars of Emergence*, pp. 253, 257–9; Christopher Duffy, *Frederick the Great: A Military Life* (Routledge and Kegan Paul, 1985), pp. 60–66, 68–72.

30. Browning, *War of the Austrian Succession*, pp. 251–4.

31. Hochedlinger, *Austria's Wars of Emergence*, pp. 254–6.

32. Black, *Britain as a Military Power*, p. 65.

33. Romney Sedgwick, ed., *The History of Parliament: The House of Commons, 1715–1754*, 2 vols (HMSO, 1970), vol. 1, pp. 19–78; John Cannon, *Parliamentary Reform, 1640–1832* (Cambridge: Cambridge University Press, 1973), p. 30.

34. John Cannon, *Aristocratic Century: The Peerage of Eighteenth-Century England* (Cambridge University Press, 1987), pp. 93–123.

35. John Brooke, *The History of Parliament: The House of Commons 1754–1790: Introductory Survey* (Oxford University Press, 1968), pp. 1–81.

36. Linda Colley, *In Defiance of Oligarchy: The Tory Party, 1714–60* (Cambridge University Press, 1982), pp. 85–117.

37. Harry T. Dickinson, *Liberty and Property: Political Ideology in Eighteenth-Century Britain* (Weidenfeld and Nicolson, 1977), pp. 121–62.

38. Szechi, *Jacobites*, pp. 64–5.

39. Daniel Szechi, *1715: The Great Jacobite Rebellion* (Yale University Press, 2006), pp. 77–101.

40. Colley, *In Defiance of Oligarchy*, pp. 177–235. Cf. Cruickshanks, *Political Untouchables*, pp. 36–78.

41. Frank J. McLynn, *The Jacobite Army in England 1745: The Final Campaign* (Edinburgh: John Donald, 1983), pp. 34–183.

42. McLynn, *Charles Edward Stuart*, pp. 170–72; Colley, *In Defiance of Oligarchy*, pp. 243–60.

43. Paul Kléber Monod, *Jacobitism and the English People, 1688–1788* (Cambridge: Cambridge University Press, 1989), pp. 197, 198–9, 201–2, 206–9, 216–17.

44. David Greenwood, *William King: Tory and Jacobite* (Oxford: Clarendon, 1969), pp. 235–6.

45. McLynn, *Charles Edward Stuart*, pp. 327–454; Colley, *In Defiance of Oligarchy*, pp. 285–8.

46. Geoffrey Holmes and Daniel Szechi, *The Age of Oligarchy: Pre-Industrial Britain, 1722–1783* (Longman, 1993), pp. 277–9.

47. William Ferguson, *Scotland 1689 to the Present* (Edinburgh: Mercat, 1994

reprint), pp. 137–48; Daniel Szechi, *George Lockhart of Carnwath, 1681–1731: A Study in Jacobitism* (East Linton: Tuckwell, 2002), pp. 127–31; Ronald Sunter, *Patronage and Politics in Scotland, 1707–1832* (Edinburgh: John Donald, 1986), pp. 148–60.

48. John Stuart Shaw, *The Political History of Eighteenth-Century Scotland* (Macmillan, 1999), pp. 72–4.

49. John L. McCracken, 'The Political Structure, 1714–60', in T.W. Moody and William E. Vaughan, eds, *A New History of Ireland, IV: Eighteenth-Century Ireland* (Oxford: Clarendon, 1986), pp. 72–8.

50. Daniel Szechi and David Hayton, 'John Bull's Other Kingdoms: The Government of Scotland and Ireland', in Clyve Jones, ed., *Britain in the First Age of Party, 1680–1750: Essays Presented to Geoffrey Holmes* (Hambledon, 1987), pp. 268–74.

51. Szechi and Hayton, 'John Bull's Other Kingdoms', p. 278; Holmes and Szechi, *Age of Oligarchy*, pp. 230–31.

52. John L. McCracken, 'Protestant Ascendancy and the Rise of Colonial Nationalism', in Moody and Vaughan, *New History of Ireland*, pp. 105–18; Szechi and Hayton, 'John Bull's Other Kingdoms', pp. 273–6.

53. Szechi and Hayton, 'John Bull's Other Kingdoms', pp. 276–7; Holmes and Szechi, *Age of Oligarchy*, pp. 232–3.

54. Ó Ciardha, *Ireland and the Jacobite Cause*, pp. 32–3, 183, 185, 189–90, 194–8, 203–4, 206–9, 223–30, 259–70, 271–310, 313–15.

55. Ibid., p. 33.

56. Robert B. McDowell, 'Colonial Nationalism and the Winning of Parliamentary Independence, 1760–82', in Moody and Vaughan, *New History of Ireland*, pp. 202–3.

57. Allan I. Macinnes, *Clanship, Commerce and the House of Stuart, 1603–1788* (East Linton: Tuckwell, 1996), pp. 211–14; John Prebble, *Culloden* (Penguin, 1974 reprint), pp. 142–285.

58. Macinnes, *Clanship*, pp. 215–16; Bruce Lenman, *The Jacobite Risings in Britain, 1689–1746* (Eyre Methuen, 1980), pp. 275–81.

59. Christopher Duffy, *The '45* (Cassell, 2003), pp. 530, 531, 534; Doron Zimmerman, *The Jacobite Movement in Scotland and in Exile, 1746–1759* (Basingstoke: Palgrave Macmillan, 2003), pp. 23–38.

60. Zimmerman, *Jacobite Movement*, pp. 75–146.

61. McLynn, *Charles Edward Stuart*, pp. 410–11, 413–14. Cf. Zimmerman, *Jacobite Movement*, p. 112.

62. Zimmerman, *Jacobite Movement*, pp. 57–9, 62–3, 113–14.

63. Lenman, *Jacobite Risings*, p. 268; Zimmerman, *Jacobite Movement*, pp. 57–9; McLynn, *Charles Edward Stuart*, pp. 314, 325.

64. Martin Haile, *James Francis Edward: The Old Chevalier* (J.M. Dent, 1907), p. 417; John S. Gibson, *Lochiel of the '45: The Jacobite Chief and the Prince*

(Edinburgh: Edinburgh University Press, 1995 reprint), pp. 158, 166, 167; Zimmerman, *Jacobite Movement*, pp. 43, 83.

65. Lenman, *Jacobite Risings*, p. 255; McLynn, *Charles Edward Stuart*, p. 129; Leah Leneman, *Living in Atholl: A Social History of the Estates, 1685–1785* (Edinburgh: Edinburgh University Press, 1986), pp. 232–3.
66. Lenman, *Jacobite Risings*, pp. 274–7.
67. Ibid., p. 289; Bruce Lenman, *The Jacobite Clans of the Great Glen, 1650–1784* (Methuen, 1984), pp. 177–8.
68. Lenman, *Jacobite Clans of the Great Glen*, pp. 187–211.
69. Monod, *Jacobitism*, pp. 330–40.
70. Ibid., pp. 199, 201, 204–9.
71. Macinnes, *Clanship*, pp. 169–72.
72. Szechi, *Jacobites*, pp. 85, 90–116; Szechi, *1715*, pp. 77–87.
73. Szechi, *1715*, pp. 54–6.
74. McLynn, *Charles Edward Stuart*, pp. 387–93, 416–40.
75. Duffy, *The '45*, pp. 352, 523.
76. Ó Ciardha, *Ireland and the Jacobite Cause*, pp. 205, 255, 264, 267, 336, 374, 376.
77. Ibid., pp. 375, 378.
78. Edward Gregg, 'France, Rome and the Exiled Stuarts, 1689–1713', in Edward Corp, with Edward Gregg, Howard Erskine-Hill and Geoffrey Scott, *A Court in Exile: The Stuarts in France, 1689–1718* (Cambridge: Cambridge University Press, 2004), pp. 11–75; Szechi, *Jacobites*, pp. 90–104, 107–11.
79. McLynn, *Charles Edward Stuart*, pp. 311–12, 313–14, 317, 320–22.
80. Zimmerman, *Jacobite Movement*, pp. 120–58.
81. Starkey, *War in the Age of Enlightenment*, pp. 127–8.

Index

271